LAOS: War and Revolution

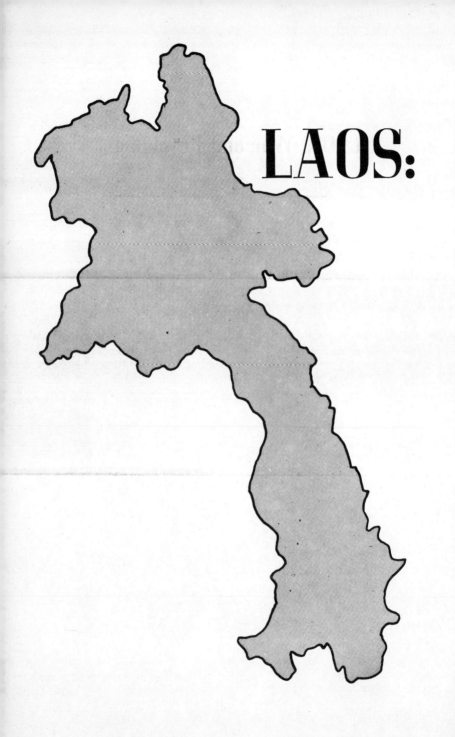

LAOS:

War and Revolution

Edited by

Nina S. Adams and Alfred W. McCoy

A publication of the
Committee of Concerned Asian Scholars

HARPER COLOPHON BOOKS
Harper & Row, Publishers
New York, Evanston, and London

FIRST EDITION: Harper Colophon Books

LIBRARY OF CONGRESS CATALOG CARD NUMBER: 76–140188

CONTENTS

MAPS

Preface

The Laotian conflict, despite its implications for American policy in Asia and its impact on the kingdom itself, has been consistently overshadowed by the war in Vietnam and continually unpublicized in the United States. Lack of information has been coupled with a general apathy toward a quiet war fought in a faraway country at a tolerably low cost in American lives. Furthermore, a distinct effort has been made by consecutive American administrations to deemphasize the scope and intensity of the conflict and to obfuscate the moral and political issues it raises. As the Indochina war expands, it becomes more and more imperative that information and opinions about the war in Laos reach the American public. This book represents an attempt to answer the need for information.

Although not all the contributors subscribe to our general outlook, this book was produced under the auspices of the Committee of Concerned Asian Scholars (CCAS), which is a national organization founded in 1967 by people concerned professionally and politically with Asia. The Vietnam War originated and escalated amid the silence, and thus, we feel, with the complicity, of the vast majority of Asian specialists in this country. CCAS was formed in order to counter this impression of scholarly approval of the war and related policies. By attempting to inform and mobilize members of the teaching profession, graduate students, undergraduates, and the general public, CCAS hopes to stimulate broader and more informal discussion of Asian issues.

This book is truly the product of a cooperative effort. The editors are first and foremost indebted to Cathleen R. McCoy and Leonard P. Adams II for their efforts as editors, proofreaders, innovators, and general morale boosters. We are also grateful to Cathleen for truly heroic feats of typing. Although we are, of course, responsible for the final manuscript and any errors it may contain, many people contributed nobly to the task of editing, revising, and translating articles, including Lydia and Brian Fegan, Michael Vickery, Richard H. Swain, Emelia Isaacson, Edward Fallon, Truong Buu Mai Van, Michelle Condominas, and Susan Brockman. We are indebted to Elizabeth O. Kyburg, Evelyn Middleton, Susan Darrach, Martha Mandel, Ann Morgan, and Eve Spangler for the many hours they spent typing the manuscript. Professor Harold C. Conklin of Yale gave us much helpful advice. We wish to thank David Obst of Dispatch News Service for his efforts in finding a publisher and Mark Lynch for his generous advice. In addition we wish to thank Annick Lévy, Daniel Hemery, and Professor Jean Chesneaux for their suggestions and continual assistance in obtaining manuscripts from France.

And finally, we wish to acknowledge an anonymous Western Union operator. When the editors attempted to send a cable to Vientiane, Laos, she first denied that such a place existed. After further investigation she then informed us that in her book, Vientiane was listed as a part of Vietnam.

New Haven, Connecticut NINA S. ADAMS
June 30, 1970 ALFRED W. MCCOY

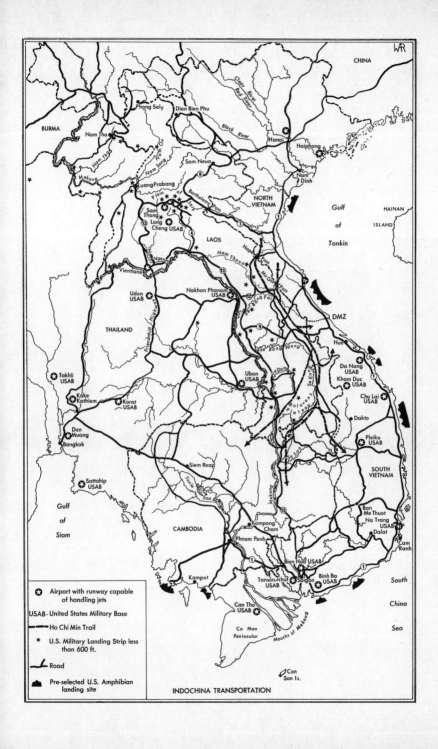

INDOCHINA TRANSPORTATION

Introduction

Noam Chomsky

For 15 years the United States has been conducting an increasingly bitter war against the people of Laos—surely one of the most grotesque episodes of modern history. By virtually any standard of national development that one might invent, the United States and Laos—halfway around the globe from each other—would stand at opposite ends of the scale. The population of the United States is 70 times that of Laos, while its gross national product is 6,000 times as great. Using any other indices, the disparity is about the same. Laos is among the poorest countries of the world. In many ways, it has barely emerged from feudalism. Much of the population has still not developed the germs of national consciousness. Simple peasants live hardly above the subsistence level in their scattered villages, unaware of the existence of Laos, let alone the United States.

Laos received its independence at the Geneva Conference in 1954. After a shaky and troubled start, a Government of National Union was formed, involving all competing factions. Free elections were held in 1958 to select 21 delegates for the National Assembly. Ambassador Graham Parsons assured the American Congress that it would receive "value for money" with the defeat of the Neo Lao Hak Xat (NLHX), the political party of the left-wing Pathet Lao guerrillas[1]—"communists," in American political terminology. But despite (perhaps even because of) the enormous American "aid" program, the NLHX and its allies won 13 seats, while the right wing won 5, with the remaining seats going to the traditional parties. Nine of the 13 NLHX candidates were elected, and Prince Souphanouvong, the

---

1. Cited in Jonathan Mirsky and Stephen E. Stonefield, "The United States in Laos," in Edward Friedman and Mark Selden, eds., *America's Asia* (New York: Pantheon, 1970). An excellent analytic review of the recent history of Laos.

head of the NLHX, received the largest vote. An American campaign of subversion was undertaken immediately, and within months a new cabinet was formed by the "right-leaning neutralist" Phoui Sananikone, a wealthy Lao businessman who quickly expressed his sole allegiance to the "Free World." Though more satisfactory to the American government, he was still by no means sufficiently reactionary, and shortly thereafter he too was overthrown and the extreme right took over. The strong man of the new regime was General Phoumi Nosavan, the favorite of the CIA and the Pentagon and a relative of the military dictator of Thailand, Marshal Sarit, who was also receiving substantial American support (while rapidly amassing a personal fortune—estimated at $137 million when he died in 1963).

As he reported quite frankly in congressional testimony, Ambassador Parsons worked tirelessly to prevent the formation of a coalition government that would represent the existing political forces in Laos. Though his efforts, combined with those of the CIA and the American military mission (disguised as civilians), did succeed in establishing a government of the extreme right, they succeeded in nothing else, since the left continued to grow in strength and popular support. In the words of the State Department *Background Notes* (March 1969), "By the spring of 1961 the NLHX appeared to be in a position to take over the entire country." Faced with the collapse of its policies of subversion, the American government agreed to join in a new Geneva conference and to support a new government of National Union, headed by Prince Souvanna Phouma. After suffering a series of assassinations of their leaders in Vientiane the NLHX members returned to the northern provinces that had been under Pathet Lao control for a decade. In May 1964 the Pathet Lao took the Plain of Jars and the bombardment of Laos began from the "privileged sanctuaries" that the United States had established in Thailand. Nine months later these bases would be used (secretly) for the regular bombardment of North Vietnam as well.

Since that time Laos has been bombed more intensively than Vietnam. Despite vast efforts at population removal through bombardment and ground sweeps, over one-third of the population remains in areas administered by the Pathet Lao. The conditions of their existence are described by Jacques Decornoy (article 25). The United States also established guerrilla bases throughout Pathet Lao–controlled territory, as well as navigational posts near the border to facilitate the all-weather bombardment of North Vietnam. Since 1968, when Decornoy's articles were written and the regular bombing of North Vietnam was terminated, the attack on Laos has been intensified. In Senator Symington's accurate phrasing, when the air attack against North Vietnam was ended,

At the same time, we were increasing in secret the air strikes against Laos. In fact, as the general just said, which I knew, orders were that if you did not need the planes against Vietnam, use said planes against Laos.[2]

In 1969, as infiltration fell off along the Ho Chi Minh Trail in southern Laos, much of the bombing was shifted to the north, again in secret.[3] The bombing in northern Laos has no direct relation to the war in South Vietnam. Rather, as T. D. Allman reported in the *New York Times* (Oct. 1, 1969), "The main United States targets, according to sources in both the Laotian Government and the Pathet Lao rebels, are the rebel economy and social fabric." Direct reports by refugees and visitors make clear that this judgment is fully accurate. The purpose of the bombardment was explained quite adequately by Allman:

The bombing, by creating refugees, deprives the Communists of their chief source of food and transport. The population of the Pathet Lao zone has been declining for several years and the Pathet Lao find it increasingly difficult to fight a "people's war" with fewer and fewer people.

During the same years, the CIA established a private "clandestine army," made up largely of Meo mountain tribesmen. In

---

2. Hearings before the (Symington) Subcommittee on United States Security Agreements and Commitments Abroad of the Committee on Foreign Relations, U.S. Senate, 91st Congress, 1st Session, Part 3, November, 1969, p. 713.

3. Some relevant facts are revealed in the Symington Subcommittee Hearings, *ibid.*, Part 2, October, 1969, p. 464 and elsewhere.

the fall of 1969, after a savage aerial bombardment, the clandestine army swept through the Plain of Jars, destroying and plundering, in the first significant modification of territorial boundaries since 1964. This was encouraging to American government observers. Senator Javits commented: "This is one war that is successful."[4] Senator Symington, long an advocate of air power, regarded these victories as a vindication of his position. The bombardment of North Vietnam, he argues, was unfair to the United States because there were too many restrictions, but in Laos "we use the military without shackles," and the results are therefore much more satisfactory.[5] Only briefly, however. By January 1970 the United States realized that it was not going to be able to hold the Plain with the CIA army. The population was removed and the area turned into a free fire zone. It is estimated that about half the population, including most of the young men and women, went over to the Pathet Lao, despite the abominable conditions of life under constant American bombardment. The refugees, who were, perhaps, the wealthiest peasants in Laos, subsist in miserable camps near Vientiane.

I visited one of the camps in April with several journalists. A few days ago, I received a letter from one of them, describing a more recent trip to the same camp:

If [the refugees] had stayed at home on the Plain of Jars they might have been bombed to jelly; they admit that. They also know that here the bellies of their children are swelling, that muscles are slacking, that the "red spots" are running rampant from hut to hut, that most of the infants have mass scabs and raw flesh on their scalps, that pustules have popped out on the flesh of even the older children and adults, that thick yellow mucous streams constantly from the nostrils and that lips and noses have been rubbed raw, that probably a majority of the children have eyelashes caked with excreting eye infections; they know these things because they can't escape from them. They know they are dying here.[6]

Literally. Ten have died—three children, seven adults—since

4. *Ibid.*, Part 3, p. 792.
5. *Ibid.*, pp. 780 ff., 790.
6. Don Ronk, Vientiane, June 13, 1970.

my visit in April to this camp of perhaps 400 people. But no matter. "This is one war that is successful."

In the territories still held by its protégés, the United States maintains a regime of total corruption. For the tiny elite who live in luxury on American dole or by graft and corruption, for those (mostly foreigners) who control commerce and what there is of a productive economy, there are plenty of commodities and amenities. American "aid" has succeeded in corrupting the elite and involving it in the American war but not in developing the basis for a viable society.

The target of the American attack in northern Laos is the Pathet Lao which, as everyone admits, is the only political organization in Laos with a popular base, comprising the only elements in Laotian society that have any reasonable plans, that offer any realistic hope for social and economic development within the framework of genuine Laotian nationalism.

Of course, the matter is not put in these terms in official American government propaganda. The claim is that the United States is defending Laos from North Vietnamese aggression. It is surely true that the North Vietnamese are not likely to tolerate an American puppet state on their borders, complete with CIA bases used for war against Vietnam and an army wholly supported by the American taxpayer. But despite diligent efforts, the United States government and its scholars in the RAND corporation and elsewhere have yet to produce any significant evidence to substantiate their claims.[7] In fact, as Fred Branfman proves in article 12, available data support an entirely different estimate of the various forces involved in combat in Laos. What is not in doubt, however, is that in defending Laos from "North Vietnamese aggression" the United States has driven much of the population into caves and refugee camps, created a dependent consumer economy, and imposed the rule of the most corrupt elements of Laotian society. At the same time, through subversion, violence, and terror, the United States has attempted,

---

7. What evidence I could find, with the assistance of U.S. Embassy officials in Vientiane, is discussed in my book *At War with Asia* (New York: Pantheon, 1970), chap. 4.

so far without success, to destroy the only indigenous forces trying to establish a basis for a healthy economy and social life.

The basic facts are summarized with stark clarity by Jacques Decornoy:

The Americans accuse the North Vietnamese of military intervention in the country. But it is they who speak of reducing Laos to zero, while the Pathet Lao exalt the national culture and national independence.

And, we may add, the Americans are in fact well on their way to reducing Laos to zero, while the Pathet Lao have made a valiant effort to bring Laotian society into the modern age.

The techniques of the American war have varied over the years; the aim persists. There is, to be sure, an element of lunacy in this relentless attack by the great superpower of the Western world on a poor and helpless people. There is an element of cynical rationality as well. However bedecked with farcical expressions of goodwill, the attempt to subjugate Laos is merely one component in the long-term effort to dominate Indochina, a crucial theme in American imperial policy in the postwar world. Since 1962 the war in southern Laos has been an extension of the Vietnam War. In part, Laos is being destroyed in an effort to buy time for the Thai elite that has served as the main support for American aims in Southeast Asia—a fact that is more or less conceded by an Administration spokesman.[8] Furthermore, as Fred Branfman explains in article 12 of the present book, Laos is serving as a test site for the experimental investigation of counterinsurgency, yielding insights that can be applied elsewhere in the world to suppress indigenous movements of national liberation.

In Laos, we find in relatively pure form the major features of counterrevolutionary intervention as designed by the gendarme of the world. In Laos, the indigenous political forces of the "rebels" have been separated from their base in the peasantry by "forced-draft urbanization," that is, the direct application of military power to drive the population from their homes and

8. See, for example, the Symington Subcommittee Hearings, Part 2, p. 564, one of the few places where there are glimmerings of coherence in Ambassador Sullivan's curious testimony.

to concentrate them in areas where, it is hoped, they can be controlled by the regime that serves as a local façade for American power. Beyond the reach of American-supported ground forces, bombardment of unprecedented savagery has undone the hard work of social and economic development and replaced the hope for progress with a prayer for survival. And, best of all, it has been done in secret. No grand exposures, no detailed reporting on the scene by journalists and TV crews, none of the exposure in the media that has plagued the similar American effort in Vietnam. The murder and destruction have been carried out in delightful obscurity, so much so that even the Chairman of the Senate Foreign Relations Committee was unaware until October 1969 of "this big war in Laos," and "had no idea we had a full-scale war going on."[9] And the ordinary citizen is naturally still less aware.

Of course, we live in an open society, and therefore all will ultimately be revealed. The history books may, some day, be reasonably accurate. The peasants of Laos, rotting in refugee camps, huddling in their caves, may take comfort in this fact.

A further advantage of the Laotian model of repression is that it is relatively inexpensive in American lives. Only some 200 Americans are listed officially as killed in action in Laos since 1964, and another 200 as missing in action or as prisoners. In Laos, apart from the victims of the American bombardment, Asians are being killed by Asians. For the imperialist power, this is a far more satisfactory "scenario" than Vietnam. There it was learned that the population at home is likely to be restless when too many Americans are killed.

The tactic of setting the natives at each other's throats—called "Vietnamization" in its latest reincarnation—is a venerable one. In general, conquerors prefer quisling governments to direct rule not only on grounds of efficiency but also so that aggression can be masked as defense of a legitimate government against subversion inspired from outside. A standard technique is to use a native elite or minorities, sometimes imported from a neighboring country, to administer or to maintain order. And quite often it is possible to exploit latent ethnic, religious, and class an-

9. *Ibid.*, Part 3, p. 673.

tagonisms in the conquered territories. The American government is as skilled as its predecessors in the use of such devices. In the Indochina war, every potential antagonism has been raised to the level of a bloody conflict. The Meo have been incited to fight alongside Nationalist Chinese, Thai, and other mercenaries against the Pathet Lao. It appears that the Meo have been decimated by this cynical policy. In South Vietnam, Khmer mercenaries are used to repress the indigenous forces of the National Liberation Front (NLF), while ARVN troops, along with mercenaries from the Cambodian minority in Vietnam and now Thai troops (necessary, as Premier Lon Nol explains, because his officers may still be loyal to Sihanouk),[10] are sent into Cambodia to help contain a rising insurgency. More than 11,000 Thai troops have been stationed in South Vietnam and some 5,000 are reported to be in Laos, in part to defend the American-imposed regimes, but in part to receive training which, it is hoped, will serve them well when they are called upon to repress their own domestic insurgency. The American-supported regime of Lon Nol in Cambodia,[11] in a despicable effort to win over the mass of the peasantry, launched a pogrom against Cambodians of Vietnamese origin which is estimated to have taken more than 5,000 lives. The same American government that never tires of reiterating its concern over the "bloodbaths" that might conceivably occur if it were to relieve South Vietnam from American bombardment and military occupation, quickly sent in an invading army, not to stop the bloodbath, but to defend Lon Nol. The blood debt incurred by the desperate coup regime in Phnom Penh may yet be repaid in a still more horrifying way.

10. Ralph Blumenthal, *New York Times*, June 16, 1970, citing "well-informed sources."

11. Perhaps "American-imposed regime" might be a more accurate term. A full account of American involvement in the March 18 coup in Cambodia is yet to be written. That there was some involvement seems evident, if only from the fact that the Khmer Serei were infiltrated into the Cambodian army shortly before the coup. These forces, organized and supported by the CIA, were previously "at war" with Cambodia under Sihanouk. One can hardly avoid the suspicion that they were introduced into the Cambodian army to strengthen the right in preparation for the coup.

The two most dynamic societies in the region, the Thai and the Vietnamese, have been driven toward war by the American use of Thailand as a military base for its attack on Vietnam and by the use of Thai mercenaries throughout Indochina. Again, the legacy of this cynical manipulation of ethnic fears and rivalries may be grim and long-lasting. In South Vietnam and Thailand, the mountain tribesmen have been uprooted and assaulted by the local accomplices of the United States, while in Laos, the CIA-USAID exploitation of the Meo, in the name of "protecting the Meo from Communism" and "defending the Free World from aggression," is likely to lead to their disappearance as an organized community. In South Vietnam, the Catholic community has provided the main support for the successive regimes imposed by the United States, while, in neighboring Cambodia, Lon Nol spoke of a war of religions (Buddhism versus Communism) as he sent the Cambodian army to slaughter the native Vietnamese, who constitute the overwhelming majority of the Cambodian Catholic community. Throughout the region, native elites, dependent on American money for their sustenance and American arms for their survival have been drawn into a bitter war against their own people.

Not all of the problems of Indochina result from American intervention and aggression. But it is striking that precisely those indigenous groups that show real concern for social and economic development, that have the capacity to mobilize the mass of the population, that have succeeded in overcoming and resolving ethnic conflicts are the target of the American attack. This has been true in Vietnam and Laos, and it will no doubt prove true in Cambodia as well.

In these respects, the United States merely follows the traditional pattern of great power intervention. What is remarkable is only the scale of the attack and the amazing inability of Americans to see the plain facts, their persistence in believing that somehow they are engaged in an exercise in benevolence as they expend two million tons of ordnance a year in Indochina, destroying towns and villages, "generating" millions of refugees, cratering and defoliating the landscape, and demolishing every painfully won achievement of the indigenous popular forces.

Part I

The Setting: The Land and Its People

1

Contours, Cultures, and Conflict

Richard S. D. Hawkins

> Hanoi is not threatened by Laos; it runs risks only when it
> moves its forces across borders.—Richard Milhous Nixon,
> March 6, 1970
>
> It [Laos] was a state by diplomatic courtesy.—Arthur M.
> Schlesinger, Jr., A Thousand Days

The problem of how to define the physical limits of political
groupings has plagued men for as long as they have struggled
for power and property. The ready availability of maps demar-
cating national bounds in gaudy colors has by no means eliminated the problem. Most of today's bitterest and most durable
conflicts involve a dispute over delimitation of territory; the
Arab-Israeli struggle, the Kashmir dispute, and the brief battle
between Russians and Chinese for Chen Pao/Damanskii Island
are recent examples. It should not be surprising, then, that territorial limitation is very much a part of the war in Laos.

There are several kinds of territorial limits. We are all familiar
with the legal concept of a *border*—a line defined by treaty, and
marked on maps. A *boundary* is also linear, but its function is
to contain and limit, and it conveys the notion of a territorial
barrier beyond which a state cannot expand. A *frontier* is never
a clearly defined line but usually a zone of indefinite depth in
which a neighboring state exercises some influence. The usual
implication is that a nearby state is expanding into the frontier
zone, often an area of low population density. In common par-
lance, the United States shares a border with Canada; a
boundary separates one's own property from that of his neighbors; and the American West was formerly a frontier.

In diplomatic practice it frequently occurs that two relatively
powerful neighboring states may not share a common border and
may find that it is in their interest not to do so. In this case they

may agree, formally or tacitly, on the maintenance of a *buffer zone,* a piece of geopolitical insulation which insures the parties against potential territorial conflicts. Usually a buffer zone consists of part or all of a politically and militarily weak third area. The creation of a buffer zone is seldom a guarantee of serenity for the third party, since it usually implies tensions between the unfortunate buffer's powerful neighbors.

Laos presently serves as a "buffer zone and battleground" for the manipulations of the United States and six surrounding nations as well as a battlefield for its own fragmented elite. A mere reading of the names of states which share borders with Laos is enough to suggest that its only alternatives are neutrality or chaos: North Vietnam and South Vietnam to the east; Cambodia to the south; Thailand to the west; Burma to the northwest; China to the north. The rugged terrain of Laos, its internal political division, its diversity of peoples and languages, its small population, and its strategic location make it ideally suited for a protracted guerrilla struggle.

A brief glance at the surface of Laos is sufficient to explain many of its present difficulties. On the map, the outline of Laos resembles a tree, its large trunk rooted in eastern Cambodia, its stunted crown bending westward into the high winds of change blowing out of North Vietnam (see map, page xiii). Few maps, however, give an adequate impression of the precipitous slopes and tumultuous rivers, the thick vegetation on the lower hills, the few roads which dissolve into quagmires during the summer rainy season, the pockets of irrigated rice grown in small river plains by tribal Tai, the burned-off patches in the forest where other groups raise dry rice and root crops on slopes of up to 45 degrees or more, or the peaks above 3,000 feet where the Meo and Yao raise their opium poppies. Wild is the only word for most of Laos.

Population density is highest in the narrow valley of the middle Mekong, from Luang Prabang down to the Khong Falls at the Cambodian border. This is the home ground of the Lao people, a group of wet-rice growers oriented toward the Mekong, closely related in culture and language to the Thai of the Bangkok area. More ethnic Lao live on the Thai side of the river than in Laos proper. A small minority of the Lao constitutes the elite of Laos. This tiny fraction of the population is further split by rivalries and feuds between families and personalities. The control of the Lao elite does not extend far from the major cities, and probably a majority of Laotians (citizens of Laos, of whatever ethnic heritage) owe allegiance only to their village.

Laos today harbors in its 91,425 square miles a population variously estimated at up to three million; the most reasonable figure is generally agreed to lie somewhat under two million. The great population centers of Indochina are the deltas of the Mekong south of Saigon and of the Red River, in the Hanoi area, where population density reaches 3,500 per square mile in the most fertile tracts. Even the relatively populous river valleys of Laos average fewer than 100 people per square mile. The hill areas may shelter as few as two per square mile. Migrating groups have frequently pushed into Laos, meeting little resistance because of this low population density.

The geographically homogeneous belt of uplands which stretches from the Vietnam-China border west as far as the valley of the Irrawaddy in Burma is occupied by a great diversity of ethnic groups. Most of the surface of Laos is in this hill zone and in its offshoot, the Annamite Chain, which runs southeast almost as far as Saigon, separating the area of Mekong Lao influence from that of the Vietnamese. Such points of population concentration as exist in this upland zone are found in the numerous river valleys. These are inhabited largely by peoples of the Tai race, which includes the Chuang and Nung of southern China, the Shan of Burma, the Thai (Siamese), and in Laos, the Lao, Black Tai, Red Tai, Tai Neua, and others. Non-Tai groups favor higher altitudes. Upland Mon-Khmer tribes, such as the Loven, So, and Bru of southern Laos and their relatives to the north, the Lamet and Khmu, are the most "backward" of the Laotian groups, living in small villages and growing dry rice and maize by the techniques of shifting cultivation. (The culture of these groups is actually quite complex and well adapted to their environment.) Interspersed among the northern Tai and Mon-Khmer populations are groups of Tibeto-Burmans belonging to such tribes as Akha, Lolo, and Lahu, and tribes

which have migrated southward from China, including the Miao
(Meo) and Yao (Man). The region of northern Laos shown on
the colorful ethnolinguistic map of mainland Southeast Asia
published by the Human Relations Area Files resembles a Jack-
son Pollock painting.

The different groups tend to favor certain altitudes. Theoretically,
one could walk uphill from a given river and pass through Lao
villages, then those of Lamet and Akha, finally reaching Meo
settlements just beneath the highest peaks. Coexistence under
these conditions has not always been peaceful. In a sense, the
entire hill region is a frontier zone. Subject to incursions of new
groups over the centuries and the scene of frequent revolts
against lowland control, it is an area that strong kingdoms have
often tried to dominate.

Communications throughout the hill region are terrible by
modern standards, but this has not prevented frequent migra-
tion of small hill groups. The fact of their scattered distribution
means that a Meo of Sayaboury province, southwest of Luang
Prabang, feels more closely related to another Meo of the Cao-
bang region of North Vietnam than to his near neighbor in a
Khmu village. The borders separating the modern states of mainland Southeast Asia bear little relationship to the distribution
of the hill populations.

Since the remarkable tribal patchwork of the northern regions
of Southeast Asia defies the imagination, not to mention the
boundary surveyor, geographic features have been used to define Laos' borders. Its border with North and South Vietnam
largely follows the watershed of the Annamite Chain. Because
the land is too rugged for easy communications, the influence
of the Laotian government has never been strong along this
boundary; it is now openly conceded to be in Pathet Lao control. The borders shared with China and Burma are equally
unpopulated and permeable. The Chinese border traces the
watershed of the Nam Ou, a small river. Most of the border
between Sayaboury province and northern Thailand also follows
the Mekong watershed. But from the west of Vientiane down
almost as far as Pakse, the border between Laos and Thailand

follows the mainstream of the Mekong, the natural focus of trade and communication for the entire region.

However, political borders are not the sole determinants of the situation; natural boundaries still exert a strong influence. The Mekong Development Project, a TVA-like complex of dams planned to bring flood control, irrigation, and hydroelectric power to the region, transcends national boundaries and embraces the entire Mekong basin. Its outlines on the map encompass almost all of Laos, Cambodia, and northeast Thailand, as well as portions of southern Vietnam. Overlooking the potential wealth of the area, critics of the American presence tend to regard Indochina only as a battleground upon which the United States struggles to protect its other Asian interests. However, the agricultural and industrial potential of the Mekong basin is great, and President Johnson, for one, knew that this potential could not be realized without the development of cheap electric power.

Although one side wages a fluid guerrilla struggle while the other modifies techniques of positional warfare, the ultimate goal of all parties is still control of territory. There can be no lasting truce until the battleground is finally divided and a suitable and lasting border is achieved where none now exists.

BIBLIOGRAPHY

Auvray, Georges, "Les voies de pénétration au Laos," *Bulletin des Amis du Laos,* I, 1 (September 1937), pp. 45–47.

Coedes, Georges, *The Making of Southeast Asia.* Berkeley: University of California Press, 1967.

Croizat, Victor J., "The Mekong River Development Project: Some Geographical, Historical, and Political Considerations," RAND Corporation, Unpublished, n.d. [1967?].

Fisher, C. A., *South-East Asia.* London: Methuen, 1966.

Hall, D. G. E., *A History of South-East Asia.* New York: St. Martin's Press, 1968.

Gouvernement Général de l'Indochine (compiled by Lt.-Col.

Tournier, Résident Supérieur), *Notice sur le Laos français.* Hanoi: Imp. F.-H. Schneider, 1900.

LAMB, ALASTAIR, *Asian Frontiers.* London: Pall Mall, 1968.

LATTIMORE, OWEN, *Inner Asian Frontiers of China.* Boston: Beacon Press, 1951.

LEBAR, FRANK M., GERALD C. HICKEY, and JOHN K. MUSGRAVE, eds., *Ethnic Groups of Mainland Southeast Asia.* New Haven: Human Relations Area Files Press, 1964.

PANIKKAR, K. M., *Asia and Western Dominance.* London: G. Allen and Unwin, 1959.

SOLOMON, ROBERT L., "Boundary Concepts and Practices in Southeast Asia." Santa Monica: RAND Corporation, December 1969 (RM-5936-1-ARPA).

2

The Lao

Georges Condominas

Translated by Malitte Matta

On an ethnolinguistic map of Southeast Asia, the Lao population appears as a slow stream following the riverbed of the Mekong. From both banks, threadlike pseudopods correspond to the progressive Lao settlement on the branches of the great river. Between Luang Prabang and Vientiane (where the river turns abruptly eastward at a right angle and then, almost as abruptly, southward) the Lao population spreads out to cover not only the left bank of the river but the greater part of eastern Thailand (*Phaak Isaan* or the "northeastern region"). This population becomes sparse near the Mekong in the south, and is confined to the region near the river banks by the time it arrives at the Cambodian border, which it crosses by a few kilometers. The Lao ethnic group is essentially a Thai-speaking population whose economy rests upon paddy field cultivation, whose religion is Theravada Buddhism, and which constituted a powerful state during the sixteenth and seventeenth centuries.[1]

The movements of history have resulted in a double paradox on Laos as a state and on the Lao as an ethnic group. This led me to write more than ten years ago, "In my understanding, the most important characteristic of Laotian ethnology, which on the sociopolitical level has repercussions which are underestimated, is that *the Lao proper represent only half of the total population of the country.*"[2] I then noted a fact which today

---

1. There is no need for me to discuss Laotian history, treated elsewhere in this volume, but for a thorough understanding of the current culture, it is useful to refer to the pertinent studies of Charles Archaimbault, notably those devoted to the annals of Champassak and Xieng Khouang.

2. Claude Gaudillot and Georges Condominas, *La Plaine de Vientiane: Rapport d'étude* 3 vols. (Paris: Bureau de Developpement Productivité Agricole, 1959), I, 42.

seems to me just as important on an international level, at least within this part of the world.

If, on the one hand, the Lao represent only one half of the population of the state which bears their name, on the other hand, it is not in Laos that they are most numerous: from estimates based on the census taken in Thailand in 1957, the Northeastern Lao (inhabitants of the right bank of the Mekong) would number five million, to which one may add one million Thai Khorat and two million Lao Yuan (of Chieng Mai) for the total of the Lao group. Even if one limits oneself to the two groups bordering the Mekong, which form only one ethnic group, strictly speaking, one must remember that *the independent Lao, even today, number less than a million while the Lao of Siam represent a mass of five million,* in constant demographic growth, and that this mass is settled on very poor land.[3]

Along the banks of the Mekong or one of its branches, or as an island in the midst of paddy fields, the Lao village appears as a group of high-stilted houses spread out in a vast orchard dotted by stands of giant bamboo or clumps of palm trees (areca and coconut in the lower regions). The principal activity is rice cultivation. The paddy fields, (*naa*), watered simply by rainfall, do not have complex systems of irrigation. The few trenches one notices have been dug for purposes of drainage. Of course, the techniques used by the Lao peasant are elaborate, as they are wherever the paddy field system is used, but they are not carried to the limits of their possibilities. Where one might expect two harvests each year, the Lao peasant is satisfied with only one. This has been seen as a cultural trait, but if so, the main factor has been the lack of demographic pressure.

Cultivation is a family enterprise depending essentially upon a human work force, with the use of animals limited to harrowing and plowing (and sometimes threshing); that is the only period of the agricultural year when complex tools appear in the fields. Sowing and harvesting require more workers, who are still obtained mainly by the reciprocal help of neighbors. The importance of paddy field culture in the life of the peasant is attested by the succession of agrarian rites (focused on the

3. *Ibid.*, p. 43.

paddy field) which coincide with the different periods of the agricultural calendar and culminate with the harvest festival.[4]

The paddy field is not the only form of cultivation. The *hay* or *swidden* is still used wherever the forest is accessible, in fact nearly everywhere. In clearings created by slashing and burning, rice seed is placed in holes (rather than sown) in soil fertilized by ashes; not only rice but also corn, manioc, and different vegetables (pepper, beans, cucumbers, etc.) are grown. The following year, these latter plants occupy a more important place than the rice, which disappears altogether from the plot the year after. The soil is not exhausted but is left fallow in order to reforest itself while another part of the forest is slashed and burned. However, abandonment of dry rice cultivation may lead to landholding, either for a long period, if fruit trees have been planted, or almost permanently if, after a few years, fields have been leveled and dikes established in order to create a paddy field.[5] In effect, the *hay* is not only a complementary form of rice cultivation and a means of cultivating other vegetables but the necessary and productive preliminary to the establishment of the paddy field (except in the lowlands, which can be transformed without the *hay* stage). Another important type of cultivation is conducted on the river banks exposed at the beginning of the dry season by the receding waters, which leave a heavy layer of alluvial deposits that are particularly fertile. These gardens or *suan* are used as kitchen gardens, or for planting tobacco, with excellent results and profits.

One must also mention the fruit trees (*agrumes,* jack fruit, mango, banana) which grow around the houses and the little squares planted with Lao onions and ginger. One sees also small boxes of herbs placed up on little columns in order to be within reach of the cook. Betel vines supported by lines of training sticks complement areca palms which grow in clearings near

4. For a description of these rites, see Charles Archaimbault, "Les rites agraires dans le Moyen-Laos," *France-Asie,* Vol. XVI (1959), pp. 1185–1194; pp. 1274–1283.

5. Georges Condominas, "Notes sur le droit foncier en milieu rural dans la Plaine de Vientiane," *Artibus Asiae,* Felicitation Volume, presented to Professor Georges Coedes, Vol. XXIV, No. 3/4 (1961), pp. 255–262.

the houses; betel leaves are used to wrap areca nuts, which Southeast Asians find delectable to chew. The space between the stilts underneath the house can have two uses: as a storage area for agricultural implements—tools, fish traps, etc.—with an empty corner where the women's looms are set up, or as a stable for buffalo and oxen, which are fenced in by wooden railings attached to the stilts of the house. The manure is periodically carried to the *suan*. In the empty space around the house there are pig pens, a granary (placed on stilts) for rice, and a shelter for the cart, which sometimes covers the rice treadmill too (when this is not installed beneath the house).

The nearby forest, which provides wood, bamboo, rattan, and various fibers used in construction and handicrafts (especially basketry, which is very important), firewood and charcoal (mainly near the town), also furnishes important ingredients of the local diet. The Lao gather an appreciable quantity of wild fruit and vegetables. The men hunt and trap game. However, fishing provides the greatest quantity of animal protein. Farming and fishing take up the greater part of the Lao peasants' work time. Everybody fishes, all year long. One has only to see the children after school, especially after a rain shower, to understand the pleasure with which they rush, with a great variety of containers, to scoop the fish, shrimp, and snails from the bottoms of ponds, canals, and even puddles. The flooded paddy fields are not forgotten—if the rice is growing, they fish only along the edges of the dikes. Fishing gear takes various forms and sizes, from lines with fish hook and simple bamboo or basketry traps (used in streams and canals) to giant fish traps and dipping nets (used in the rivers and larger ponds). We must remember that fishing is given great importance everywhere in Southeast Asia.

Only large villages have one or more shops, which are generally built at ground level. But exchanges with the outside world take place in marketplaces either in nearby towns, or at crossroads, or at crossings of paths and rivers where settlements have sprung up. People travel most often on foot but also by buffalo cart or oxcart and by boat. Today, relatively regular private bus service is available to the city, extending the trading network deeper and deeper into the countryside.

John F. Embree was struck by the loosely structured character of Lao culture.[6] This trait is perhaps most apparent in family organization, and is demonstrated by the lack of rigor in the drawing up of rules and the casualness with which they are applied. However, one finds many of the characteristics of this family organization in other great Southeast Asian cultures. On the popular level, there are no large and well-defined groups such as clans or lineages. The system of descent is nonunilineal, or cognatic: paternal and maternal kin have the same importance for the individual. There is, however, a cleavage: the kinship system differentiates between senior and junior members in each generation. But this cleavage has few practical consequences for Laotians, in contrast to what generally happens elsewhere in Southeast Asia (where this trait has a much greater importance). This dichotomy, in principle, prevents a Laotian man from marrying a kinswoman of the elder branch (*sua*) of his family, but infractions of this rule are not taken seriously. There is no rule that a couple must live with one or the other set of parents; but couples tend to live near the wife's parents, and proverbs and sayings recommend that they do so. A young couple will live in economic interdependence with the wife's family for a few years while they construct their own home and granary nearby. As a consequence, in matters of inheritance, the youngest daughter of a couple is privileged; she and her husband have remained in the home of her aged parents. After two or three years of marriage, her elder sisters have left and built their own homes. The sons have married and live elsewhere. Here also, this is not a rule but a tendency.[7]

The religion practiced by the Lao peasant, both in his daily life

6. John F. Embree, "Thailand—A Loosely Structured Social System," *American Anthropologist*, Vol. 52 (1950), pp. 181–193.

7. For a fuller discussion of these matters, see Georges Condominas, *Essai sur la société rurale de la region de Vientiane*. (Vientiane: 1962; mimeographed paper, 1968).

and in public festivals, is a harmonious blend of Buddhism and the cult of *phi* or spirits.[8] It also has traces of Hinduism wherever the Khmer (Cambodian) Empire exerted an influence. But it is very difficult to distinguish what has been derived directly from Buddhism, from what has been inherited from Hinduism, not to mention the elements of the *phi* cult that have been "civilized" by having been given Hindu names.

Attempts have been made to link Buddhism to the Lao state since its beginnings. Lao written tradition attributes the introduction of Theravada Buddhism to the first sovereign of Lan Xang, Fa Ngoum, and his wife, a Khmer princess.[9] In fact, the Buddhist doctrine already had followers in the middle of the fourteenth century, before the creation of the first Laotian kingdom,[10] and Fa Ngoum did no more than promote the diffusion of the religion on a grand scale. We know that the period of Buddhism's greatest influence coincided with the greatest height of the state in the sixteenth and seventeenth centuries. The great king Pothisarath even tried to impose it to the exclusion of the *phi* cult. By an edict in 1527 he forbade the practice of the *phi* cult in the entire kingdom. He ordered the destruction of all its sanctuaries, even that of the tutelary god of the capital, Luang Prabang, on the site of which he caused a pagoda to be constructed.[11]

The *phi* cults belong to the old Thai animist background and were enriched by elements assimilated by these settlers from the prior occupants, the proto-Indochinese. One finds cults associated with Buddhism in analagous ways in all of the neighboring countries. However, one must not envisage the *phi* cults as

8. For a more detailed analysis, see Georges Condominas, "Notes sur le Bouddhisme populaire en milieu rural Lao," *Archives de Sociologie des Religions*, Vol. XIII, No. 25 (1968), pp. 81–110; and No. 26 (1968), pp. 111–150.

9. Auguste Pavie, *Recherches sur l'histoire du Cambodge, du Laos et du Siam*, (Paris: E. Leroux, 1898), p. 32; Paul Le Boulanger, *Histoire du Laos français*, (Paris: Plon, 1931), pp. 46–47.

10. Paul Lévy, "Les traces de l'introduction du Bouddhisme à Luang Prabang," *Bulletin de l'Ecole Française d'Extrême-Orient* (BEFEO) Vol. XL, No. 1 (1958–1959), pp. 880–892.

11. Le Boulanger, *op. cit.*, pp. 72–73.

an organized religion as in the case of official religions. The word *phi* encompasses a great number of notions, which must be translated for us by words carrying a multitude of different meanings, such as "souls of the dead," "maleficent spirit," "tutelary god," "natural divinity."[12]

The *phi* are constantly present in the life of the Lao and govern many of their acts (if only because of the ability of the *phi* to inflict illness). But *phi* worship rarely involves great expenditures. The abundance of food offered at the harvest festival feasts must be considered as much a normal requirement of the large work force assembled to harvest the grain as an agrarian rite. As to the expenses incurred through an illness caused by the *phi*, they may be put under the heading of payment for medical care and magic healing practices (the wages of the medicine man being the most important item). Love potions and black magic do not, in my opinion, threaten to bankrupt their users.

We should consider as part of the *phi* cult the *sou khouan* (calling back of the soul) better known under the name *baci*. During this charming ceremony, complementary to many different rites, one of the wandering souls of an individual is called back, received with offerings, and kept in place by knotting a thread of cotton to the owner's wrist. The idea of thirty-two "souls" which underlies *baci* probably belongs to the system of representations, remodeled by Buddhism, of which the *phi* are a part. The worship of the *phi ban*, the tutelary god of the village, is the most emphatic expression of the *phi* cult and involves the participation of the entire village. He is the *genius loci*, the god of the village commons, both protector of the forests and fields and of the human and animal inhabitants which these commons support. His altar, the *ho phi ban*, made of one or two huts on stilts, is hidden in a corner of the forest near the village. The person responsible for its upkeep, the *chao cham phi ban* (the cult master of the spirit of the village), goes to pray for the well-being of the village community every fifteen days, on

12. Condominas, "Notes sur le Bouddhisme populaire en milieu rural Lao," p. 131. This article offers a detailed discussion of the points raised in the following pages which can only be treated generally here.

the waxing and waning moon. He also goes to worship at the
request of any inhabitant wishing to cure a member of his
family or to implore protection for travel; the sacrifice of *lieng
phi* (literally "feeding the spirit") is executed under the direction of the cult master.

This sacrifice literally throws the role of the *chao cham* or
cult master into relief as the intercessor for the entire community.
This ceremony, in which all the inhabitants of the village take
part, occurs twice a year: but that of the first month, which is
a sort of thanksgiving for the harvest which has just been
gathered, is never as important as the *lieng phi* of the sixth
month, performed at the onset of the rainy season just before
beginning work in the paddy fields not only to implore good
health for men and domestic animals but above all to ask for
a bountiful harvest. The ritual connected with the ceremony of
the sixth month varies from one village to another. In some
villages, it consists of a collective sacrifice in which each household offers up at least a chicken, or must contribute to a collection for the purchase of a pig, which will be eaten in the clearing
before the *ho phi ban*. On the morning of the sacrifice to the
phi ban, the village is closed off to strangers, who are warned
away by *taleo,* a kind of star of woven bamboo placed at each
point of entry to the village. However, in most of the villages
of the plain of Vientiane, the *lieng phi* is included in the *Boun
Bang Fay* or "Rocket Festival," a ceremony considered Buddhist.
Then the village is not only open to strangers but welcomes visitors from neighboring communities. Even in this case, the role
of the *chao cham phi ban* remains the most important.

It would be an error to believe that by the very importance
of his role the *chao cham* could become a rival of the abbot of
the pagoda. In fact, he is a faithful Buddhist to whom it would
not occur that the rites accomplished in honor of the spirit of
the village might be contrary to the practice of Buddhism. I
must emphasize that when he has to go to the *ho phi ban* to
worship the village spirit, the *chao cham* goes first to make an
offering to the monks. Often the *chao cham phi ban* fulfills the
duties of the master of the cult of the "beneficent spirit of the

monastery" (*chao cham phi khoun vat*). This spirit is the soul of the first abbot of the monastery (*vat*). His altar is a tiny building on stilts not more than two feet high placed in a bushy corner of the *vat*. The *chao cham* must recount there all of the important happenings in the life of the parish (men entering or leaving the monastic order, the beginning of a journey, the stay— even brief—of strangers, etc.). The cult of the beneficent spirit of the monastery seems to be a tie between Buddhism and the cult of the *phi*.

As important as the cult of the *phi* may be in the Lao village, Buddhism remains the dominant factor on the religious and sociological level. Buddhism is responsible for the most striking physical feature of the settled area. The only relatively open space (and the largest) is the courtyard of the monastery. Beyond the buildings stand some fruit trees and, in the case of ancient pagodas, a great banyan, the Tree of the Buddha's Enlightenment. Furthermore, the only brick building in the village was, at the time of my investigation in 1959–1960, the sanctuary (*sim*) of the monastery. Indeed the *vat* is both *the symbol and the center of the rural collectivity*.[13]

The creation of a monastery follows a certain pattern. When the farmers who have cleared an area of the forest and created paddy fields consider their hamlet large enough to justify replacing their field huts with permanent houses, their first preoccupation is to "animate" this new community by the installation of a *vat pa*. This "forest monastery" will attest to the social unity of the group of houses. Henceforth this is not a collection of pioneers but a community possessing a common center of interest which will be at the same time the forum and the temple and which will serve as its emblem and symbol in the eyes of strangers. The group of houses originally built for the clearing of the forest have detached themselves from their older village to become a new parish. The same thing occurs when the people living on the outskirts of a rapidly growing settlement wish to form an autonomous quarter.

13. Condominas, *La Plaine de Vientiane*, p. 80.

The "forest monastery" (called this even when juxtaposed to the village as a new quarter) consists of a simple house on stilts, the monastic dormitory (*koutchi*), which will offer shelter to the monk (or monks) who has agreed to live there. As it develops and the hamlet acquires a larger work force, the inhabitants build a *sala*, a larger square building on short stilts with a steep roof. The following stage is particularly important; up to this point the village's own work force is sufficient. Now the construction of the sanctuary (*sim*) requires supplementary effort: the village must become not only capable of assembling a work force but also able to raise money, in order to buy materials such as brick and tiles, etc., and to pay the salaries of specialized workers such as bricklayers and sculptors. This means that the village community has further developed, reaching a level of prosperity and repute sufficient to attract cash gifts and to warrant the collection, during its festivals, of a large amount of money for the temple. The sanctuary is built by stages as funds become available; therefore the construction may take several years. But once the sanctuary has been completed, the *vat* and therefore the village may hope to attract a larger number of monks and novices, thereby acquiring even greater merit and prestige. Above all, they may arrive at the stage much desired by every monastery, that of having a *sim* where ordination ceremonies may be held.

Like all monasteries, the Lao *vat* is, of course, a group of buildings dedicated to the religious life. But in fact it is more than that, for it is really the focus of the life of the community. The *sala* is the site of village meetings whether they concern well-digging, electing the chief of the village, the upkeep of paths and canals, or the organization of a village festival. The *vat* also houses the latter; when it is held, it overflows the court-yard because of the crowds arriving from neighboring villages. The *vat* drum not only calls to prayer but alerts the inhabitants in case of danger. The well in the courtyard is always public, while those beyond the walls often belong to private owners. The racing shell which will represent the village in rowing races during the Water Festival is housed beneath one of the buildings of the *vat*. The *vat* also serves as a warehouse for the tools and materials destined for collective use. And the passing traveler will be housed in the *sala* and in the morning will share the monk's meal.

The *vat* is not only the forum, the fairground, the warehouse, and the traveler's lodging, but for centuries it housed the only local school. The young boys who entered as novices learned mathematics as well as how to read and write Lao, then Pali. One may say that Pali, the sacred language of Theravada Buddhism, plays the role of Latin in the Catholic Church. The creation of lay public schools during the French protectorate naturally reduced the pagoda's role as a primary school. But very often classes are still held in the *sala*, when the funds necessary for the construction of a school have not yet been found. Furthermore, the young monks still naturally consider teaching as an inherent part of the monastic vocation, and it is they who are asked (as in 1962, for example) whenever an extension of the school program must be put into effect.

Nevertheless the traditional religious teaching is maintained in the *vat* at the same time as lay instruction is dispensed by the state. It is possible for students to then go on to the renovated and expanded monk-directed Pali schools located in the more important monasteries of each district. Eventually this course of instruction culminates in the Institut Buddhique in Vientiane. However, one must not exaggerate the significance of studying Pali and dogma on the level of the rural *vat*. Most of the time knowledge is confined to the mechanical recitation of phrases, at best generally understood with no true appreciation of the content of the Pali words; greater emphasis is given to phrases that seem charged with magic powers.

In spite of these deficiencies, the period spent in the pagoda remains of major importance in the education and cultural integration of the Lao. While today few men receive their primary education as novices, all continue to be marked by the moral and religious education dispensed by the *vat*, and by virtue of having spent longer or shorter periods of time as monks. One can readily understand how important this period in a man's life is for the formation of his personality. The moral standards inculcated during his childhood (not only what he was taught directly but also what he grasped from adult conversations and from sermons heard at the temple when he accompanied his parents there on feast days) suddenly become tangible rules to which he must submit in order to enjoy spiritual progress. He undergoes the trials of voluntary ugliness, asceticism and chastity, self-imposed contemplation and meditation upon his own nature and the words of the Buddha. In short, he tries to learn perfect detachment and will unconsciously be influenced by the fact that he is most highly regarded by society when he exists in a state of material poverty. One can understand how deeply these norms, absorbed at the end of highly impressionable adolescence, will affect him. The values to which he is exposed in the *vat* are respect for all life, understanding which creates a profound tolerance, deep faith (without a desire to proselytise, for one respects another's opinions), and individualism (for everyone must find his own means of salvation). But very often the experience in the monastery also fosters indifference to others, disinterest, nonchalance—in short, the surprising *bo pen nhang*, which is at the same time a great *savoir-vivre* and a block to all real effort.

The importance of the *vat* depends upon the considerable significance of the monk in Lao spiritual life. He makes it possible for the layman to accomplish daily the meritorious act par excellence: the giving of alms. A Lao author, reflecting on his religion, has written

Hed boun (do good, give an offering), that is to say acquire merit for a future life and if possible attain final Nirvana . . . and to whom should one give an offering if not to monks, these direct representatives of Buddha, his living images on earth.[14]

The giving of alms similarly constitutes the base of all festivals. These permit donors to acquire prestige in the eyes of their neighbors while also gaining merit for the afterlife. Only in the

---

14. Thao Nhouy Abhay, "Le Bouddhisme Lao," *France-Asie*, Vol. XII (1956), pp. 917–935, p. 922.

presence of monks can one accomplish the meritorious acts which play such an essential role in one's life.

The religious state is open to all, and the ideal remains for each man to enter holy orders. A Lao will do everything possible in order to wear the monastic habit at least once during his lifetime. From the minimum age of ten until the age of twenty, one can only be a novice. Once one has reached twenty years of age, he will be accepted as a monk if he has not killed or stolen and does not have a skin disease. The postulant *does not have to pronounce perpetual vows* but may leave the community at will. The ability of every man to pass at will from the lay to the religious state and vice versa creates even tighter bonds between the monks and the rest of the population.

Before and after a period of life in the *vat* devoted to austerity and detachment, one can continue accomplishing good works: the fact that others are living in the saffron robe permits one to continue acquiring *boun* or merit each time one makes an offering. Indeed, the man who enters holy orders provokes an immediate increment of merit, not only for himself, but also for others such as his dead parents and the donor—who may or may not be a relative—who provides the necessary accoutrements for his new vocation. After having become a monk, the offerings of food that he receives provoke a more diffuse increment of merit for the daily donors. During major festivals, there will once again be an increment of merit as massive as at the time of ordination. The monk remains the object of the offering whether the gifts are addressed directly to him or to his monastery. Therefore we must examine what is involved in giving alms to the monks.

One of the rules of Buddhist monastic life is to beg for one's food. The classic image of monks sees them walking in single file, clad in their saffron robes, with the faithful kneeling before them and putting single handfuls of food into the large begging bowls which they carry. In the countryside, this offering is generally carried to the *vat;* the villagers bring meals to the monks twice a day, at seven and at eleven in the morning. The monks must fast from noon until the following morning.

During certain festivals of the Buddhist calendar, gifts of a different nature are offered along with food; for example, monastic habits at the time of entry into and withdrawal from a Buddhist retreat. But offerings to the monastic community take on their deepest meaning during certain festivals, or *boun,* which are decided upon by an individual or by the village. The offerings affirm the prestige of some, manifest the unity of the collectivity, or accomplish both simultaneously.

Among the offerings made to the monks, there is a special category which is found in each *boun* and which appears to be almost a salary, or at least a gratuity, for a particular service. These are called *bang,* and consist of small cornucopias of banana leaf containing a pair of small candles or sticks of incense, flowers, and a sum of money (the amount depends on the generosity of the donor). The benediction of the monks is asked on almost every occasion and, each time, one distributes one *bang* to each monk present. Certain family occasions (the inauguration of a house, for example) involve only an offering of food and a distribution of *bang.* But these two elements are included in all other ceremonies, both private ones and collective *boun* offered by the village. It is significant that the Franco-Lao phrase "faire une *boun*" simply means "faire la fête" in its most common construction. The word *boun* serves to define any ceremony of which the object is to obtain merit.

Another element of each *boun,* a kind of spiritual counter-offering and justification on a mystical level of the offering of the donor is the reading of the *salong* (a kind of palm-leaf book), which relates the number of merits acquired by the donor. The contents may vary according to the nature of the offering. It would be correct to consider the *salong* as a written confirmation of the counteroffering described therein. Thus the relations between monks and laymen are based upon a continuing series of exchanges; on one side material gifts such as food and clothing; on the other side spiritual counterofferings of merit for future lives. These counterofferings, however, are also in a sense material, because they modify the conditions of life after the future rebirth. In this light, the *bang* now appears as only a feeble echo moving in the opposite direction; it is a small offering to give

thanks for the merits received, a response to the important cere-
monial gift just offered by the monks.[15]

As we have seen, Buddhism permeates the entire existence of
the Lao peasant, as much in daily life as in the explosion of
festivals which break its pattern. It is not only the days with their
double offerings of food but the months and years whose rhythm
is marked by that of the pagoda. The eighth and fifteenth days
(the fifteenth only in the region of Vientiane) of the waxing and
the waning moon are holidays (*van sim*); not only is work in
the fields suspended, but the offering of food is supplemented by
listening to readings of sacred texts. The three months of Buddhist retreat (from the full moon of the eighth lunar month—
July—to that of the eleventh lunar month—October), at the height
of the rainy season, represent a more austere period of life for
the monks and lead the layman more often to the monastery.
The retreat begins and ends with important public ceremonies.
Many men choose this moment to enter the order. Buddhism
thereby marks the principal hours of the day, the important
phases of the lunar month, and the beginning and end of the
rainy season, while remaining the dominant element in all special
celebrations.

Apart from religious ceremonies, when the central focus is the
ritual offering made to the monks, the lay festivities have nothing
to do with asceticism or continence. Public festivities reach their
peak in the two village festivals of *Boun Pha Vet* (Festival of
Vessantara) and *Boun Bang Fay* (the Rocket Festival). The
latter is a fertility rite transformed into a Buddhist ceremony.
As a matter of fact, in many villages the *Phi Ban* festival coin-
cides with the *Boun Bang Fay*. The Lao consider the rocket
festival, in spite of its symbolism and its songs and dances celebrating life and eroticism, a Buddhist festival commemorating
the triple anniversary of the Birth, the Illumination, and the
Death of the Buddha. The whole village takes part along with
the population of neighboring villages. Each village (or rather
its monastery) builds a giant rocket for this occasion and brings

---

15. Condominas, "Notes sur le Bouddhisme populaire en milieu rural Lao."
p. 113.

it with great ceremony to the courtyard of the local *vat*. The principal part of the celebration takes place there; however, the firing of the rockets takes place outside the courtyard. The rocket which makes the longest flight brings prestige to the monastery which constructed it, and thus to its village. The best rocket builders are found among the monks, for other elements of the population have little time for such an occupation.

The *Boun Pha Vet* may be compared with a French or Italian village festival, although it is not a celebration for a patron saint who varies according to the locality but for a single personage everywhere, the Prince Vessantara. As a result, the festival is not given at a fixed date; it depends upon a decision made by the assembled villagers. As in the case of the Rocket Festival, several villages join in; the inhabitants accompany their monks, who participate in the uninterrupted reading of the next-to-last incantation of the Buddha. The most important collective festival, then, consists primarily of listening to recitations of the remarkable actions of this prince who vowed to give all that should be asked of him and went so far as to give up his children and wife. His charity and detachment, carried to the utmost limit, serve as the most significant example of conduct because they are the central motif of the most important rural festival.

This huge assembly of monks permits the organization of religious ceremonies, of which the most important is ordination. The same festive gathering also permits nonreligious activities such as cock fights, Lao plays, and love-song competitions (which take place in the courtyard of the *vat*), not to mention the banquets and drinking bouts inspired by the meeting of friends and relatives from other villages, if only to return the welcome offered by the latter during their own *Boun Pha Vet*.

The spiritual life of the Lao peasant oscillates between the two poles of the religious life of the village: the monastery, and the altar of the tutelary god. On the one hand, the *ho phi ban*, a single or double hut hidden in the forest, stands for the territory of the village and represents that aspect of nature which sustains the rural collectivity. On the other hand, the *vat* comprises the only structures of much importance in the village. In the oldest and richest villages, the *vat* contains a building in masonry, the only one of its kind in the settlement. It is in the *vat* that collective life unfolds simply and that the monks attempt to realize the ideal of Lao culture.

I observed in 1959 that a good deal of the American aid offered for rural development was, to the great disappointment of the donors, used by the villages to rebuild or beautify the pagoda in preference to other undertakings of common interest.[16] Why this would be so has been explained above. In part it is because the individual layman sees his support of the monks and their monastery as the surest means of his salvation by the acquisition of merit. But, above all, the *vat* not only represents the unity of the village but also serves to express all aspects of its collective life.

The rural world of Laos knows above all the autonomous cell, that is, the village living around its *vat;* of the town and the city, the market is best known. To the villager, questions of administration and parliamentary representation remain the concern of a small number of more or less westernized city dwellers. The latter are the principal beneficiaries of foreign economic—and military—aid, and successors to the class of nobles and mandarins.[17]

Even the massive intrusion of dollars into the Lao economy (which wiped out local handicrafts) was unable to destroy, up until a few years ago, the character of this rural society, where the fame attached to the pagoda was of more importance than material wealth. Lao rural society is remarkable for its lack of clear stratification. The difference in levels of wealth was hardly significant, since newly wealthy peasants often left for the city, which offered more promising possibilities for action than the village. One might also say that the lack of differentiation which appears in family relations, marriage, choice of residence, and land tenure arrangements, and which is reflected in village administration and even in the religious syncretism, remains not

16. Condominas, *La Plaine de Vientiane,* pp. 84–85.
17. See Condominas, *La Plaine de Vientiane,* for a discussion of the relations between the peasant society and the mandarin class. For an analysis of the administrative organization of the villages, see Condominas, *Essai sur la société rurale de la region de Vientiane,* part III.

only the most general characteristic of rural society but its best protection against subjugation by the representatives of urban society.

BIBLIOGRAPHY

ANUMAN RAJADHON, *Life and Ritual in Old Siam: Three Studies of Thai Life and Customs.* Translated and edited by William J. Gedney. New Haven: Human Relations Area Files Press, 1961.

ARCHAIMBAULT, CHARLES, "Les annales de l'ancien royaume de S'ieng Khwang," in *Bulletin de l'Ecole Française d'Extrême-Orient* (BEFEO), Vol. LIII, No. 2 (1967), pp. 557–673.

"L'histoire de Champassak," in *Journal Asiatique*, 249, 4 (1961), pp. 529–595.

"Les rites agraires dans le Moyen-Laos," in *France-Asie*, Vol. XVI (1959), pp. 1185–1194; pp. 1274–1283.

"Le sacrifice du buffle à Vat Ph'u," in *France-Asie*, Vol. XII (1956), pp. 841–845.

BLANCHARD, WENDELL, *Thailand: Its People, Its Society, Its Culture.* New Haven: Human Relations Area Files Press, 1957.

CONDOMINAS, GEORGES, *Essai sur la société rurale de la region de Vientiane.* Vientiane: 1962; mimeographed paper, 1968.

and CLAUDE GAUDILLOT, *La Plaine de Vientiane: Rapport d'étude.* 3 volumes. Paris: Bureau de Developpement Productivité Agricole, 1959.

"Notes sur le Bouddhisme populaire en milieu rural Lao," in *Archives de Sociologie des Religions*, Vol. XIII, No. 25 (1968), pp. 81–110; and No. 26 (1968), pp. 111–150.

"Notes sur le droit foncier en milieu rural dans la Plaine de Vientiane," in *Artibus Asiae*, Felicitation Volume, presented to Professor Georges Coedes, Vol. XXIV, No. 3/4 (1961), pp. 255–262.

EMBREE, JOHN F., "Thailand—A Loosely Structured Social System," in *American Anthropologist*, Vol. 52 (1950), pp. 181–193.

LAFONT, PIERRE-BERNARD, "Introduction du Bouddhisme au Laos," in *France-Asie*, Vol. XVI, No. 1 (1958–1959), pp. 890–892.

LE BOULANGER, PAUL, *Histoire du Laos Français: Essai d'une étude chronologique des principautés Laotiennes.* Paris: Plon, 1931.

Lévy, Paul, "Le sacrifice du buffle et la prediction du temps à Vientiane," in *France-Asie*, Vol. XII (1956), pp. 846–858.

"Les traces de l'introduction du Bouddhisme à Luang Prabang," in *BEFEO*, Vol. XL (1940), pp. 411–424.

Nhouy Abhay, Thao, "Le Bouddhisme Lao," in *France-Asie*, Vol. XII (1956), pp. 917–935.

Pathoumxad, Kruong, "Organisation de clergé Bouddhique," in *France-Asie*, Vol. XII (1956), pp. 936–945.

Pavie, Auguste, *Recherches sur l'histoire de Cambodge, du Laos et du Siam*. Paris: E. Leroux, 1898.

"Présence du Royaume Lao," in the special issue of *France-Asie*, Vol. XII, Nos. 118–120 (March, April, May 1956).

Tambiah, S. J., "The Ideology of Merit and the Social Correlates of Buddhism in a Thai Village," in E. R. Leach, ed., *Dialectic in Practical Religion*. Cambridge Papers in Social Anthropology, No. 5. Cambridge: Cambridge University Press, 1968.

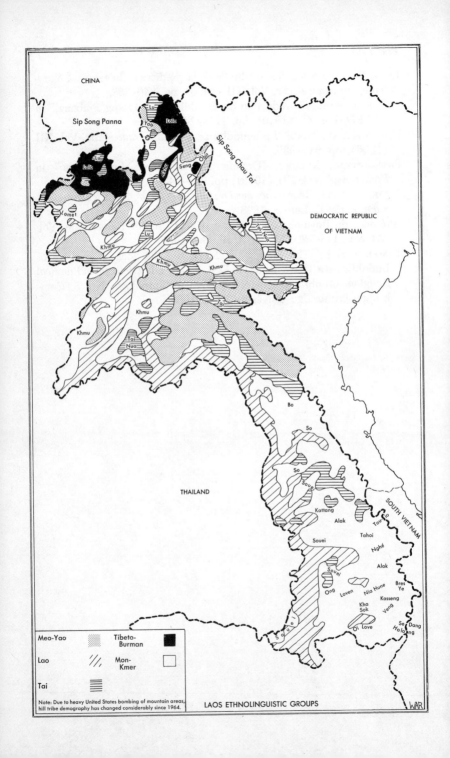

CHINA

Sip Song Panna

Lu
Yao

Lolo

Lu
Lolo

Lamet

Khmu

Khmu

Khmu

Khmu

Seng

Sip Song Chau Tai

DEMOCRATIC REPUBLIC
OF VIETNAM

Tai
Nua

Bo

So

So

Souei

Kattang

Souei

Alak

Souei

Souei

Ong

Loven

Nia Hune

Kha
Sok

Oi Love

THAILAND

Tahoi

Nghé

Alak

Kasseng

Yeng

Tau Oi

Bres
Ye

Se
Ha

Dang
Lang

SOUTH VIETNAM

Meo-Yao

Lao

Tai

Tibeto-
Burman

Mon-
Kmer

Note: Due to heavy United States bombing of mountain areas,
hill tribe demography has changed considerably since 1964.

LAOS ETHNOLINGUISTIC GROUPS

WAR

3

The Many Languages and Cultures of Laos

Guy Moréchand

The ethnic diversity of the population of Laos makes nation building there a far more complex process than elsewhere in Southeast Asia. Social and political changes which have already begun must inevitably destroy the traditional ways of life and cultures of the various groups who populate the area. The broad lines which change will follow may be clear enough, even to outsiders. But though the origins and distribution of the peoples of Laos and the differences among them are obscure, even to the Laotians themselves, they will have important effects on the details of future change, and are worth looking at here.

In some multiethnic nations, war against a common external enemy may weld the peoples together. But the war in Laos is at the same time a civil war, an ideological war, a war in which different minorities have aligned themselves with one side or another for local advantage, and above all a war in which foreign powers have, for their own ends, exploited ethnic differences, setting ethnic groups, or factions of ethnic groups, at each others' throats. Foreign intervention does not "help" unify a Laotian nation, but sides with particular ethnic groups, classes, factions, and individuals in a complex and unpredictable country.

The peoples of Laos have different origins, languages, ways of gaining their living, traditional ways of life, and different mental universes. I will examine these differences, keeping in mind that few people really know all the groups, and even indigenous Lao or montagnards confuse peoples who have similar appearance and clothing.

The most reliable criterion for distinguishing ethnic groups is language. Fortunately, studies of several of the languages of Laos have been published, and by linguistic methods we can discern the degree to which the various ethnic groups are related—their subdivisions, centers of diffusion, and culture areas.

There are five language families in this part of Asia; Sino-Tibetan, Tai, Austro-Asiatic, Austronesian, and Meo-Yao. The first four are spoken by large numbers of people who spread across South, Southeast, and East Asia and the adjacent islands. Sino-Tibetan comprises the languages of the ethnic Chinese, Tibeto-Burman, and Karen, and it is spread widely over China, Tibet, Burma, and the northern parts of Vietnam, Laos, and Thailand. Tai is strongly represented in the mountain valleys of South China and in parts of North Vietnam. It is the language of the most numerous lowland people of Thailand, and it is represented in Burma and found as far away as Assam. Austro-Asiatic (Mon-Khmer) includes not only the Vietnamese and Cambodian languages, but also those spoken by montagnards of the Annamite Chain, the Cardamones, and other mountainous areas in South China, Thailand, and Burma. It is found in Malaysia, the Nicobar Islands, and India. Austronesian (or Malayo-Polynesian) is found in the Annamite Chain as far north as Pleiku-Kontum, and includes most of the languages of the Philippines, Indonesia, and Malaya. It is the only one of these five language groups not found in Laos. Meo-Yao is spoken by only 5 to 6 million people scattered in small villages above 3,000 feet in highland areas throughout the southern provinces of China (Szechuan, Hunan, Kweichow, Yunnan), the northern portion of Vietnam, in Laos, Thailand, and possibly Burma.

This tremendous linguistic diversity is striking evidence that Laos was in a main path of Southeast Asia's great human migrations and incorporated elements of most of the cultures which fashioned Asia.

But to understand contemporary Laos one must consider the living "ethnic groups" derived from these historic and prehistoric migrators. These groups comprise persons who speak a common language, dress alike, think and act with reference to a common scale of values, observe the same ritual, possess the same oral or written tradition, share a common technical heritage, observe the same customs, consider themselves descended from a common ancestor, and in general think of themselves alone as men, and of outsiders as devils. The best criterion for distinguishing one group from another is again language.

The Tai language family branched out from a common cradle extending over South China, Hainan, and the Vietnamese frontiers, where one finds today groups speaking the most archaic of the Tai dialects (Mu-lao, Kelao, Li, Laqua, Tsin Lo). The present Kwangsi Autonomous Region of the Peoples Republic of China includes the Kung, the Deng, the Shui, and the Mao Nam. In about the thirteenth century, Tai groups settled the Chao Phraya (which eventually became Siam), while farther west the Shan and Hkamti settled in Burma and Assam.

The Lao Tai are the largest single ethnic group in Laos, constituting somewhat less than half its population. The country was named for the Lao Tai who settled along the lowlands of the Mekong Valley about the thirteenth century. They later adopted elements of Indian culture, particularly the Buddhist religion. Today they are the peasants who grow wet rice and live in small villages where traditional life centers around the Buddhist *vat* (compound). They were long ruled by a hierarchy of petty princelings who are now well represented in the civil and military elite which runs the Royal Laotian Government (RLG) areas.

Other less culturally developed ethnic Tai groups, who have little in common with the Lao Tai, are also found in Laos. The Lu on the Yunnan border are a well-defined unit with a well-developed hierarchy of traditional rulers. The Tai Neua (North Tai) are found in Sam Neua province, while the Tai Deng (Red Tai) are located in Yunnan. The Tai Dam (Black Tai) inhabit the area around Dien Bien Phu. In the past all have been at war with one another, and the Tai language group should not be seen as a harmonious social or political unit.

The Austronesian (Mon-Khmer) peoples, who formerly occupied the land, were pushed back or subjugated by the Tai; they are called Kha, which means "slave" in Lao. Most of them belong to the Palaung-Wa branch (which includes the Yin and Kawa of China, Palaung and Wa of Burma), their largest subdivision being Khmu (or Phou Teng). They occupied the territory of the former kingdom of Luang Prabang where they are still an important group. In Vietnam the Xa Cau or Khan and, farther south, the Phong are Mon-Khmer speakers. The Kui and So who are found in the southern provinces of Laos as well as Cambodia and Thailand, and finally, north of the Khmu, the Lamet are important groups.

The Meo-Yao originated somewhere near Kweichow, China, where they include four linguistic divisions: northern Meo or Hmau, western Meo or Hmong, central Meo or Hmu, and the little known eastern Meo. Only the Hmong language is spoken in Laos, where the Hmong consider the term "Meo," used by the Lao, demeaning. The Meo are subdivided according to details of dress and decoration into White and Green Meo—who are really one group—and the Black Meo, about whom little is known. The Yao, called Man in Laos, are not numerous. They speak two main languages, Mien and Mun, and can also be distinguished by details of dress and clothing.

Meo and Yao groups came into Laos only a century and a half or so ago to settle on lands above about 3,000 feet. There they practice the shifting cultivation of upland rice, maize, and opium as a cash crop. Until recently they avoided involvement with lowlanders except for trade. Today the Meo are split into two factions: one fighting with the Pathet Lao; the other, following Vang Pao, constitutes a large proportion of the CIA-backed Armée Clandestine which has figured in the struggle for the Plain of Jars area. (The politics of the Meo involvement in Laotian conflicts are discussed in detail in article 6, by McCoy and in article 12, by Branfman.)

Finally, a few Tibeto-Burman-speaking groups have also come down from Yunnan. The Yi or Lolo number over 4 million in China. In Laos, Phunoi, Akha (Puli-Akha, Kha-ko), and the Mosu or Lahu (related to the Nakhi) live close to the Burmese and Chinese borders near Muong Sing and Houei Sai.

Along the northern borders, Kuan Hua or upland Chinese and Lao serve as lingua francas among Meo-Yao and Tibeto-Burman montagnard peoples, who speak mutually unintelligible languages. Ethnic differences based on language remain a barrier to communication and unity among the peoples of Laos. Mixed villages exist only as recently constructed artificial centers—the missionary village of Ban Nam Ngao or the CIA-created military and refugee camps like Sam Thong or Long Chen. Cross-ethnic marriages occur only among a few less traditional families.

In Vietnam and Thailand this ethnic diversity is less important because Vietnamese and Tai form overwhelming majorities compared to the relatively few members of the ethnic minorities. But in sparsely populated Laos the Lao Tai probably number less than 1½ million out of a population of less than 3 million. The statistics are unreliable—and probably deliberately inflated or deflated at times. The Khmu supposedly number about 750,-000 and the Meo about 300,000. What is clear is that the montagnards altogether number about the same as the Lao Tai, but, whereas the Lao are relatively homogeneous, the diverse montagnard groups are little known and difficult to approach—let alone manipulate for either their own development or that of a Laos in the making.

To generalize, then, today the Lao Tai live along the lowlands of the Mekong and its tributaries. They have permanent irrigated rice fields and live in long-settled villages, often with remarkable stone religious architecture in their Buddhist *vats*. They live under a hierarchical, traditional, feudal rule, which today is complicated by government officials, merchants, and an officer class that is drawn from the elite and follows a largely Westernized style of life. The montagnards live in upland areas where the majority cultivate rice and maize. Since they use slash and burn agriculture, they must periodically shift their villages to new land. For the montagnards, family and clan are the only important social groups, and they look to shamans for supernatural assistance, protection, and augury.

The montagnards were neglected by the dominant Lao during the colonial period. Today they desire entry into the modern world. A few Khmu and Meo flirted with the Christian missions. Some members of all groups have been attracted by the Pathet Lao; and others have sided with the RLG, which has recently begun to take an interest in offering them an education.

The prolonged war has been one of the most important factors in ending the isolation of the montagnards. The land they occupy has become a battlefield, and their manpower (or at least denying it to their opponent) has become important to each side. Many have been attracted by the chance of pay and promotion in forces such as the Armée Clandestine. The fate of Meo groups around the Plain of Jars, who suffered the full horrors of war as the battle lines shifted, demonstrates the dangers of picking a side which loses even a local campaign. Even in a peaceful nation these groups would have faced inevitable anguish during the transition from an isolated traditional way of life to participation in the uncertain future of a new nation; but outside intervention has, as usual, changed anguish to catastrophe.

Part II

The Historical Development of Modern Laos

4

The Laotian Conflict in Perspective

Philippe Devillers

Unfortunately, the long and involved history of Laos is quite unknown in the West. The tribes of Austronesian (or Indonesian) stock, who have lived in the middle and upper Mekong Valley and its tributary basins since prehistoric times, have faced Tai invaders thrusting southwards and southeastwards since the ninth century A.D. The Tai (Lao branch) ousted the Austronesian Kha ("slave") tribes from the valleys, settled in the plains and formed a kingdom, Lan Xang, with Luang Prabang as its capital. Unable to maintain an efficient centralized rule over such a wide area, they imposed feudal suzerainty over local princes and chiefs, many of whom were not Lao. Many small principalities (*muong*) were able to survive as vassals of the Luang Prabang kings. In 1563 the capital of Lan Xang was moved from Luang Prabang to Vientiane, but rivalries between branches of the royal family offered Burma, Siam, and Vietnam opportunities to intervene in Laotian affairs. To gain protection from Vientiane, the feudal princes of Xieng Khouang (located around the Plain of Jars) became vassals of Vietnam. In 1696 the king of Vientiane himself became a vassal of the Vietnamese, who helped him to regain his throne from pro-Siamese usurpers.

For decades, Siam and Vietnam fought for suzerainty over Vientiane and Luang Prabang. In 1826 the king of Vientiane, who had sided with the Vietnamese and was bitterly hostile toward the Siamese, attacked Siam, but his army was defeated. In retaliation, the Siamese captured and destroyed Vientiane, imprisoned the king, and deported the population by the tens of thousands to the east bank of the Mekong. The kingdom of Vientiane was then annexed to Siam, although many of its former vassals went over to Minh Mang, the emperor of Vietnam, who extended his sovereignty over the Tran-ninh and Cammon regions (see article 5 by John K. Whitmore). However, he gained little since the Siamese had already devastated the region and deported its population. At the same time, the Siamese had imposed a protectorate over Luang Prabang. Around 1850 Meo tribes, coming from south China, entered Laos and settled on highlands in the Tran-ninh and Sam Neua regions.

In 1884 the French imposed their protectorate over Vietnam and claimed suzerainty over the Laotian princes. In the name of Vietnam, and at Hue's request, the French pushed westward, concluding alliances and treaties with the king of Luang Prabang and local chiefs, which forced the Siamese to withdraw to the west bank of the Mekong. (See article 6, by McCoy.) While the kingdom of Luang Prabang became a French protectorate in 1887, the various *muong* in the area between the Vietnamese border and the Mekong were regrouped into provinces (*khoueng*) under direct French authority. In 1899 the French set up a new administrative entity, Laos, which included the kingdom of Luang Prabang as well as the *khoueng*. Laos became a part of the Indochinese Federation. In August 1941 the French concluded a new treaty with the king of Luang Prabang, agreeing to give him three provinces (Vientiane, Xieng Khouang, and Sam Neua). Prince Phetsarath of the royal family of Vientiane became premier of the enlarged kingdom. Meanwhile, the four southern provinces remained under direct French control.

On March 9, 1945, the Japanese overthrew the French in Indochina. The Japanese "persuaded" King Sisavang Vong and Prince Phetsarath to proclaim the independence of the kingdom of Luang Prabang on April 8, 1945. (See article 7, by Adams.) After the Japanese surrender in August, Phetsarath announced the reunification of Laos through the merger of the kingdom of Luang Prabang and the four southern provinces. On October 4, 1945, he asked the Allied Powers to recognize the independence of Laos. But on October 10, King Sisavang Vong dismissed Phetsarath at the request of French officers who had managed to return to Luang Prabang. Shortly thereafer a Laotian People's Assembly convened in Vientiane and decided to form the Provisional Government of Pathet Lao (Pathet Lao literally means the "State of Laos"). This government denounced all treaties with France, and on October 20 deposed the king and selected

Prince Phetsarath as head of state.[1] Prince Souphanouvong, half brother of Phetsarath, was appointed defense minister, and a treaty of friendship and alliance between the Democratic Republic of Vietnam (DRV) and the Pathet Lao was signed a few days afterwards.

However, French forces returned, defeated the Lao-Vietnamese forces in Thakhek, and recaptured Vientiane (April 24, 1946) and Luang Prabang (May 13, 1946). Phetsarath and his Lao Issara (Free Lao) political followers fled to Bangkok, where they set up a government in exile. Siding with the French, King Sisavang Vong asked Savang Vatthana, his son (the present king), to form a new cabinet. On August 27, 1946, an agreement was signed with the French: southern Laos was merged with the kingdom of Luang Prabang into the Kingdom of Laos, under the authority of King Sisavang Vong. Autonomy was granted to Laos, as a state belonging to the Indochinese Federation and the French Union. Since the economy and finances remained under French control, many French advisers continued to work in the Laotian administration at various levels. Elections for a constituent assembly took place on December 15, 1946, and a constitution was promulgated on May 11, 1947. Technically, Laos had become a constitutional monarchy, with a Western-style parliamentary regime. But the situation remained tense. Many Laotian officials, educated as servants or members of the royal house or of the northern aristocracy, defined autonomy as the freedom to subordinate the hill tribes (Meos, Khas, etc.) and the southern provinces to their bureaucratic power and trade interests. Since the French advisers generally supported the tribes and the more Westernized southerners, the northern aristocrats met strong resistance, which forced them to ask for more "independence."

Tensions also developed among members of the Phetsarath government-in-exile in Bangkok. Defense Minister and Commander in Chief Souphanouvong called for an alliance with Ho Chi Minh against the French and in February 1949 formed a

1. The king formally abdicated on November 10, 1945, agreeing to recognize the legitimacy of the Pathet Lao government.

"political front" around the Lao Issara armed forces. However, his half brother Souvanna Phouma (public works minister) and Katay Don Sasorith were listening to Thai and American advice and consequently favored a compromise with the French. After the French had given "independence" to Laos as an Associated State (July 18, 1949), the Lao Issara government in Bangkok decided to dissolve itself on October 24, 1949, despite Phetsarath's opposition. Its members flew to Vientiane, where they received a jubilant welcome.

On February 6, 1950, the French transferred sovereignty to Laos. The next day, the United States and Great Britain recognized the Laotian Associated State and the Vientiane government. Although the pro-French Boun Oum cabinet was succeeded on February 24 by a new one, led by Phoui Sananikone, a member of a prominent Vientiane family already in touch with American interests, the French advisers and military men remained in control. Indochina was at war, and the French still hoped to force the Ho Chi Minh resistance government to surrender to Emperor Bao Dai (head of state in the Associated State of Vietnam). In 1951 the "Bangkok group" (composed of former right-wing Lao Issara) won the elections, and on November 28, 1951, Souvanna Phouma became premier, with Phoui Sananikone and Katay Don Sasorith as prominent cabinet members.

Meanwhile, Prince Souphanouvong had joined his forces with those of Ho Chi Minh and had found new allies among the hill tribes engaged in resistance to the Royal Laotian Government. On August 13, 1950, the first Congress of the Peoples of the Pathet Lao met in northeastern Laos and formed the Laotian United Front and a Provisional Resistance Government to take over the duties of the Lao Issara Government recently disbanded in Bangkok. Souphanouvong became head of the Provisional Resistance Government, whose aims were the liberation and total independence of Laos and the formation of a coalition government to establish unity and peace.

In September 1950 the Pathet Lao government settled in Sam Neua province and on March 11, 1951, probably at Ho Chi Minh's headquarters in Vietnam, concluded an alliance with the

Vietnamese and Cambodian liberation movements. Since Souphanouvong already had the support of Sithone Komadom, leader of the southern Kha tribes, the Pathet Lao was able to expand its guerrilla activity along the entire Vietnamese border, from Phong Saly in the north to the Bolovens Plateau in the south. And, in the northeast, a "liberated zone" was taking shape.

In March 1953 General Giap's People's Army (the Viet Minh) swept into northern Laos, forcing the French to withdraw from the city of Sam Neua. There Souphanouvong established the Pathet Lao Government, which claimed to be the only legal government for the state of Laos. Alarmed by Giap's offensive in the direction of the Mekong, Thailand and the United States prepared to meet the threat. The Thai called for UN intervention, but President Eisenhower chose another course of action. Washington, seeking to draw Laos into a military alliance, pressed France to relinquish its control over Laotian defense matters and foreign affairs and to grant Vientiane total independence. On October 22, 1953, France recognized Laos as "an independent and sovereign state."

In the spring of 1954 Giap's army moved westward once more, threatening Luang Prabang as well as the Mekong valley towns and allowing the Pathet Lao guerrillas to enlarge their "liberated zones" in both the northeast and the south. Right-wing politicians, encouraged by the CIA, maneuvered to oust the Souvanna Phouma cabinet in order to replace it by a "stronger" one which would call for Thai and American intervention. The French did not allow the maneuver to succeed. The cabinet was merely reshuffled, Souvanna Phouma was replaced, and the leader of the pro-American faction, Phoui Sananikone, became foreign minister. Phoui was later to lead the Royal Laotian Government delegation at the Geneva Conference (May–July 1954).

At Geneva the Western powers made it clear from the start that they would not accept any participation by the Pathet Lao Government. And neither Russia nor China insisted on it. (See article 8, by Marek Thee.) In June 1954 Peking agreed to recognize the Royal Laotian Government and respect the independence and unity of Laos in exchange for the military neutralization of Laos and the integration of the left-wing forces into the political structure of the country. The cease-fire agreement was signed on July 21, 1954, and went into effect on August 6.

THE LONG STRUGGLE FOR INTEGRATION AND UNITY

According to this Geneva agreement, the Viet Minh forces had to withdraw from Laos in three months. Pending a political agreement on integration, Pathet Lao forces were to be regrouped in the provinces of Phong Saly and Sam Neua. Laos pledged not to grant bases to any foreign power (except France, which was allowed to keep a few training areas), not to allow any foreign troops to come to Laos, and not to enter into any military alliances. General elections were scheduled to take place in August 1955. The sensitive task of merging the RLG and Pathet Lao forces remained. Since they retained military control of the two northern provinces, the Pathet Lao leaders could bring two valuable cards to the Royal Government political bargaining table. They were not likely to accept the reinstatement of aristocratic and bureaucratic power in the hill tribe areas where they had set up "people's committees."

However, the pro-American faction had already gained ground in Vientiane. A few weeks after the rather mysterious murder of the pro-French Defense Minister Kou Voravong (August 18, 1954), Souvanna Phouma was forced out of office. Since Phoui Sananikone was not yet ready to take office with full responsibilities, Katay Don Sasorith, a right-wing nationalist, became premier. After January 1, 1955, American aid poured directly into Laos and was no longer channeled through French intermediaries. American advisers arrived to help set up a new banking system, for which a number of right-wing politicians were trained in "banking" and "foreign trade" operations.

By March 9, 1955, Premier Katay had agreed to allow the Pathet Lao to participate in the next elections in exchange for the integration of their military units into the Royal Laotian Army. After China and the Democratic Republic of Vietnam gave assurances to Laos at the Bandung Conference (April 1955) that they would respect the Geneva Agreements, Katay suggested he was ready to negotiate a nonagression pact with China. This neutralist trend was opposed by the American embassy, the conservative faction, and Crown Prince Savang. (See article 9, by Ackland.) With their encouragement, some local Royal Army commanders staged incidents with Pathet Lao units. American correspondents and press agencies gave these incidents wide publicity, suggesting that the Communists were violating signed agreements in an attempt to prepare for the conquest of the "Free World's Laotian outpost."

Increasingly wary of the right wing's intentions, Pathet Lao leaders refused to agree to any reestablishment of the Royal Government's authority in the two provinces unless an overall political settlement was reached. The Katay cabinet then decided to hold the elections only in the area under its control. Surprisingly, however, these elections (December 25, 1955) produced a majority, not for the right-wing "hawks," but for the moderate neutralists led by Souvanna Phouma.

In order to encourage political integration through the formation of a coalition government with the Vientiane forces, the Pathet Lao made a major political move. Obviously drawing inspiration from the recently formed North Vietnamese Patriotic Front, the Pathet Lao decided to replace the Provisional Government of Pathet Lao with a political organization, the Laotian Patriotic Front, or Neo Lao Hak Xat (January 6, 1956). On March 22, 1956, Souvanna Phouma formed the new "nationalist" cabinet and pledged to work for national unity through negotiation and for peaceful relations with all countries, including the Democratic Republic of Vietnam (DRV). In July 1956, Moscow recognized Laos.

In only ten days of talks (August 1–10, 1956), Souvanna Phouma reached a general agreement with the Patriotic Front: (1) Hostilities would cease everywhere in Laos. (2) Sam Neua and Phong Saly provinces, as well as Pathet Lao armed forces, would recognize the authority of the Royal Government. (3) By-elections would be held to fill new seats to be created in the Assembly. (4) A Government of National Union would be set up with the Front's participation. This government would pledge to follow "a policy of peace and neutrality," according to the five principles of peaceful coexistence. It would maintain good relations with all countries, would not enter into any alliance, or accept foreign troops or bases in the country.

Next, Souvanna Phouma went to Peking and Hanoi, where he signed joint declarations confirming the principles agreed upon with the Patriotic Front. Detailed talks with the Front's leaders followed and, despite tough American and right-wing opposition, a final agreement was concluded on November 2, 1957. Prince Souphanouvong then offered the two Pathet Lao provinces of Phong Saly and Sam Neua to the king and, on November 19, 1957, the National Assembly approved the coalition government just formed under Souvanna Phouma's premiership. Souphanou-vong and Phoumi Vongvichit, two of the Front's major leaders, were given ministerial posts (economic affairs and religious affairs). On February 18, 1958, Pathet Lao armed forces were integrated into the Royal Army. A few weeks later, after a hot electoral campaign, the Front and its ally, the small neutralist Santiphab Party, won 13 of the 21 new seats in the by-elections (May 4, 1958). The American embassy and the Laotian conservative faction were stunned. From then on, every major decision of the Laotian government would have to be approved by the Front.

The "New Class" of wealthy officials, bankers, merchants, and military felt their positions and privileges threatened by the very presence of a leftist minister for economic affairs, supported by 13 vocal members in the Assembly of 59 seats. The special and highly profitable links with Thai and American business interests (the work of U.S. intelligence in the Laotian central administration) could be continued only if the Patriotic Front was kept out of the government, or even better, out of the capital. Thus, in order to "keep Laos in the Free World" it was necessary to break the coalition and prevent the left from sharing power again.

With the CIA's help, young and dynamic elements of the New Class formed the Committee for the Defense of National Interests (CDNI). In July a hostile vote in the assembly forced Souvanna Phouma to resign, and on August 18, 1958, Phoui Sananikone, the senior leader of the pro-American faction, formed a new cabinet, one in which the Front was no longer represented. The November 1957 agreement was broken. Immediately after assuming office, Phoui Sananikone and his young New Class ministers shifted Laotian policy far to the right: they dismissed all the Front's members and sympathizers from the administration, and even put Souphanouvong and Vongvichit under house arrest; they entered into talks with the Ngo Dinh Diem government in Saigon and the Chiang Kai-shek regime in Formosa; and they asked for an immediate sizable grant of American financial aid.

However, because the U.S. Congress had some doubts about the way previous aid programs had been administered in Laos, it decided in January 1959 to send a bipartisan fact-finding mission to Vientiane. By a curious coincidence, at this very time, the Sananikone government announced that North Vietnamese army units had crossed the border and taken villages in the Tchpone area. Hanoi denied the charge and offered to discuss it through the mediation of the International Control Commission (ICC). Vientiane refused, demanded the withdrawal of North Vietnamese troops prior to any talks, and said that the ICC had long since fulfilled its mission and had no further business in Laos (February 11, 1958). At the same time, the general staff of the Royal Army was attempting to disperse and neutralize former Pathet Lao cadres and soldiers who had been integrated into the army.

In a last-minute attempt to avoid liquidation, the last Pathet Lao battalion, which was still awaiting integration, escaped into the jungle. In July 1959 the Phoui Sananikone government outlawed the Patriotic Front and jailed Souphanouvong, Vongvichit, and the Front's deputies. On July 20, Pathet Lao armed forces took the offensive to recapture Phong Saly and Sam Neua provinces. The Vientiane government called for UN intervention, charging that Hanoi was giving massive support to the rebels.

In September the UN sent a fact-finding mission to Laos. When the mission failed to find evidence of any serious Vietnamese interference, it became increasingly clear that Vientiane had deliberately spread false rumors and information to alarm American public opinion in order to get money and aid from

Washington. UN Secretary General Dag Hammarskjöld paid a visit to Vientiane on November 10, stationed a personal representative in the city, and urged Sananikone to get rid of his "hawks." From then on, Laos was to suffer through almost continuous struggles between the moderates (of both sides) and a group of right-wing hawks and their faceless advisers who were determined to prevent a new settlement with the left.

Just as he was preparing to follow Dag Hammarskjöld's suggestion, Sananikone was forced to resign by a group of generals led by his own defense minister, Phoumi Nosavan. A general election was organized, and the two right-wing organizations led by Sananikone and Phoumi Nosavan won all 59 seats (April 24, 1960). This closed the door to any new negotiations with the left; and after Souphanouvong and the other Front leaders escaped from jail on May 24, 1960, a resumption of the war between Vientiane and the Front seemed unavoidable. However, some junior officers were unwilling to accept this turn of events. On August 9, 1960, Captain Kong Le and his paratroopers took control of the capital, Vientiane and forced the National Assembly and the king to reappoint Souvanna Phouma as premier. Souvanna Phouma declared he was ready to resume the policy of neutrality and to negotiate immediately with the Patriotic Front.

Backed by the Americans, Phoumi Nosavan and the right wing launched a strong offensive against Vientiane from their southern base of Savannakhet. They obtained the support of King Savang in Luang Prabang and Touby Ly Fong, the Meo leader in the northeast. Lacking money, weapons, and various supplies, Souvanna Phouma accepted Soviet aid, which was flown from China to the Kong Le stronghold in the Plain of Jars. But General Kouprasith Abhay's forces in Vientiane rose against Souvanna Phouma and Kong Le and forced them to withdraw from the capital. Phoumi's army, the Assembly, and the king agreed to entrust the government to Prince Boun Oum. Washington immediately granted him official recognition (December 16, 1960). Now, however, the Laotian civil war had taken on an international character, since Peking and Moscow still considered Souvanna Phouma's government to be the only legitimate one and they continued to give aid to its army under the command of Kong Le.

In February 1961, after two months of a strong Pathet Lao and neutralist counteroffensive, it became clear that peace could be restored only through the reconstitution of a coalition government committed to a policy of neutrality, guaranteed by the major powers. (See article 10, by Mirsky and Stonefield.) John F. Kennedy gave up the Eisenhower-Nixon policy, which had permitted only a "broadening" of the Boun Oum Government. After weeks of talks at various levels, especially between Washington, Moscow, and London, it was decided to urge the factions to negotiate a cease-fire, which the ICC would control, while an international conference would discuss the problem of Laotian neutrality. At the same time, the Laotian factions would negotiate to form a new coalition government, which could speak for all of Laos.

An agreement on the cease-fire was signed on May 13, 1961, and a 14-power conference opened in Geneva three days later. On June 22, in Zurich, the three Laotian princes (neutralist Souvanna Phouma, leftist Souphanouvong, and rightist Boun Oum) agreed to form a new Government of National Union. On December 18, 1961, West and East in Geneva agreed on the conditions of Laotian neutrality. But because of right-wing resistance the three factions did not finish bartering their shares in the coalition government until June of 1962. A cease-fire went into effect on a line which bisected Laos from north to south. The next day the king appointed the new coalition government, headed again by Souvanna Phouma. On July 23 the international accords on Laotian neutrality were signed in Geneva.

Laos proclaimed its neutrality and its intent to follow a policy of peaceful coexistence. In addition it pledged *not* to let any foreign troops enter its territory, any power to establish bases on its soil, or any power to protect it or bring it into an alliance. On the other hand, the 14 powers pledged to respect Laos' neutrality, to abstain from interfering in its domestic affairs, and to help maintain its independence and neutral status. Foreign

troops and other military personnel were to leave the country
before October 7, 1962.

Laos Between Colonialism and Destruction

On October 7, 1962, Souvanna Phouma expressed satisfaction
over the implementation of the agreements. Foreign forces, he
said, had left the country, "except [for] a few people who are
expected to leave soon." Moscow and Peking, however, accused
the United States of simply putting its military advisers in plain
clothes. Washington published a denial and retorted by saying
there were still North Vietnamese military units in eastern and
northern Laos. Fortunately, this sour exchange did not prevent
the three Laotian factions from agreeing on the unification of
their armed forces (November 28, 1962) and deciding that unanimity would be required for any decision involving foreign
affairs, defense, or administrative appointments (February 10,
1963).

Clearly this was more than the right-wing diehards and their
American advisers could accept. Resuming their provocative tactics, they harassed the left in an attempt to force it to split from
the coalition or to "commit aggression." On April 1, 1963, Foreign Minister Quinim Pholsena, a left-neutralist, was assassinated.
In the capital, harassment of leftists by army units created such
insecurity that the Front's ministers and their aides decided to
leave for the northeast. Joint work between the three factions
in the capital was no longer possible. Although this was exactly
what the military and civilian right wing and the CIA wanted,
they have since maintained that "leftist obstruction had para-
lyzed government work." (See article 11, by Porter.)

For months the American CIA had been organizing and supporting Meo guerrillas against the Patriotic Front. When the
Front retaliated by attempting to consolidate its forces with the
neutralist forces on the Plain of Jars, hostilities flared up again
and American planes, recently "supplied" to Souvanna Phouma,
began reconnaissance flights over the Front's zone (October
1963).

Souvanna Phouma did his best to resume negotiations with Souphanouvong and restore cooperation between the three factions within the framework laid by the Geneva Agreements of 1962. He met with Souphanouvong and even went to Peking and Hanoi in April 1964, where he found conciliatory Communist attitudes. The day after his return to Vientiane, however, the army took control of the capital (April 19, 1964) and imposed its rule and policies. Souvanna Phouma bowed to the ultimatum and merged the neutralist faction with the right wing, immediately giving Laotian "neutrality" a distinctive pro-Western flavor. In May 1964, while the Patriotic Front called vehemently for an immediate reconvening of the Geneva Conference, the U.S. Air Force started daily reconnaissance and bombing raids over the mountain area. Because this was an election year in the United States, military escalation had to be done quietly—at least until November.

A few days after the Gulf of Tonkin incident and the subsequent Senate resolution, a new Laotian conference opened in France, at La Celle St. Cloud (August 24, 1964). On November 21, after several weeks of fruitless talks, the Vientiane delegation left France: Lyndon Johnson had just been elected President and it had served its purpose. A new U.S. ambassador, William Sullivan, arrived in Laos, and a new policy of bombing and escalation came to Indochina. On January 13, 1965, the U.S. Air Force suddenly attacked and razed Ban Ban, a village on the Laotian-Vietnamese border. This was the beginning of the great escalation which became apparent in Vietnam a few weeks later.

Although events since then are well known, they still need to be seen in perspective. In Laos the right wing (old and new) and its American advisers and allies were and are still determined to prevent the return of any kind of coalition formula. Therefore, they have blocked—and they still block—every attempt to resume serious negotiations. Their strategy is to present conditions they know to be unacceptable to the other side. But the Americans have little to fear. Since the army (regular forces and mercenaries) is paid exclusively by U.S. aid (through the American embassy and various agencies), as are the corrupt politicians who work with it, the United States virtually controls the state machinery of the kingdom. The right wing is assured of U.S. and Thai support because neither Washington nor Bangkok can "afford to let North Vietnam overrun Laos"!

The war in South Vietnam and the U.S. bombing offensive have forced Hanoi to rely heavily on the Ho Chi Minh Trail (which runs through Laotian jungles) to bring supplies to the southern insurgents. Consequently, for the past five years the U.S. Air Force has been bombing eastern Laos, the traditional home of many hill tribes. Hundreds of thousands of refugees have had to leave their villages, fields, and valleys for shabby camps under RLG police control and American supervision. Thousands of American advisers helped draft, direct, and implement these "programs." Although subjected day and night to this war of destruction, the Patriotic Front and its neutralist nationalist allies, the Laotian People's Liberation Army, have held their own and persisted in carrying out a "protracted war strategy" and in demanding that the 1962 Agreements be respected.

Yet there is no indication that the Laotian tragedy is approaching a finale. Wishing both to create a buffer zone between Thailand and Vietnam and to cut the supply lines between North and South Vietnam, the American airmen, like the Thai generals of the nineteenth century, are systematically destroying the capacity of a large part of Laos to support human life. The Lao elite consider this destruction an acceptable price to pay for the security of the New Class and for the continuation of the profitable business between the "commercial interests" of Bangkok and those of Vientiane, Savannakhet, or Pakse. Although the strategic and moral interests of the Free World are said to justify this policy, no one has yet dared to question the power and activities of the Thai-Lao-American "military-financial complex" which lie at the roots of the establishment of this Mekong valley satrapy.

It remains to be seen if a "scorched-earth policy" of this sort can continue to be implemented by a democratic nation such as the United States, even under the cover of a "hidden war." The Thai war of destruction in Laos in 1827–1832 is more than a black spot in Asian history, the image of Thailand has been stained by it forever. When the facts come to light and become more widely known, the Laotian Case, 1945–1970, will probably become, along with the war in Vietnam, one of the most appalling "success stories" of Western enterprise in Asia—something a "silent majority," feeling guilty of complicity and cowardice, will certainly not like to discuss.

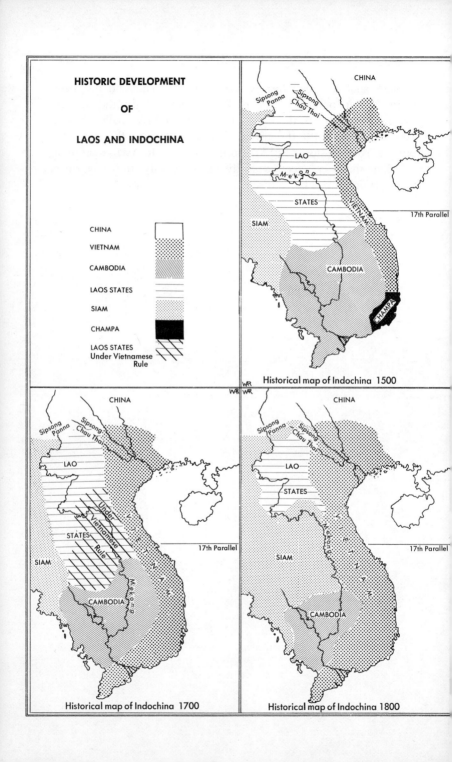

HISTORIC DEVELOPMENT

OF

LAOS AND INDOCHINA

CHINA

VIETNAM

CAMBODIA

LAOS STATES

SIAM

CHAMPA

LAOS STATES
Under Vietnamese
Rule

Historical map of Indochina 1500

Historical map of Indochina 1700

Historical map of Indochina 1800

5

The Thai-Vietnamese Struggle for Laos in the Nineteenth Century

John K. Whitmore

Those who are interested in the problems of the present kingdom of Laos should be aware of some of the fluctuations in meaning of the term "Lao" and a few of the details of the remote past of the geographic area today called Laos.[1]

For present purposes it would be of little value to discuss the etymology of the word "Lao" or the origin of the people who now bear that name. Suffice it to say that the Lao people belong linguistically to a very large group called "Thai" when the inhabitants of modern Thailand are meant and usually Tai or Dai when those inhabiting Laos, Vietnam, or China (as minority groups in the latter two) are designated. The dates of entry into their present locales and the routes of their migrations are still matters of controversy, but they may have occupied most of their present area from at least the early centuries of the Christian Era.

Politically, large parts of present-day Thailand and Laos were part of the Cambodian Empire, which was centered at Angkor from the ninth to the fourteenth or fifteenth centuries. The first Thai political entities, judging from inscriptions which have been preserved, date from the late thirteenth and the fourteenth centuries. At the height of the Angkor Empire, in the late twelfth and early thirteenth centuries, present-day Laos, along the Mekong River, was under Cambodian control at least as far north as Vientiane and possibly farther. At that time the territory to the east had not become Vietnam, but from midway between the 17th and 19th parallels southward to the Mekong Delta was the state of Champa, whose people spoke a Malayo-Polynesian language and had an Indianized culture similar to that

1. The introductory section, pp. 53–55, was prepared by Michael Vickery.

of the Khmer of Cambodia. Vietnam at that time was restricted to the northern half of present-day North Vietnam.

The history of most of the Lao area for the next 300 to 400 years is not well established. Local chronicles speak of the founding of independent kingdoms in the thirteenth and fourteenth centuries, but the accuracy of most of these accounts may be questioned. What needs to be remembered for our purposes is that by the time (the sixteenth century) fairly good records are available concerning relations between the Lao states and their neighbors in Burma and central Thailand and with the first European travelers (the seventeenth century), "Laos" meant all of what is today called Laos plus present northern and northeastern Thailand. This large area included a number of independent or partly independent royal states and principalities. The states of Chieng Mai, Lamphun, Lampang, Chieng Sen, Nan, and Phrae in northern Thailand were independent from the fourteenth century, if their own traditional accounts are accurate; were dominated by Burma after the mid-sixteenth century; were independent again at the beginning of the eighteenth century; and came under full Thai control in the nineteenth century. To the east, in the area of present-day Laos, were the major states of Luang Prabang, Vientiane, Xieng Khouang, and Champassak. There were also a large number of smaller principalities in this region which were at times dominated by the larger states and at times maintained a precarious independence under their own hereditary rulers. Information on the Lao states included in present-day northeast Thailand is extremely scanty until the nineteenth century. Control by the central Thai government over the area began only under King Taksin (1776–1782). It was extended under his successors of the Chakri dynasty but did not become complete until the reign of King Chulalongkorn (1886–1910). As an illustration of the vicissitudes of these territorial entities, one might cite the well-informed nineteenth-century European observer who wrote that Korat, only 160 miles from Bangkok, was ruled by its own "little king," and that the most important states were Phy Khiey and Suvannaphum, which even many Thai might have difficulty locating on a map today.

The logic of the use of the term "Lao" for all this vast area lies in the recognition by its neighbors, Vietnam, Burma, Thailand (Siam), and Cambodia, and by early European travelers and officials, of an essential cultural and linguistic homogeneity which made all of the peoples and states of this area more similar to one another than to any of their neighbors, including their close linguistic relatives in central Thailand. It is also essential to note that in those days the Mekong River was not a boundary. All of the Lao states lying along it, such as Chieng Sen, Nan, Luang Prabang, Vientiane, and Champassak extended over territory on both sides.

Within the states surrounding Laos certain developments essential to a discussion of conflicts in modern times should be noted. By the end of the sixteenth century, and perhaps earlier, Cambodia had shrunk to within its present boundaries and had ceased to exert any political influence over Laos. Burma dominated northern Laos for most of the sixteenth to late eighteenth centuries and was of importance in the politics of Luang Prabang and Vientiane as well.

The first half of the nineteenth century saw increased competition between two strong and expanding states on the Southeast Asian mainland. Siam and Dai Nam (now Thailand and Vietnam) sought to extend their influence over the politically weak areas lying between them, the present states of Laos and Cambodia. In earlier centuries the kingdoms of Lao Lanchang (Lan Xang) and Khmer (Cambodian) Angkor had been the equals of their eastern and western neighbors, but during the seventeenth and eighteen centuries they gradually lost ground to the rising Thai and Vietnamese powers.

Around the turn of the nineteenth century, following periods of chaos, new dynasties rose in Siam and Vietnam. The founding kings of these two dynasties had known each other during their respective struggles for power, and throughout their reigns felt sufficiently close to give each other personal advice. During this time, from the 1780s to the 1810s, a certain stability existed in the buffer zone between them. By the end of this period the Cambodian king paid tribute to both states, as did the Lao princes (*chao-muong*) of the states of Vientiane and Luang Prabang.

The entire area of what is now considered the state of Laos
was made up of small political centers known as *muong*. These
were generally centered in the valley areas among the hills and
tended to control the territory surrounding their particular valley, as well as more extensive territory if they had sufficient
resources and a good leader. Luang Prabang to the northwest,
Vientiane in the center, Champassak to the south, and Xieng
Khouang in the northeast were the most important of these
numerous *muong*. The first three of these states lay along the
Mekong, with Vientiane located in an area which, ever since
the French appeared, has formed the Thai-Lao border. Xieng
Khouang included the Plain of Jars, the largest relatively flat
area in upland Laos. It lies in the eastern mountain area which
separates the northern part of Vietnam (Tonkin) from its central section (Annam). Because of their natural domination over
valley areas that produced rice surpluses, these four states generally held sway over their smaller neighbors in the surrounding valleys.

The Thai-Vietnamese struggle of the 1820s and 1830s evolved
around the center of Laos and the three northern states; the
southern Lao princes, dominated by the Thai, played only minor
roles in the conflict. At the end of the eighteenth and the beginning of the nineteenth centuries, Vientiane held the upper hand
among the Lao states. Even though it had lost a good number
of its southern and western *muong*, as well as the Emerald
Buddha, the symbol of its realm, to the new and expanding
Thai dynasty, the latter granted Vientiane and its ruler, Chao
Anou, control over Champassak in 1821. Vietnam showed its
proprietary attitude toward the Plain of Jars by giving it to
Anou's supervision. Luang Prabang had been weakened by
Bangkok in retaliation for its disloyal dealings with the Burmese in earlier decades and, while still autonomous, it was no
longer the equal of its southern neighbor, Vientiane.

The struggle that broke out in Laos in the 1820s centered
on Vientiane and involved all of central Laos and the forces of
both the Thai and the Vietnamese states. In 1826 Chao Anou,
ruler of Vientiane, took advantage of a slight, real or imagined,
which he received during a visit to Bangkok as an excuse to

avenge all the wrongs done to his state and himself by the Thai. He attacked the Thai directly and moved swiftly toward Bangkok, spreading the word that the English were attacking from the sea. His son, ruling at Champassak, brought southern Lao troops to his support, and he almost reached Bangkok before the Thai recovered from their surprise. The Thai armies then struck back at both the Vientiane and Champassak forces. Chao Anou's son fled east and hid with the Kha mountain peoples before being captured by Thai troops. The Thai thereupon took over the administration of Champassak and dismembered it by giving greater power to subordinate *muong* at the expense of their former overlords and placing the *muong* more directly under Bangkok's control.

As the Thai, joined by the forces of Luang Prabang, seized their territory, Chao Anou's forces began to fall back to the *muong* of Xieng Khouang. The ruler of Xieng Khouang, who was a vassal of Chao Anou, readily gave aid and comfort to the refugees. Chao Anou himself fled to Vietnam and sought troops from Emperor Minh Mang to help him regain his state. Throughout the affair, the emperor continued to believe that the Thai monarch would be content merely to chastise Chao Anou, who had initiated the conflict, and leave the matter there. The Thai forces, however, did not stop at Vientiane, but continued to penetrate deeper into Lao territory in search of Anou.

Since the Thai kept coming, the debate among the Vietnamese began in earnest. Le Van Duyet, the powerful warlord of the southern frontier, sought every opportunity to extend Vietnamese influence westward at the expense of the Thai state. In this instance he insisted on Vietnam's responsibility to its tributary states, especially Vientiane, which was a "gateway" of the empire. To accomplish this, Duyet was prepared to attack the Thai from the rear, via Cambodia, as they pressed toward Laos. Minh Mang, however, preferred to deal diplomatically with the Thai to resolve the situation—but only if Bangkok ceased its advance and fell back. Otherwise, the Vietnamese troops would move to stop them. Meanwhile, the Thai troops kept moving, and the Vietnamese sent a protest as they advanced their own troops, with Anou following in their wake.

At this point Xieng Khouang, caught between the two advancing forces, of the Thai and Luang Prabang on the one hand and of the Vietnamese and the remnants of Vientiane on the other, eagerly sought Vietnam's aid. Minh Mang decided that aid should be given lest panic set in and worsen the situation. He felt the best course would be to take advantage of the situation and tie the plateau into the empire, thus scaring off the Thai forces. After all the territory had once belonged to the Vietnamese empire, which now needed control of this important strategic gateway. Yet the emperor remained uncertain as to exactly how he should deal with the Vientiane affair.

This indecision had no consequence, however, as Luang Prabang ceased its harassment of Xieng Khouang. Minh Mang viewed this as a response to the advance of his troops, who, despite their small numbers, seemed to have had an effect. He chose to leave only a small force on the Plain of Jars. When the Thai indicated they had pardoned Anou for his acts, Minh Mang released him after scolding him for the maladministration of his state. An imperial letter was sent to Bangkok, and Vietnamese troops escorted Anou back to his domain, while the emperor continued to maintain his faith in his diplomatic relations with the Thai state.

Although the threat of war had declined, the balance of power in Laos had changed. Vientiane was no longer the major *muong* of the Lao territories. It had been greatly humbled and had lost much of its power. Champassak and Xieng Khouang were no longer under its hegemony. The Thai had taken control of Vientiane and had begun to dismember Champassak, while the Vietnamese had established themselves on the Plain of Jars. Luang Prabang had gained greatly from its alliance with Bangkok and was taking advantage of the situation to expand its power into lesser *muong* to the east. Minh Mang responded by sending a letter warning Luang Prabang against further expansion. The latter, we are told in Vietnamese records, trembled and asked pardon. Xieng Khouang became the Vietnamese prefecture of Tran-ninh, belonging to Nghe-an province, and other *muong* also sought to become tributaries of Vietnam. The *muong* of Laos had broken off all contact with Vientiane, lost their autonomy, and become evenly divided between the Thai and Vietnamese.

Luang Prabang continued its attempt to build power, and in 1828 word came to Hue of the accumulation of stocks for an attack on Tran-ninh. Preparations were made to guard the Plain of Jars against this threat. The commander at Tran-ninh was sent to set matters in order in the surrounding territories which recognized Hue's role. Gradually, the Vietnamese built up their own position in the mountains, organizing the administration there, accumulating local rice and men, with the Plain as the headquarters for the entire area.

Once again, however, Chao Anou's actions upset the balance. A fight had broken out between Lao and Thai over rice stored in Vientiane. On hearing of the incident, Minh Mang correctly foresaw that the Thai forces would come storming back and that Anou had no chance of stopping them. He decided to abandon Anou and instead tried to placate the Thai. Immediately, other strategic *muong* lying between Xieng Khouang and Vientiane (some of which were Thai tributaries) came and asked to join the Vietnamese Empire. Minh Mang accepted their tribute and brought them into the administrative organization of his state, forming them into prefectures (*phu*) and districts (*huyen*) with their own leaders or officials.

Because of the Vientiane incident, the Thai forces repeatedly attacked Anou's base and eventually forced him again to seek Vietnamese aid. Minh Mang was unreceptive, and told Anou to make the best of his situation and defend himself.

Shortly thereafter, Vientiane fell and Chao Anou fled. Minh Mang immediately began to move troops into the outer areas of Vietnamese control, those which had only recently been drawn into the administrative network. The Thai, furious at Anou's repeated treachery and determined to punish him, allied with the Lao to hunt him down. However, these expeditions turned out to be unnecessary. The ruler of Xieng Khouang (Chao Noi, a former vassal of Anou) became suddenly fearful of the Thai thrust, seized Anou, and turned him over to the Thai. With this act, the entire border situation calmed down.

Thus, a span of three years again changed the old situation

of the Lao states. Much of Vientiane's population was removed
to Thai territory, its throne was left vacant, and the old *muong*
essentially ceased to exist. Champassak too had lost its autonomy
and a number of its tributary *muong*, while Xieng Khouang had
become a prefecture of Vietnam's Nghe-an province. Only Luang
Prabang had maintained its autonomy.

At this time, the Vietnamese did not seem to realize the extent to which their limited presence in the Lao hills had led
various Lao princes, Chao Noi in particular, to feel insecure
and to doubt the commitment of Hue. After turning Anou over
to the Thai, he no doubt feared retribution from Hue, and this,
together with the Vietnamese administrative hold on his territory, led to a certain edginess in his relations with the Vietnamese capital. He did not pay his year's tribute and pleaded
ill when asked to appear at court. He was attempting to move
gracefully out of the Vietnamese orbit now that the immediate
Thai danger had disappeared. Minh Mang, however, had him
arrested, tried, and executed.

The Lao hills remained quiet for four years. Luang Prabang,
in favor with both the Thai and the Vietnamese, stood high on
the list of tributary states in Hue, even above Cambodia. Vientiane lost its royal family and status as a *muong*, and the Vietnamese yoke sat heavily on Xieng Khouang. Hue did not appoint
a new *chao-muong* for Xieng Khouang until 1832. Meanwhile,
the Vietnamese official and his troops stationed there requisitioned everything in sight, oppressed the notables and the population, and ignored local custom. The Vietnamese assigned
"proper" family names to the Lao leaders, and they maintained
only a small garrison of several hundred men around the Plain
of Jars, since they assumed the territories were grateful and
at peace.

In 1833 rumors of Thai plans to invade Vietnam began to
take concrete form. The Lao peoples' fear and suspicion of the
Vietnamese were increasing; in addition, famine struck the Lao
hills. The court at Hue appears to have been less worried about
Lao problems than about the possibility of Vietnamese "pirates"
establishing bases in the Lao hills in order to strike against the
lowlands. The Vietnamese garrison at the Plain of Jars remained

small. Then Luang Prabang ceased paying tribute, and some of its men, armed, appeared at Tran-ninh to trade. The court became suspicious and gave orders for its outposts to stay alert.

Relations between Luang Prabang and Hue became strained, and the restlessness in the hills increased. More local chiefs took flight and moved to Thai territory. But when Luang Prabang did send tribute, Vietnamese vigilance relaxed, and Minh Mang agreed to the Lao request that the people of a certain *muong*, who had fled to Tran-ninh earlier, be permitted to return to Luang Prabang. Thus, the movement away from Vietnamese territory continued, right under the eyes of Hue. Leaders who had fled sent men back to draw others out. Word of Thai strength passed through the hills.

Toward the end of the year a Thai officer and a Lao prince announced explicitly that they were going to invade the outer territories under Vietnamese sway. The Thai forces began to move. Using local disaffection with Vietnamese control as their own pretext, the Thai opened a northern front at the same time that they fought the Vietnamese for control of Cambodia. Thai troops also struck across the central mountains into the Cam-lo area, in the western part of Quang-tri province in Vietnam.

New year 1834 came and went, with Minh Mang responding slowly. The Thai–Luang Prabang forces (500 Thais and 4,500 Lao) pressed on toward the Plain of Jars, easily gaining control of the Vietnamese territories beyond Tran-ninh. The Plain itself, with its difficult entry and Vietnamese fortifications, was another matter. Vietnamese troops easily repulsed the Thai attacks. At this point, the *chao-muong* of Xieng Khouang rebelled, caught the Vietnamese completely by surprise, and massacred their garrisons. According to the Xieng Khouang chronicle, the *chao-muong* had actively sought Thai intervention.

Since the geopolitical relationship of the Plain of Jars to Vietnamese strength was obvious, the Thai decided here, and elsewhere on the periphery of Vietnam, to remove the population and to lay waste the area, intending to deprive the Vietnamese forces of as much support as possible upon their return. In this way, Bangkok ensured a definite buffer around the domain which it had so meticulously carved out. The Thai promised the men of Xieng Khouang neighboring territory on the other side of the Mekong, and they agreed to move. But they were driven deeper into the Thai state and forced to settle where they could be easily controlled by the Thai. Some, however, were able to break away and return home.

By the time new Vietnamese forces, sent by an outraged Minh Mang, worked their way back into the Lao mountains, all they found were villages burned to the ground. The Vietnamese then set about establishing a new post and regrouped the approximately 20 per cent of the population which remained. As the Vietnamese ventured beyond the Plain in pursuit of the Thai, they found their other posts and nearby villages also destroyed and the population gone. Again, they reestablished their posts and regrouped the remnants of the population, although they left the posts to the north vacant. Indeed, confronted by this traditional Southeast Asian tactic of removing conquered populations, the Vietnamese, coming from the overcrowded delta, considered themselves victorious since they now held the land. Their morale rose, because they believed the Thai had withdrawn in fear of the great army of the Vietnamese Empire. For the Thai, who held sway over underpopulated frontiers, it was the population that mattered. By the end of the year the Vietnamese had completely reestablished themselves with the usual small number of troops and had set up an even more extensive administration using local dignitaries.

The Thai, aided strongly by Luang Prabang, continued to harass the mountain areas on the western frontier of Vietnam. Luang Prabang was now the only one of the four major Lao states to retain any autonomy, to be relatively powerful, and to possess a royal house of its own. The *muong* of Xieng Khouang had ceased to exist, only the Vietnamese prefecture of Tran-ninh remained (though the Xieng Khouang royal family was reestablished 17 years later, in 1851). Luang Prabang, with Thai support, wasted no time extending its hegemony throughout the northern Lao realms. It pushed northeast all the way to the outer reaches of Hung-hoa province, west of Hanoi, and even drew tribute from the old segments of Xieng Khouang.

The Thai must have been encouraging Luang Prabang to do

what it could to involve Vietnamese troops on the northern part of the western border of Vietnam. Hue recognized the move for what it was and continued to refuse to commit any large numbers of troops to the Lao region. Meanwhile, as the struggle for Cambodia continued in the south, the Thai continued to apply as much pressure as they could elsewhere. In Cam-lo, opposite central Vietnam, they harassed the border areas; to the north, they raided the outposts on the fringes of the Plain of Jars and supported Luang Prabang in its forays farther north.

In 1835 the Thai mounted a major campaign in the Tran-ninh area and against the outer limits of Hung-hoa. The Thai used Lao leaders who had fled to them from Vietnamese-controlled territory as spokesmen in an attempt to draw more people away from the Vietnamese forces. Only when extensive Thai-Lao attacks began along the entire northern front from Tran-ninh to Hung-hoa did the Vietnamese begin to move against them. After this late start the Vietnamese quickly drove the Thai from northern Laos. As the Thai withdrew from the field, Luang Prabang became much less belligerent and remained content with its new gains.

In the following years peace returned to the Lao hills, and the remainder of the population rebuilt their communities. In the northeast section of Laos, the Vietnamese maintained a firm hold, applying "love and reason" and lessening any friction that might otherwise have led to inter-*muong* warfare. The areas most remote from Vietnam were virtually depopulated. Closer in, around the Plain of Jars, about half the population remained. Only in the far north were any of the *muong* fully populated. Dislocated elements of the population came to be troublesome for the Vietnamese, and the Lao inhabitants in Thai territory continued to draw their fellows over to join them. A weary Minh Mang, tired of the perpetual upheavals among the "barbarians," gave strict orders to handle the "detestable" elements severely and to move them to a place where they could be controlled and separated from the Lao on the other side to forestall collusion between them.

In 1837 Luang Prabang staged a final raid against a *muong* north of Tran-ninh, but Minh Mang merely expressed his disapproval. Later that year a Luang Prabang envoy sought Vietnamese support for one aspirant in a Luang Prabang succession struggle—the other having Bangkok's recognition. Minh Mang found this contrary to his Confucian views and, righteously indignant, expelled him and rejected future Luang Prabang tribute.

Thus, after a decade of intense involvement with the various Lao *muong,* the strongly Confucianized Vietnamese of the Minh Mang period had not adjusted to Southeast Asian politics. In their minds there were "civilized" rules for the conduct of interstate relations, which could not be breached, even for political advantage. The great Vietnamese Empire could and must stand above questionable activities. The Vietnamese forces, however, remained in the Lao hills at their base of Tran-ninh and in the *muong* immediately adjacent to their own territory. These areas, particularly the Plain of Jars, were ruled in accordance with local custom. In the decade that followed, the Vietnamese presence gradually lessened until by the 1850s Xieng Khouang had once again become a barbarian state whose local ruler received a mandate from Hue. Even so, Vietnamese official geographies up until 1909 continued to list Tran-ninh and its fellow Lao prefectures as part of the official administrative structure of the Vietnamese state. In reality, Luang Prabang, the only remaining Lao power, had asserted itself, demanding and receiving tribute from the newly rearranged *muong.* A claimant to the throne of Xieng Khouang sought aid from Bangkok and Luang Prabang, but was told by the latter that the Vietnamese were aware of the situation and would not allow it. In the 1860s, when a new *chao-muong* succeeded to the throne of Xieng Khouang, he received his mandate from both Hue and Luang Prabang.

This political balance, so like that of the early part of the nineteenth century (although along different lines), dissolved in the chaos of the 1870s. Hue lost control of its northern mountain areas as Chinese bands of brigands and refugees surged throughout the hills and down into the lowlands. These renegades took the Plain of Jars, defeating a Vietnamese army in the process, and devastated Xieng Khouang. The population scattered westward to Luang Prabang, to the region of Vientiane, and all along the Mekong, though as always, some remained to pay the occupier's fees. Bangkok sent an army in an attempt to restore peace to the area. Once again the Thai drove the refugee Lao of Xieng Khouang deeper into Thailand; many died of an epidemic on the way. The Thai-Lao troops did, however, stop the Chinese bands at the Mekong near Vientiane after hard fighting. Money and opium changed hands and the Chinese left the Plain of Jars.

Thereafter, because the weakened Vietnamese court was constantly preoccupied with the French, the Thai held the upper hand throughout the Lao states. Yet guerrilla warfare continued as local people around the Plain fought against both Chinese bandits and rebellious Kha tribesmen. This warfare lasted until Thai and Luang Prabang troops came to their aid and suppressed the disruptive elements; but this time, they removed the Xieng Khouang royal family to Bangkok and occupied the Plain. The French were now bogged down in Tonkin and, with no rivals, Bangkok took over Xieng Khouang, although remnants of the royal family eventually found refuge with the French. As the Thai continued their attempt to bring all the Lao *muong* into the Thai state, they moved to take over Luang Prabang and the western portion of northern Laos. The French, following the missions of Auguste Pavie, from 1887 to 1893 (see article 6 by McCoy), took advantage of Lao pleas and the old Vietnamese tributary claims to take control of Lao territory themselves and, as the Vietnamese had done before them, to install their own residents over the local officials. Following confrontations with the Thai and the English in the 1890s, the Lao *muong* became French; Luang Prabang remained the only Lao state with even pretensions of autonomy, becoming the capital of a united Laos after World War II.

This nineteenth-century Thai-Vietnamese rivalry clearly presages some of the major strategic and political issues of today's conflict. The most important point is that, given the strategic relationship between the Plain of Jars and the northern half of Vietnam, no Vietnamese state can afford to leave itself vulnerable by allowing hostile forces to hold this plateau. And, as Alexander

Woodside has observed,[2] no Vietnamese state can afford to allow hostile forces to dominate any particular element of an upland population that spills over into the hills of Vietnam, because this makes possible infiltration by hostile elements. Woodside has noted that it is no coincidence that the areas that sustain the Vietnamese-supported Pathet Lao movement (such as Sam Neua and Tran-ninh) are those border territories which Minh Mang seized in reaction to Thai penetration of the Lao states. These are reasons, to quote him, "why, whether we like it or not, no Vietnamese government, Communist or non-Communist, is ever going to follow a policy of 'hands off Laos.'" As for Thailand, we may say exactly the same thing regarding the (Lao) Mekong territories of Luang Prabang, Vientiane, and Champassak. In our century, as in earlier ones, stability is possible only if Vietnam and Thailand reach a mutual, if tacit, resolution of their centuries-long conflict over Laos. Stability can be sustained only if the great powers cease to fish in troubled waters.

SOURCES

Archaimbault, Charles, "L'Histoire de Champassak," *Journal Asiatique* 249, 4 (1961), 529–595.

——, "Les Annales de l'Ancien Royaume de S'ieng Khwang," *BEFEO,* 53 (1967), 557–673.

Excerpts and text of the *Dai Nam Thuc Luc* (Vietnamese annals).

Nguyen Sieu, *Phuong Dinh Du Dia Chi.* Saigon translation, 1960.

Phan Huy Chu, "Du Dia Chi," in Vol. I of *Lich Trieu Hien Chuong Loai Chi.* Hanoi translation 1960 (geography section of the major Vietnamese compendium).

Vella, Walter, *Siam Under Rama III, 1824–1851.* Locust Valley, N.Y.: J. J. Augustin, 1957.

Woodside, Alexander B., "Vietnam and Laos: The Continuing Crisis," paper presented at American Historical Association meeting, Washington, D.C., December, 1969.

Wyatt, David K., "Siam and Laos, 1767–1827," *Journal of Southeast Asian History,* 4, 2 (1963).

2. A. B. Woodside, "Vietnam and Laos: The Continuing Crisis," paper presented at American Historical Association meeting, Washington, D.C., December 1969, p. 4.

6

French Colonialism in Laos, 1893–1945

Alfred W. McCoy

Throughout more than a half-century of colonial rule, the kingdom of Laos remained a quaint, neglected backwater of France's Indochina empire. While 40,000 Frenchmen crowded into Saigon and the Mekong Delta to compete for jobs ranging from governor to traffic cop, the French colonial administration often found it difficult to get enough men to fill the meager 100 positions that were allotted to Laos on the general Indochina budget. Those Frenchmen who did agree to go to Laos often went for a short term, having been promised that they would be remembered on the promotion lists in later years for having endured this hardship. This attitude was reflected in their work, for French colonial officials in Laos generally spent most of their time chasing the local women, seeking or avoiding addiction to alcohol or opium, and dreaming of their return to Saigon or Hanoi.

Although this reaction to Laos was typical of most of the French colonial officials who served there, it was by no means true of all of them. Indeed, because so many of their countrymen did so little, Laos was a place where a dynamic and pioneering official could assume authority and have an impact far beyond his years and official rank. Since most French officials were content to let Laos flow along undisturbed so long as the opium smuggling did not reach outrageous proportions, everybody paid his taxes, and there was no rebellion in the hills, French policy in Laos was the work of a very few men.

In fact, it might more correctly be said that the French legacy in Laos was the work of two men: Auguste Pavie and Charles Rochet. It was the dedicated explorer Auguste Pavie who conducted his "conquest of hearts" in the 1880s and 1890s by trekking barefoot across the hills and river valleys of Laos seeking trade routes, tribal alliances, and political relations. With a unique combination of warm sympathy and hard political bargaining, Pavie was able to win Laos away from Thai control and secure it as a French colony by forging a series of political alliances with the Lao royal courts and the highland tribal federations. Pavie also served as the colony's first governor; the administrative and political relations he established remained the basis of French rule until 1940. Pavie believed himself the father of all the Lao and called them "my dear children" in his letters. He and his successors treated the Lao as charming but incompetent children, denied them all effective political authority, and kept them in a state of prolonged national adolescence.

However, in 1940, when Japan's influence spread throughout Southeast Asia, bringing with it the shock waves of Pan-Asian nationalism, the delicate structure of French paternal rule was shattered. Backed by Japan, Thailand proclaimed itself the homeland of the Tai race (which includes the Lao) and began a campaign to win over the Lao. The French responded by having Charles Rochet launch the Lao national movement. Through education, literature, and mass rallies, Rochet revived the Lao sense of national identity. The French then gave the Lao greater political authority and hoped that by giving a little they could hold Laos forever. However, once awakened, Lao national consciousness grew dramatically—to the point where Laos desired and achieved its independence in 1945. However, achieving independence so quickly after having been dominated for so long left Laos a shaken, nervous, and factionalized society. Even though Pavie had furthered France's interest by making the Lao think of themselves as French, and Rochet had sought to do the same by reminding the Lao that they were Lao, both men inadvertently promoted tension and conflict that are still present in Laos today.

THE FRENCH CONQUEST OF LAOS

The French conquest of Laos in the 1880s and 1890s was the last stage of 35 years of French expansion in Indochina. It was not their interest in Vietnam, Laos, or Cambodia which involved the French, but rather their interest in China—in particular in the vast potential of Chinese markets. The French had watched with envy while Britain secured enormous profits through domination of the China trade and with bitterness as they noted that France's consumption of one-half of Shanghai's and one-third of Canton's silk exports in the 1870s (and over one-half of all of China's silk exports in the 1880s) was one of the major reasons that the China trade was so profitable for England. England's control over Hong Kong (Canton) and Shanghai meant that the silk was shipped on British vessels to London before it could be shipped to France—all to England's profit. Thus, the French sought a port of their own in Indochina which could be used as a base from which France's shipping could challenge England's. More ambitiously, they sought a back door to China which would entirely avoid the English-dominated ports.[1]

In 1858 the French sent the first of several naval expeditions to Danang to secure it as a port for French shipping. However, since Danang was so close to the royal court at Hue, Vietnamese resistance was strong and the French were unable to secure their position. Finally, in July of 1861 the French captured Saigon, established a permanent garrison, and began their annexation of Cochin China (Saigon and the Mekong Delta). Saigon was not only a suitable port, but it had the advantage of being close to the mouths of the Mekong, which the French believed would give them their backdoor to southwest China. Acting on these beliefs, in 1866 the French colonial administration dispatched an expedition to explore the Mekong River and assess its feasibility as a trade route to southern China. Although the one surviving leader of the expedition, Francis Garnier, reported in 1868 that the Mekong was too long and had too many rapids to be of any use for navigation, he asserted that the Red River, which ran from south China to the Tonkin Gulf, was a good alternate route.

However, because of the shock of its defeat in the Franco-Prussian War in 1870 and the subsequent turmoil in French

1. John Laffey, *French Imperialism and the Lyon Trade Mission*. Ph.D. thesis (Cornell University, 1966).

domestic politics, it was not until 1882 that a French expedition set off from Saigon to conquer the Tonkin delta. The Vietnamese emperor was disturbed by the French expedition and resisted, ordering his garrisons to fight and forging a military alliance with the Ho armies. The Ho were remnants of a Chinese messianic revolutionary movement (the Taipings) who had been forced to retreat into the hills of northern Vietnam and Laos following their eviction from China ten years earlier. Despite stiff Vietnamese resistance, by August of 1883 the French armies had bombarded and occupied the royal capital. They completed their conquest of all of Vietnam by imposing a French protectorate on the remaining parts of the country.

With the conquest of the Tonkin delta and the assumption of a protectorate over the Vietnamese imperial court, French involvement in Laos became inevitable. By establishing a protectorate over the imperial court, France fell heir to traditional Vietnamese claims on Laos. More significantly, the hills of northern Vietnam and Laos had become the refuge for rebellious imperial court officials who allied themselves with the Ho armies and the Tai Tribal Federation in order to combat the French. Until these groups were subdued, travel and commerce between French possessions and southern China would be impossible.

Both the conquest of Tonkin and the assumption of Vietnamese claims in Laos served to bring France into direct contact and conflict with Thai and British expansion. In 1886 Upper Burma fell to the British. And at about that time the Thai sent troops into Laos to defend their claims in the area. The French realized that their commercial control over south China would be greatly weakened if Britain and its Thai client were able to gain control over the Mekong and develop a competing trade down its course to northeast Thailand, where goods could be shipped overland to Bangkok. The French had also begun a new series of explorations for navigable channels on the Mekong, and there was hope that the Mekong too might give France another access to China. One French colonial official, exulting at the prospect of wealth that awaited France's conquest of the Mekong valley, declared:

One quick glance at the map will show that the Indochinese Union forms a neat package, bordered by natural frontiers which are: the Annamese Sea on the south and east; the great Mekong River, on the west and north; the Chinese frontier on the north. . . . The rights of protectorate favor our own national products. In this way we assure ourselves a monopoly on trade with 27,000,000 people. The minimal transit tax and a light tariff in transit goods will develop exchange currency with Yunnan, Kwangsi, and Kwangtung, and will give us a clientele of 40,000,000 Chinese at a minimum. The general trade traffic will give us a base of 67,000,000 consumers.[2]

Several times during its most intense period (from 1886 to 1893), the struggle for the Mekong valley almost sparked war between England, Thailand, and France. However, the competing interests were ultimately reconciled by diplomatic agreements hastened to completion by a few minor skirmishes. Throughout the contest England remained the calmest of the rivals, for it held the ultimate power to decide the outcome of the conflict. England dominated Thailand, ruled Burma and the Indian subcontinent, and controlled the largest portion of the China trade. The English navy would impose a settlement if diplomacy failed.

England's major goals were to keep the French at a comfortable distance (by preserving a buffer between British and French territories in northern Burma and Laos) and to maintain the independence of Bangkok and the Menam valley, where all of its commerce with Thailand was conducted.[3] In contrast, the French were desperate to expand their relatively meager holdings by gaining what they imagined to be an easily exploitable river empire. They were willing to risk war to gain these ends.[4] Thailand simply wanted to hold what it already had. Luang Prabang, central Laos, and lower Laos (Champassak) were its clients. Since without England's support Thailand would ultimately have to yield, and England felt there was little worth fighting for, France seemed to have the upper hand in Laos.

2. Charles Lemire, *Le Laos Annamite* (Paris: Librairie Coloniale, 1894).
3. Claire Hirschfield, "Struggle for the Mekong Banks," *Journal of Southeast Asian History* (March 1968), p. 49.
4. *Ibid.*, p. 48.

However, because France lacked a cabal of officials, missionaries, or merchants capable of forging an alliance with a Lao political group, and because many of its troops were tied down suppressing the Vietnamese Royalist Rebellion, France had, apparently, no means by which to conquer Laos. Even if the French had had sufficient strength for a military conquest, a direct clash with Thailand might have drawn in England—a contest France would certainly have lost. Thus, in 1886 the French were faced with the alternatives of making a peaceful conquest or postponing their effort until some future date by which time Thai influence might be reestablished. It was Auguste Pavie who made this peaceful conquest possible.

The struggle began on September 21, 1886, when Thailand's King Chulalongkorn announced that he was sending an army to the Laotian principality of Xieng Khouang and the Sip Song Chau Tai cantons (the Tai Federation; the name literally means "the 12 cantons" [regions]) of Lai Chau, Son La, and Dien Bien Phu to put down the Ho armies that were ravaging the area. This was actually a thinly disguised attempt to reestablish Thai control over Laos, and the French responded to the challenge nine days later when Auguste Pavie set out for Luang Prabang. In this first mission, Pavie was accompanied by only eight Cambodian assistants whom he had recruited in Phnom Penh.[5]

Although at first glance this may not have seemed like an even match, Pavie was more than equal to the task. He had first come to Indochina in 1869 as a regular army sergeant. He later became a telegraph operator and developed a strong interest in Southeast Asian cultures while stationed at the end of the line in a racially diverse corner of Cambodia.[6] Pavie's study won him a job as a survey geographer for the colonial government, and his wide travels gave him the ability to adapt quickly to Indochina's diverse peoples and grasp the subtleties of their local politics.

On September 30, 1886, the French government sent Pavie on

5. Paul le Boulanger, *Histoire du Laos Français* (Paris: Librairie Plon, 1931), p. 257.

6. Albert de Pouvourville, *Auguste Pavie* (Paris: Larose, 1933), pp. 11–13.

his first trip to Laos. He and his Cambodian assistants arrived in Luang Prabang the following February. There he tried to make contact with the royal court and to begin establishing political relations with the king; but the Thai kept Pavie under close surveillance, and he suffered several weeks of absolute failure.

In May 1887 the Thai expeditionary force withdrew most of its troops from Laos and the Sip Song Chau Tai and returned to Bangkok with hostages from the ruling Deo family of the Sip Song Chau Tai and from the royal courts at Luang Prabang and Xieng Khouang. However, the leader of the Tai Federation, Deo Van Tri, reacted rather differently than the Thai had expected. On June 7, 1887, Deo Van Tri and 600 of his Ho allies arrived in Luang Prabang and drove off the Thai garrison. For three days, Deo Van Tri sacked the city to avenge the kidnapping of his brothers. On June 10 the Ho set fire to the Royal Palace and a number of the Buddhist temples and began to drive the population from the city. In the confusion the 76 year-old king, Oun Kham, was left in the burning palace until Pavie's Cambodian assistant, Keo, risked the flames to carry him out of the palace and down to the banks of the Mekong, where Pavie and the city's population were embarking. Pavie accompanied the king downstream, and when they reached a refuge at Paklay he and his assistants tended the sick king, conducted a search for the royal archives, and helped organize the settlement of the refugees. After three months together, Pavie records that Oun Kham assured him that

our kingdom is not a conquest of Thailand. Luang Prabang, wanting protection against all attacks, voluntarily offered its tribute. Now through Thailand's interference, our ruin is complete. Now if my son consents, we will offer tribute to France, sure that it will guard us against all future evils.[7]

Pavie had gained an important ally for France.

Pavie devoted the remaining months of his first mission (which lasted until 1889) to the subjugation of the Sip Song Chau Tai

7. Boulanger, *op. cit.*, p. 269.

and the destruction of the Ho armies which were still the dominant power in the area. In the fall of 1887 the French launched a sizable military expedition up the Black River from Hanoi in an attempt to suppress Deo Van Tri and his Ho allies. Pavie arrived in the area in January 1888 and began a much more successful campaign. It was Pavie's feeling that the Tai were tired of incessant warfare and would willingly exchange a military alliance with the Ho for a peaceful alliance with the French. Therefore, he began negotiations with the various Tai chiefs, and in October secured the release of Deo's brothers from the Thai in Bangkok in exchange for the Tai-French alliance. When they lost their major ally, the Ho soon surrendered and, in Deo Van Tri, Pavie gained another invaluable friend for France.[8]

By the time his first mission ended, Pavie had forged two powerful political alliances which were to serve as the ultimate basis for France's claims in Laos. At the outset of his second mission (1889–1891) the colonial government, recognizing the importance of his work, gave Pavie a greatly expanded staff (20 colonial officials) and considerable financial support. The Pavie mission, accompanied by representatives of a commercial company called the French Syndicate of Laos, began a scientific exploration of Laos' peoples, products, and geography and the construction of a systematic network of political relations with the local leaders.

With their claims and their presence firmly established, the French moved to secure formal recognition of their position. During negotiations with England over the Mekong problem in 1892, the British made it quite clear that they would do nothing to prevent French seizure of Lao territories east of the Mekong.[9]

In February 1893 Pavie became the French representative in Bangkok, and in May the French used one of the perennial "incidents" between Thai and French troops as an excuse to send three columns of troops into central and southern Laos. The arrival of these troops provoked even more serious "incidents,"

8. *Ibid.*, p. 283.
9. Hirschfield, *op. cit.*, p. 30.

which then served as the French pretext for dispatching three gunboats up the Menam River to Bangkok. On July 12, 1893, the Thai garrison at Paknam hit one of these ships with an artillery barrage, and this incident was used by pro-imperialist elements in the French Assembly to secure an ultimatum demanding the cession of all Lao territories east of the Mekong. By October the Thai had yielded to this pressure. They assured French hegemony in the Mekong basin by ceding all lands on the east bank of the river. French control over the east bank territories was confirmed in 1896 when the British gave up the idea of a buffer zone in upper Laos and yielded the east bank to the French in exchange for a guarantee of the security of the Menam valley. Later, in exchange for the 25-kilometer neutral zone along the Mekong's west bank, the Thai gave the Laotian provinces of Champassak and Sayaboury to the French in 1904 and 1907.[10]

THE ESTABLISHMENT OF FRENCH CONTROL

For the French, Laos was defined by the eastern half of the Mekong River basin, and boundaries were carefully drawn to conform with the exact limits of the Mekong watershed. When the colonial government demarcated Laos' common borders with Burma, China, and Vietnam, the survey teams simply determined the limits of the Mekong's watershed and adopted these as the borders of Laos. In reality, the French borders meant absolutely nothing to the people of Laos. What the French thought of as a clearly defined political unit was one of the most racially and politically complex areas of Southeast Asia. The Lao themselves accounted for only about 45 per cent of the total population, while the remainder was composed of Meo, Kha, and Tai tribes in the north and about 60 different Kha tribes in the south. People of the same tribe, political grouping, and often the same family were separated by the arbitrary border. Indeed, in their insistence in defining Laos in terms of the Mekong basin the

10. *Ibid.,* pp. 49–52.

French completely ignored existing political structures and carved a colony out of segments of existing states and federations.

The consequences of this policy can best be seen in the French treatment of the Lu Federation and the six cantons of Sam Neua province. In northern Laos the French created a politically unstable situation by annexing two cantons from the great Lu state, the Sip Song Panna (literally, "the 12,000 rice fields"). The Lu were a highly developed people who spoke a language similar to Lao and Thai, had adopted Buddhism from Burma, but were most influenced by Chinese culture. About two-thirds of all Lu males could read and write in Chinese characters, and their highly centralized court bureaucracy was based on Confucian organizational principles. The Sip Song Panna extended from northern Laos and Burma along the Mekong River into China's southern Yunnan province.[11] Although its borders had changed considerably through its 1,000-year history, in the 1890s the Sip Song Panna occupied 6,000 square miles and consisted of 28 cantons, each of which was surrounded by rolling hills that spread off to the east and west of the Mekong. The Lu lived in the cantonal valley states, each of which was dominated by a local hierarchy directly subordinate to the Lu capital at Ch'eli. While the Lu valley dwellers made up only about half of the population in each canton, they maintained friendly political relations with the minority tribes who lived in the hills.[12] By annexing one Lu canton in Nam Tha province and another in Phong Saly, the French aroused tremendous resentment among the Lu, which later produced two major insurrections.

While the western half of the territories which make up Sam Neua province are a part of the Mekong River basin, the eastern half is drained by rivers that flow into the Tonkin Gulf. Accordingly, in 1896 the French governor of northern Laos announced that the eastern half of Sam Neua province would be

11. William Clifton Dodd, *The Tai Race* (Cedar Rapids, Iowa: Torch Press, 1923), p. 187.
12. Frank M. Lebar, Gerald C. Hickey, and John K. Musgrave, eds., *Ethnic Groups of Mainland South East Asia* (New Haven: Human Relations Area Files [HRAF], 1964), pp. 207–212.

transferred to Vietnam. In doing so the French ignored the fact that since the thirteenth century the Black and Red Tai populations of these cantons had shared a common history, culture, and political structure. The Tai in the eastern canton began a mass exodus to the west, and when the eastern canton became virtually depopulated by 1903 the French finally reunified the area.[13]

When the French acquired Laos in 1893 they still entertained the fantasy that it would be a profitable river empire. The colonial government's delusion was shared by the French Syndicate of Laos, whose Parisian backers supplied 100,000 francs in capital, 15 tons of trading goods, and 10 trading posts along the Mekong. Within two years the venture collapsed, because the Mekong proved a poor transportation route and the French merchants failed in competition with the Chinese for Laos' 400,000 poor customers.[14]

With the collapse of the Syndicate, responsibility for administration fell upon the colonial government. In 1895, 14 provinces were created and placed under governors for upper and lower Laos, but four years later they were unified under a single governor, who directed a highly centralized administration in Vientiane. Although Laos' first governor, Auguste Pavie, had promised the king of Luang Prabang his autonomy, the French governor assumed absolute authority, and the artificial distinction the French made between indirect administration in the kingdom of Luang Prabang and direct administration in the rest of Laos was little more than legal fiction.

After the dream of instant wealth faded, the French resigned themselves to maintaining order and managing their administration as inexpensively as possible so that it would not become too much of a strain on the general Indochina budget. Since one of the largest expenses of any colonial budget was the support of European officials at their normal standard of living,

---

13. André Boutin, "Monographie de la Province des Houa-Phans," *Bulletin des Amis du Laos,* #1 (September 1937), Hanoi, p. 72.

14. Lucien de Reinach, *Le Laos* (Paris, 1911). Translated by HRAF, p. 9; Pierre Grossin, *Notes sur L'Histoire de la Province de Cammon* (Hanoi, 1933), p. 42.

the French kept their colonial staff in Laos to such an absolute minimum that in 1904 the contingent of 72 officials was the smallest anywhere in the French Empire. With so few men the French had to conduct their administration by adapting themselves to the Lao feudal court structures in the lowlands and by manipulating the tribal-racial hierarchies in the mountains.[15]

In the lowland areas the traditional Lao political structure provided a convenient means for carrying out this policy. The five major lowland principalities had a uniform administrative system with villages grouped into districts (*tasseng*), and districts grouped into cantons (*muong*). The French simply grouped the cantons into provinces and guaranteed the loyalty of the Lao officials by assuming the right to approve all appointments and by making officials swear their traditional Buddhist oath to the French Republic instead of to their king.[16] The most subordinate positions in the provincial bureaucracies (translators, low-level clerks) were manned by the Gallicized Lao elite, the middle-level positions by French-educated Vietnamese, and the very highest positions were reserved for French officials. So efficient was this system that in 1938 there were only three French officials (commissioner, assistant commissioner, and military officer) in all of Saravane province; and these three successfully administered 6 cantons, 36 districts, and 596 villages.[17]

Although the French administration held all substantive power, the colonial government preserved the traditional royal families and used them as religious symbols to maintain popular compliance with French administration.[18] Out of the five great royal houses of Laos, only three had survived the turmoil of the nineteenth century; Xieng Khouang, Champassak, and Luang Prabang. (See article 5, by Whitmore.) Because of the special relationship between Pavie and the royal family of Luang Prabang, the French ended two centuries of aristocratic compe-

15. *Ibid.*, p. 372.
16. *Ibid.*, pp. 125–127.
17. Joel Halpern, "Population Statistics and Associated Data," *Laos Project Paper* #3 (Los Angeles: UCLA Press, 1961), Table XIV.
18. François Iché, *Le Statut Politique et International du Laos Français.* Ph.D. thesis (Université de Toulouse, 1935), p. 198.

tition by reducing the kings of Xieng Khouang and Champassak to governors, thus leaving Luang Prabang the only kingdom in Laos. Although they had no legal right to do so, the French further extended their control over the kings and princes by approving their successors, thus making sure that an heir favorable to France would emerge. For example, when Prince Kham Huang of Xieng Khouang instigated the local Meo rebellion against the French in 1896 to protest his demotion to governor, the French merely had him deposed, replacing him with a member of another branch of his family who had served as a French official in Vietnam and Laos.[19]

Although over half of the population of Laos was hill tribes, the French lacked the manpower, finances, and interest to deal with these widely scattered peoples. The French demanded heavy taxes, opium, porters, and corvée road work from these tribes, but gave them absolutely nothing in return. This exploitative attitude was explained by a French colonial official who traveled extensively in the hills of southern Laos. According to him,

it does not seem . . . that this savage race, indolent, superstitious, non-progressive, can be called upon to play an important role in Indochina. It seems that they will be of no use for our civilizing actions, for which they will create nothing but obstacles. Their pathetic weakness will not permit them, after all, to maintain their position against the more active races of Vietnam and Laos, who are encircling and penetrating more and more each day. . . . It is a positive good for our colonization that this exodus be heightened under our direction and the savage races will be blended with their neighbors into a mestizo race which, resisting the mountain climate better than the Laotians and Vietnamese, will be able to realize all of the resources of this region.[20]

In order to have the hill tribes deliver the taxes, porters, opium (or whatever was demanded of them) regularly and

19. Charles Archaimbault, "Les Annales de L'Ancien Royaume de S'ieng Khuang," *Bulletin de L'Ecole Française d'Extrême-Orient* (1967), pp. 595–596.

20. M. A. Lavalée, "Notes Ethnographiques sur Diverses Tribus," *Bulletin de L'Ecole Française d'Extrême-Orient* (1904), p. 311.

reliably without incurring the expenses of any kind of direct relationship, the French used a system of cross-racial administration which established a brutal ethnic hierarchy, and, especially in northern Laos, pitted the various ethnic groups against each other. The French used traditional racial hierarchies where they were strong, reinforced them where they were weak, and created them where they did not exist. This system of control without direct contact had another advantage for the French. By deflecting peoples' anger at the race above or below them on the scale, the French administration was able to exploit extremely independent and volatile groups without ever incurring any direct hostility. However, the condition of the mass of the tribesmen on the lower rungs of the hierarchy was little better than slavery, since their traditional subordination was compounded by heavy French taxes which produced unbearable demands on their meager resources.

The Lamet tribe of southern Nam Tha province provides a clear example of how this cross-racial administration worked. The Lamet were a Kha tribe whose 4,000 members lived in a hundred or so villages that were located on the southern border of the province. The Lamet were not particularly aggressive and had paid their tribute of beeswax regularly to the Thai without coercion from any chiefs or tribal leaders. When the French arrived, they created a hierarchy by appointing a Lamet in each village as a combination tax collector-chief and by creating a special Lamet canton (*muong*) whose administrators and tax collectors were Lu. Thus, a Lamet village chief (never really accepted by his village as a legitimate leader) reported to a Lu tax collector who was responsible to a Lao canton chief who in turn probably dealt with a Vietnamese bureaucrat subordinate to one of the four Frenchmen in Nam Tha province. The French appointed the Lu as administrators because they were literate and had experience dealing with the Lamet. But, as with many interracial hierarchical relationships, the Lu overtaxed for their personal profit, sold titled positions to rich Lamet at high prices, levied disproportionate fines for small offenses, and took every step possible to extort from the Lamet. When the situation reached the crisis stage, the French were able to pacify the

Lamet simply by replacing the Lu district chief with a French-educated Lao.[21]

Similarly, the French administered the Meo through Tai and Lao intermediaries. The colonial government never made its demands (for the opium tax, a heavy head tax, corvée labor, or food requisitions) through French officials. Thus, when the Meo rebelled in 1919 against tax demands (which in many cases were inflated because of Lao-Tai corruption), it was the Lao who were massacred, not the French.[22] French officials were able to make contact with Meo at will and were able to draw off much of the rebels' support merely by offering direct French administration.[23]

In a situation where the French dealt directly with a minority group, they themselves were the target of protest. The French supervised the Chinese minority in Laos through "congregations" whose leaders were directly responsible to French provincial commissioners. Therefore, in 1914, when Chinese merchants became angered at increased taxation on opium marketing, they assaulted the French garrison at Sam Neua and tried to avenge themselves on French officials.[24]

Thus, if a racial or territorial group was aggressively independent, did not have a distinct political hierarchy that could be manipulated, and was unwilling to be dominated by any other ethnic group, it could maintain its independence from the French. Unfortunately for them, not many of the Laotian hill tribes displayed these characteristics, and even those who did had to put up a long and costly resistance to maintain their autonomy.

THE FRENCH ADMINISTRATION OF LAOS, 1893–1940

Once the speculative bubble of the Laotian *Eldorado* burst in the 1890s and the French realized that there were no easy pro-

21. Karl G. Izikowitz, *Lamet* (Göteborg: Elanders Boktryckni Aktiebolag, 1951), p. 346.
22. Barthelemy, *Note sur la Décentralisation Administrative et une Politique des Races au Laos* (Paris), p. 140.
23. F. M. Savina, *Histoire des Miao* (Hong Kong, 1930), pp. 238–239.
24. Boutin, *op. cit.*, p. 74.

fits to be made, Laos became the neglected stepchild of Indochina. Some Frenchmen shared the view of Governor General Paul Doumer, who declared that Laos "constitutes the agricultural, forestry, and possibly the mineral reserve of our Indochina, and . . . will be called to a brilliant future."[25] But even such perennial optimists postponed that future to an indefinite date. Since the French regarded the hill tribes as savages and the Lao as charming but incompetent children, the little economic and social development that did take place in Laos was not done by or for the Lao.

Although colonial governments everywhere boasted of the vast improvement in the health conditions of the natives through the introduction of modern medicine, similar claims could not be made in Laos. The limited French medical facilities consisted of one hospital in Vientiane, clinics in each provincial capital (staffed by one European doctor and a Vietnamese assistant), and an occasional paramedical clinic in one of the larger outlying cities. The hospital and clinics served the Europeans, government officials, and the few Lao who lived in cities. (The Lao were a minority of the urban population.) The public health corps tried merely to prevent the spread of plagues which might eventually reach the cities. The French failed to reduce Laos' infant mortality rate, and during the last 12 years of French administration the number of medical facilities and personnel declined steadily.[26]

Because the French had little use for educated Laotians, by 1940 there were only 7,000 primary school students in a colony of one million people. Not a single high school was constructed. Rather than spending funds to develop a modern school system, in 1907 the French decided that the traditional two or three years of religious education at the local Buddhist temple would suffice.[27] In 1933 there was an attempt to hand out chalk, blackboards, and some training to the teaching monks, but those who received training were hired by the colonial administration, and

25. Paul Doumer, *L'Indochine Française* (Paris, 1930), p. 292.
26. Boutin, *op. cit.*, p. 118. Charles Rochet, *Pays Lao* (Paris: Jean Vigneau, éditeur, 1946), p. 61.
27. *Bulletin de L'Ecole Française d'Extrême-Orient* (1907), pp. 412–413.

the program died. In 1932 Prince Phetsarath summed up the French effort by saying,

the official monk schools have degenerated into training schools for administrative employment. As for the pagoda schools, they have never been organized except on paper, there has never been any effective authority responsible for them, and they continue to function as before.[28]

France's greatest scheme for Laos involved the construction of a complete, all-weather road network linking Laos with Vietnam, thereby enabling the future development of the country and permanently denying Laos to Thailand. Since Laos' natural route to the sea was across northeast Thailand to Bangkok, French road construction across the rough Annamite mountains was an attempt to defy geographical reality, and the difficult task was only partially completed. The road construction was done with forced labor drawn from the whole male population and was bitterly resented. The Lao could not see any logic in this grandiose master plan, which ignored the fact that all of their commerce was conducted between neighboring villages on footpaths and not between Saigon and Vientiane.[29] Since the extensive roads were built for the future by a presently small population, villagers often had to travel 20–30 miles from their homes to the construction site, where they were driven hard by civil engineers eager to set new construction records. Often the demands were so heavy, as in Phong Saly province from 1917 to 1924, that whole districts fled until the work was finished.[30]

The self-supporting village economy of over 90 per cent of Laos' inhabitants was virtually untouched by the French. Most of the new urban commerce generated by the French presence was taken over by the Chinese, any new crafts were dominated

28. Etienne Boul, "La Rénovation des Ecoles de Pagode au Laos," *Bulletin General d'L'Instruction Publique* (September 1933), p. 6.

29. Norton S. Ginsberg, ed., *Area Handbook on Laos* (New Haven: HRAF, 1955), p. 101.

30. G. Ayme, *Monographie du Ve Territoire Militaire* (Hanoi: Imprimerie d'Extrême-Orient, 1930), pp. 126–127.

by the Vietnamese, and the technicians that were needed were either French or Vietnamese.[31] Although the French introduced coffee growing in the Bolovens Plateau and substantially improved the opium-growing methods in Xieng Khouang province, they made few attempts to improve the production of Laos' staple crops—rice and maize—and thus had little impact on Laos' major economic activity—agriculture.

The one resource the French did develop was tin, mined at Nam Pathene in Khammouan province. These mines had been worked for centuries by Lao, who dug shallow trenches in the highland river banks and sent the tin to the Gulf of Siam, where it was used as fish-net ballast. In 1923 European prospectors discovered its potential; by 1937 a French company had induced the colonial government to build two roads to the coast of Vietnam through the Mughia and Nape passes and was exporting 939 tons of tin per year (out of 1,602 tons for all of Indochina). However, the mine's 6,000 laborers and craftsmen were almost entirely Vietnamese and all the technicians were either Vietnamese or French. The Lao received no profit, training, or employment, and eventually would be left with nothing more than a large hole in a mountainside.[32]

Under most colonial systems the Europeans supervised the development of a large urban center which increased in size as the rural residents migrated to the cities and adapted to urban living. But in this area of Indochina, the French had so little interest in working with the native population that the Laotians became a minority in their own cities, and the cities remained inconsequential enclaves surrounded by an unchanging village society. The French populated the cities with Vietnamese merchants and traders to the point that in 1943 the capital, Vientiane, was 53 per cent Vietnamese (42 per cent Lao, 4 per cent Chinese); its second largest city, Thakhek, was 85 per cent Vietnamese (10 per cent Lao, 4 per cent Chinese); and its third largest city, Pakse, was 62 per cent Vietnamese (14 per

31. Joel Halpern, "The Role of the Chinese in Lao Society," *Laos Project Paper #1, op. cit.,* pp. 2–12.
32. Charles Robequain, *The Economic Development of French Indochina* (New York: Oxford University Press, 1944), p. 261.

cent Lao, 23 per cent Chinese).[33] The language of the cities was Vietnamese or French, and the Lao were even prevented from establishing a newspaper for fear that it might generate discontent. Much of the hostility of the present-day Lao elite and urban populace toward the Vietnamese stems from this colonial experience.

After 1898 the fiscal administration of Indochina was managed through a unified general budget. The cost of maintaining even Laos' small number of colonial officials on a European standard of living was so high that Laos had to be subsidized through the general budget. The colonial administration in Saigon never accepted the idea that any colony could be a net loss and maintained constant pressure on its officials in Vientiane to increase Laos' tax revenues. The officials in Vientiane responded by levying an increasingly heavy head tax on every male between the ages of 18 and 60, by demanding an average of 15 days of corvée labor a year (which could be redeemed by paying another head tax), and by extracting heavy fines for even minor legal offenses. This was not very successful, however, for the tax was so heavy that most Laotian village, district, and canton officials were willing to underreport the local population on the annual census (to the extent that French population estimates in some areas were 35 per cent too low.)[34] In 1900 direct taxation collected only 300,000 francs out of a total administrative budget of almost 2 million francs.[35]

The French tried to remedy this fiscal disaster by using the same method they had adopted in other parts of Indochina—the development of a government monopoly on the manufacture and sale of opium. While the French may have neglected the economic development of Laos, in the rest of Indochina from 1900 to 1925 they built a costly railway network, a complete highway system, schools, universities, and impressive colonial administrative centers. This was the period in which most of

33. Joel Halpern, "Population Statistics and Associated Data," *op. cit.*, Table #58.

34. Eric Piertrantoni, "La population du Laos de 1912 à 1945," *Bulletin de la Société des Etudes Indochinoises,* Vol. XXVII, #1 (1953), p. 27.

35. Reinach, *op. cit.*, p. 382.

Vietnam's economic infrastructure was developed, but it was also a time when French private and governmental capital showed little interest in colonial development. The colonial administration solved this problem by establishing a government opium monopoly in 1899 which had the sole right to grow, import, manufacture, and sell opium in Indochina. Through its 5,000 opium dens and shops the opium monopoly generated between 20 and 50 per cent of all of Indochina's revenues from 1898 to 1925 and was largely responsible for the economic development of the colony.[36] Although the monopoly's sale of opium in Laos produced only 150,000 francs in 1900, by 1904 it had increased to 350,000 francs, and its steady rise over the years solved most of Laos' fiscal problems.[37]

But the significance of opium for Laos soon went far beyond its own internal consumption and particular budgetary problems. Although most of the opium which the monopoly sold came from China, India, or Persia, the monopoly did promote the improvement of agricultural techniques among the Meo of Laos. Xieng Khouang province was given a monopoly on legally grown opium in Indochina.[38] To the French this seemed like an ideal solution of Laos' economic dilemma, for a small amount of opium could bring a high return and profits could be made despite poor transportation.

By legalizing and promoting the consumption of opium among the peoples of Indochina (it was illegal for a European to consume opium) and selling their opium at the highest possible price, the French also created a huge demand for less expensive opium and indirectly promoted an enormous smuggling trade. While only Xieng Khouang province participated in the legal opium trade, all of northern Laos grew opium for the contraband trade. The Chinese merchants who crossed Laos' loosely guarded borders with their opium-loaded mule trains from Burma and China were willing to supplement their profits by

36. Jacques Dumarest, *Les Monopolies de L'Opium et du Sel en Indochine*, Ph.D. Thesis (Université de Lyon, 1938), pp. 5–6.

37. Reinach, *op. cit.*, pp. 211, 385.

38. Dumarest, *op. cit.*, p. 20.

exchanging silver, cloth, and utensils for Laotian opium.[39] Although the French took vigorous action to suppress this trade on the Vietnam-China border in the late 1920s (thereby increasing the monopoly's sales ninefold in northern Vietnam), the French ignored Laos' long, difficult frontiers. Through this oversight the French made Laos into a smuggler's haven and started the contraband opium trade, which today is managed by the CIA and its airline, Air America.[40] (See also article 14, by Scott and article 15, by Feingold.)

LAOTIAN RESPONSE TO THE FRENCH

While the French administration of the lowland Lao met with indirect resistance, it rarely encountered any direct, violent opposition. The French gained Lao compliance by taking advantage of the charisma of Lao kings and princes, by ruling through the effective Lao administrative hierarchy, and by defining all of their demands in terms of traditional Lao customs. The Lao had been administered by some form of centralized government for centuries and were used to accepting outside authority. In contrast, the French made harsher demands on the upland peoples and generally had little respect for their customs, leaders, and political traditions. There were a series of upland revolts beginning in 1896, reaching a peak between 1910 and 1916, and finally dying out in the late 1930s, all of which expressed resistance to almost every aspect of the French program.

In southern Laos the French administration of the highland tribes quickly provoked a massive rebellion which lasted for 35 years. The uprising was centered in the Bolovens Plateau and was led by the Alak tribe, who worked as weavers and merchants for the other Kha tribes of the region.[41] Although the revolt took the form of a messianic religious movement, the Alak and their allies (the most important of whom were the Loven, another Kha tribe) bitterly resented French attempts to collect

39. *Ibid.*, p. 136.
40. *Christian Science Monitor*, May 29, 1970.
41. Lebar, Hickey, and Musgrave, *op. cit.*, p. 135.

taxes and regulate their commerce. They were, essentially, fighting for political independence.

The revolt began in January 1901 when a group of Kha crossed the Mekong from Thailand into Saravane province, successfully avoided French troops trying to force them back into Thailand, and made contact with the Alak villages near Thateng on the northern edge of the Bolovens Plateau.[42] Under the leadership of the Loven tribesman Ong Keo the revolt spread so quickly that by April French Commissioner Remy was forced to try to repress it by attacking its base area at Thateng with only the weak Saravane garrison. The French force was heavily assaulted by over 1,500 armed Kha and escaped only after a bitter battle and heavy losses.[43]

Ong Keo was soon joined by the great Alak leader Komadom, and the rebellion gained such momentum that in June Remy wired from Saravane for reinforcements saying, "It is a general uprising, all the villages on the Plateau are deserted, the rebels have formed seven groups, stronger than 1,000 men each."[44]

In June the rebellion spread into Vietnam as Sedang rebels attacked the French garrison at Kontum. In April of 1902 it reached its peak when several thousand unarmed Laotians assaulted the provincial capital at Savannakhet and were gunned down by French troops, who killed over 150 Laotians.[45] The movement lost much of its strength soon thereafter, for the French built a series of blockhouses around the edge of the Plateau, burned most of the region's crops, moved villages out of the area, and drove the rebels off the Plateau and eastward into the mountains.[46]

In 1907 the French launched a major campaign to destroy the rebel stronghold and succeeded in forcing Ong Keo to surrender and swear his loyalty to France. But they failed to capture

42. M. Colonna, "Monographie de la Province de Saravane," *Bulletin des Amis du Laos* #2 (1938), Hanoi, p. 86.
43. Boulanger, *op. cit.*, p. 345.
44. Colonna, *op cit.*, p. 86.
45. Boulanger, *op. cit.*, p. 346.
46. André Fraisse, "Les Villages du Plateau des Bolovens," *Bulletin de la Société des Études Indochinoises* (1951), p. 58.

Komadom and his Alak followers, who escaped to the Phou Luong ridge on the northeast edge of the Bolovens Plateau. Ong Keo's submission was only temporary; he fled to Thailand, where he gained new support, and then returned to Laos. In 1910 through the leader of the royal house and governor of Champassak, Chao Nhouy, the French arranged for negotiations between Ong Keo and a French representative, Fendler. Knowing that the Kha would not touch his head when they checked for weapons, Fendler hid a pistol in his helmet, and when the bodyguards had backed away he shot Ong Keo.[47]

Komadom carried on a small resistance movement at Phou Luong until 1934 when he suddenly began to gain masses of new followers. The depression had affected the hill tribes severely because the relative value of the coffee and spices they sold declined sharply in relation to the cloth and iron they purchased.[48] Poverty and hunger swept the Plateau, and in their wake Komadom's movement gained new strength. In 1935 whole districts began abandoning their villages to join Komadom. The French responded in the spring of 1936 with a massive pacification campaign which climaxed in an attack on Phou Luong and the capture of Komadom's son, Si Thon. Four months later the movement ended when Komadom was shot by French militia as he was fleeing into Attopeu province.[49] However, the outcome of this rebellion still influences Laotian politics, for Komadom's son is now vice-chairman of the Pathet Lao for the southern hill peoples, and the son of the Champassak governor, Chao Nhouy, is a present-day right-wing leader, Prince Boun Oum.[50]

By their annexation of the Lu cantons Muong Ou (northern Phong Saly province) and Muong Sing (Nam Tha province) the French aroused a great deal of initial resentment, which passed when they granted these areas their autonomy immediately after the annexation. However, as the French began to

47. Wilfred Burchett, *Mekong Upstream* (Hanoi: Red River Publishing House, 1957), p. 242.
48. Izikowitz, *op. cit.*, p. 313.
49. Colonna, *op. cit.*, p. 87.
50. Pierre Gentil, *Remous du Mekong* (Paris, 1950), p. 119.

renege on these commitments and to assume the right to raise taxes, appoint officials, and station troops, hostilities arose which soon led to rebellion. As the French moved to assume greater authority in the Lu areas of Phong Saly province, they met with the opposition of Lu canton chief Va Na Poum. He became such an administrative bother that in 1908 the French commissioner sent troops to arrest him and send him to Vientiane for trial. Instead the Lu evicted the French from Muong Ou, tried to assassinate the commissioner, and sought to reestablish their independence. In 1910 the French dispatched counterinsurgency specialist Nollin (fresh from the 1907 campaign against Ong Keo) and some colonial troops to Muong Ou to reestablish their authority. Nollin attacked Muong Ou and succeeded in capturing Va Na Poum, who was killed in a skirmish a short time later when the Lu tried to set him free.[51]

In 1914, when the French representative in the Lu canton of Muong Sing encroached upon the authority of the canton chief, Phra Ong Kham, the Lu began to plot the assassination of the French official. The plot was discovered in December and Phra Ong Kham and his supporters retreated into the Sip Song Panna, raised an army, and returned to lead a rebellion. It was not until 1916, after the French had sent three large, costly military expeditions into Muong Sing, that Phra Ong Kham was finally defeated and driven back into the Sip Song Panna.[52]

From 1914 to 1916 the most violent of all the revolts against the French swept across northeastern Laos and northern Vietnam, temporarily removing whole provinces from French control. The revolt was the result of an alliance between Chinese opium merchants who were being harassed by the opium monopoly, and Tai from Vietnam's Sip Song Chau Tai who were angered at the excesses of the Deo family and French administration. The revolt began on November 11, 1914, when 40 Tai and 40 Chinese attacked the French garrison at the city of Sam Neua, slaughtered the colonial troops, and captured the city. A neighboring French garrison that tried to recapture the city

51. Ayme, *op. cit.*, pp. 113–114.
52. Boulanger, *op. cit.*, pp. 356–357.

was ambushed and repulsed, and it was not until December that regular troops from Vietnam were able to retake Sam Neua.[53]

The rebels retreated into Vietnam, and after launching unsuccessful attacks on the French garrisons at Son La and Dien Bien Phu, fell back into Phong Saly province in Laos. The French had administered Phong Saly as a special military district and their rule had been particularly harsh. The hill tribes were bitter because of the heavy demands made upon them for food, porters, and taxes. The Lu had recently finished their own revolt, and the southwest corner of the province was filled with Tai refugees who had fled from the harshness of the Deo-French rule in the Sip Song Chau Tai.[54] Forty rebels led by a Chinese mule driver captured Muong Ou without a shot. After the Lu drove off the French officials, the Tai joined the rebels willingly, and by February 1915 this rebel band had captured nearly the whole province.

In March 1915 the French sent two companies of troops into Phong Saly to deal with the rebels. Several months later, after suffering a series of inconsequential victories and partial losses, they withdrew.[55] By December 1915 the French realized that their continued possession of the province was in question. They mustered two regular colonial army regiments from Hanoi comprising over 5,000 troops, 1,600 pack mules, and several batteries of mountain artillery. After two months of heavy fighting this expedition managed to restore French control by driving the rebels into China.[56]

In Xieng Khouang province the French presence had made Lao dominance over the Meo unbearable. In 1919 the Meo unleashed a bloody revolt. One colonial officer explained its causes this way:

One day the warlike temper of the Meo revived itself and there were good reasons for that; crushing taxes, heavy tithes on the opium;

53. Boutin, *op. cit.*, p. 73.
54. Commander Deporte, "Les Origines de la Famille de Deo Van Tri," *Bulletin des Amis du Laos* #4 (Hanoi, 1940).
55. Ayme, *op. cit.*, p. 116.
56. *Ibid.*, p. 121.

requisitioned horses which were not paid for. And always these lower officials and petty chiefs brandished before the Meo the scarecrow of the French bogeyman. One day, despite the scarecrow, the coup came and the revolt struck.[57]

The revolt began among the Vietnamese Meo in July 1919. It spread to Laos when a fleeing rebel Meo from Vietnam, Batchay, took refuge in Xieng Khouang province and called upon the Meo to establish an independent kingdom with its capital at Dien Bien Phu. The tough Meo began a devastating assault on all Lao, Tai, and French installations in the province and created a genuine crisis for the colonial government. The local garrisons sent in to quash the revolt had been ambushed and defeated by September, and so regular troops from Saigon and Hanoi had to be dispatched. These troops launched a systematic "pacification" program—moving villages, burning crops, and incarcerating the Meo population—with such success that by March of 1921 Batchay had lost most of his support. He was finally betrayed to the French and killed.[58]

All of these revolts ultimately failed because they were scattered, isolated events which usually involved only one segment or one region of the mountain populations. They remained fractional minority revolts which in most cases failed to get the support of other minorities, or more important, the support of the Lao plurality. These revolts would remain the localized outbursts of countless racial and regional splinters until some larger movement could unify their dissidence and harness it to a higher cause. Unwittingly it was the French who supplied this cause, and they did it with the "Lao Movement."

The Great Awakening, 1940–1945

With the rise of Thailand's "Pan-Thai" movement and the apparent willingness of the Japanese to sacrifice French Laos to the expansionist aims of its Bangkok ally, the Vichy French realized that they would have to make some effort to reinforce

57. Henri Roux, "Les Meo or Miao Tseu," *France Asie* #92–93 (January–February, 1954), p. 404.
58. Boulanger, *op. cit.*, pp. 358–360.

their position. In January 1941 the Thai gave vent to their growing militance by attacking several French naval vessels in the
Gulf of Siam. Although the military outcome was not clear,
the Japanese imposed an armistice (concluded in Tokyo, January 31, 1941) which forced France to cede all Laotian territories
west of the Mekong (Sayaboury and Champassak provinces).
This created a political crisis for the French two days later when,
meeting with the French governor of Laos and Crown Prince
Savang Vatthana, Governor General Admiral Decoux learned
that King Sisavang Vong was considering his resignation. This
would have been a major blow, for without the Lao royal presence to bolster the declining French position, the loss of Laos
to Thailand was a distinct possibility.

Decoux visited Laos the following month, met with the king,
and offered him a number of concessions to assuage his grief at
the loss of two productive provinces. Decoux agreed to guarantee
the existence of the kingdom of Luang Prabang with a treaty of
protectorate, to add three more provinces (Nam Tha, Xieng
Khouang, and Vientiane) to the three provinces which then
constituted the kingdom, and to give Laos a certain amount of
political autonomy.[59]

Since what Decoux really offered the king was a tiny separate
budget, an advisory legislature, and three powerless cabinet
positions, something more was needed to save Laos for France.[60]
To parry the thrust of Pan-Thai nationalism across the Mekong,
Decoux sought to use as a counterthrust something the French
had stifled in the Lao for over 45 years—Lao nationalism.

This [Lao national] movement was responding to a pressing necessity.
An intense and dangerous Thai propaganda was developing along the
Mekong River against us, and the question was posed whether our
Laotian protégés, troubled and touched by the defeat of France, might
yield to the solicitations of Bangkok, and turn their regard to their
brothers of the Thai-Lao race, or on the contrary remain loyal to us,
and constitute an unmoveable rock under the shadow of our pavilion.
. . . The Lao propaganda, addressed itself in reality to all the Laotians,

59. Admiral Decoux, *A la Barre de L'Indochine* (Paris, 1949), pp. 292–
297.
60. Katay Don Sasorith, *Le Laos* (Paris, 1953), p. 55.

the Siamese as well as the French, and developed, in all forms, the exalted theme of the "great Lao homeland" which will one day group all of the children, temporarily separated, of this vast family under the folds of the French flag.[61]

Decoux felt that if the national movement were correctly managed, it would make the Lao eager for modernization and for the return of the west bank territories, both of which occupied Vichy France was now too weak to guarantee.

Decoux chose Charles Rochet as the midwife of the Lao movement. Rochet was a colonial official who had come to Laos six years before, developed a deep affection for the Lao, and become embittered at the French for their neglect of the country. Under Rochet the Lao movement tried to arouse national sentiment among the younger Lao elite through a cultural renaissance of Lao literature, music, and dance, creation of a national development program, and participation in patriotic gestures such as marches and mass rallies.[62] The movement's leaders met weekly at Rochet's home in Vientiane, where they mapped out new strategies for generating ethnic pride among the lowland Lao. The movement's solid accomplishments included the construction of over 7,000 schools (more than had been built in the previous 47 years), significant expansion of a declining health system, and publication of the first Laotian newspaper. Rochet himself looked at the movement as a last desperate attempt to save Laos from extinction. In making this effort he aroused the hostility of the more conservative colonial officials, who rightly claimed that Rochet was arousing dangerous sentiments.[63] Whatever the French may have thought of him, Rochet aroused emotions in the young Laotian elite which they had never been allowed to express. As one Lao diplomat explained in his 1960 memoirs,

No Lao teachers, students, or farmers, will ever forget the name Charles Rochet. We cannot ever forget this man who was very different from other French. We will never forget that in 1945 . . . every

61. Decoux, *op. cit.*, p. 409.
62. *Ibid.*
63. Rochet, *op. cit.*, p. 41.

student had to get up early in the morning, salute the flag, and do drilling exercises. And every Sunday we went to the Lao Association Lawn to drill. We also sang songs, Boy Scout songs, and other songs—songs that would not let us Lao forget that Laos still exists in the world. . . . M. Rochet gave a start to the young Lao who are now helping their country. He also gave birth to Lao dramatic plays, the Lao Club, and the *Lao Yai* bulletin which has made the Lao feel gratitude and appreciation toward him more than any other European except M. Pavie. . . . We will never forget that we used to wear our blue shirts and our white shorts with a Lao emblem on our pockets, which is the symbol of the Young Lao. We were well disciplined, which gave us the feeling that Lao can rule themselves rather than the French or Vietnamese and also we speak the same language.[64]

For decades the French had succeeded in making the Lao elite think of themselves as the children of France, but with even this slight taste of the heady wine of ethnic pride a whole generation of the elite was lost to France. Forces of racial and national pride were aroused which could no longer be denied and which would make it impossible for the French to maintain their position in Laos.

However, while the highland peoples were ignored by the Lao movement, other forces of change swept through the hills of northern Laos. Two of these—opium trade and guerrilla warfare—were to have equally serious consequences for the future of Laos.

After the fall of France in 1940 and the establishment of the French Vichy government by the Nazis, Indochina came under greater and greater Japanese control. By the time of the Japanese attack on Pearl Harbor, the French and Japanese had established a joint administration and Indochina had become a base both for Japanese attacks against Chiang Kai-shek's forces in southwestern China and the Japanese advance into Indonesia. While this arrangement satisfied most French colonial officials, it caused enormous problems for those who had to manage the opium monopoly. Indochina was now cut off from its major

64. Anonymous, "Smiles and Tears," quoted in Joel Halpern, *Government, Politics and Social Structure in Laos,* SEAS Yale University Monograph Series #4 (New Haven, 1964), pp. 149–150.

opium sources in southwest China, the Middle East, and Burma. Indochina would face an incredible social crisis if it had to deal with the massive withdrawal problems of several hundred thousand addicts, and it would face a fiscal crisis if it were deprived of this important source of revenue.

The solution to the problem was found in northern Laos. Previously the French had bought some opium from the Meo of Xieng Khouang province but had generally allowed most of the opium in northern Laos to become contraband rather than undertake the enormous military costs involved in suppressing the illegal trade. Now rather than ending the contraband trade, the French tried to take it over. French officials scoured every ridge and mountain top in northern Laos for poppy fields, offered the Meo, Yao, and Tai tribes fantastic prices for their produce in an attempt to outbid the smugglers, and even supplied seeds and instruction to tribes and villages who had not previously grown opium. Since these tribes prized the silver which the French offered in exchange as jewelry for their women and as a mobile form of savings, they began to neglect their food crops for the poppy fields to such an extent that malnutrition and even starvation began to plague the opium growers.[65] The French-induced bonanza also initiated serious conflict in the previously harmonious mountain villages as clans and families fought with each other for the enormous rewards of this lucrative trade.

In late 1944 and early 1945, as the Free French prepared for the liberation of Indochina, they set up guerrilla bases in the wild mountain terrain of the Indochinese uplands. When French forces in Calcutta planned their operations for Laos, they realized that European commandos would be easily detected by the Japanese and that the lowland Lao were ill-suited to the difficult highland life.[66] Thus, as the French organized their guerrilla forces and began parachute drops of supplies and commandos in late 1944, they sought out the hill tribes, the only people

65. Rochet, *op. cit.*, pp. 106–108.
66. Michel Caply, *Guérilla au Laos* (Paris: Presses de la Cité, 1966), p. 56.

who could make effective mountain guerrillas. Thus, tribes who had been at odds with each other for a half century because of the French cross-racial administration, and clans or families who had been fighting each other for the opium rewards, were now armed and organized with modern military weapons. The resulting conflict produced permanent cleavages in Laotian society which are still being worked out today.

How opium and armaments promoted major divisions among the mountain peoples can be seen most clearly by using the example of the Meo of Xieng Khouang province. In the current Laotian conflict the Pathet Lao vice-chairman for the northern hill peoples is the Meo leader Faydang, a member of the Lo clan from Nong Het village in Xieng Khouang province. The political leader of the Meo in General Vang Pao's CIA army is the Meo leader Touby Ly Fong, a member of the Ly clan from Nong Het village.[67] As a part of their program to prevent a repetition of the 1919–1921 Meo uprising, the French had established an independent Meo district *(tasseng)* with its headquarters near the Plain of Jars at Nong Het. The district leader was a Meo whose appointment was approved by the French. It was his duty to deliver the Meo opium quota to the Lao canton chief at Ban Ban (usually the canton chief was a member of the Xieng Khouang royal family) who in turn delivered it to the French provincial commissioner at Xieng Khouang City.[68] By the late 1930s power at Nong Het was shared between the wealthier, more established Lo clan (Faydang's), which was allied with the Luang Prabang royal family, and the rising Ly clan (Touby's), which was allied with the French and the Xieng Khouang royal family.

The alliance between the Lo and the Ly clans broke up when the daughter of the leader of the Lo clan who had married Touby's father (Ly) died after complaining several times about being mistreated. After the split, Prince Phetsarath (a member of the Luang Prabang royal family and later leader of the Lao Issara, a forerunner of the Pathet Lao) asked the

67. Dumarest, *op. cit.*, p. 61; Savina, *op. cit.*, pp. 237–239.
68. Archaimbault, *op. cit.*, p. 660.

French to give the important position of district leader to the Lo clan, and Faydang's father was given the appointment.[69]

However, with the Japanese occupation and the increased demand for opium, the French wanted a close ally at the vital Nong Het opium center. Faydang's father was removed from the position of district leader, and a member of the French-educated Ly clan (Touby's) was appointed.[70] As the French began to study their reoccupation of Laos in late 1944, they realized the paramount strategic importance of the Plain of Jars. On March 4, 1945, they parachuted commandos and supplies into a secret camp which had been established for them by Touby Ly Fong and his Meo followers.[71] When the French liberation of Laos turned into a campaign of recolonization aimed at destroying the Lao Issara, it was only natural that Faydang would join with Phetsarath and the Lao Issara. Although Faydang's alliance with Phetsarath's more conservative Lao Issara was based as much on these factional splits as it was on his dislike of the French, his subsequent alliance with Souphanouvong's Pathet Lao was made on a much more sophisticated ideological basis. Nonetheless, a simple clan conflict, which in traditional Meo society would have been resolved by splitting the village and separating the clans, has become instead a permanent cleavage which has helped to fuel 25 years of civil war.

In April 1945 the Japanese terminated fifty years of French colonialism by having King Sisavang Vong declare Laos independent. But by manipulating racial and regional factions, the French managed to return to power after Japan's surrender. However, the movement which had developed through Laos' wartime experience created nationalists who refused to return to colonial status. Some eventually allied with the traditional dissidents of the upland tribes to create a strong national revolutionary movement—the Pathet Lao.

69. *Ibid.*

70. G. Linwood Barney, "The Meo of Xieng Khouang Province, Laos," in Peter Kunstader, ed., *Southeast Asian Tribes, Minorities, and Nations* (Princeton: Princeton University Press, 1967), pp. 273–275.

71. Caply, *op. cit.*, pp. 58, 82.

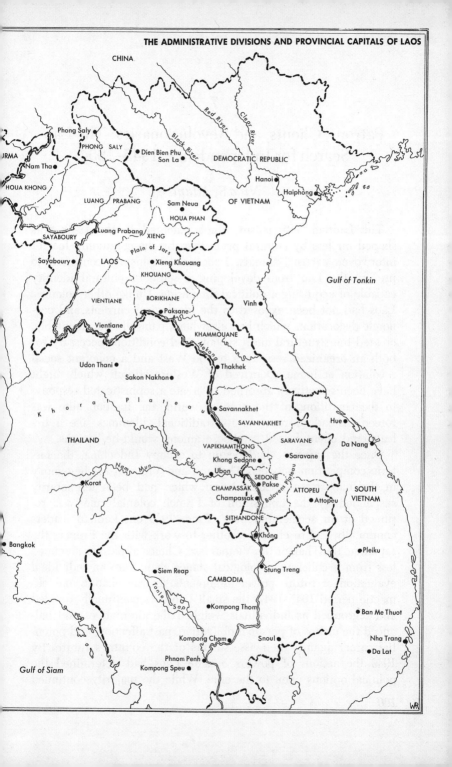

THE ADMINISTRATIVE DIVISIONS AND PROVINCIAL CAPITALS OF LAOS

7

Patrons, Clients, and Revolutionaries: The Lao Search for Independence, 1945–1954

Nina S. Adams

The Laotian nationalism which emerged in the 1940s was shaped far less by cultural pride than by the continuing fear of interwoven external threats. Location and history conspired to prevent the Lao from developing a sense of cultural identity capable of acquiring a political dimension. Unlike other colonies, Laos had not been exposed to the ideological currents and economic dislocations which had elsewhere, painfully but inevitably, created the structural and psychological conditions necessary for both an organized resistance to the West and a coherent social revolution at home. Deprived of Western stimuli which might have been selectively absorbed to create a sophisticated response to the conditions of the postwar world, the Laotian elite was forced instead to react to its traditional dilemmas like a beleaguered client forced to choose among would-be patrons.

Once the Japanese had begun to occupy Indochina, the historic competition between Thailand and Vietnam for hegemony in the Lao states—a competition which had been temporarily suspended by the imposition of French colonial rule—was resumed at an accelerated pace. From 1940 on, Laotian leaders continually had to choose whether to work with the French, the Japanese, the Thai, or the Vietnamese. Choice of patrons stemmed less from a coherent ideological stance than from an individual evaluation of future power alignments. In the chaotic and climactic period 1945–1947, the small Lao elite continually divided and regrouped as individuals weighed the alternatives and balanced the claims of personal obligation, past affection, and potential career against their assessments of the country's future. By 1949 the actions of powers outside Laos had determined the political options open to the elite. While the majority continued their nonideological drift toward the power which would safe-guard a limited Laotian independence and guarantee elite prerogatives, a significant minority of the national and local leadership moved from the rhetoric of immature defensive cul-turalism to the ideology of modern social revolution. In each case, the choice of a patron group was inextricably linked to the perception of the greatest evil and promise of the most direct assistance. Purely ideological choices of allies, made on the basis of abstract calculations and theoretical affinities, were a luxury denied to all Laotians by virtue of the complex situation which continually engulfed them.

France's assumption of control in Indochina had frozen the conflicts of earlier years, allowing the Lao and Cambodians respite from the continual Thai-Vietnamese wars fought on and for their diminishing territory. Given the artificial political unity created by the French in Indochina, the Lao faced the recurrent but seemingly unpressing problem of differentiating themselves culturally from three other peoples: the Vietnamese, with whom they were educated and on whose soil many lived while acquir-ing an education; the Thai, from whom they were now politically and economically if not culturally estranged by virtue of the French presence; and the French, whose intellectual and eco-nomic dominance was seemingly irreversible despite the fact that Laos was ruled indirectly by a handful of French administrators. While the abuses of the French administration were apparent to many of the Lao and montagnards, the elite which served the French remained unconcerned. They benefited from the educa-tional and career opportunities offered by the French system while retaining the prestige, income, and feudal power guaran-teed by French support of traditional society in the provinces and principalities.

The arrival of the Japanese in Indochina in 1940 abruptly trans-formed what seemed to be a quiet situation. As in Vietnam, the Japanese merely added an additional supervisory layer to the existing colonial system of rule, but they changed the power balance in the area by supporting the Thai drive to regain terri-tories reluctantly ceded to France in 1904 and 1907. The short Franco-Thai War of 1940–1941, halted by Japanese intervention, forced mediation in favor of Thai claims, removed a portion of Lao territory from French control, and stimulated the French to sudden concern with Laotian development and loyalties.

More important, the growth of Thai power created an alternative set of possibilities in the minds of many of the Lao elite. Limited independence under Japanese or Thai aegis suddenly seemed conceivable. There could be, and now was, a divergence of opinion among educated Lao regarding ways of responding to powers that had the potential to assume control. Northerners and those educated in French schools sought to use France's weakened position to extract concessions and enhance the importance of Laos within the Indochinese Federation. One man who saw things this way was Prince Souphanouvong. He apparently believed that the advent of the Vichy regime under Admiral Decoux (who had been named governor general of Indochina in 1940) offered an opportunity for talented Indochinese to advance steadily into positions previously reserved for the French. In a warm letter to Decoux[1] the prince described the glories of closer Franco-Indochinese collaboration which would benefit both sides (not the least the French) by ensuring them the sincere loyalty of their protégés.

Members of the southern elite, traditionally linked to Thailand, saw another possible result of France's decline. In contrast to those whose major interest lay in working with the French, students at the College Pavie in Vientiane saw the Japanese arrival as heralding the beginning of the end of French hegemony. Tham Sayasithsena and 50 other young Laotians attempted an amateur coup against the French administration in Vientiane in 1940. The failure of this coup sent them into exile in friendly Thailand,[2] where several joined the Thai army and received commissions.

---

1. *Indochine,* No. 133, March 18, 1943. I am indebted to Michael Vickery for bringing the full text of this letter to my attention.
2. Paul F. Langer and J. J. Zasloff, *Revolution in Laos: The North Vietnamese and the Pathet Lao* (Santa Monica: The RAND Corporation, September 1969, RM–5935–ARPA. Prepared for the Advanced Research Projects Agency, Department of Defense), p. 30. Tham Sayasithsena (or Saingsithena) became Assistant Defense Minister in the Lao Issara government of

Choices open to the Laotians multiplied as a result of the Japanese preemptive coup of March 9, 1945, against the French. Throughout Indochina, the Japanese imprisoned French military and civilian officials, completely replacing them with Japanese and Indochinese functionaries. Laotian leaders again divided, each seeing different options and choosing his allegiance accordingly. Those who consistently collaborated with the Japanese did so by choice; men such as Nhouy Abhay and Katay Don Sasorith felt Japanese protection was needed against Vietnamese ambitions, which would grow once France was totally eliminated from the scene. Nhouy's new journal, *Lao Chaleun,* which appeared for the first time on March 22, argued that it was necessary for yellow races to unite against the whites and insisted on the desirability and strong possibility of Lao independence in the very near future.[3] Even though many provincial officials and members of local administrations, for example Kou Abhay and Prince Boun Oum, shared Nhouy's fear of the Vietnamese, Japanese brutality had reinforced their loyalty to the French.

The new fears and internal conflicts created by the March 9, 1945, coup influenced decisions regarding foreign relations. The sudden disappearance of the top echelon of the civil service opened the way for ambitious Vietnamese, the dominant group of "indigenes" in the colonial civil service, to assume virtual control of several urban areas. Their arrogance, long noted and resented by the Lao, and their eagerness to consolidate their hold, particularly in areas bordering Vietnam, alarmed both pro- and anti-Japanese Lao. Prince Phetsarath, premier and viceroy,

---

October 1945. Immediately prior to that time, he worked with Bongsi Ratakul in the Lao-Pen-Lao anti-Japanese resistance movement in central Laos. For details on the Lao-Pen-Lao, formed by Oune Sananikone, see footnote 9. Much of the information on Laotian leaders involved in the early independence groups is taken from "Background of the Neo Lao Hak Xat" in *Say Kang* (official organ of Souvanna Phouma's Neutralist Party) issues dated October 2, 9, 16, 23, and 30, 1965, and November 7, 13, 20, and 26, 1965. Again, I am deeply indebted to Michael Vickery, who located and translated this article, then permitted me to consult his notes. Information on Tham Sayasithsena appears on page 6, October 2, 1965, as well as page 3 of the same issue.

3. Michel Caply, *Guérilla au Laos* (Paris: Presses de la Cité, 1966), p. 175.

and Crown Prince Savang Vatthana, men who disagreed firmly on matters concerning future independence from France, were, for once, in accord on the Vietnamese threat. Taking advantage of the Japanese takeover, Phetsarath began removing Vietnamese functionaries from their posts and evacuating them from Laos.[4] Savang, told by the Japanese to proclaim the end of the French protectorate, called on the population of Luang Prabang to revolt against the Japanese.[5] Neither man achieved his aims, for the Japanese hurriedly marched troops into Luang Prabang, exiled Savang to Saigon, and forced King Sisavang Vong to declare independence on April 8, 1945. And with the return of full Japanese control, the Vietnamese administrators once more had protectors who watched benignly as Lao administrators were prevented from freely administering their assigned areas.[6]

Even more alarming to the Laotians, the Japanese sanctioned the April 12, 1945, creation by the Vietnamese of the *phu* (prefecture) of Tran-ninh, a repeat of the procedure by which, 118 years before, the Laotian Xieng Khouang area had been absorbed by Vietnam. But in May 1945 Prince Say Kham, who was pro-French, re-created the Lao Phuoun, a militia composed mainly of former members of Charles Rochet's Lao Movement (See article 6, by McCoy). On August 10 this militia unit destroyed the independent Vietnamese organization in the city, and the Japanese then agreed to future Lao control, at least in theory, of the urban administration.[7]

The removal of the French from urban areas and administrative posts did not mean their disappearance from the political scene. In Laos, unlike Vietnam and Cambodia, both the lowland and the hill peoples offered protection to the French who had escaped the Japanese purge. Laotians also abetted the Free French commandos who had stayed quietly in the hills since late 1944. Commando units, usually consisting of a single Frenchman

---

4. *Ibid.*, p. 177.
5. Arthur Dommen, *Conflict in Laos* (New York: Praeger, 1964), p. 18.
6. Caply, *op. cit.*, p. 178.
7. Caply, *op. cit.*, p. 140. For a full treatment of the Thai-Vietnamese maneuvers in Tran-ninh in the nineteenth century, see article 5, by John K. Whitmore, in the present book. Caply, *op. cit.*, p. 206.

with 12 or so Lao or tribesmen, were scattered throughout Laos and worked successfully with the montagnards as well as with Lao officials. Their function, as defined by the Free French command, was to remind the populace of the continuing French presence, gather intelligence, and prepare for the reestablishment of colonial rule. The commando groups performed their first two assignments effectively despite their small numbers and their lack of equipment (even after liaison teams of Force 136 were parachuted in during May and June 1945).[8] Their presence did, in fact, influence Laotians, for whom the anti-Japanese and anti-French resistance groups operating with either Thai or Vietnamese backing provided yet another political option.

Most Western-language accounts of 1945–1946 focus on events in the capital, conveying the impression that a single united group backed Phetsarath in a largely personal dispute with the king and a small clique. In fact, numerous and competing, albeit minuscule, nationalist groups (as often interlocking in membership as standing in opposition to each other) emerged in the major provincial capitals of Laos during the summer of 1945. Again their lack of unity stemmed from lack of unanimity on the question of future relations with the French, Thai, and Vietnamese. The Lao-Pen-Lao, one of the most important groups, was formed in the south and had close links to the Free Thai movement headed by Pridi Phanomyong (who made contact with the American OSS in 1944).[9] Its major organizer, Oune Sananikone, who had lived in Thailand since 1941, made extensive contacts in Laos after forming a base among the refugees on the Thai bank of the Mekong.[10]

8. Bernard B. Fall, *Anatomy of a Crisis: The Laotian Crisis of 1960–61*. Edited, with an epilogue, by Roger M. Smith (Garden City, N.Y.: Doubleday, 1969), p. 33 (hereafter cited as Fall, *Anatomy*). For a full account of the adventures of one team pursued by the Japanese through eastern Laos, see Valmy (pseud.), "Parachutistes et Partisans dans la Brousse Laotienne" in *Indochine-Française*, No. 28 (February 1947), pp. 24–26.

9. While Caply uses the name Lao-Pen-Lao only to designate the group formed by Oune Sananikone in southern Laos with Thai encouragement, the articles in *Say Kang* use Lao-Pen-Lao to refer to the resistance government formed in the fall of 1945 by combining three groups, including the Lao Issara, whose name is generally applied to the entire coalition.

10. Caply, *op. cit.*, pp. 222–226.

His organization, which particularly annoyed the French, favored reliance on Thai protection to prevent the French return and to forestall Vietnamese expansion.[11] Many of those whom he contacted shared his fear of the Vietnamese, yet also distrusted the Thai and were unwilling to break with the French. Lines of underground communication between individuals of varying viewpoints were maintained; given the family relationships among members of the Lao elite in 1945, as later, political differences did not mean estrangements or betrayals.

Many of the Laotians who joined or were contacted by the anti-French groups nonetheless remained cautious in their dealings with the commandos. Prince Phetsarath, who kept informed of the activities of the Lao-Pen-Lao, and who knew of the other groups which were gradually uniting to form the Lao Issara (Free Lao), encouraged the nascent independence movement but refrained from playing an active role until he could assess the strength of both the Lao-Pen-Lao and the French.[12] By September 1945 he had decided that these anti-French groups were likely to succeed, and he and Ngon Sananikone accepted the leadership of the Lao Issara at the Vientiane meeting of representatives of all these groups.[13] The coalition of groups had, for the moment, decided to leave politics undiscussed; they would create resistance groups aimed at the French but would not yet try to agree on their future relations with any of the contending forces.[14] The group did not confront the issue of total versus limited independence from France.

Phetsarath and many of the other leaders shared a firm belief that the situation in Laos was quite different from that in Vietnam in 1945; Laos had first to protect itself from extinction, whereas no such threat to Vietnam existed. The militance of the Ho Chi Minh government in Hanoi was not echoed in either Luang Prabang or Vientiane, where members of the elite were acutely conscious of potential Thai threats as well as of the discrepancy in sophistication and power between themselves and the Viet-

11. Langer and Zasloff, *op. cit.*, p. 32.
12. Caply, *op. cit.*, p. 226.
13. *Say Kang* (October 2, 1965), p. 3.
14. Caply, *op. cit.*, p. 227.

namese. Despite his reluctant assumption of the leadership of a movement for almost total autonomy, Phetsarath never really altered his 1945 view that "we still have need to lean on a strong power in order to protect ourselves against the designs of our neighbors both in the east and in the west, in the north and in the northwest."[15]

Japan's surrender came suddenly in August 1945, and once again the real and potential balance of forces in Laos was in doubt. On August 15 the Japanese troops and administrators left hastily for Thailand. Pursued and harassed by French-Lao guerrillas, they also sought to escape the tender attentions of the Nationalist Chinese 93rd Division, which was planning to enter Laos and Tonkin to accept the Japanese surrender.[16]

The Japanese departure opened the way for the various groups of French paratroopers to influence events in the capital. The French immediately made plans to reassume symbolic control. In Vientiane, Captain Fabre contacted Phetsarath and attempted to make arrangements for French reentry into the city. But on August 31 Phetsarath, annoyed at the former French resident (who had proclaimed his return in the most tactless manner possible) informed him that he no longer had any authority in Laos. On September 1 Phetsarath announced that the declaration of independence of the previous April was still in force. Backed by the coalition of independence groups, Phetsarath took another unilateral step; on September 15 the kingdoms of Luang Prabang and Champassak were declared united.

Meanwhile a group under Colonel Imfeld had arrived in Luang Prabang to reassert French influence over the king. At the same time Phetsarath became head of the coalition of the Committee of the People, the Lao-Pen-Lao, and the Committee for a Free Laos,[17] the French were seeking supporters among the Lao. On October 10, 1945, the king wired Phetsarath, removing his titles of premier and viceroy. Two days later, the Phetsarath group, constituted as the Defense Committee, voted a provisional consti-

15. Langer and Zasloff, *op. cit.*, p. 32.
16. Fall, *Anatomy*, p. 33.
17. Langer and Zasloff, *op. cit.*, p. 33.

tution, formed a Provisional People's Assembly, and nominated a new government of Lao Issara. Phaya Khammao, the former governor of Vientiane province, became premier. By October 20, 1945, the assembly had deposed the king for refusing to recognize the new regime.

Both sides realized a solution had to be reached lest the tiny elite group find itself totally powerless in the face of the French and completely discredited in the eyes of the population. As Bernard Fall describes it, "Personal emissaries and couriers traveled to and fro between Luang Prabang and Vientiane; politicians changed their opinions from day to day on the basis of rumors and tempting counter-offers; while at the same time the news of the progressing French and Laotian troops added an element of panic to the whole proceedings."[18] Gradually a settlement was reached. The Lao Issara agreed on the need to retain the monarchy, and the king in return placed himself under the authority of the provisional government. It was decided that the king would be enthroned as ruler of a united Laos in Luang Prabang on April 23, 1946.

Despite the farcical aspects of these proceedings, the ability of the Laotians to deal with each other in political contexts was increasing. Knowing the weakness of the nascent nationalist bloc, the group in Vientiane welcomed the November 1 arrival of Prince Souphanouvong, who brought with him a small group of Viet Minh soldiers and advisers. Souphanouvong was appointed minister of national defense in the new government and became commander in chief of the armed forces as well. During his journey up the Mekong he had already begun successfully recruiting Laotians and resident Vietnamese for the resistance forces.[19] However, the appearance of Souphanouvong's group had led to clashes between Laotian activists and his Vietnamese followers, a problem which was only temporarily solved by moving to friendlier Savannakhet.[20] The organization he was building was not the only one in Laos, and his policy of dealing with the

18. Fall, *Anatomy*, p. 37.
19. Dommen, *op. cit.*, p. 23.
20. Langer and Zasloff, *op. cit.*, p. 44.

Viet Minh gradually became the principal source of disagreement with the Lao Issara.

In early 1946 the French began to move back into Laos in force. The signing of the Chungking Agreement with Chiang Kai-shek's government on February 28 foreshadowed the rapid withdrawal of all Chinese warlord troops from Tonkin and Laos. Conclusion of the March 6 agreement with Ho Chi Minh's government released French forces for the reoccupation of Laos.[21] By April 24, the day after the king's inauguration, they had retaken Vientiane. Despite savage Lao Issara resistance in Savannakhet and Thakhek, the French expeditionary force had easily prevailed over the smaller, lightly armed partisans. By September 23, 1946, the French had reoccupied the last provincial capital (along the Thai border) and were in complete control of Laos.

The Lao Issara government, headed by Prince Phetsarath and Phaya Khammao, had fled to Thailand in late April 1946. Once forced into exile, three distinct factions emerged, only two of which were readily reconcilable. The third, led by Prince Souphanouvong, gradually came to disagree with the prevailing Lao Issara viewpoint on almost every issue. The schism within the Lao Issara became even wider than that existing between the exiles and those men who returned to French Laos (such as Nhouy Abhay) or those who chose to remain there under reoccupation (such as Outhong Souvannavong). The latter felt that as a minor undeveloped country, Laos needed the guidance of a great power. Wisely, the king had chosen tutelage under France and would continue to work for improvement without envisioning total independence.[22]

The Phetsarath faction hoped for a royal government in a

21. The March 6, 1946, agreement with Ho Chi Minh's Democratic Republic of Vietnam provided that the French would be able to land 40,000 troops in Tonkin unopposed, on the understanding that within five years all of these forces would have been withdrawn. In exchange, the French pledged to hold a referendum to unite the three sections of Vietnam. Ho Chi Minh himself had difficulty in persuading the Viet Minh leadership to accept the agreement. For a full account of this period, see Jean Lacouture, *Ho Chi Minh: A Political Biography* (New York: Random House, 1969).

22. Outhong Souvannavong [Savannavong] letter to Prince Phetsarath, October 2, 1945, in *Indochine-Française*, No. 18 (March 1946), pp. 44–45.

basically independent Laos under limited French protection. Prince Souvanna Phouma and his followers wanted to negotiate with the French for full independence. These two, and most of the members of the Lao Issara, shared a common distrust of the Viet Minh and a lack of interest in social change within Laotian society. A minority of the Lao Issara, grouped around Prince Souphanouvong, were willing to use Vietnamese support to wage an armed struggle for total independence from France.[23] Manifesting little faith in French sincerity, this latter group came to share the Viet Minh view that the war for independence involved all of Indochina.

All the Lao Issara exiles shared the belief that Laos was incapable of gaining freedom unassisted. But the exiles could not agree on which power was best suited to aid them. Souphanouvong, who had few illusions about Vietnamese ambitions, nonetheless felt that a strong Lao Issara under his own or similar leadership could control the Vietnamese influence accompanying proffered aid. But in order to do this the group in Bangkok would have to move beyond pamphleteering; it had to prove itself a viable resistance force within Laos by sustaining direct armed actions against the French. Given French strength, this meant a long hard struggle which initially required foreign support[24] and the use of non-Lao personnel. Such strategic thinking was alien to most of the leaders in exile; not only did it imply direct dealings with the Vietnamese and the minorities of Laos, it also implied the creation of an ideology and program envisioning goals beyond the creation of a new governmental façade designed to prolong the retention of lowland Lao elite privileges.

The publications of the Lao Issara movement in exile lacked any concern with modernization and social change. The chief propagandist, Katay Don Sasorith produced a flow of polemical essays dealing with abstract issues and calling on the French

23. Fall, *Anatomy*, p. 42; Langer and Zasloff, *op. cit.*, p. 53.

24. Langer and Zasloff, *op. cit.*, p. 42; Bernard Fall notes that Souphanouvong's position was bolstered by his ability to work with the approximately 60,000 Vietnamese refugees who settled in the Mekong Valley after fleeing from the French. Fall, *Anatomy*, p. 42.

public to put an end to "sterile, dishonorable [and] murderous" colonial wars.[25]

Katay's attacks on the French colonial system contained few references to the future; he did not attempt to prescribe how Lao society and economy should be transformed after independence. After strongly rejecting Marxism as materialist and aggressive, his interest in economics was limited to abolition of the French trade monopolies (with hints that these might, with modifications, revert to Laotian control) and to a strong defense of the natural advantages of Laotian trade via Bangkok rather than Vietnam.[26]

There is little doubt that the political disagreements among Lao Issara leaders were exacerbated by the often petty frictions which afflict any exile group. When the final break between the Lao Issara and Souphanouvong's group occured in May 1949, the acrimonious exchanges between the latter and Katay included references to personal as well as political tensions. In response to charges that his dealings with the Viet Minh had been kept secret from the rest of the group so that no one could be sure to what extent the Lao were now indebted to the Vietnamese, Souphanouvong replied angrily:

As to the various conventions and agreements entered into with the Ho Chi Minh government, they cannot be placed on the agenda until the day when there will exist a Lao Issara government worthy of that name "Free Laos," i.e. a government which has the support of a strong

25. Thao Katay (Don Sasorith), *L'Amitié ou La Haine!* (Bangkok: Lao Issara publication, 1949), p. 3, taken from *Bang-fai,* his newspaper, #3. In publishing order, Katay's books were: *Pour Rire Un Peu: Histoires vécues,* 1947; *Laos: Le pivot idéal contre le communisme,* 1948; and *L'Amitié ou La Haine!,* 1949. In all three, his most abusive language was reserved not for the French but for those of his compatriots who served them as officials in Laos. Thus, the dedication in his first book reads in part: "To the Prince Savang Vatthana, the incompetent apprentice dictator and traitor to his country." His second book was dedicated to America and its tradition of democracy. His last book was dedicated to Charles Rochet and was subtitled *Pour une entente Franco-Lao contre le colonialisme désuet et périmé.*

26. For example see the selections in Katay's *L'Amitié* from *Bang-fai* #21, p. 35, "Comment les colonialistes Français se font de l'argent en Indochine." See also *Bang-fai* #39 and #41, entitled "Liberté! Liberté Chère! Combat avec tes défenseurs."

majority of the Lao population engaged in the resistance movement
and made up of politicians of some stature. Ho Chi Minh will never
talk with bluffers or pseudoresistance fighters. He would use those
simply as instruments of his Indochinese policy or of Vietnamese
victory.[27]

The consistent reappearance of traditional rivalries among and
within princely families may also have been a factor in estrang-
ing Souphanouvong from his brothers. But this unicausal explanation of his behavior has been given far too much emphasis,
particularly by cash-and-carry scholars who cannot envision any
pragmatic or ideological reasons for a sane man to work with
the Viet Minh. Langer and Zasloff, who suffer a peculiarly RAND
variety of this particular blindness, offer a psychological explanation of Souphanouvong's perverse actions and attitudes. After
suggesting that, like many of his historical predecessors, he
sought Vietnamese aid to put him in power over rivals who had
Thai backing, they then presume that his unfortunate background
impelled him into the communist camp. Inferring that he was
less-favored by his father than were his brothers since his mother
was a commoner, they add that while being educated and influenced in Vietnam he was rejected by a French metisse (mixed
blood); finally, they mention, correctly, that upon his return to
Indochina, despite his brilliant scholarly achievements in France,
he was given a low-ranking post accompanied by an insultingly
insufficient salary.[28]

In explaining Souphanouvong's move to the left of others about
whose backgrounds less is known, Freudianism is dropped in
favor of the political scientist's most hackneyed explanation for
the rise of revolutionary movements—that is, status hunger. When
Langer and Zasloff deal with Souphanouvong's royal associates
like Prince Souk Vongsak and his more plebeian comrades like
Kaysone and Nouhak, they see this insidious appetite at work.
Thus those whose birth and education put them almost but not
quite at the top of society sought Vietnamese help to jump that

27. Langer and Zasloff, *op. cit.*, p. 58.
28. *Ibid.*, p. 42.

last small way to total power. And the others, who lacked status and the possibility of attaining it, needed the Vietnamese if they were ever to hope to achieve power.[29] Faced with this facile nonsense, it is far easier to assume that the split within the Lao Issara reflected differences of opinion regarding the changing political and military situation in Indochina. It could be expected that an increasing gap would grow between verbose exiles debating in urban areas and activists participating in military operations along the Thai border. The latter began to work with non-Lao peoples for the first time, learning from dynamic Viet Minh cadres who imported a new political style and world view and dealing continually with the realities of supply and command.

Souphanouvong's forces, Lao Issara, driven into Thailand in April 1946, immediately began armed forays back across the Mekong, seizing arms, kidnapping village notables, and harassing the French who crossed the Thai border in hot pursuit.[30]

While the raids into Laos from Thailand began as a series of sporadic gestures, Souphanouvong and his Viet Minh advisers soon set up a more organized program of partisan activity, including the development of "factories" to supply bases, which rapidly became self-sufficient.[31] In August 1946[32] the Resistance Committee of Eastern Laos was set up under Viet Minh auspices. The Lao Issara reluctantly approved the formation of this group, which relied on the Vietnamese. While the more publicized raids over the Thai border received the greatest attention from the French, as well as from later writers dealing with the period, the organization of resistance groups along the Vietnamese border

29. *Ibid.*, p. 61. The authors take an extremely condescending view of the Lao elite: "In contrast to the Vietnamese, even the educated Lao rarely are intellectuals or even avid readers. The desire for intellectual achievement, in the Western sense, plays little part in the life of the Lao elite . . . the public speeches of the [Pathet Lao] movement's leaders are remarkable for their lack of ideological content and terminology. One can only conclude that ideology, for the revolutionary as well as the nonrevolutionary Lao plays a distinctly subordinate role." p. 26.

30. *Indochine-Française,* July 1946.

31. Dommen, *op. cit.,* p. 30.

32. *Say Kang* (October 23, 1965), p. 11; Langer and Zasloff, *op. cit.,* p. 50.

slowly but quietly became significant. The bases which were established grew, by late 1948, into "military zones" which thereafter tied down French troops needed elsewhere to combat the Viet Minh. They also served as the headquarters from which armed propaganda teams and cadres could be directed to gradually build the "people's power bases,"[33] which were of increasing importance as the Pathet Lao developed into a strong popular movement and organized government in the countryside of eastern Laos.

While Souphanouvong had concentrated on the organizational and military problems of the independence movement, his colleagues in Bangkok paid far more attention to political developments at home, carefully analyzing each French proposal for changing the status of Laos. On March 24, 1945, the Free French government had announced a new colonial policy designed in part to preclude any UN attempt to impose international trusteeship on its colonial possessions. The French Empire was to be transformed into the French Union which would offer opportunities for both national and personal advancement within its confines. While changes in economic and administrative policy were at first envisioned (but never, in Laos, actually implemented), no political changes were foreseen.[34] A joint Franco-Lao commission, set up in June 1946 to discuss unresolved issues, soon confirmed that all political, economic, and military authority would remain with the French. The French did concede the unity of Laos under the king of Luang Prabang and agreed that elections would be held within a year to nominate a constituent assembly. On August 27, 1946, Savang Vatthana signed the empowering documents establishing a *modus vivendi* with the French.[35] The new arrangements within the French Union were totally unacceptable to the Lao Issara. One faction of the exile

33. Dommen, *op. cit.*, p. 31; Langer and Zasloff, *op. cit.*, p. 52.

34. Ellen J. Hammer, "Blueprinting a New Indochina," *Pacific Affairs*, Volume XXI, #3 (September 1948), pp. 252–263, p. 252. Throughout the summer of 1945, French colonialist periodicals such as *Indochine-Française* were preoccupied with the possibility that the United States might lead a move to force the UN to assume trusteeship responsibilities in Indochina.

35. Dommen, *op. cit.*, p. 28.

group attempted to establish direct contact with the French in Saigon but soon failed.[36]

On March 15, 1947, the Laotian Constituent Assembly was convened. With considerable assistance from French observers and advisers, a document was drawn up which provided considerably less real independence than the earlier rebel constitution of 1945.[37] The constitution was promulgated by the king on May 11, 1947, and the first National Assembly met on November 26, 1947. At this point an exchange of letters began between the king and the president of France, aimed at "perfecting" the details of Laotian autonomy. With considerable fanfare, both the French and the Royal Laotian Government celebrated the culmination of these executive agreements in a General Convention signed July 19, 1949. Further "perfection" proving necessary, letters were again exchanged, and in October 1953 negotiations quickly led to the signing of a Treaty of Amity and Association. In fact, total independence for Laos came only after the French defeat in the Indochina War had forced the convening of the Geneva Conference.

While only a few of the Lao Issara exiles had been impressed enough by the constitutional developments of 1947 to return home,[38] the General Convention of 1949 had a far greater effect on men anxious, in Fall's words, "to share in the proceeds as well as the glory of effectively governing a country."[39] On September 30, 1949, the Vientiane government sent a letter to Souvanna

36. Dommen, *op. cit.*, p. 29, describes the attempt to use Baron Patrick Surcouf to contact the staff of Admiral Thierry d'Argenlieu in Saigon. Surcouf met with the Lao Issara in November 1946, but was kept waiting in Saigon until March, when it became clear that his mission had failed.

37. The daily communiqués issued during the deliberations of the Constituent Assembly identify the Frenchmen involved in the discussions. These may be found, along with all basic documents including the electoral law, the constitution, amended suggestions, and inaugural speeches, in *L'Assemblée Constituente Laotienne 15 Mars–10 Mai 1947* (Saigon: Imprimerie de l'Indochine, 1948). Dommen, *op. cit.*, p. 33; Fall, *Anatomy*, p. 38.

38. (Thao) Katay, "Aux Compatriotes Lao Réfugiés en Terre Etrangère," in *L'Amitié ou La Haine!*, p. 50, reprinted from *Bang-fai* #17, offers examples of Lao officials who upon their return found French guarantees against reprisals to be worthless.

39. Fall, *Anatomy*, p. 43.

Phouma pledging a warm welcome and full amnesty to the exiles should they return. Shortly thereafter the French authorities echoed and reinforced the offer. On October 24, 1949, the Lao Issara in exile solemnly disbanded so that the following day its members could embark for Vientiane. The group which had chosen to dissolve itself no longer included Souphanouvong and his followers, who had in January begun to form their own group: the Progressive People's Organization for Lao Issara. Souphanouvong's angry exchange of letters with Katay in May 1949 and formal resolutions of expulsion from the Lao Issara merely ratified the split which had in fact begun several years earlier, merely deepening with the passage of time.

The signing of accords between France and Laos in the summer of 1949 encouraged Souvanna Phouma and the Lao Issara in their belief that the French intended to cooperate with indigenous Lao leaders to develop the country. Souphanouvong's group, however, deduced that the French found concessions necessary in order to pacify a rear area during the course of their intensifying war with the Viet Minh.[40] In light of this analysis, and undoubtedly repelled by the limited nature of the French concessions and the avidity with which the Lao Issara had accepted them, Souphanouvong moved to strengthen the armed forces at his command and to ally them more closely with those of the Viet Minh. In August 1950 a First Resistance Congress, held on Vietnamese soil at Tuyen Quang, set up the new regime of Pathet Lao (Lao state). Its political arm, the Neo Lao Issara (Laotian Freedom Movement) was created in November 1950. The significant portion of its program included the following statement:

Internal Policy: 1. Widen the circle of unity throughout the country to include those of all races and religions, of both sexes and all ages, to defeat the French imperialists and their puppet governments and to make the country independent, free and strong. 2. Open the opportunity for people of all tribal groups to the right of liberty and democracy for all. 3. Eliminate illiteracy which makes men deaf and blind. 4. Develop handicrafts and commerce. 5. Sweep out the backward

---

40. Dommen, *op. cit.*, p. 34, sees this as a reason for the French moves.

colonial rule. 6. Get rid of gambling and drunkenness. 7. Develop guerrilla forces into regional forces, and further develop these into a national army.[41]

While only scattered information exists regarding the nature of later agreements concluded between the Pathet Lao and the Viet Minh (i.e., that of March 11, 1951),[42] it seems clear that the two groups intended to coordinate their efforts against the French and to permit their forces to be used on each other's territory. At the same time, their arrangements were political. Envisioning the formation of new core and mass groups, within Laos and linked to the Viet Minh, these understandings aimed at developing the popular base and mass understanding needed to undertake social revolution. The alliances which were forged became directly significant in the winter and spring of 1953, when the Pathet Lao assisted Viet Minh forces in threatening northern Laos and the capital cities of Vientiane and Luang Prabang. The Laotian guerrillas provided a critical margin of support, supplying the guides, intelligence, rice, and backup forces which enabled the Viet Minh to make a successful military and political thrust into the area.[43]

Then, as later, the Indochinese resistance forces did not aim at seizing and retaining territory but rather at further over-extending French resources. At the same time, their advance enabled the guerrillas to spread propaganda and extend the areas in which their cadres could operate in the future. In 1954 the Viet Minh and Pathet Lao repeated their previously successful tactics; the French were forced into the political decision to defend northern Laos at the cost of tying down increasing num-

41. Langer and Zasloff, *op. cit.*, p. 67.
42. The best summary of available information on the growth of the Pathet Lao, its political program and military strategy, is found in Bernard B. Fall, "The Pathet Lao: A Liberation Party," in Robert Scalapino (ed.), *The Communist Revolution in Asia* (Englewood Cliffs, N.J.: Prentice-Hall, 1964). See also Donald Lancaster, *The Emancipation of Indochina* (London: Oxford University Press, 1961), and Hugh Toye, *Laos: Buffer State or Battleground* (London: Oxford University Press, 1968).
43. Fall, *Anatomy*, pp. 50–56, offers a good brief account of French and Viet Minh military operations. See also Lancaster, *op. cit.*, p. 262, and Fall, in Scalapino, *op. cit.*, p. 179.

bers of troops. The climax came with the battle of Dien Bien Phu, undertaken for the same reasons, to which the French had little choice but to commit themselves. That battle not only concentrated French forces far from where they were needed, but placed them in an indefensible position. The fortress fell on May 8, 1954, and its collapse signaled the end of French rule in Indochina. While little of the fighting in the Indochina War had taken place on Laotian soil, the existence of a Laotian independence movement and the demands of a client Laotian state had combined to hasten the final defeat of French forces facing the Viet Minh. It may well be that a similar, albeit unintended, collaboration will eventually halt if not defeat the Americans fighting the Second Indochina War.

It is tempting to view the period from 1945 to 1954 as one in which segments of the Lao elite moved slowly away from French patronage to the new forms of clientship with neighbors who had traditionally extended such options but who now were buttressed financially and militarily by powers still farther removed from the scene.[44] Certainly this is the view accepted by those who support the American efforts to fill a "power vacuum" or create a human vacuum in various sectors of Indochina. While the symmetry of this hypothesis is tempting, it dismisses the practical and ideological elements introduced on one side but not duplicated on the other between 1945 and 1954.

The moderates of the Lao Issara, like their compatriots who chose consistent collaboration with the French, reproduced a very traditional pattern, seeking effective patronage not only to safeguard the kingdom but perhaps more important to protect their privileges as an elite group. Despite their choice of exile, most of the Lao Issara maintained a stance which readily permitted them to reintegrate themselves into the elite politics of a far from independent Laotian client state. Their return to Vientiane in 1949 set the stage psychologically for their later acceptance of anti-communist premises and forces including the

44. H. B. Fredman, *Laos in Strategic Perspective* (Santa Monica, Calif.: The RAND Corporation, 1961), Memorandum P–2330, p. 7.

French, the Thai, and lastly the Americans. The necessary personal and political compromises had long since been accomplished and rationalized. A lack of ideology and social concern allowed the easy transformation of a moderate political nationalism keyed to the achievement of Laotian independence into an increasingly conservative political, economic, military, and psychological dependence. The Laotians came to see clientship as necessary to the preservation of their elite model of government from increasingly effective attack and counterorganization by the Pathet Lao.

Prince Souphanouvong and those who followed him in his shift to the left were also, although to a far lesser extent, accommodating themselves to a traditional pattern—acquiring external assistance in order to obtain internal power. But in the relationship formed with the Viet Minh, the element of patronage was strongly modified by the shared ideology. Pathet Lao members gained not only material assistance and technical advice but also a variety of political techniques and practices aimed at mobilizing the population, engendering total social change, and transforming the individual and collective will.

The nature of their social and political goals modified the patronage extended by the Viet Minh to the Pathet Lao into a nontraditional form. Between 1945 and 1954 the focus on the Vietnam theater of operations in the Indochina War meant that Viet Minh aid was confined to occasional partnership in limited ventures. Equally significant, the terrain of much of Laos made it difficult for the Viet Minh to supply and supervise Pathet Lao groups. The French, Thai, and Americans could far more readily provision and control their clients via Thailand.

Thus of sheer necessity, much must often be left to the local initiative —not only the initiative of Souphanouvong himself but even the initiative of his own local commanders.[45]

For the Laotians, there was never any choice but to accept a measure of foreign assistance in full recognition of the fact that

45. Fall, in Scalapino, *op. cit.*, p. 191.

such aid would never be offered through altruism and without implicit Laotian obligations. What distinguished the offers was the price demanded and the reasons put forward for accepting it. In both these spheres, there soon emerged a clear-cut difference between Souphanouvong and Souvanna Phouma as well as between the patrons with whom they worked.

8

Background Notes on the 1954 Geneva Agreements on Laos and the Vientiane Agreements of 1956–1957

Marek Thee

THE PAST AND PRESENT COURSE OF EVENTS

Three times in the history of the Indochina conflict agreements were reached for the settlement of the Laotian problem: at Geneva in 1954, at Vientiane in 1956–1957, and again at Geneva in 1962. All of these agreements had three basic presuppositions in common—neutrality, national reconciliation, and democracy. In fact, from agreement to agreement these assumptions and principles were spelled out in ever greater clarity and detail. This striking similarity indicates that perhaps these three settlements shared a common solution which accurately reflected the deeply felt needs of the Laotian situation. However, each of these agreements ultimately failed. Parts of the provisions were never implemented, others were violated, and all of them were ineffective.

Since Laos is an integral part of the Indochina region and a vital strategic axis in any larger war, it is not surprising that the Laotian conflict and the protracted struggles in Vietnam have been closely related. The kingdom of Laos played a crucial role in France's Indochina War and now plays an equally significant role in the present Indochina conflict. With foreign interference having such a large impact on Laos' internal political life, it would seem impossible to isolate and extract the Laotian settlement from the wider course of events in Indochina.

Yet, the history of the past negotiations and the study of the agreements which have been concluded provide important clues for a general appraisal of the Indochina conflict. Understanding of the present course of events can be improved by studying the circumstances in which the 1954 Geneva Accords and the subsequent Vientiane Agreements were negotiated, concluded, and violated. However, the historical and political evidence on Indochina and Laos is still not complete. In particular, very little has been written on the Vientiane Agreements, their contents, and background.[1] It may therefore be useful to trace the history of these events and focus some attention on the early period of American involvement in Laos.

The Secret Understanding of the Western Powers, 1954

The 1954 Geneva Agreements on Laos consisted of six documents:[2]

1. The Agreement on the Cessation of Hostilities in Laos.
2. The Final Declaration of the Geneva Conference.
3. The Declaration by the Royal Government of Laos concerning Article 3 of the Final Declaration. This established "measures permitting all citizens to take their place in the national community" with full civil rights and elections to be held sometime in 1955. The Royal Government "declared itself resolved to take the necessary measures to integrate all citizens, without discrimination, into the national community and to guarantee them the enjoyment of the rights and freedoms for which the Constitution of the Kingdom provides" and "affirmed that all the Laotian citizens may freely participate as electors or candidates in general elections by secret ballots."
4. The Declaration of the Royal Government of Laos concerning Articles 4 and 5 of the Final Declaration. These articles dealt with foreign aid and introduction of war materials into Laos and prohibited Laos from entering into any military alliances. The

1. For instance, Arthur J. Dommen in *Conflict in Laos* (New York: Praeger, 1964) does not mention the term "Vientiane Agreements," while Hugh Toye in *Laos: Buffer State or Battleground* (London: Oxford University Press, 1968) attributes this term to only two out of ten agreements reached between the Royal Laotian Government and the Pathet Lao in 1956–1957.

2. *Text in Further Documents Relating to the Discussion of Indo-China at the Geneva Conference,* June 16–July 21, 1954. Command Paper 9239 (London: Her Majesty's Stationery Office [HMSO], 1954).

Royal Government pledged that "during the period between the cessation of hostilities in Vietnam and the final settlement of that country's political problems, the Royal Government of Laos will not request foreign aid, whether in war matériel, in personnel or in instructors, except for the purpose of its effective territorial defense and to the extent defined by the agreement of the cessation of hostilities."

5. The Declaration by the Government of the French Republic concerning Article 10 of the Final Declaration, which dealt with the withdrawal of the French troops from Laos.

6. The Declaration by the Government of the French Republic concerning Article 11 of the Final Declaration in which France pledged respect "for the independence and sovereignty, the unity and territorial integrity of Cambodia, Laos and Viet Nam."

The distinctive feature of these agreements was a general lack of precise provisions for the political solution of the conflict. The only detailed document concerned itself with the cessation of hostilities. Although the others mentioned the political conditions for achieving peace and particularly stressed the clauses aimed at neutralizing Laos, they were so vague and general that they failed to establish the framework for a political settlement. Since they were a compromise solution arrived at after a long and bitter war, the agreements concentrated mainly on the military provisions for a cease-fire and provided only general principles for political reconciliation. The use of the term "neutrality" accurately reflected the spirit of the agreements—it was not even mentioned.

Looking back on the circumstances in which these agreements were negotiated, one wonders if the Western powers may not have welcomed or even cultivated this vagueness and lack of precision. There certainly was no willingness in the Western capitals to neutralize Laos or to allow a real national reconciliation. The *spiritus movens* of the Western strategy at that time was U.S. Secretary of State John Foster Dulles. Obsessed by his conspiratorial monolithic view of Communism and by the image of an expansionist Communist China, Dulles ignored the local, national, and social realities of Indochina and shaped his policy in terms of global political power and military strategy. Dulles aimed at eventually transforming Laos into a forward military position on the Chinese border.

THE HISTORICAL EVIDENCE

In the final stages of the First Indochinese War Laos achieved importance as a pivotal strategic axis which determined to some extent the general military equilibrium of the whole Indochinese peninsula. It was largely in order to defend Laos that the French High Command decided to fortify the upland valley of Dien Bien Phu on the Laotian-Vietnamese border. Matters became so critical that in the spring of 1954, just before the fall of Dien Bien Phu, the U.S. State Department was willing to "internationalize" the war by the "united action" of all the Western powers.[3] Believing that Western interests could only be defended by a military solution, Dulles opposed the convening of the Geneva Conference. Accordingly, on April 4, 1954, President Eisenhower wrote to Winston Churchill:

Our painstaking search for a way out of the impasse has reluctantly forced us to the conclusion that *there is no negotiated solution of the Indochina problem* which in its essence would not be either a face-saving device to cover a French surrender or a face-saving device to cover a Communist retirement. The first alternative is too serious in the broad strategic implications for us and for you to be acceptable.[4]

After failing to get its allies to consent to widening the war, the United States finally acquiesced to holding the Geneva negotiations. However, Dulles viewed them only as a means to achieve a necessary pause in the fighting in order to regroup Western forces and to build new positions of strength for a later confrontation. He unveiled this strategy to his British colleagues in a confidential meeting at Geneva on May 1, 1954. The British foreign secretary, Sir Anthony Eden, noted in his memoirs:

    3. See letter of President Eisenhower to Winston Churchill in Dwight D. Eisenhower, *Mandate for Change 1953–1956* (Garden City, N.Y.: Doubleday, 1963), pp. 346–347.
    4. *Ibid.*, p. 346. Italics added.

I said that we must really see where we were going. If the Americans went into the Indo-China war, the Chinese themselves would inevitably step up their participation. The next stage would be that the Americans and the Chinese would be fighting each other and that was in all probability the beginning of the third world war. . . . Our American hosts then introduced the topic of the training of Vietnamese forces to defend their own country. Whatever the attractions of this scheme, they admitted that it would take perhaps two years to finish. The problem was what would happen meanwhile. When Lord Reading asked Mr. Dulles what he thought about this, he replied that they would have *to hold some sort of bridgehead,* as had been done in Korea until the Inchon landings could be carried out. Lord Reading commented that this meant that *things would remain on the boil for several years to come,* and Mr. Dulles replied that *this would be a very good thing.*[5]

The "bridgehead" strategy of letting "things remain on the boil for several years to come" was later consecrated by an agreement among leading Western powers. This was done in two stages— first by a formal British-American understanding and later by a tripartite agreement including France. The first step was taken in the latter part of June 1954 at the Anglo-American conference in Washington in which Winston Churchill and Anthony Eden participated. At this meeting, the two nations decided to set up in perfect secrecy—since the Geneva Conference was going on at the same time—a study group for the establishment of the South East Asian Treaty Organization. (These meetings bore fruit several months later when SEATO came into being on September 6, 1954, barely seven weeks after the conclusion of the Geneva Accords.) Furthermore, at this same Washington conference Britain and the United States agreed upon seven confidential conditions for a settlement at Geneva. According to Eden, the two clauses of this agreement which concerned Laos stipulated that the armistice

3. Does not impose on Laos, Cambodia, or retained Vietnam any restrictions materially impairing their capacity to *maintain stable non-*

5. *The Memoirs of the Rt. Hon. Sir Anthony Eden* (London: Cassel, 1960), pp. 112–113. Italics added.

communist regimes; and especially restrictions impairing their right to *maintain adequate forces* for internal security, to import arms and to *employ foreign advisers.*

4. *Does not contain political provisions which would risk loss of the retained area to communist control.*[6]

In other words, through the Washington agreement, Britain and the United States resolved that no political provisions, such as free elections, should be allowed to endanger the existence of regimes designed to serve the military "bridgehead" concept. This naturally precluded any national reconciliation which tolerated free political activity for the left or the participation of the Pathet Lao in government.

The Washington Anglo-American understanding was soon transformed into a formal Anglo-French-American agreement. This was achieved as a result of diplomatic conversations conducted in Paris on July 13 and 14, 1954, by Dulles and his French and British counterparts, Mendes-France and Anthony Eden. President Eisenhower noted this significant achievement rather succinctly:

Foster succeeded in obtaining agreement to a position paper which was essentially the same as that agreed between the United Kingdom and the United States at the time of the Churchill visit.[7]

Eden is more explicit. Recounting the discussion in Paris on July 13 and 14, Eden writes:

Mr. Dulles . . . said that even if the settlement adhered to the seven points faithfully, the United States still could not guarantee it. . . . To this Mendes-France replied that the United States would not escape the dilemma by refusing to appear at Geneva. Since they were already represented at the conference, they would have to make a decision in any case. He repeatedly emphasized that Dulles' suspicion about a departure from the "seven points" was wholly unjustified. . . . In the end, Mr. Dulles told us that he would give us his final answer on the following day. . . . On the following morning Mr. Dulles and I first met together and had some discussion on the kind of documents which

6. *Ibid.,* p. 133. Italics added.
7. Eisenhower, *op. cit.,* p. 370.

might be exchanged, based on drafts which he had prepared of a joint "position paper." It was decided that this should be reduced to one document setting out the attitudes of the United States and French Governments, and that I should express in a separate letter my general agreement. A conference followed at the Quai d'Orsay, where Mr. Dulles announced that Mr. Bedell Smith would be returning to Geneva in the very near future to share in the work of the conference. The documents were put in shape, signed and exchanged after luncheon at the American Embassy.[8]

It is important to note that the Western powers made their decisions barely a week before the conclusion of the Geneva Accords. Documents of both the Washington and Paris meetings were kept secret from the world and the text of the "joint position paper" Dulles presented at Paris has yet to be released. The seven-point Washington agreement was made public in 1960 in the Eden memoirs and later in the book by Jean Lacouture and Philippe Devillers on the end of the First Indochina War. The French authors made this comment about the text of the agreements:

This astounding text, which preceded the agreements of July 20th, was kept in no less amazing secrecy: one cannot find a better proof for the existence of a common Western doctrine.[9]

Of primary importance for the subsequent course of events in Indochina was the fundamental difference between the letter and spirit of the Western secret understanding and that of the Geneva Accords concluded a week later. Post-Geneva history clearly evidences the reality that developments did not follow the scenario outlined in Geneva but rather the strategy fixed in Washington and Paris. The policy to leave things "on the boil for several years to come" also played into the hands of the hawkish circles in the capitals of the great Eastern powers, which were only too eager to have the United States follow in France's footsteps and wear out its military forces in a protracted guerrilla

8. *Memoirs* (Eden), *op. cit.*, p. 139.
9. Jean Lacouture and Philippe Devillers, *La fin d'une guerre: Indochine 1954* (Paris: Editions du Seuil, 1960), p. 245.

war for which the United States was neither prepared nor able
to win.

THE AFTERMATH OF GENEVA

As was mentioned earlier, the central and most detailed document of the 1954 Geneva Accords on Laos was the agreement on
the cessation of hostilities. This document, characteristically
enough, was not signed by any Laotian. Brigadier General Delteil,
as commander in chief, signed for the French Union Forces in
Indochina, and Vice-Minister of National Defense of the Democratic Republic of Vietnam Ta Quang Buu signed for the commander in chief of the Fighting Units of Pathet Lao and for the
commander in chief of the People's Army of Vietnam. However,
the real heirs to the agreement were the Royal Laotian Government (RLG) and the Pathet Lao (which in 1956 became a
political party with the name of Neo Lao Hak Xat—the Patriotic
Front of Laos).

Article 13 of the agreement on the cessation of hostilities provided for the withdrawal of the foreign forces—the French and
the Vietnamese volunteer units—from Laos. This operation, in
accordance with Article 4a, had to be completed within 120 days.
In the meantime, according to Article 14, "pending a political
settlement," the widely dispersed fighting units of the Pathet Lao
were supposed to concentrate themselves in the two northern
provinces of Phong Saly and Sam Neua. After the withdrawal of
the foreign forces and the regroupment of the Pathet Lao units,
the poorly defined "political settlement" required by Article 14
became the key problem in implementing the Geneva Accords.

But a "political settlement" was conceivable only in the framework of national reconciliation and in the spirit of the Final
Declaration of the Geneva Conference, which provided for
"fundamental freedoms" (Article 3), neutrality (Articles 4 and
5), and protection against "individual and collective reprisals"
(Article 9). However, the realization of these goals was made
impossible by a series of events in and outside Laos.

First, on September 6, 1954, barely seven weeks after the
conclusion of the Geneva Accords, the South East Asian Treaty

Organization came into being and placed Laos within its "protective orbit." This move contradicted the concept of a neutral Laos and was censured by the 1962 Geneva Agreement on Laos, which stated that all the signatories, including the five big powers, were to "respect the wish of the Kingdom of Laos not to recognize the protection of any alliance or military coalition, including SEATO."[10]

In the same month these external problems were compounded by a severe Laotian cabinet crisis following the assassination of Minister of Defense Kou Voravong, a leading advocate of the Geneva Accords. The government of Prince Souvanna Phouma resigned and a new cabinet was formed in November headed by Katay Don Sasorith, a tough supporter of SEATO with clear Thai and U.S. leanings. Recalling this episode at the plenary session of the Geneva Conference on June 14, 1961, Prince Souvanna Phouma said:

Immediately after the conclusion of the Geneva Agreements the Government over which I presided entered into negotiations with the Pathet Lao in order to reintegrate the combatants of this patriotic movement into the national community, but foreign interference into our internal problems compelled me to resign.[11]

The change of government was followed by the opening of the United States Operation Mission (USOM) in Vientiane on January 1, 1955. As U.S. military assistance to Laos grew to represent the highest per capita American foreign aid anywhere in the world and as the whole state budget of Laos became dependent on U.S. financial support, American officials began to assume direct control over RLG policies.

Under these circumstances, negotiations between the Royal Laotian Government and the Pathet Lao encountered serious difficulties. While the Royal Government pressed for a prompt reintegration of the two northern provinces controlled by the Pathet Lao and avoided any discussion of the political questions

10. Treaty Series No. 27–1963, *Declaration and Protocol on the Neutrality of Laos*, July 23, 1962. Command Paper 2025 (London: HMSO, 1963).

11. Gouvernement Royal du Laos, Ministère de l'Information, *Pour un Laos Pacifique, Indépendant et Neutre*, pp. 15–16.

involved in the implementation of the Geneva Accords, the leadership of the Pathet Lao made reintegration conditional upon prior political adjustments. With the intensification of RLG military activities against the Pathet Lao zones in 1955, it became evident that the Katay government, encouraged by the United States, had abandoned the "political settlement" in favor of a military solution to the problem. This shift was spelled out by John Foster Dulles after the February 1955 SEATO conference in Bangkok and his subsequent visit to Vientiane. In his report on the Asian tour, referring to the situation in Sam Neua and Phong Saly, Dulles emphasized that the Katay government

is worried lest, if it suppresses the Communists within, it will be struck by the Communists from without. I hope that the worry is now allayed by their better understanding of the protective nature of the Manila Pact.[12]

To some extent, emphasis on a military solution played into the hands of the Hanoi-supported Pathet Lao. It allowed them to buy time, to dig in deeper in the northern provinces, and to strengthen their forces in preparation for a vigorous political comeback.

Military clashes in 1955 between the forces of the Royal Government and Pathet Lao created a tense situation. It was to the credit of the International Commission for Supervision and Control (the ICSC is more commonly called the ICC) that a more serious military conflict was prevented and peace prevailed.

In December 1955 the Katay government, without heeding the demands of the Pathet Lao for a revision of the electoral law and without waiting for the reunification of the country, conducted separate parliamentary elections in the ten provinces under government control. But the results were disappointing to Katay, and the newly elected National Assembly refused to reappoint him prime minister. After a five-week ministerial crisis a new government was formed in March 1956, headed again by Prince Souvanna Phouma. The new cabinet declared "as its preoccupation

12. Text in U.S. Department of State, *The Conference of the Manila Pact Powers*, February 23–25, 1955.

number one the settlement of the Pathet Lao problem . . . in order to achieve reconciliation through patriotism and loyalty."[13]

In fact, in the spring of 1956 a slow but steady process of rapprochement between the parties was set in motion. The negotiations, which dragged on till November 1957, produced ten agreements specifying the general formula for a "political settlement" as envisaged in Article 14 of the Geneva cease-fire agreement for Laos. To commemorate the place where these agreements were negotiated and signed, they came to be called the Vientiane Agreements.

THE VIENTIANE AGREEMENTS

The 1956–1957 negotiations in Vientiane between the Royal Government and the Pathet Lao touched on a wide range of problems and dealt with internal as well as external questions. The main impetus for the discussions came from the Pathet Lao. Being the weaker party, the Pathet Lao wanted to reassure itself that the reconciliation would be real, that they would be given the possibility for free political activity, that there would be no reprisals, and that the country would adopt a genuine neutralist policy. The following is a partial list of the documents which constituted the Vientiane Agreements:

1. Joint Declaration of the Delegation of the Royal Government of Laos and the Delegation of the Pathet Lao Forces, signed on August 5, 1956, by Prince Souvanna Phouma and Prince Souphanouvong.[14]

2. Joint and Final Declaration of the Delegation of the Royal Government of Laos and the Delegation of the Pathet Lao Forces, signed by both princes on August 10, 1956.[15]

---

13. Declaration of Prince Souvanna Phouma before the National Assembly on February 28, 1956, *Third Interim Report on the Activities of the International Commission for Supervision and Control in Laos*, July 1, 1955–May 16, 1957 (New Delhi: Government of India Press, 1958), Appendix to Annexure 5.

14. *Ibid.*, Annexure 7.

15. *Ibid.*, Annexure 8.

3. Agreement on the Measures to Be Taken for the Implementation of the Cease-Fire, concluded by the delegations of the parties in the Joint Military Committee on October 31, 1956.[16]

4. Agreement of the Joint Political Committee on the Question of Peace and Neutrality, signed on November 2, 1956.[17]

5. Agreement Between the Political Delegation of the Royal Government and the Political Delegation of the Pathet Lao Forces Relating to the Measures for the Guarantee of Civil Rights, of Nondiscrimination and of Nonreprisal for the Members of the Pathet Lao Forces and Ex-Participants of the Resistance and Measures for the Integration of the Pathet Lao Cadres and Ex-Participants in the Resistance in the Administrative and Technical Services of the Kingdom at All Levels, signed on December 24, 1956.[18]

6. Joint Communiqué of H.R.H. Prince Souvanna Phouma, Prime Minister of the Royal Laotian Government and H.R.H. Prince Souphanouvong, Representative of the Pathet Lao Forces, signed on December 28, 1956.[19]

7. Agreement Between the Political Delegation of the Royal Government and the Political Delegation of the Pathet Lao Forces on the Electoral Law, signed on February 21, 1957.[20]

8. Joint Communiqué by H.R.H. Prince Souvanna Phouma, Prime Minister of the Royal Government and H.R.H. Prince Souphanouvong, Representative of the Fighting Units of the Pathet Lao Forces, signed on November 2, 1957.[21]

9. Agreement on the Reestablishment of the Royal Administration in the Provinces of Sam Neua and Phong Saly, reached between the Political Delegation of the Royal Government and the Political Delegation of the Fighting Units of the Pathet Lao, concluded on November 2, 1957.[22]

---

16. *Ibid.*, Annexure 10.
17. *Ibid.*, Annexure 11.
18. *Ibid.*, Annexure 12.
19. *Ibid.*, Annexure 13.
20. *Ibid.*, Annexure 15.
21. *Fourth Interim Report on the Activities of the International Commission for Supervision and Control in Laos,* May 17, 1957–May 31, 1958 (New Delhi: Government of India Press, 1958), Annexure 14.
22. *Ibid.*, Annexure 15.

10. Military Agreement on the Integration of the Fighting Units of the Pathet Lao Forces into the National Army, signed by the representatives of the Joint Military Committee on November 2, 1957.[23]

The first five agreements dwelled in great detail on all the aspects of national reconciliation, internal democracy, and the foreign relations of Laos. Of special significance was the agreement on the policy of peace and neutrality (Agreement Number 4, above) which stated: "The two Parties unanimously acknowledge that the achievement of a policy of peace and neutrality is of great importance and is closely connected with the destiny of our fatherland." Article 1 of the agreement stipulated that Laos would "foster friendly relations and establish diplomatic relations in accordance with the five principles of peaceful coexistence with all countries, irrespective of their political systems." The main consideration here was the establishment of a neutral balance in the foreign relations of Laos and, especially, the development of peaceful and friendly relations with all of Laos' neighbors. While Laos already maintained diplomatic relations with all the Western powers and many other countries, including South Vietnam, the Royal Government had not established relations with the socialist countries, which included its two neighbors—the People's Republic of China and the Democratic Republic of Vietnam. The Royal Government also refused to enter into diplomatic relations with either the Soviet Union, cochairman of the Geneva Conference, or Poland, a member of the International Commission for Supervision and Control in Laos. The Pathet Lao felt that this situation was fraught with dangers for the future of Laos. The November 1956 agreement on the policy of peace and neutrality tried to correct this distorted diplomatic posture by introducing the spirit of Geneva into Laotian political life.

The Vientiane Agreements provided for the reunification of the country and the formation of a government of national union with Pathet Lao participation. The first seven of the Vientiane

---

23. *Ibid.,* Annexure 16.

Agreements were ratified unanimously by the National Assembly on May 29, 1957, and the last three were approved by the Assembly on November 19, 1957, at the same time it proclaimed a new coalition government with Prince Souvanna Phouma as prime minister and Prince Souphanouvong as minister of planning.

This agreement was achieved despite continuous U.S. opposition to the policy of national reconciliation and neutrality throughout the whole period of the Vientiane negotiations. During the 1959 congressional hearings before the Subcommittee on Foreign Operations and Monetary Affairs it was revealed that the United States had struggled hard to prevent the formation of a coalition government. This was freely admitted by former U.S. Ambassador to Laos J. Graham Parsons, by Assistant Secretary of State for Far Eastern Affairs Walter S. Robertson, and by Under Secretary of State for Economic Affairs C. Douglas Dillon. Pointing to the coalition government Robertson stressed that "we did everything we could to keep it from happening."[24]

In its attempts to prevent the coalition government from forming, the U.S. Department of State enlisted the aid of other SEATO members, including Great Britain and France, who were obligated to lend their support by the 1954 Paris agreement. In the early stages of the Vientiane negotiations all the Western powers expressed, in varying degrees, their dissatisfaction to the RLG over the contents of the agreements which had been concluded with the Pathet Lao. In a note directed to the three Western powers on February 22, 1957 (the day after the signing of the seventh Vientiane agreement), the Royal Laotian Government expressed concern about the disparity of attitudes shown by the Western powers toward the Vientiane negotiations. The RLG said that these opposing views tended to "create uneasiness in the public opinion, to hamper the delicate task of the Royal

24. *Committee on Government Operations, House of Representatives; United States Aid Operations in Laos: Hearings before the Foreign Operations and Monetary Affairs Subcommittee,* March 11–June 1, 1959, 86th Congress, 1st Session (Washington D.C.: Government Printing Office, 1959), p. 196.

Government, and, finally, to endanger the desirable settlement of the Pathet Lao problem."[25]

In a coordinated diplomatic response on April 16, 1957, the United States, Great Britain, and France presented identical notes to the Laotian ambassadors in Washington, London, and Paris which expressed total disapproval of the agreements concluded with the Pathet Lao.[26] The notes maintained that the Pathet Lao "have sought to place extraneous conditions upon their acceptance of the authority of the Royal Government and upon their reintegration into the national community," and intimated that these conditions were contrary to both the Geneva Agreements and the resolution of the International Control Commission (ICC) of January 7, 1956, dealing with the reestablishment of RLG administration in the northern provinces. The notes went on to express confidence that the Royal Laotian Government "will continue in its determination that the political future of the Kingdom of Laos shall not be dictated by dissident groups enjoying no constitutional status."[27]

The publication of the notes of the three Western powers exposed the extent to which pressure had been mobilized against the RLG's reconciliation with the Pathet Lao. This move precipitated a new ministerial crisis which resulted in the resignation of Prince Souvanna Phouma's government on May 31, 1957, and the subsequent suspension of negotiations with the Pathet Lao. On August 9, 1957, after three unsuccessful attempts by Katay, Phoui Sananikone, and Bong Souvannavong to form an alternative government, Prince Souvanna Phouma was asked to form a new government which finalized the Vientiane Agreements.

The International Control Commission played an important

25. "Note sur le règlement du problème 'Pathet Lao' et sur la position des puissances occidentales au regard de ce problème," *Lao Presse*, April 25, 1957, p. C.

26. *Ibid.*, pp. D, E; English text in *Department of State Bulletin*, May 13, 1957, pp. 771–772.

27. Text in *Third Interim Report on the Activities of the ICSC in Laos, op. cit.*, Annexure 3.

role during this period and reacted strongly to the disruptive moves of the Western powers, which challenged its peacekeeping role. The Third Interim Report to the cochairmen states that "it was clear to the Commission by the end of April that the Parties had encountered difficulties of various kinds . . . and the Commission felt it necessary to encourage the Parties further to come to a speedy solution and accordingly on 16 May 1957 it adopted the following resolution."[28]

The wording of this unanimously adopted ICC resolution constituted a direct response to the April 16 notes of the Western powers and a reaffirmation of the spirit of the Geneva and Vientiane agreements. Noting "with concern and regret" the difficulties encountered by the negotiating parties, the resolution stated the Commission's conviction "that a political settlement should be achieved as a result of full and free discussions between the Parties" which "should remain free to discuss and determine between them what is most equitable and acceptable." The Commission also "noted with satisfaction" the agreements and their terms of negotiation "are not contrary to the Geneva Agreement and the resolutions adopted by the Commission, including that of January 7, 1956." Further, the resolution stated that the Commission "considers important the implementation of the agreements necessary for the political settlement" and "recommends to the Parties that the negotiations now in progress between them should be continued with the utmost vigour in an atmosphere of existing goodwill and mutual understanding until a final settlement on all outstanding points is reached with the least possible delay."

On July 15, 1957, disturbed by the protracted government crisis and suspension of negotiations, the International Control Commission adopted a new resolution. It recalled the May 16 resolution, took note of the unanimous approval by the National Assembly of the agreements signed by the parties between August 1956 and February 1957, and urged the parties "that they should consider important the full implementation of all the

28. *Ibid.*, Chap. I, para. 20.

agreements necessary for the final settlement of the Laotian problem."[29] The Commission's initiative at that time was instrumental in surmounting the internal political crisis. It helped to renew the negotiations and form the Government of National Union.

Yet the United States, Thailand, and the other SEATO members could not accept the settlement. Their growing uneasiness was increased after the supplementary National Assembly election held in May 1958 in which the Neo Lao Hak Xat gained 9 of 21 contested seats, and the Party of Peace and Neutrality (allied with the Neo Lao Hak Xat) won an additional 4 seats. Alarmed by these results, the U.S. Mission in Laos decided to put an end to the coalition government experiment. In his Geneva speech of 1961 Prince Souvanna Phouma described the developments of 1957–1958 in the following way:

The policy followed by my government received full approval of the Lao people. In fact, the war raged in Laos from 1949, and everyone aspired to peace and understanding between all the Lao. However, this policy met with opposition of certain member states of SEATO. The Government of National Unity with the participation of the Pathet Lao ministers which I succeeded to form, did not last long. Soon came an announcement threatening to cut our aid. Such pressures provoked my resignation. Mr. Phoui Sananikone who replaced me deviated clearly from the road of neutrality and adopted a pro-American policy. To begin with, he gave permission to install in our country American military advisers and instructors, he authorized Taiwan to open a consulate general in Vientiane and raised the level of the Saigon representation—a body which existed from the preindependence period—to the level of an embassy. What was more grave, he introduced a policy of discrimination towards the Pathet Lao whose leadership was even put in prison although several of them were members of the National Assembly. And all this brought fatally to the revival of the civil war.[30]

29. *Fourth Interim Report on the Activities of the ICSC in Laos, op. cit.,* Annexure 2.

30. Gouvernement Royal du Laos, *Pour un Laos Pacifique, Indépendant et Neutre, op. cit.,* p. 16.

In the next stages of the Laotian conflict, foreign interference grew progressively greater, widening the internal rift and complicating both internal and external issues. The result of this foreign interference was that the Laotian civil war came to serve as a prelude to the second Indochina conflict and drew Laos into this larger struggle.

9

No Place for Neutralism: The Eisenhower Administration and Laos

Len E. Ackland

In 1954, when the battle of Dien Bien Phu put an end to French colonialism in Indochina, the United States did not even have a diplomatic mission in Laos. Yet, by 1960 the United States and the Soviet Union were on the verge of a major confrontation in this small, isolated Asian country of less than three million inhabitants.

During the period from 1954 to the end of the Eisenhower Administration, Laos had become a testing ground for American counterinsurgency and "nation-building" programs which blossomed fully in Vietnam. And many of the features which marked these later U.S. programs—the conflicts between various American bureaucracies vying for power, the king-making adventures, and the overwhelming ignorance of the actual problems facing the indigenous populations—first surfaced in Laos.

When we look back at this period, two major questions stand out: (1) How did the United States come to perceive an interest in Laos? (2) What was the form and character of the involvement that followed from these perceptions?

Laos was intrinsically important to no one but the people who lived there. The economic interests that spokesmen for three consecutive administrations have mentioned with regard to Southeast Asia do not apply to Laos, a land whose major resource is opium. There is no close cultural affinity between Americans and Laotians, which might cause us concern about that country's future. On the contrary, Americans have paid no attention to the people, customs, values, or desires of the Laotians, as is evidenced in a bitter statement by Prince Souvanna Phouma. In January 1961 he condemned one of the chief archi-

tects of Eisenhower's Laos policy as a man who "understood
nothing about Asia and nothing about Laos."[1] The sad reality
is that the substance of Souvanna Phouma's stinging indictment
of the American ambassador to Laos—and, by extension, of the
whole American policy—is true.

Those policy makers viewed Laos as a piece of strategic real
estate in the battle between Communist and anti-Communist
forces. By a curious rationalization, Americans had already transformed the French colonial war in Indochina into a fight to
preserve the "Free World." In his memoirs, President Eisenhower
gives us insight into the "true meaning" of that war:

At this time, the spring of 1953, our main task was to convince the
world that the Southeast Asian war was an aggressive move by the
Communists to subjugate the entire area. To make this clear was a real
necessity: our people as well as the citizens of the three Associated
States of Indochina had to be assured of the true meaning of the war.[2]

The world remained unconvinced. At the Geneva Conference
in 1954, the settlement of the war was reached when the participants agreed (with the notable exceptions of the United States
delegation and the Saigon observers) on a neutralized Laos and
Cambodia and a temporarily partitioned Vietnam. The conference participants took note of two unilateral declarations by the
Royal Government of Laos which stated that it would request
no foreign military aid, join no military alliances, integrate all
citizens into the national community, and allow no foreign bases
on its soil unless its national security was threatened. In a separate Laotian cease-fire agreement, the Pathet Lao, who will be
discussed more fully below, were not recognized as a "resistance
government" but still as "Pathet Lao Fighting Units." Under
Article 14 of this agreement the Pathet Lao was given 120 days
to regroup their troops in Phong Saly and Sam Neua provinces,
which border North Vietnam. The International Control Com-

1. *New York Times,* January 20, 1961.
2. Dwight D. Eisenhower, *Mandate for Change 1953–1956* (Garden City,
N.Y.: Doubleday, 1963), p. 168.

mission (ICC) was empowered to supervise the observance of the agreement terms.[3]

The United States, however, was unwilling to accept the idea of a neutral Laos, since its map showed Laos as a key "domino" situated between the Communist states of China and North Vietnam and the Free World nations of Thailand, Cambodia, and South Vietnam. After all, Eisenhower's famous Domino Speech of April 14, 1954, had been specifically directed at Indochina.[4] Secretary Dulles interpreted the Geneva Accords not as providing for a neutralist solution in Indochina but as a deal in which, by handing over half of Vietnam to the Communists, he had "eliminated the possibilty of a domino effect in Southeast Asia" by "saving" Laos and Cambodia.[5] These countries were to be added to the Free World roster.

Thailand pushed for a nonneutral, pro-Western Laos since its leaders felt threatened both by their traditional Vietnamese enemies and by the Chinese to the north. American policy toward Laos cannot be understood unless we are aware of the degree to which our actions were dictated by the perceived interests of the Thai leaders. The United States commitment to Thailand put Washington "under a continuing compulsion to take actions disproportionate to the intrinsic strategic value of Laos."[6] Thailand viewed Laos in terms of the metaphor used by the assistant secretary for Far Eastern affairs, who described it as "a finger thrust right into the heart of Southeast Asia."[7]

3. "Further Documents Relating to the Discussion of Indochina at the Geneva Conference, June 16–July 21, 1954." Miscellaneous No. 20 (1954), Command Paper (CMND.) 7239 (London: HMSO, 1954).

4. Eisenhower and Dulles developed the strategy of "massive retaliation," designed to deter Russian aggression anywhere in the world by threatening all-out war. Simultaneously, Eisenhower emphasized the need to strengthen individual countries in order to keep the dominoes from falling. This approach converged with the thinking of those members of the American bureaucracy who advocated what Army Chief of Staff Maxwell Taylor called "flexible response."

5. *Life* magazine, January 16, 1956.

6. Arthur J. Dommen, *Conflict in Laos* (New York: Praeger, 1964), p. 68.

7. Quoted in Oliver E. Clubb, *The United States and the Sino-Soviet Bloc in Southeast Asia* (Washington, D.C.: The Brooking's Institution, 1962), p. 60.

America first maneuvered to pull Laos away from neutrality by integrating it into John Foster Dulles's collective security scheme. Only two months after the Geneva Conference, the SEATO (Southeast Asia Treaty Organization) protocol designated Laos (as well as Cambodia and the "free territory under the jurisdiction of the State of Vietnam") eligible for the protection provided under its Article IV and for the economic assistance under Article III. The fact that the Laotians were far from overjoyed about their new foster parent was underlined in a statement by Nhouy Abhay, a former foreign minister: "If SEATO came in there would be international war and this country would be the battleground. Nobody really wants that."[8]

However, the desires of a tiny country carried no weight in Washington's ponderous deliberations. Having associated Laos with SEATO, the next U.S. move was to strengthen the country in order to forestall the possibility of a Communist takeover. The question in Washington concerned *how* to best become involved, not *whether* to become involved.

According to Roger Hilsman, a top Kennedy adviser, in 1954 the United States could have chosen to support any of three leaders: Souvanna Phouma, then prime minister, who advocated strict neutrality and Pathet Lao participation in the government; Phoui Sananikone, who advocated pro-Western neutrality and no Communist participation in the government; or Colonel Phoumi Nosavan, who desired an alliance with the United States and elimination of the Communists.[9] With a superb display of inconsistency and bad coordination, the United States managed to support each of these alternative men at one time or another during the next few years—and sometimes more than one was supported simultaneously by different segments of the American bureaucracy.

To accomplish the U.S. goal of building up Laos, a program of economic and military aid was devised. American economic aid had been channeled to Laos since the signing of an economic

8. Quoted in E. H. S. Simmonds, "The Evolution of Foreign Policy in Laos since Independence," *Modern Asian Studies* (January 1968), p. 8.

9. Roger Hilsman, *To Move a Nation* (Garden City, N.Y.: Doubleday, 1967), p. 106.

cooperation agreement in September 1951. By an exchange of diplomatic notes in July 1955 the United States and the Royal Government of Laos completed an agreement "to further the economic cooperation objectives [of the 1951 agreement] and to *promote the effective defense of the Kingdom of Laos.*"[10]

Serious disagreement arose in Washington over the interpretation of promoting "effective defense" in Laos. Secretary Dulles and the State Department favored the creation of a 25,000-man army both as an "agent of modernization" and as a "trip wire" to Communist aggression. The latter meant that although the army could not be expected to stand up to larger Communist forces, it would resist enough to dramatize the situation and allow outside intervention. The Pentagon opposed this plan, arguing that it would be better to expand the police forces to about 15,000 men, since such a small army would be useless in the event of a Chinese or North Vietnamese attack. The military also believed that any effort to create a strong Laotian army would require American advisers—a clear violation of the Geneva Accords. The Pentagon reluctantly went along with Dulles after being promised that a Military Assistance Advisory Group (MAAG) mission would be set up under the guise of a Programs Evaluation Office (PEO) attached to the economic aid mission. This move was made despite its violation of the Geneva Accords and the fact that the PEO façade fooled no one.[11]

Thus, during the late fifties, over 80 per cent of the annual American aid to Laos of $40 million went to the Royal Laotian Army (RLA). Laos became the only foreign country in the world where the United States supported 100 per cent of the military budget. The army itself "became more political than anything else—a focal point for graft, the principal lever for ambitious men plotting coups, and a symbol of governmental repression in those villages to which it did, intermittently, pene-

10. Robert F. Randle, *Geneva 1954: The Settlement of the Indochinese War* (Princeton, N.J.: Princeton University Press, 1969), p. 514, note. Italics added.

11. See Dommen, *op. cit.*, pp. 98–104, for a detailed account of American support for the Laotian Army; Hilsman, *op. cit.*, p. 112.

trate."[12] This American client army came to be a major instrument of U.S. involvement in the internal affairs of Laos.

As mentioned above, the creation of the RLA was justified on the ground that it would work for change and be effective in signaling Communist aggression. The "trip wire" was important because of the SEATO provision which called for allied consultation only in the event of "Communist aggression." Washington regarded the Pathet Lao as the spearhead of Communist aggressive aims in Laos and viewed it as little more than an agent of Moscow or Peking. But this picture did not conform to the reality in Laos.

The Pathet Lao movement, which had grown out of the liberation struggle against the French, was officially founded in 1950. The heart of the Pathet Lao was a small group of Laotian members of the Indochinese Communist Party. The party had been established by Ho Chi Minh in 1930. The Pathet Lao were led by the non-Communist Prince Souphanouvong, a royal Laotian prince and half-brother of Souvanna Phouma.[13] This movement received its greatest support from the hill people of Laos who had no great love for the wealthier lowlanders controlling the Royal Government. In 1953 the Pathet Lao and their Viet Minh allies began fighting the French in Laos and established a regime in Sam Neua province. It was this action which caused the French High Command to fortify the narrow valley of Dien Bien Phu in hopes of preventing the fall of northern Laos.

The Soviet Union had little to do with the Pathet Lao. Russia, while granting support to the Viet Minh, had shown little interest in Laos or Cambodia until 1951, when they became apprehensive that French troops based there created a danger to the Viet Minh and Chinese.[14] Still, Russia remained far in the background, since it did not consider any of its vital interests at stake.

The Democratic Republic of Vietnam (DRV) and China were closer to the Pathet Lao, but the Geneva Conference showed

12. Hilsman, *op. cit.*, p. 113.
13. Hugh Toye, *Laos: Buffer State or Battleground* (London: Oxford University Press, 1968), p. 106.
14. Charles B. McLane, *Soviet Strategies in Southeast Asia* (Princeton, N.J.: Princeton University Press, 1966).

how easily the desires of the Pathet Lao were given short shrift by its allies. Early in the Geneva Conference the Chinese and the DRV pushed to seat both the Pathet Lao and the smaller Cambodian insurgent force. On June 10 Anthony Eden stated that the issue of Viet Minh troops in Laos and Cambodia threatened to cause a breakdown in negotiations. Six days later Chou En-lai visited Eden and declared that the Viet Minh could be persuaded to remove their troops from Laos and Cambodia, and that China could recognize the two royal governments, provided there were no American bases in these kingdoms. That afternoon Chou made a formal proposal to that effect, which was accepted by the other conferees.[15]

The Soviet Union, China, and the DRV were quite satisfied with the Geneva provisions for a neutral Laos. At the 1955 Bandung Conference, Pham Van Song affirmed that the Democratic Republic of Vietnam considered the settlement in Laos "a question of internal order which the royal government of Laos and the Pathet Lao are entirely free to solve in the best way possible."[16] As the United States began its program to insert Laos into the defense perimeter of the Free World, it appears that none of the Communist powers had designs on Laos. Many Laotian leaders were also ready to work toward the accommodation and reconciliation foreseen in Geneva, and wished to achieve the peaceful neutralism that the Conference had laid out for their country.

A Coalition Is Built—and Destroyed

While Washington was debating how best to support its aims in Laos, Prime Minister Souvanna Phouma took steps in September 1954 toward opening negotiations with the Pathet Lao. His government fell after the assassination of Kou Voravong, his minister of defense, who shared his views. Souvanna Phouma later said that his fall was caused by foreign interference.[17]

15. King C. Chen, *Vietnam and China, 1938–1954* (Princeton, N.J.: Princeton University Press, 1969), pp. 310–311.

16. Quoted in Randle, *op. cit.*, p. 514.

17. Toye, *op. cit.*, p. 107.

The new government formed in November under Katay Don Sasorith, a wealthy man of partly Vietnamese origin, drew Laos much closer to both the United States and Thailand. Katay did nothing to help resolve the internal conflicts in his country. In April 1955 he broke off talks with the Pathet Lao concerning the administration of the two provinces under their control. Attempts by the RLA to enter these two provinces aborted. Without serious negotiations the Pathet Lao were not going to simply turn themselves over to an unsympathetic government. The elections originally called for by the Geneva Conference took place in December, but without the participation of the Pathet Lao.

After the December elections Katay could not muster up the two-thirds Assembly majority then needed to form a new government; Souvanna Phouma was again chosen prime minister in March 1956. The prince began this term by stating a policy of settling the "Pathet Lao problem" and achieving a "general reconciliation through patriotism and loyalty." "No effort shall be spared," he said, "so that negotiations with the adverse party [may] be crowned by the royal reconciliation longed for by all."[18] The Pathet Lao had also helped create a more favorable climate for negotiations. On January 6 they had issued a manifesto declaring the desirability of forming a united front, implying a coalition with the Royal Government, and had simultaneously announced the formation of a political organization, the Neo Lao Hak Xat (NLHX).[19]

Efforts by both sides resulted in a preliminary agreement between the Pathet Lao and Royal Government in August. During the same month Souvanna Phouma traveled to both Peking and Hanoi, announcing that his policy for Laos was one of "peace and neutrality." Such a sudden change from Katay's visibly pro-Western stance sent shivers of dread through the United States and Thailand.

Negotiations between the Laotians still had many difficulties to stumble over. In March 1957 Prince Souphanouvong prema-

18. Quoted in Randle, *op. cit.*, p. 520.
19. Dommen, *op. cit.*, p. 84.

turely demanded recognition from Moscow, Peking, and Hanoi and also introduced a Chinese offer of substantial economic aid to Laos.[20] Not only did the talks with Souvanna Phouma break down, but the latter resigned after a vote of no confidence from the Assembly. Again his opposition was unable to form a government, and Souvanna Phouma returned as prime minister in August.

Renewed talks in September led the Pathet Lao and Royal Government to sign the Vientiane Agreements on November 12, 1957. On the military side the most important article provided for the integration of 1,500 men from the Pathet Lao units into the Royal Laotian Army and the discharge of the remaining forces. The political agreements provided for the integration of the administration of the two Pathet Lao-controlled provinces after the creation of the Government of National Union. A compromise was worked out according to which the province of Sam Neua would receive a Royal Lao governor and a Pathet Lao deputy, and Phong Saly a Pathet Lao governor and a Royal Lao deputy. Other articles granted the Neo Lao Hak Xat the freedom to exercise democratic rights throughout the country.[21]

On November 18 Prince Souphanouvong formally returned the provinces of Phong Saly and Sam Neua to the authority of the king. The next day the Laotian Assembly unanimously agreed on a coalition government, the Government of National Union. Included in the government were two Pathet Lao: Prince Souphanouvong, minister of planning, and Phoumi Vongvichit, minister of religious affairs.

The Laotian agreement to form a coalition government received widespread praise from the world, with the United States introducing the only sour note in the form of a terse State Department warning about the dangers of coalition with the Communists.[22] American officials had blatantly worked to frustrate the settlement. J. Graham Parsons, the American ambassador to

20. Simmonds, *op. cit.*, p. 13.
21. Bernard B. Fall, *Anatomy of a Crisis* (Garden City, N.Y.: Doubleday, 1969), p. 78.
22. Simmonds, *op. cit.*, p. 13; Fall, *op. cit.*, p. 81.

Laos, testified before Congress: "I struggled for sixteen months to prevent a coalition."[23]

The coalition seemed promising for Laos. By January 1958 the Royal Laotian Army had occupied both Phong Saly and Sam Neua provinces. A special ceremony was held on February 18, 1958, on the Plain of Jars, where 1,501 members of the Pathet Lao units were integrated into the RLA and another 4,284 troops processed for discharge.[24]

Developments on the political front also gave cause for optimism. The Assembly's supplementary elections held on May 4 were billed as a test of the degree of success with which the dispute in Laos had moved from the battlefield to the ballot box. The NLHX campaigned under the banner of Laotian unity and peace and promised to put an end to the corruption in Vientiane. The "old guard" parties and the military combined to campaign as the Lao Ruam Lao (Laotian Peoples Rally). In what was to become a typical American reaction to problematic situations in Laos, Ambassador Parsons reached for the U.S. bankbook. As a result, the United States spent $3 million on "Operation Booster Shot," designed to increase the popularity of the government by flooding rural Laos with goodies. But such a sudden injection of funds was more likely to cause an inflationary embolism and could not make up for the mismanagement of American economic aid that had preceded this election and was to continue far into the future. For example, of $480.7 million granted to Laos in the fiscal years 1955–1963, only $1.9 million was spent on agricultural improvement.[25] Corruption and misuse of funds aided the recruiting appeal of the Pathet Lao in the countryside. As for Operation Booster Shot, Bernard Fall reports that this super plan backfired when the NLHX pointed to the merchandise and told the peasants, "This is what you've been deprived of for so long."[26]

---

23. House of Representatives Committee on Government Operations, "United States Aid Operations in Laos: Hearings March 11–June 1, 1959." (Washington, D.C.: Government Printing Office, 1959), p. 195.

24. Fall, *op. cit.,* p. 82.

25. Dommen, *op. cit.,* p. 107.

26. Fall, *op. cit.,* p. 85; Dommen, *op. cit.,* p. 109.

When the final vote was counted, the NLHX had won a startling 9 out of 21 contested seats. The victory created no immediate threat to the royalists since the Pathet Lao and their allies controlled only 13 of 59 Assembly seats, but many pro-Westerners were jittery. A short time after the elections, Souvanna Phouma called for adjournment of the ICC (International Control Commission), since Laos had "fully accomplished" the pledges made at Geneva to hold elections. On July 20, 1958, despite the protests of the Polish delegate, the ICC adjourned *sine die*.[27]

The United States registered its displeasure with the election results in two ways. The CIA backed the Laotian right wing in forming the Committee for the Defense of National Interests (CDNI) in June.[28] This Committee, no more than a U.S.-front organization, served as Colonel Phoumi Nosavan's ladder to the rank of general and the fortune which accompanies this position in Laos. The CIA was to remain loyal to their protégé even after a change of administrations. The CIA's John Hazey, adviser and personal adherent of Phoumi, was only withdrawn in February 1962, at the urging of Ambassador Harriman, who was trying to force Phoumi to the negotiating table.[29] Then the United States withheld aid payments to the Royal Government —a hard blow to an economy whose other major sources of income were opium exports and smuggled gold. On July 23 Souvanna lost a vote of confidence and resigned.

With CDNI support Phoui Sananikone built a new government in August 1958, adding four CDNI members and excluding the two Pathet Lao ministers who had had positions in the Government of National Union. Phoui developed his own special kind of neutrality, one which "does not imply a neutrality on the ideological plane: We are anti-communists."[30] The government shifted further to the right with the addition of Colonel

27. Randle, *op. cit.*, p. 523.
28. Hilsman, *op. cit.*, p. 115.
29. David Wise and Thomas B. Ross, *The Invisible Government* (New York: Random House, 1964), p. 153.
30. A. M. Halpern and H. B. Fredman, "Communist Strategy in Laos." Memorandum prepared by the RAND Corporation, June 14, 1960.

Phoumi Nosavan and two other army officers in January 1959. That same month Phoui Sananikone obtained permission to rule for one year without a National Assembly. He immediately declared that he was searching for methods to dismember the NLHX, but although several deputies left town, Prince Souphanouvong remained in Vientiane.[31]

A month later Phoui Sananikone renounced the section of the Geneva Accords which restricted the amount of foreign military aid that Laos could receive, thus opening the door to increased American aid. The U.S. State Department supported Phoui's statement and responded by setting up a training section in the PEO, despite protests from the Soviet Union that the United States was inciting the Laotian government to violate the Geneva Accords.[32]

In April Phoui began a concerted effort to destroy completely the NLHX and by mid-May moved to forcibly integrate the two Pathet Lao provinces into the domain of the Royal Laotian Government. The crisis peaked in May after Phoui issued an ultimatum to the two Pathet Lao battalions to integrate with the RLA immediately. The First Battalion complied, but the crack Second Battalion sifted through an RLA cordon and fled, taking their families and belongings into North Vietnam. Key NLHX leaders including Prince Souphanouvong were placed under house arrest in Vientiane.

The coalition Government of National Union was dead, and civil war was imminent. In July the Pathet Lao forces counterattacked, and war once again came to Laos. Two RAND analysts conclude the following about the total breakdown of the coalition government that provoked civil war:

In retrospect it is apparent that the Sananikone government precipitated the final crisis that led to war in Laos; it is also apparent that while the Sananikone government knew, at the time, that it was running a serious risk of open conflict with the NLHX and its mentors in

31. Hilsman, *op. cit.*, p. 120.
32. Toye, *op. cit.*, p. 124.

Hanoi, the pattern of Communist behavior up through mid-May had not been sufficiently belligerent to deter it. To each of the successive crises the Communist replies had been primarily verbal.[33]

Correct as far as it goes, the government-financed study quoted above overlooks the American role in the collapse of the Laotian coalition. The American ambassador had openly labored against the coalition; the U.S. cutoff of economic aid had brought about the fall of Souvanna Phouma's government and cleared the way for Phoui Sananikone; the CIA underwriting for the CDNI had given Phoui at least a temporary base of support; and the State Department seems to have been instrumental in Phoui's renunciation of the Geneva Accords. These American activities grew out of the refusal to accept any political solution in Laos that suggested Communist participation or influence. Through this intransigence in the political sphere, the United States severely limited its options and started down the muddy trail of military solutions for the problems of Indochina.

Although China and North Vietnam were troubled by the events occurring along their borders, neither of these powers desired a collision with the United States.[34] Still, the specter of Communist aggression was created by the distortions of the Laotian government and irresponsible journalism in the American press. According to the newspapers and reports from the Royal Laotian Government in the summer of 1959, Chinese troops were massing on the frontier and Viet Minh troops were swarming over Laos, an assessment which the State Department accepted completely.[35] By mid-September the fighting had reached a stalemate, and a UN fact-finding committee sent to Laos did nothing to clear up the situation. The United States had taken the opportunity to send an additional hundred military advisers to the PEO, pumped the RLA up to 29,000 men, and increased military aid by 30 per cent over the 1958 figure.[36]

33. Halpern and Fredman, *op. cit.* p. 51.
34. *Ibid.*, p. 38.
35. Fall, *op. cit.*, pp. 137–140; Dommen, *op. cit.*, p. 123.
36. Toye, *op. cit.*, p. 129.

COUP AFTER COUP

Internal power struggles continued in Vientiane. The CDNI began exerting pressures on Phoui to launch an all-out effort to destroy the Pathet Lao, but Phoui was reluctant to drive the country deeper into civil war. In December 1959 Phoui decided to dismiss the all-too-influential CDNI ministers. But the Americans were unwilling to accept any turn toward moderation in Laos, and the PEO and CIA advised Phoumi Nosavan (now a general) to stage a coup, which he dutifully did.[37] No attempt was even made to hide the fraudulent nature of the elections that were staged by Phoumi in April 1960. Setting the precedent for later "free elections" in South Vietnam, Phoumi and his advisers set up rigorous qualifications for candidates and gerrymandered districts in order to circumscribe any NLHX gains.[38]

Angered at the sight of the American colonization of Laos, the diminutive nationalistic paratrooper Captain Kong Le drove Phoumi out of office in August. Kong Le announced the aims of his coup: to bring an end to the civil war; to remove foreign troops from Laos; and to suppress those who were "making their harvest off the backs of the people."[39] Following Kong Le's seizure of power the king appointed Souvanna Phouma as prime minister and hoped to avoid renewed fighting by allowing General Phoumi Nosavan to hold the portfolios of both deputy prime minister and minister of the interior.

The next episode is a perfect example of the crosscurrents in American policy toward Laos. Winthrop G. Brown, the new U.S. ambassador to Laos, supported Souvanna Phouma, while the former ambassador, J. Graham Parsons, now the assistant secretary of state for Far Eastern affairs, used his new position to favor his old Laotian friend General Phoumi Nosavan. The Pentagon maintained their support of Phoumi, and the CIA

37. Roger Smith, in *Asian Survey* (January 1963); Dommen, *op. cit.*, pp. 127–128.
38. Dommen, *op. cit.*, p. 129.
39. Quoted in Toye, *op. cit.*, p. 141.

used their own private air corps—Air America—to give Phoumi's troops a military supply system.[40]

In September, operating from his base at Savannakhet in southern Laos, Phoumi formed a "Revolutionary Committee" chaired by Prince Boun Oum, a venerated leader from the south. Shortly after this move, Marshal Sarit Thanaret, the prime minister of Thailand and a relative of General Phoumi, placed a Thai blockade on goods flowing to Souvanna Phouma's government. The United States resorted to its favorite tactic of applying pressure on troublesome Laotian governments and suspended the Royal Government's monthly payment on October 7.[41]

Parsons flew to Vientiane on October 12 to try to persuade Souvanna to break off the new round of negotiations with the Pathet Lao, but had no success. However, thanks to the intercession by Ambassador Brown, a compromise was offered Souvanna Phouma. Aid would be resumed if Souvanna would allow the United States to continue providing General Phoumi with military assistance. In return Phoumi promised to send his forces only against the Pathet Lao. Souvanna agreed, only to be ousted by Phoumi two months later.[42]

Kong Le's neutralist troops, who had fully supported Souvanna Phouma, now joined forces with the Pathet Lao and quickly captured the Plain of Jars. A new chapter in the civil war had begun.

At this juncture the Eisenhower-Dulles scenario, which in 1954 had mapped Laos out as a battleground between the forces of Communism (i.e., the USSR) and the forces of the Free World (i.e., the USA), had come closer to reality. In December, following the precedent set by the United States, the Soviet Union began supplying one of the Laotian belligerents —Kong Le. In fact the Soviet Union had reacted with restraint to the blatant intervention which the United States had been conducting in Laos for years. The world could only regard the

40. Dommen, *op. cit.*, p. 154.
41. Hilsman, p. 125.
42. Dommen, p. 159; Hilsman, p. 124.

Americans as being naïve, foolish, or utterly devious when it read this bland State Department pronouncement on January 7, 1961:

> The Lao nation is entitled to an opportunity which it has never had since its birth to develop in an atmosphere of peace and tranquillity, with an assurance that its national efforts will not be thwarted by predatory threats from without. The history of its struggles to date reveals the incontrovertible fact that there never has been any threat to the security of Laos but that which has come from its Communist neighbors. These efforts to undermine its national integrity have been insidious and constant.

> The United States on its part has contributed considerable wealth and effort to help this new nation develop its economy and its social and political institutions. It is recognized that this effort is of little avail if the nation does not have the capability of protecting itself from attacks from without and the maintenance of security against disruptive influences from within. In the spirit of the Geneva Agreement which ended the war in Laos in 1954, and with the full cooperation and at the request of all successive governments, the United States has worked toward these objectives.[43]

43. "State Department Statement, January 7, 1961." *Department of State Bulletin,* January 23, 1961, p. 117.

10

The Nam Tha Crisis: Kennedy and the New Frontier on the Brink

Jonathan Mirsky and Stephen E. Stonefield

When he came to the presidency in January 1961, John F. Kennedy faced a dangerous situation created largely by the United States: a Laos divided into ardent right and left wings with a vacuum in the center caused by the deliberate American eradication of a genuine neutral alternative. Washington had deliberately linked itself, not once but twice, to an illegitimate rightist government bolstered by an unresponsive army.

On August 9, 1960, twenty-six-year-old paratroop captain Kong Le staged a coup in Vientiane. Maintaining that "Lao must stop killing Lao," he asserted that in fighting against the Pathet Lao his troops had never encountered a North Vietnamese or Chinese. By his coup Kong Le drew attention to the central factor in Laotian politics: there existed in Laos a genuine struggle between competing groups, with only Souvanna Phouma, who was recognized by all sides, holding the political framework together. By mid-August, in response to Kong Le's demands, the National Assembly passed a unanimous vote of no confidence against the CIA-supported regime dominated by General Phoumi Nosavan. Phoumi moved his headquarters back to his home base in Savannakhet while Souvanna Phouma was once again installed in Vientiane as prime minister.

Alliances were forming, with Phoumi and the generals on one side, while the Pathet Lao looked to Souvanna with whom they had signed a cease-fire on September 7.

For its part, the Bureau of Far Eastern Affairs in Washington considered Kong Le a probable Communist and looked with dubiety on the

This is a revised version of the authors' article appearing in *America's Asia*, Mark Selden and Edward Friedman, eds., to be published by Pantheon Books, a division of Random House, Inc. Copyright © 1970 by Random House, Inc.

neutralist solution. Nowhere was the pure Dulles doctrine taken more literally than in this bureau. . . . (The Director) in 1959 was J. Graham Parsons who (as ambassador) had been applying those principles so faithfully in Laos. . . . As for the Defense Department it was all for Phoumi.[1]

As Kennedy's policy planners analyzed it, the geographic significance of Laos lay in the fact that it provided one of the four "roads" from China through Southeast Asia.[2] United States policy was to continue to concern itself with the containment of China. The Laos situation, indeed, presents in microcosm the basic continuity of policy from Eisenhower to Kennedy, from Dulles to Rusk. Although Kennedy would occasionally complain to his friends that he had been saddled with the Indochinese involvement, ex-Assistant Secretary of the Air Force Townsend Hoopes' opening passages in *The Limits of Intervention* make plain that the new president's preoccupation with "stopping China" did not differ from those of his predecessors.[3] Kennedy's policy, too, was grounded on "the implicit assumption that henceforth Washington would be predisposed to view an effort to overthrow the existing order anywhere as a national-liberation war fomented by and for the benefit of Russia or China."[4] In accusing the Russians and Chinese of interfering in Laos during the Eisenhower years, Kennedy lied. In his increasing conviction that "insurgency" had taken the place of the Russian "threat," he led the way for years of American *counterrevolutionary* activity ranging from B–52 raids against "guerrilla strongholds" to the assassination of key individuals or "neutralization" (as it is called by the creators of the Phoenix program of counterterror in southern Vietnam). Kennedy's celebrated "grace" should not disguise his leadership in the continuum of cold-war politics and practices.

One-time White House aide Arthur Schlesinger, who expends

1. Arthur M. Schlesinger, Jr., *A Thousand Days* (Boston: Houghton Mifflin, 1967), p. 305.
2. Roger Hilsman, *To Move a Nation* (Garden City, N.Y.: Doubleday, 1967), pp. 93–94, 129, 134; A. J. Dommen, *Conflict in Laos* (New York: Praeger, 1967), p. 202.
3. Townsend Hoopes, *The Limits of Intervention* (New York: McKay, 1969), pp. 7–24.
4. *Ibid.*, p. 15.

considerable effort to present Kennedy's "clear historical view of Laos," quotes the new president as saying that Laos was not a land "worthy of engaging the attention of the great powers." Nonetheless, although Kennedy remained convinced of the importance of Laotian neutrality,

> he knew that the matter was not that simple any longer. The effort had been made, American prestige was deeply involved, and extrication would not be easy . . . it was essential to convince the Pathet Lao that they could not win and to dissuade the Russians from further military assistance.[5]

Schlesinger's analysis contains much unintended irony. His own description of the Eisenhower period makes plain the role of the United States in provoking the Pathet Lao and the Russians, both of whom had been willing to recognize the neutralist government overthrown by Washington in 1960.[6]

During the last months of the Eisenhower period the Pentagon and CIA continued to build up Phoumi Nosavan by supplying aid directly to all Royal Laotian Army units, except those of Kong Le.

> Souvanna could be supported, as head of the legally constituted government of Laos, but at the same time it would be United States policy to attempt to persuade him to abandon his policy of "true" neutralism and the effort to form a government of national union and to adopt instead the pro-Western neutralism so long advocated by . . . the United States.[7]

In the last few months of the Eisenhower administration the Department of Defense and Assistant Secretary of State J. Graham Parsons advised the White House that the best way to maintain America's position in Laos was to seek a military solution by backing General Phoumi Nosavan. Although the American embassy in Vientiane urged full support for Souvanna, on

5. Schlesinger, *op. cit.*, pp. 307–308.
6. Hilsman, *op. cit.*, p. 131, supports the interventionist line: "The United States had to be fully determined to intervene if it became necessary. This in turn meant that . . . our determination had to be backed with concrete movements of troops." Hilsman writes as if U.S. policy up to 1961 had been "hands off Laos."
7. Hilsman, *op. cit.*, p. 123.

October 7, 1960, Washington ignored this advice and suspended economic aid to Vientiane while it continued its military aid to General Phoumi in Savannakhet. Five days later Parsons arrived in Laos to offer Souvanna a bargain: resumption of aid in exchange for a compromise. Souvanna should end his negotiations with the Pathet Lao, deal with Phoumi, and move his capital to Luang Prabang, where, as Arthur Dommen noted, "Washington felt that the King would exert a conservative influence on the government."[8]

Souvanna considered all Parsons' points unacceptable, pointing out that continued American aid to Phoumi undercut the authority of the very government Washington purported to recognize. In December 1960 Russian planes began to deliver military equipment and oil to the Royal Laotian Government. But by December 9 Souvanna had fled in despair to Cambodia, where he issued an angry statement: "What I shall never forgive the United States for is the fact that it betrayed me . . . the Assistant Secretary of State (Parsons) is the most nefarious and reprehensible of men. . . . He and others like him are responsible for the recent shedding of Lao blood."[9]

With Souvanna Phouma's unifying presence gone from the scene, General Phoumi moved up the east bank of the Mekong from Savannakhet to Vientiane and on December 31, 1960, drove Kong Le's forces out of the city. Kong Le retreated to the Plain of Jars, where he established his command headquarters and began a tenuous political alliance with the Pathet Lao, who were also in the area. The Soviets transferred their airlift to the Plain of Jars and gave Kong Le the logistics, munitions, and material support they had earlier given Souvanna Phouma.

FAILURE AND ESCALATION

Soon after assuming office in early January 1961, President Kennedy dispatched American AT–6 Harvard trainer aircraft outfitted as fighter bombers in the wake of false reports of Viet

8. Dommen, *op. cit.*, p. 159.
9. *New York Times,* January 20, 1961.

Minh aggression.[10] However, his decision at the same time to replace PEO (Program Evaluation Office) officers with 400 Special Forces personnel (White Star Mobile Training Teams) from Okinawa was more important in terms of escalating the conflict. This decision is an early application of the counterinsurgency theories propounded by Roger Hilsman and others who hold that by using Mao Tse-tung's *techniques* either side in a civil war should be able to win.[11] As in Vietnam in 1961, the impending embarrassment of a weak ally's defeat provoked in Washington a drive to enlarge the struggle and forsake the possibility of a political solution.

In their histories of the Kennedy administration, Arthur Schlesinger and the former assistant secretary of state for Far Eastern affairs, Roger Hilsman, present a picture of a frantic administration badly informed, desperate to achieve success—or at least to avoid failure—and buffeted by conflicting advice.[12] Although at his first press conference in early 1961 President Kennedy declared that Laos should be free of great power intervention, he took heart from CIA reports in February that Phoumi would soon drive Kong Le and the Pathet Lao from the Plain of Jars. When this drive failed, the president decided to accept Ambassador Brown's more favorable evaluation of Souvanna Phouma. But Souvanna's recent trips from Cambodia to Hanoi, Peking, and Moscow, seeking assurances for his legitimate claims to authority, confirmed long-held views in Washington. "The State Department, having driven him to the Communists, now flourished his itinerary as proof of his perfidy."[13] Souvanna in fact was desperately continuing his search for support of a neutralist regime.

Both the Americans and the Russians were by now deeply engaged. The State Department composed a statement for the Lao king proclaiming a policy of nonalignment and calling for guarantees of Laotian integrity from his neighbors. At the same

10. *New York Times*, January 13, 1961; for the false reports see *New York Times*, January 27, 1961.
11. Hilsman, *op. cit.*, p. 413 ff.
12. Schlesinger, *op. cit.*, p. 307 ff.; Hilsman, *op. cit.*, pp. 127 ff.
13. Schlesinger, *op. cit.*, p. 308.

time the Soviet deputy foreign minister assured Averell Harriman that not since the Bolshevik Revolution had Moscow attached such importance to a foreign operation.[14] Moscow, seeing Washington's determination to upset neutralism in Laos, had become determined to prevent a decisive shift to the right.

In late February and March 1961 the Pentagon, frustrated by the dismal performances of the Royal Laotian Army, put forward bold schemes for landing a division of marines on the Plain of Jars ("We can get them in all right," said General Lemnitzer. "It's getting them out that worries me.") or sending up to sixty thousand troops into the area south of Vientiane, to hold the lower Mekong. These plans were ultimately dismissed as unfeasible and because they were too "limited."[15] This new caution stemmed in part, as we shall see, from the Bay of Pigs fiasco.

Kennedy, although questioning "why we have to be more royalist than the king," remained determined to avoid "any visible humiliation over Laos."[16] His oldest British friend, David Ormsby-Gore, cautioned him in February that "the United States . . . had done its best to destroy Souvanna Phouma, who represented the best hope of a non-Communist Laos, and instead was backing a crooked, right-wing gang; the impression of Washington always rushing about to prop up corrupt dictators in Asia could not have happy consequences."[17] Nonetheless, on March 23, 1961, Kennedy told a press conference that peace was dependent on a "cessation of the present armed attacks by externally supported Communists," and that "the security of all of Southeast Asia will be endangered if Laos loses its neutral independence."[18]

In Washington the President saw [Soviet diplomat] Gromyko at the Rose Garden [in March], took him to a bench in the Rose Garden, and observing that too many wars had arisen from miscalculation said that Moscow must not misjudge the American determination to stop aggression in Southeast Asia.[19]

14. *Ibid.*, p. 309.
15. Hilsman, *op. cit.*, p. 128.
16. Schlesinger, *op. cit.*, p. 310.
17. *Ibid.*, p. 313.
18. *New York Times*, March 23, 1961.
19. Schlesinger, *op. cit.*, p. 312.

What Kennedy could never grasp was that the United States was playing the aggressive role. American policy makers, then as now, habitually used American "defensive" rhetoric to disguise intervention. (For Chinese relations with Laos at this time see the appendix at the end of this article.)

ESCALATION

On March 29, 1961, Averell Harriman, who earlier than most Americans saw the need for a negotiated settlement, reported to Kennedy that the optimum plan would be to give at least conditional support to Souvanna Phouma. He argued that the best settlement for Laos was neutralization by international agreement, guaranteed by both the West and the Soviet Union.[20]

But Kennedy's strategy was to combine the Pentagon's force with Harriman's conciliation. In March he decided to alert the Seventh Fleet and to send five hundred additional troops to northeast Thailand, 35 miles from Vientiane, while at the same time he endorsed a British proposal for negotiations.[21] It was becoming evident that negotiations would have to take place, because French opposition to U.S. policy in Laos had resulted in SEATO's refusal to back a multinational intervention.[22]

By the middle of April 1961, Kennedy had undergone the Cuban humiliation. Fearful that the Russians (and the American voters) might judge him weak in yet another crisis, he instructed American advisers to wear uniforms in the field with the Royal Laotian Army (a symbolic change in policy) and sanctioned a substantial increase in troop movements in Laos. Both Hilsman and Schlesinger make plain the president's reason for escalating United States' activities in Laos: his failure at the Bay of Pigs, which he feared would make him appear irresolute. However, Kennedy grew increasingly aware of the dangers of the Pentagon, which after its initial reluctance seemed even prepared to

---

20. Schlesinger, *op. cit.*, p. 313; Dommen, *op. cit.*, p. 204.
21. Schlesinger, *op. cit.*, pp. 311–312; Dommen, *op. cit.*, p. 192.
22. Schlesinger, *op. cit.*, p. 312.

land thousands of troops with no certainty of their safety thereafter. For the military, afraid of the "no-win" potentialities of counterinsurgency, even nuclear intervention appeared attractive. At a National Security Council meeting in April 1961, General Lemnitzer stated: "If we are given the right to use nuclear weapons, we can guarantee victory." Kennedy's later judgment on this advice was that "since he couldn't think of any further escalation, he would have to promise us victory."[23] Despite what Hilsman refers to as "nicely balanced political and military moves on Laos," the fact remains that from the standpoint of success, Kennedy—again in Hilsman's words—"could hardly win."[24] And Richard Nixon remembers President Kennedy as saying, "I don't see how we can make any move in Laos, which is 5000 miles away, if we don't make a move in Cuba, which is only 90 miles away."[25]

What Kennedy feared—especially after Cuba—was humiliation and *loss*. In May, while preparing to send 10,000 marines to the Laotian theater, Kennedy recalled the French debacle at Dien Bien Phu: "I can't take a 1954 defeat today," he then told an aide. He therefore told Khrushchev in Vienna that "the (Laos) commitments had been made before he became President, why they were undertaken was not an issue here." At this conference Kennedy revealed the shallowness of his own concern for new foreign policy directions and the depth of his determination to avoid admissions of error. At his best Kennedy could recognize miscalculation—in Cuba or in Laos—but he remained obdurately committed to the broad policy directions laid down by his predecessors.

THE ROAD TO GENEVA: 1961–1962

In a speech at the United Nations in September 1960, Prince Sihanouk proposed that Laos and Cambodia should form a guaranteed neutral zone to safeguard themselves from foreign inter-

23. *Ibid.*, p. 312.
24. Hilsman, *op. cit.*, p. 134.
25. Quoted in Schlesinger, *op. cit.*, p. 314ff, from *Reader's Digest*, November 1964; Hilsman, *op. cit.*, p. 134.

ference. Souvanna Phouma concurred with this proposal.[26] On
December 15 Nehru suggested to Britain and the Soviet Union
that the International Control Commission (ICC) should be
reactivated in view of the renewed fighting after Kong Le's coup
and the great amount of foreign intervention.[27] Seven days later,
the Soviet Union in response proposed a reconvening of the 1954
Geneva Conference[28] but gained no support from the Western
powers. New Year's Day 1961 brought another appeal by Prince
Sihanouk for a conference on Laos to be attended by the original
Geneva members, the ICC nations (Canada, Poland, India),
Thailand, and Burma.[29] Finally, on April 24, 1961, Britain and
the Soviet Union called for a cease-fire and subsequent conference to settle the Laotian problem.

Geneva Convenes

By May 3, 1961, all three parties—Phoumi, Souvanna, and
Souphanouvong—had subscribed to the cease-fire, and eight days
later the newly reactivated ICC confirmed the armistice.[30] With
the guns silent, on May 16, 1961, the conference convened. The
idea of partitioning Laos according to the Vietnamese model

26. S. Simmonds, "Independence and Political Rivalry in Laos, 1945–
1961," in Saul Rose (ed.), *Politics in Southern Asia* (London, 1963), p. 191.

27. Documents Relating to British Involvement in the Indo-China Conflict, 1945–1965, Command Paper (CMND.) 2834, pp. 26, 154–155.

28. *International Conference on the Settlement of the Laotian Question,*
May 12, 1961–July 3, 1962, CMND. 1828, pp. 3 ff.

29. *Ibid.,* CMND. 1828, p. 4.

30. For the importance of a cease-fire before the conference could get
under way, see Arthur Lall, *How Communist China Negotiates* (New York:
Columbia University Press, 1968), esp. p. 47. Lall points out, p. 48, that
accepting a cease-fire, and abandoning the demand that the U.S. and Thailand withdraw from Laos as a precondition for talks, constituted an important
concession by Peking. Lee Chae Jin feels, however, that going to Geneva
constituted a net gain for Peking and that Peking knew this to be so. Indeed,
Lee states, it was the U.S. which had much to lose: (1) The conference
might result in recognition of the Pathet Lao; (2) Chinese participation
would enhance China's international prestige; (3) Negotiations in Laos might
lead to a settlement in South Vietnam. Lee, *Chinese Communist Policy in
Laos: 1954–1965* (University Microfilms, 1967), pp. 165 ff. As will be seen
below, however, the Chinese seemed positively in favor of a neutral Laos,
even at the possible expense of the Pathet Lao.

was never considered, because of the existence of a middle faction in the Laotian dispute (absent in the 1954 Vietnamese situation), and the general desire for a neutral coalition government.[31] During the Geneva Conference, on June 3 and 4, John F. Kennedy and Nikita Khrushchev met in Vienna. In what was otherwise a thoroughly unpleasant and acrimonious series of exchanges, both men agreed on the importance of a neutral Laos.[32]

LAOS DURING THE GENEVA CONFERENCE (1961)

Although the disagreements between Laotian factions in the summer of 1961 were confined primarily to the political arena, on June 6 Kong Le led neutralist forces against Meo tribesmen who, having been built up by Phoumi Nosavan and the CIA, were supplied entirely by air. The Meo were accompanied by American advisers; Kong Le considered the presence of such hostile forces in his area, together with supply flights over his positions, to be provocative.[33] American supply flights and Special Forces teams helped destroy the cease-fire.

A situation of this sort might have been foreseen: on May 20 the ICC had described the fragility of the cease-fire. What constituted a provocation, the report stated, seemed difficult to determine, but it added that flights over the territory of an opposition group were always regarded as hostile acts.[34] On June 6, 1961, Kong Le routed the Meo, causing a five-day suspension of the Geneva talks. Continued outbreaks of military activity in Laos were to plague the conference to the end.

The seating of a Laotian delegation at Geneva created immediate difficulties when the three factions could reach no agreement on coalition formulas. It was finally agreed that until a coalition government was formed representatives from Laos

31. George Modelski, *SEATO: Six Studies* (Melbourne, 1962), p. 21; for a general diplomatic "appreciation" of Geneva see Arthur Lall's study cited in footnote 30, *passim.*

32. Schlesinger, *op. cit.,* p. 340; Hilsman, *op. cit.,* p. 136.

33. Hugh Toye, *Laos: Buffer State or Battleground* (London: Oxford University Press, 1968), p. 177.

34. Modelski, *op. cit.,* p. 61.

would be seated if sponsored by other powers.[35] The Phoumi-backed government under its premier, Boun Oum, refused to participate when the Soviet Union sponsored a delegation headed by Souvanna Phouma and his chief aide Quinim Pholsena, while China supported Souphanouvong and a member of the Neo Lao Hak Xat (Pathet Lao political body) Central Committee, Phoumi Vongvichit. After the three princes, Boun Oum, Souvanna, and Souphanouvong, met in June at Zurich in a futile attempt to resolve their differences, Vientiane sent as representatives Phoui Sananikone and Pheng Norindr.[36]

WASHINGTON

President Kennedy, increasingly disillusioned with Phoumi and relying on Harriman's recommendations, looked to Souvanna Phouma to act as a "third force." Souvanna, who was also favored by the Soviet Union and supported by Peking, had not spurned the West.[37] Dean Rusk, addressing the Geneva delegations on May 17, 1961, outlined the American position.[38] To ensure a "genuinely neutral Laos," he maintained, three main points demanded settlement.

First, the conference needed to draw up an acceptable definition of neutralism—"more than mere nonalignment"—while also insisting on the withdrawal of all foreign military personnel and "free choice" for the Laotians. This position amounted to Washington's definition of "neutralism." Schlesinger attempts to contrast the Dulles view with Kennedy's: "Thus, where Dulles saw neutralism as immoral, Kennedy felt that the new states . . . were naturally . . . indifferent to the 'moral issues' in the cold war. . . ." The new president, however, did not share this indifference. "He felt . . . that the third world had now become

35. Modelski, *op. cit.*, p. 15; Lall, *op. cit.*, states, p. 56: "Privately, all delegations were agreed that it was necessary to have all three Laotian wings represented at the Conference table."

36. Modelski, *op. cit.*, p. 15.

37. Toye, *op. cit.*, p. 176; Schlesinger, *op. cit.*, p. 314, describes Kennedy's invitation to Souvanna; Secretary Rusk, by making himself unavailable, caused the visit to be canceled.

38. Text in Department of State *Bulletin*, No. 1145, June 5, 1961.

the critical battleground between democracy and communism."
What, then, did Kennedy offer the new nations? "By making
national independence the crucial question [he] invited the
neutrals to find common interest with us in resisting communist
expansion,"which he feared. It is clear, the New Frontier rhetoric
of Kennedy, Rusk, Hilsman, and Schlesinger envisioned neutralist
countries joining an American crusade to save the world from
communism, while Washington provided the muscle and money
and the neutrals looked on approvingly. A genuine independence
which also leaned to the left was as inconceivable to the graceful Kennedy circle as to the messianic Dulles. Schlesinger points
out that "the new policy brought clear gains. The Kennedy strategy ended the alliance between the neutralists and the Pathet
Lao," as they had intended. Secondly, Rusk advocated the creation of a strong ICC, with full access to all parts of Laos. This
constituted Washington's most substantive demand at the conference. Finally, Rusk called for an economic and technical aid
program "administered by neutral nations from the area."[39]

LAOS: ATTEMPTS TO UPSET THE CEASE-FIRE

On October 18, 1961, the king authorized Souvanna Phouma
to form a new government. His appointment followed the agreement reached by the three princes at Zurich on June 22, four
months earlier.[40] General Phoumi Nosavan, increasingly sensitive to growing disfavor in Washington, mounted a series of
probing actions into neutralist territory beginning in October.
And the agreement regarding Souvanna's new government
proved meaningless, for in December Phoumi Nosavan's representative Boun Oum twice withdrew his endorsement and
ultimately refused to participate in further formal discussions.[41]

39. Schlesinger, *op. cit.,* pp. 468–469, 478. Rusk's position seems similar
to that of Peking delegate Ch'en Yi. While Washington and Peking insisted
on neutrality, there is little evidence to support the American claim.

40. Text of the Zurich Agreement in *International Conference on the
Settlement of the Laos Question,* May 12, 1961–July 23, 1962, CMND. 1828,
pp. 13–14.

41. Toye, *op. cit.,* p. 175.

By January of 1962 Phoumi's military drive had collapsed.[42] His tactics were designed, however, not to win ground but to tear apart the fragile cease-fire, upset the Geneva discussions, and force the hand of the United States.[43] In these actions he was almost certainly encouraged by the CIA.[44] Hilsman describes American policy at this time as "properly ambiguous. . . . If it was Phoumi . . . who broke the cease-fire, the United States would probably intervene." Yet it was American assistance which afforded Phoumi his power.[45] Phoumi's star began to decline. Harriman had been to Laos, and by the end of 1961, Washington, which wanted reliable allies, began to apply the kind of economic pressure to the rightists it had hitherto used to destroy Souvanna Phouma.[46] In February 1962 United States economic aid to the Phoumi–Boun Oum government was stopped. Phoumi, desperate to retain his power, set up the old cry of Viet Minh aggression, charging that now Chinese and Russian troops were operating in Laos. As in the past, these reports proved false.[47] Washington, although not taken in by Phoumi's maneuvers, continued to send him military aid.[48]

Harriman's persuasion was reinforced by Phoumi's brother-in-law, Marshal Sarit of Thailand. Sarit, who had opposed efforts for a neutral coalition in Laos, had received assurances from Washington. In March 1962 Thai Foreign Minister Thanat Khoman conferred for a week with Dean Rusk about Laos and Thailand. On March 6 the two issued the now famous communiqué which significantly altered the official United States–SEATO commitment to Thailand: America promised to come

42. Bernard Fall, *Street Without Joy* (London, 1964), p. 338.

43. Oliver E. Clubb, *The United States and the Sino-Soviet Bloc in Southeast Asia* (Washington, D.C., 1962), p. 67; Hilsman, *op. cit.*, p. 137.

44. Hilsman, *op. cit.*, p. 137; and Roger Smith, in George McT. Kahin (ed.), *Governments and Politics of Southeast Asia* (Ithaca, N.Y.: Cornell University Press, 1964), p. 559, note 83. For an authoritative allegation of direct CIA involvement with Phoumi, see *The Times*, London, 24, 25, 31 May 1961; summarized in Toye, *op. cit.*, p. 184.

45. Hilsman, *op. cit.*, p. 137.

46. *Ibid.*, p. 139.

47. Toye, *op. cit.*, p. 180.

48. Smith, in Kahin, ed., *Governments and Politics of Southeast Asia, op. cit.*, p. 559, note 86.

to Thailand's aid in a case of "Communist aggression," without the "prior agreement" of other SEATO members. In other words, Washington pledged unilateral intervention in Thailand, an arrangement which guaranteed future American involvement in Thai affairs.[49]

Phoumi remained reluctant to join the coalition, even though Marshal Sarit, on March 24, in the presence of Harriman, recommended to Phoumi that he do so. At the same meeting Harriman cautioned Phoumi that the rightists were almost "finished in Laos." The meeting produced no tangible result.[50]

Hilsman and Schlesinger strive to show that Kennedy wanted a neutral solution, but it is clear that this awakening originated only from the forced recognition of the incapacity of the rightists, not through a genuine desire for an uncommitted Laos.[51] The unwillingness of Kennedy to cut loose from the right in Laos led inevitably to the near-catastrophe of Nam Tha.

NAM THA

During 1962 while the Geneva diplomats were drafting most of the conference resolutions, in Laos the rightists of Phoumi Nosavan prepared their final military effort. In the spring, Phoumi had concentrated more than 5,000 troops at the northwest city of Nam Tha, which lies in a mountain river valley 15 miles from China. He appeared to be using Nam Tha for a show of his own strength and as a test of Department of Defense and CIA commitment to him.[52] As Pathet Lao forces advanced in the direction of Nam Tha, taking over the Phoumist supply airstrip at Muong Sing, reports came from Laos charging that Chinese troops were aiding the Pathet Lao. Although United

49. Frank C. Darling, *The United States and Thailand* (Washington, D.C., 1965), p. 207, text in Department of State *Bulletin*, March 26, 1962.

50. Dommen, *op. cit.*, p. 216; Hilsman, *op. cit.*, pp. 140–141; Toye, *op. cit.*, pp. 181–182.

51. Max Frankel, *New York Times*, May 12, 1962.

52. Smith, in Kahin, ed., *Government and Politics of Southeast Asia, op. cit.*, p. 559, note 86.

States military sources at first confirmed these reports, State Department officials denied them.[53]

On May 6, 1962, Pathet Lao forces launched a limited offensive against Phoumi's Nam Tha garrison, forcing the rightists and the American Special Forces team to evacuate the post. Although "Colonel Edwin Elder, the commander of the Nam Tha MAAG [Military Assistance Advisory Group] detachment, immediately warned, with the coolness of the professional soldier, that there was 'no evidence that the Chinese or (North) Vietnamese had participated in the attack',"[54] rumors of foreign invasion spread.

The State Department immediately charged the Pathet Lao with violating the cease-fire; but Washington sources privately asserted that, even though Phoumi was warned by Washington that his aggressive buildup was dangerous, he had continued his maneuvers and then "provoked" the Nam Tha invasion.[55] Furthermore, the Pathet Lao had issued several warnings through Souvanna Phouma, stating that unless Phoumi's buildup stopped, they would counterattack.[56]

While the State Department charged cease-fire violation and on May 8 urged Moscow to restrain the Pathet Lao[57] (as if the Kremlin controlled the Laotian leftists), Phoumi's troops fled across the Mekong into Thailand. Secretary of Defense Robert McNamara, conferring with Thai leaders in Bangkok, heard from Defense Minister Thanom Kittikachorn that the fall of Nam Tha posed a threat to Thailand; Marshal Sarit assured McNamara, however, that Thailand possessed sufficient troops along the border to meet any emergency.[58]

In his May 9 news conference, President Kennedy stated the Pathet Lao action to be a "clear breach of the cease-fire." In the president's view there were two courses open to the United

53. *Washington Post,* May 6, 1962; *New York Times,* May 6 and May 8, 1962.
54. Fall, *op. cit.,* p. 339.
55. Frankel, *New York Times,* May 7, 1962; *Washington Post,* May 7, 1962.
56. *Ibid.*
57. *New York Times,* May 9, 1962.
58. *Washington Post,* May 9, 1962.

States: (1) successful negotiations; (2) military intervention. As he told reporters, "Let's not think there's some great third course."[59]

As Kennedy advisers met constantly, the situation in Laos became more chaotic. Fleeing Phoumist troops infected the garrison of Ban Houei Sai on the Thai border with such panic that "Ban Houei Sai was announced as having fallen into Communist hands at 0300 on May 11, 1962, *while in actual fact no organized enemy unit was within thirty miles of the town.*"[60] Max Frankel reported in the *New York Times,* "The United States has written off the Right-wing Laotian Army as useless against the pro-Communist forces and is therefore losing interest in supporting the army's leaders politically."[61] He further stated that Kennedy and State and Defense Department aides had concluded that only "the credibility of United States power" could help the West's bargaining position in Geneva.[62]

The "threat" which faced the Kennedy administration, then, was not the new "crisis" in Laos, but the possibility of diminished American influence in Southeast Asian affairs. Washington, still hoping to undermine a genuinely neutralist solution, translated Phoumi's provocation of the Pathet Lao at Nam Tha into a communist attack, "a large-scale probe, a major although still-limited violation of the cease-fire . . . [predicting] as they went up the ladder the pace of military encroachments (by the Communists) would accelerate toward a military take-over of the whole country."[63] The pattern of escalation following a marked failure emerged once more. Again a crisis developed in Laos, again the agents of the United States appeared chiefly responsible; and in the process, the Kennedy strategists eventually found an opportunity to further extend America's military commitment in Southeast Asia.

Although by now the *New York Times* and the *Washington*

59. *New York Times,* May 10, 1962.
60. Fall, *op cit.,* p. 339, italics in original; Dommen, *op. cit.,* p. 218, reports the same.
61. *New York Times,* May 12, 1962.
62. *Ibid.*
63. Hilsman, *op. cit.,* p. 141.

Post (to name only two) had made clear the manufactured nature of the Nam Tha "crisis," the administration split along "political" and "military" lines. Hilsman, who appears unaware to this day that no aggression had taken place, discusses the "political" thinking of the State Department:

What we needed was a package of moves that would signal to the Communists that if they continued on a military course, we would occupy the Mekong lowlands and the territory held by the Royal Lao Government up to the cease-fire line.[64]

America's intentions according to the "political advocates" should be indicated by ordering the Seventh Fleet to the Gulf of Siam and dispatching troops to Thailand. This view was presented to Kennedy before the National Security Council met on May 10, 1962. Hugh Toye, almost alone of all authorities, points out that the rightists had been successful:

Phoumi had worked for the Nam Tha and Ban Houei [Sai] fiasco, bizarre even by Laotian standards, because after the suspension of American aid, his only hope had been to lose a Mekong town and thus involve the West militarily on his side. . . . The West . . . was obliged to consider the effects in Siam of the abandonment of Ban Houei Sai, which is immediately across the Mekong from Siamese territory.[65]

Yet, although Thailand had not expressed public concern for its security,[66] Washington remained determined to use the situation in Laos to expand American military power into yet another Southeast Asian nation, and the war in Vietnam accelerated the pace by which other countries in the area were brought within the American sphere.

On the other hand, the "military" advocates at the Pentagon recommended (in addition to diplomatic maneuvers and moving the Seventh Fleet) American support for Phoumi and the use of military force either all out, *including nuclear attacks on China,* or not at all.[67] Ever since 1958 the Pentagon had ex-

64. *Ibid.,* p. 143.
65. Toye, *op. cit.,* p. 183.
66. *Washington Post,* May 9, 1962; *New York Times,* May 12, 1962.
67. Hilsman, *op. cit.,* pp. 142–147.

pressed its fear of bogging down in a limited action. This latter policy found support from former President Eisenhower, who advocated putting substantial numbers of American troops into Laos. What is noteworthy about the Eisenhower proposal is Kennedy's conviction that the former president's support would make it "easier to send troops at least to Thailand."[68] Kennedy ordered the Seventh Fleet to deploy in Southeast Asian waters, although Thailand had not publicly expressed concern for its security. Washington remained determined to use the situation in Laos to expand American military power into yet another Southeast Asian nation. The National Security Council met on May 12, 1962, with McNamara and General Lemnitzer, just returned from Thailand, present. Both supported troop movements, supplemented by communications and supply improvements in Thailand. Kennedy accepted this plan,[69] although he would later claim that the United States moved into Thailand "at the decision of the Thai government."[70]

Thereafter positions hardened. The dominant Defense Department view was an "all-or-nothing" formula, while the State Department tended to favor the "political" solution. Presidential adviser Walt Rostow advocated considering the bombing of North Vietnam.[71] McNamara, in meetings on May 13 and after, sided with the military view, asserting that if troops were used, they should occupy the panhandle of Laos all the way to North Vietnam. Unless the communists surrendered immediately, North Vietnam should be bombarded by land, sea, and air power. In the case of Chinese intervention, nuclear retaliation would probably be the American course.[72] It should be remembered that a public policy of cease-fire, negotiations, and neutrality underlay these apocalyptic projections.

The "political" view held that intervention which passed the cease-fire line would gather no international support, "Thus, the 'political' proposal came down to occupying the Mekong

68. *Ibid.*, pp. 144–145.
69. *Ibid.*, p. 145.
70. *New York Times,* May 18, 1962.
71. Hilsman, *op. cit.*, p. 146.
72. *Ibid.*, p. 147.

lowlands." The RAND Corporation drew up a logistical survey of the routes through Laos, which supported the "political" view. The chances of Chinese intervention, furthermore, seemed slimmest with this strategy. The "political" plan appeared sound in Washington for several reasons: most ethnic Lao lived in this agriculturally and commercially central region; the lowlands offered the most secure military position; and the United States could most easily defend Thailand from there.[73] Since Thailand was not under attack, these maneuverings underline the wider opportunities seen in the Nam Tha affair.

Hilsman's terms "political" and "military" provide an initial illusion of subtle manipulation versus heavy-handed intervention. Actually, both schemes called for an American military commitment greater than at any time since Korea. Hilsman's position at first seems realistic: "The real issue is whether there is to be an accommodation . . . between the Communist and especially the Chinese Communist world and the non-Communist world or a final showdown in which only one emerges dominant." But Hilsman then reveals his own willingness to consider seriously the second alternative: "A final showdown would present a test of will and require a grim determination in picking the time and the place."[74]

By now it was at least doubtful whether there was a crisis anywhere but in Washington.[75] Vital to an understanding of policy formulation is Hilsman's own summation of this course of action: "What the United States would do if the Chinese Communists intervened was not spelled out, but the general impression was that the recommendation would be to retaliate on the mainland with nuclear weapons."[76] This line of thought arose from the liberal Kennedy administration—a Dulles-Rusk continuum—exhibiting determination to continue American intervention in Southeast Asia; for Laos had by now become linked to the increasing United States counterinsurgency effort in South

73. *Ibid.*, pp. 147–149.
74. *Ibid.*, p. 149.
75. James C. Thomson points out in *Atlantic* (April 1968), the self-generating aspects of a "crisis" once it has been officially proclaimed.
76. Hilsman, *op. cit.*, p. 147.

Vietnam and to the establishment of American influence in Thailand. To protect these interests, the United States almost initiated a nuclear war. What emerges from the Hilsman and Schlesinger accounts of the events surrounding Nam Tha is that there was *no evidence at all* of Vietnamese or Chinese involvement; nonetheless, the National Security Council, whose members should have known of Colonel Elder's report or read the *New York Times* or *Washington Post,* acted as if an international communist force were threatening Thailand. Vietnamese and Chinese specters were used continuously in the Laos "crisis" to justify American intrusion.

The Seventh Fleet moved to action stations on May 12, 1962. A few days later 1,000 U.S. Marines on SEATO maneuvers in Thailand proceeded toward the Lao border; on May 15 Washington announced the dispatch of 4,000 more troops to Thailand. By May 16 the first detachment arrived in Bangkok, to be followed by small groups from Great Britain, Australia, and France. Although President Kennedy declared the troop movements were intended "to help insure the territorial integrity of this peaceful country," (justifying the intervention on the basis of the SEATO treaty, the Rusk-Khoman agreement, and the UN Charter), not only was Thailand in no danger, but Bangkok never requested American troops! General Paul Harkins, the American military commander in South Vietnam, met secretly with Marshal Sarit to persuade him to agree to the American deployment; on May 13 Washington still awaited Thai approval.[77]

By means, then, of the March 6 agreement of 1962, which permitted unilateral United States action, and the spurious Nam Tha "crisis," Washington managed to position its first official combat troops on the mainland of Southeast Asia. The day of the landing in Thailand, Secretary McNamara announced the creation of a new United States Military Assistance Command—Thailand—to be headed by General Harkins, who retained his post as commander in Vietnam. In the words of Deputy Defense Secretary Roswell Gilpatric, the establishment of this new foot-

77. *Washington Post,* May 14, 1962.

hold in Asia was "not just a show, not just a demonstration of force." Within a week it became evident that, regardless of events in Laos, American combat troops—including some of the United States' best counterguerrilla units—were in Thailand to stay.

By May 16 the Chinese had announced that the American deployment threatened their borders and endangered the Geneva talks.[78] But the "crisis" was over. On May 25 Premier Khrushchev again declared his support of neutralism, while on the same day Souvanna Phouma reported from Paris his agreement to participate in new negotiations. With no evidence remaining that the Pathet Lao intended to invade Thailand or break up the Geneva negotiations, from June 7 to June 12 Boun Oum, Souvanna Phouma, and Souphanouvong conferred on the Plain of Jars, finally agreeing on a new government including Phoumi and Souphanouvong as vice-premiers.[79] But a settlement in Vientiane had been delayed while the world teetered on the edge of the atomic brink, and America hammered another link into its chain surrounding Vietnam and China.

APPENDIX

CHINA'S ROLE IN LAOS

U.S. policy planners suspected China of harboring aggressive designs in Laos and used these suspicions to justify much of their own intervention in Laos. In reality, in its relations with independent Laos from 1953 to 1962, China consistently backed the neutral forces and took relatively little direct action in Laos.

At the Geneva (1954) and Bandung (1955) conferences, China had favored Laotian neutralism.[80] Peking appeared reluctant to be-

78. Lee, *op. cit.*, pp. 208–209.
79. Toye, *op. cit.*, p. 186; Dommen, *op. cit.*, pp. 220–221.
80. George McT. Kahin, *The Asian-African Conference* (Ithaca, N.Y.: Cornell University Press, 1956), p. 60.

come involved in the Laotian crisis until January 1960, and only did
then in response to the Phoumist seizure of control in Vientiane, when
China charged the United States with having installed a fascist government.[81] Later in the spring of 1960, the Chinese criticized the
North Vietnamese and Pathet Lao for placing any faith in the elections scheduled for April under rightist auspices. When the CIA-
backed military party (CDIN, Committee for the Defense of
National Interests) triumphed, Peking's analysis of American manipulation appeared justified.[82] Nonetheless, Peking declared its intention
to keep good relations with the new Vientiane government of Tiao
Somsanith, who in turn pledged to respect the Geneva Accords—a
gesture which reversed the anti-Geneva position of his predecessor,
Phoui Sananikone.[83]

Although in late fall of 1960 Souvanna Phouma again led the Royal
Laotian Government, by October pressure from Ambassador Parsons
showed that the United States continued to support the rightists.
Peking, in turn, offered its support to the Royal Laotian Government.[84]
The November 18 agreement, stressing Chinese and North Vietnamese support for Souvanna's neutralism, between Vientiane, Peking,
and Hanoi made it plain that Washington's policies had finally
achieved the very polarity in Laotian politics which American states-
men had claimed to dread.

In December Souvanna Phouma felt compelled by Phoumi Nosavan's pressure to flee to Cambodia, and the civil war increased in
severity. Peking perceived an increase in American influence on
China's borders.[85] Furthermore, Russia's aid to Kong Le posed the additional threat of Soviet influence in the Chinese sphere. The Chinese,
on December 19, cautioned Washington against what they termed "a
serious menace."[86] Nevertheless, in the same communiqué, the Chinese avoided threats of counterintervention, calling instead for a
reconvening of the 1954 Geneva powers.

On December 28, 1960, in a note to Britain and the Soviet Union,
China stated its "sacred duty" to uphold the Geneva Accords, as well
as its intention of "taking measures to safeguard its own security." At
this time Peking called for the ICC to reconvene and to deal with

81. Lee, *op. cit.*, p. 150.
82. *Ibid.*, pp. 152–153.
83. *Peking Review*, May 17, 1960; Lee, *op. cit.*, pp. 154–155.
84. *People's Daily*, October 17, 1960.
85. Lee, *op. cit.*, p. 161.
86. *Ibid.*, p. 162.

Souvanna Phouma's fleeing. The Chinese contended that the ICC could not work with the Boun Oum–Phoumi Nosavan government, which was illegal and supported by "United States armed intervention," without violating the Geneva Accords.[87]

China's terms for the reactivation of the ICC, like the Soviet Union's, were of course unacceptable to Washington, which supported Boun Oum and Phoumi Nosavan. It became increasingly apparent to the Chinese that Washington not only did not desire to see the ICC reactivated in its present form but intended, by its dispatch of the Seventh Fleet, to increase SEATO commitment to the area.[88] In February 1961, as Britain and the USSR were negotiating for a renewed ICC, Chou En-lai, in a letter to Prince Sihanouk of Cambodia, argued that the ICC, authorized only to deal with the provisions of the 1954 Accords, could not operate in the present situation and must receive new instructions from the proposed conference.[89] A neutral buffer state rather than an imposed communist one was favored by Peking, which understood that in the latter case the possibility of United States intervention would be greater.

No substantial evidence supports the American charges of aggressive Chinese intervention in Laos,[90] but Peking was at work establishing diplomatic and other ties. On October 7, 1961, a Chinese Consul general was established in Phong Saly (part of the Pathet Lao ceasefire area), and on November 5 a Chinese economic-cultural delegation set off for Laos[91] to deal with Souvanna Phouma's group.

In their "Military Papers," the Chinese Red Army presented an accurate evaluation of the situation in Laos, stating that

the Laotian revolutionary strength is greater now [1961] than before and there is a strong desire to have a government that wants peaceful neutrality. If we support this government we are actually supporting the revolutionary strength.[92]

87. Brian Crozier, "Peking and the Laotian Crisis: An Interim Appraisal," *China Quarterly* (July–September 1961), pp. 129–130.

88. *People's Daily*, January 8, 1961.

89. Crozier, "Peking and the Laotian Crisis: An Interim Appraisal," *op. cit.*, pp. 130–131.

90. Brian Crozier, "Peking and the Laotian Crisis: A Further Appraisal," *China Quarterly* (July–September 1962), p. 118.

91. Crozier, "Peking and the Laotian Crisis: A Further Appraisal," *op. cit.*, p. 120.

92. J. Chester Cheng, ed., *The Politics of the Chinese Red Army* (Stanford: Hoover Institute, 1966), p. 367.

On the basis of such an analysis, prepared for top-level internal use only, it is plain that Peking did not intend to upset the negotiations for a neutral coalition. China's willingness to neglect the Pathet Lao is apparent in this statement: "At the same time, whether it is the International Conference or the International Commission, they must deal directly with the Phouma *de jure* government."[93]

[T]he Chinese conception of neutrality, which literally means in Chinese language to "stand in the middle" . . . accorded top priority to strict military non-alignment with either bloc—freedom from alliance, bases, or protection by alliance, and to political independence and the absence of external interference.[94]

93. Cheng, *op. cit.*, p. 368. The public Chinese view, also procoalition, can be found in Arthur Lall's reports from the Geneva Conference, esp. p. 78 (cited in footnote 30).

94. Lee, *op. cit.*, p. 186 (cited in footnote 30).

11

After Geneva: Subverting Laotian Neutrality

D. Gareth Porter

When the United States signed the Geneva Agreement on Laos in July 1962, pledging support for a tripartite coalition government that gave the Pathet Lao equal representation with the right-wing forces of General Phoumi Nosavan, it seemed ready to give up the considerable leverage in Laotian politics which it had acquired over seven years of political and military intervention in that country. But a careful analysis of Laotian politics and American policy in the three years following Geneva makes it clear that the Agreement marked only a temporary and partial retreat from that intervention.

The Kennedy administration's acquiescence to a tripartite coalition government for Laos was not due to any concern for Laotian neutrality, but rather had been forced by the miserable failure of its previous strategy of backing General Phoumi's army against the alliance of neutralists and Pathet Lao.[1] The administration did not regard the Geneva Agreement as an opportunity for a graceful withdrawal from Laos but as a chance for the United States to gain a more advantageous position from which to conduct the future struggle against the Pathet Lao and North Vietnamese. As Roger Hilsman, assistant secretary of state for Far Eastern affairs under Kennedy, admitted in 1965, "We all understood perfectly well that [it] was just the starting gun. . . . If we had . . . used the negotiations as an excuse to withdraw from Laos . . . we in effect would have been turning it over to the Communists."[2]

1. The best account of that failure is in Bernard Fall, *Anatomy of a Crisis* (Garden City, N.Y.: Doubleday, 1967).
2. Roger Hilsman, Testimony in *Refugee Problems in South Vietnam and Laos,* Hearings before the Subcommittee to Investigate Problems connected with Refugees and Escapees of the Committee on the Judiciary, U.S. Senate, 89th Congress, 1st Session (Washington, D.C.: Government Printing Office, 1965), p. 328.

The alternative to withdrawal was to subvert the Geneva arrangement so that it could be used against the Pathet Lao and in favor of the U.S.-supported right wing. For although U.S. officials and their apologists have always insisted that the intentional aggression of the Pathet Lao and their North Vietnamese allies caused the breakdown of the Geneva Agreement and the coalition government, the truth is that the United States never wanted the coalition government to work as it was supposed to under the 1962 Agreements.

From the first, the United States, with the cooperation of both the right-wing military elite and "neutralist" Premier Prince Souvanna Phouma, intended to make the functioning of the tripartite government intolerable for the Pathet Lao. They hoped to accomplish this by impeding the consolidation of the Pathet Lao zones and by continuing the unilateral American supply operations to Meo guerrillas far behind Pathet Lao lines. At the same time they denied security to Pathet Lao ministers in the coalition government by indefinitely prolonging right-wing control of the capital.

The key to this squeeze play against the left was the American belief that Premier Souvanna Phouma (despite his past identification with neutralism) could be persuaded to cooperate if he received a guarantee of American support for him as head of government—something he had always been denied in the past. Averell Harriman, unlike his predecessors in the Far Eastern Bureau of the State Department who had decided that Souvanna was pro-communist, understood that he actually favored collaboration with the West against the Pathet Lao.[3]

Thus, the Kennedy administration pursued a strategy of reversing the 1961–1962 alignment of the neutralists with the Pathet Lao and creating a new rightist-neutralist coalition. Hilsman makes it clear in his account that the Kennedy administration hoped to get Souvanna to cooperate with the right wing against the left. Harriman is said to have declared on several occasions, "If Souvanna's government of national union breaks

3. Arthur M. Schlesinger, Jr., *A Thousand Days* (Boston: Houghton Mifflin, 1965), p. 517.

up, we must be sure the break comes between the Communists and the neutralists rather than having the two of them teamed up as before."[4]

The structure of the tripartite coalition agreement was, however, explicitly intended to rule out the collaboration by two factions against the third. The June 12, 1962, agreement concluded on the Plain of Jars among the three factions which had established the tripartite coalition cabinet set up the "troika" principle, under which either the rightist or the leftist deputy prime ministers could veto any decision made by the prime minister on matters relating to defense, internal policy, or foreign affairs.[5] Only if Souvanna agreed to suspend this principle of unanimity could the coalition be used against the Pathet Lao. All the evidence indicates that this is precisely what Souvanna was prevailed upon to do in the vital issue of the American airlift to the Meo guerrillas.

If the Government of National Union was to work at all, it would have to be based on the established lines of *de facto* control represented by the June 24, 1962, cease-fire. The Pathet Lao zone of control, which included most of northern and eastern Laos (see maps, pp. 210, 211), was their insurance against any attempt by the right wing to repress Pathet Lao political activities in the Mekong valley and Vientiane. Once before (1958–1959), the Pathet Lao had agreed to integrate their forces into a national army in return for participation in the National Assembly elections, only to have their leaders arrested after the election in a capital patrolled by right-wing troops.

Until right-wing control over the capital was replaced by a tripartite police force, and overall reductions in military forces were arranged as a preliminary step toward the unification of the armed forces, the Pathet Lao would logically insist on full control within its territory.

In this context, the United States insistence on maintaining a major anti-communist guerrilla force behind Pathet Lao lines

4. Quoted in Roger Hilsman, *To Move a Nation* (Garden City, N.Y.: Doubleday, 1967), p. 153.
5. *Bangkok Post,* June 13, 1962.

can only be interpreted as a sign that it preferred a new polarization of forces—and, inevitably, a renewal of the American military role in Laos—to a tripartite coalition government based on conciliation and compromise. Indeed, Hilsman himself indicates that it was understood that the U.S. policy of "protecting" the Meo from the Pathet Lao "might come to be a hindrance to implementing the Geneva Accords and achieving a truly neutral Laos. . . ."[6]

The following account will show in detail how the United States and its Laotian collaborators subverted the Geneva arrangement, forced the breakdown of the Government of National Union, and then went on to make Laos a full partner in the American-sponsored coalition of right-wing military regimes, while claiming at every turn to be supporting the Geneva Agreement.

The Geneva Conference of 1962 left one pivotal issue unresolved: anti-communist Meo tribesmen, who had been supplied with American arms, ammunition, and food up to the time of the cease-fire, remained deep behind Pathet Lao lines. The problem was not humanitarian but political, for these tribesmen (who were considered the best fighting men in all of Laos) had a long history of collaboration with France, and later the United States, against Pathet Lao and Vietnamese revolutionaries.

In fact, Meo collaboration with the French began long before the postwar struggle for independence in Indochina. Although the Meo were generally considered anti-French after their revolt from 1918 to 1922, some Meo clans related to a wealthy French-educated chief (the father of Touby Ly Fong, the present Meo chief) had worked closely with the French.[7] During the First Indochina War, members of these same Meo clans served as both commandos and regular troops under the French.[8] Other

---

6. Hilsman, *To Move a Nation*, p. 115.

7. Wilfred Burchett, *Mekong Upstream* (East Berlin: Seven Seas Publishers, 1959), p. 217.

8. G. Linwood Barney, "The Meo of Xieng Khouang Province, Laos," in Peter Kunstadter, ed., *Southeast Asian Tribes, Minorities and Nations* (Princeton, N.J.: Princeton University Press, 1967), p. 274; Fall, *op. cit.*, p. 56.

Meo tribesmen followed Faydang, the leader of a different Meo clan, who organized the Lao Xung (Meo) Resistance League and allied it with Prince Souphanouvong's Pathet Lao movement.[9]

Although U.S. policy in Laos viewed the ethnic Lao officers of the Royal Army as the primary basis of American influence, American involvement with the Meo began sometime before 1960 when U.S. Army Special Forces began advising the scattered detachments of Meo which continued to hold mountain strongholds within Pathet Lao territory.[10] The official explanation was that U.S. military "civic action teams" were engaged in "relief work" in the northern provinces of Laos before 1960,[11] but these teams were in fact the advance guard of the Special Forces White Star Mobile Training Teams, which became a major force in Laos during the Kennedy administration.

This small-scale Meo training program began to expand in late 1960 when the CIA-supported right-wing forces of General Phoumi Nosavan were in rebellion against Souvanna Phouma's neutralist government. In October 1960 a political alliance was reportedly made between Phoumi and Touby Ly Fong, who was then officially serving in Souvanna's cabinet. The Meo were reportedly promised an autonomous "Meo state" in return for helping the right wing fight the Pathet Lao.[12] The arms and supplies which cemented this alliance came, of course, from the Central Intelligence Agency, whose "private" airline, Air America, was then ferrying supplies to Phoumi on a large scale.[13]

Meo military chief Major Vang Pao drew up a plan to be put into operation when the right wing recaptured Vientiane and full-scale civil war erupted. He would have the 200 Meo villages in Xieng Khouang, controlled by Touby and himself, evacuate and move to seven mountain sites surrounding the

9. Burchett, *op. cit.,* p. 230.
10. The author has talked with a former Special Forces officer who was sent to train and advise the Meo in 1959.
11. Testimony of AID Director Rutherford Poats, in *Refugee Problems in South Vietnam and Laos, op. cit.,* p. 16.
12. Barney, *op. cit.,* p. 275; Fall, *op. cit.,* p. 189.
13. Arthur Dommen, *Conflict in Laos* (New York: Praeger, 1965), p. 154.

Plain of Jars, each of which had been selected because of its strategic potential for threatening a major enemy supply route. The Special Forces advisers with Vang Pao encouraged the move as the first step in building up a substantial guerrilla army around Vang Pao's Meo.[14]

When the neutralists were pushed out of Vientiane in December 1960 and occupied the Plain of Jars, the plan was carried out. Although the move became a major tragedy in which hundreds of refugees, without food or medication for weeks, died or committed suicide, more than 100,000 people eventually reached the new sites. A new AID (Agency for International Development) refugee relief program began immediately to supply the Meo encampments through Air America flights.[15]

In early 1961 the Kennedy administration substantially increased the number of White Star Mobile Training Teams serving with the Meo and began to help Vang Pao organize his new guerrilla force from these mountain bases.[16] As the buildup of the Meo army began, food, medical treatment, and other benefits were used to attract new recruits. AID Director Rutherford Poats later said, "As the scope of U.S. services became known, previously uncommitted hill people also moved into the redoubts."[17] The need for U.S. food assistance to Meo families after these early months arose in large part because all the younger men became soldiers and did not have time to grow food.[18] The fact that these Meo "redoubts" had a military rather than an economic purpose helps to explain the Pathet Lao charge after Geneva that there were no Meo "refugees," but only a Meo "maquis."

The supplies which the Americans sent to the Meo guerrillas became an international issue after the cease-fire of May 1961. Fighting between Meo—sometimes armed with long-range artillery flown in by U.S. aircraft—and Pathet Lao–neutralist forces, who were determined to eliminate centers of resistance within

14. Don Schanche, *Mister Pop* (New York: McKay, 1970), pp. 64–65, 80.
15. *Ibid.*, pp. 99–100.
16. Dommen, *op. cit.*, p. 184.
17. *Refugee Problems in South Vietnam and Laos, op. cit.*, p. 16.
18. See *New York Times*, January 22, 1967.

their territory, continued beyond the cease-fire.[19] Air America's continued flights to the Meo outposts were termed "provocative" by the International Control Commission in a report on May 24, 1961.[20]

By the time of the Geneva Agreement of 1962, the Meo forces had reached an estimated strength of 14,000 to 18,000 men, thus making them roughly equivalent to the Pathet Lao forces and approximately twice as large as Kong Le's army.[21]

At Geneva, U.S. negotiator Averell Harriman insisted that the supply flights to the Meo be continued, while the Pathet Lao insisted that they come to an end.[22] The final agreement left it up to the new tripartite Government of National Union to settle the issue. But before the conclusion of the Geneva Conference, Prince Souphanouvong, the leading Pathet Lao spokesman, made it clear that the left wing of the new government would insist on an end to American involvement with the Meo. He said that the coalition government had not yet discussed the U.S. airdrops to the tribesmen, but declared that they were contrary to the spirit of the decision to neutralize Laos. He pointed out that the Meo tribesmen had always been economically self-sufficient and said, "My own guerrillas have not been supplied from the air; why should these people?" Moreover, he suspected that the airdrops were being used to get arms to the Meo.[23]

While the controversy raged at Geneva, the supply flights continued. Although there is no evidence that arms were still being included in the supplies, such suspicions are easily understandable. The Air America planes were in many cases the same ones which had been used to supply right-wing military operations during the fighting and were manned by the same crews.[24]

19. Fall, *op. cit.*, p. 207; Hugh Toye, *Laos* (London: Oxford University Press, 1968), p. 177.

20. Fall, *op. cit.*, p. 225.

21. Robert Shaplen, "Letter from Laos," *The New Yorker* (October 20, 1962), p. 201; Toye, *op. cit.*, p. 177.

22. Schanche, *op. cit.*, p. 134.

23. Reuters dispatch, Radio Singapore, July 3, 1962.

24. Michael Field, *The Prevailing Wind* (London: Methuen, 1965), p. 369.

In fact, seven years later, a U.S. official admitted to Congress that the United States had supplied ammunition as well as food to the Meo after the Geneva Agreement.[25] Apparently at that time arms were not crucial to Vang Pao's army since the Meo had stockpiled an abundance of U.S.-supplied weapons during the first half of 1962.[26]

In late August, a few weeks before the deadline set by the Agreement for the withdrawal of all foreign military personnel from Laos, Communist Chinese sources let it be known that they had advised the North Vietnamese against withdrawing completely from Laos as long as the United States supplied Meo maquis in Pathet Lao territory.[27] The continuing American supply of the Meo was also the object of a special warning by Chinese Foreign Minister Chen Yi, who declared at a reception that "new and disquieting factors have developed repeatedly in the Laotian situation" and put particular emphasis on the fact that the United States had "frequently sent aircraft to intrude into the airspace of the liberated areas and airdrop local bandits and weapons into the liberated areas."[28]

On August 29 Pathet Lao spokesman Phoumi Vongvichit, the information minister in the new coalition government, warned the United States against continuing its supply missions beyond the October 7 deadline for the withdrawal of foreign military personnel. If the Americans persisted, he said, "this will be a violation of the Geneva Accord as well as interference in the internal affairs of Laos."[29]

One month later, he again warned that if the United States continued the operations beyond October 7, the Pathet Lao

25. *United States Agreements and Commitments Abroad, Kingdom of Laos,* Hearings before the Subcommittee on United States Security Agreements and Commitments Abroad of the Committee on Foreign Relations, U.S. Senate, 91st Congress, 1st Session (Washington, D.C.: Government Printing Office, 1970), p. 473. (Cited hereafter as *Laos Hearings.*)

26. Schanche, *op. cit.,* p. 134.

27. UPI dispatch, Hong Kong, *Bangkok Post,* August 25, 1962.

28. Peking Domestic Service, August 17, 1962. A few days later *Ta Kung Pao's* commentator repeated the same point, New China News Agency, August 21, 1962.

29. *Bangkok Post,* August 29, 1962.

would "suppress them." Recalling that the issue had not yet been discussed in the cabinet, he repeated the Pathet Lao insistence that the question of air support for the Meo could not be decided by Premier Souvanna Phouma alone.[30]

The Meo guerrilla threat to the security of the Pathet Lao liberated zones, which was greatest along Route 7 that linked the North Vietnamese town of Vinh with the Plain of Jars, became obvious in the latter half of 1962. In September a Western news service reported that a Meo commando team had ambushed a North Vietnamese supply convoy on Route 7.[31] The Meo themselves claim to have blown up all the bridges and mountain passes along a 15-mile stretch of Route 7 in December 1962 with the help of AID employee Edgar "Pop" Buell.[32]

As the October 7 deadline for the withdrawal of all foreign military personnel approached, attention became focused on the nominal head of the neutralist faction, Premier Souvanna Phouma. Despite the temporary alliance in 1961–1962 between the neutralists and the Pathet Lao, Souvanna remained a basically conservative, pro-Western figure who had worked closely with the right wing even after the blatantly rigged 1960 election.[33]

In his new role as head of a tripartite coalition government, he had little choice but to collaborate with the United States, which alone could save him from being overthrown by the right or being forced once again into an uncomfortable alliance with the Pathet Lao. For the first time, a U.S. administration was prepared to support him as head of government, and he was evidently willing to lean to the right if necessary in order to keep that support. This meant that he would have to violate the Plain of Jars agreement, the basis of his coalition government, by condoning the American support of the Meo.

30. *Washington Post,* September 26, 1962.
31. Arthur Dommen, UPI dispatch from Hong Kong, *Bangkok Post,* October 12, 1963.
32. Schanche, *op. cit.,* pp. 162–163.
33. Souvanna's uncompromising attitude toward the Pathet Lao in May 1960, when he was dean of an almost exclusively right-wing national assembly, is indicated by his statement that it was "unthinkable" that the Laotian government would negotiate with the Pathet Lao "rebels," *Lao Presse Edition Quotidienne,* May 20, 1960.

On September 21 a Reuters dispatch from Vientiane reported that Souvanna was "reliably understood" to have agreed that the Meo "guerrilla fighters" would starve unless the U.S. supply flights were continued, and he agreed to let the Americans continue them as long as he was able to "override the objections of left-wing leaders."[34] On October 3 Souvanna confirmed his consent to the American airdrops when he issued a statement calling on both the Soviet Union (which was supplying neutralist forces stationed on the Plain of Jars) and the United States to continue their existing supply operations until all the armies were demobilized and integrated.[35] It was later revealed that Souvanna, in a letter to the U.S. ambassador on October 1, 1962, formally requested that the flights continue.[36]

A few days after indicating his support for the American supply operations to the Meo guerrillas, Souvanna made a second major move to the right. He went before the rightist-controlled National Assembly, which neither neutralists nor Pathet Lao factions had previously recognized as legitimate, and received full power to govern for one year. Phoumi Vongvichit immediately pointed out that the Zurich agreement of 1961 had established that the assembly had no authority and that the Plain of Jars agreement of June 1962 had not changed that understanding.[37] He also indicated that not only Pathet Lao ministers, but most neutralist ministers as well, had boycotted the assembly's meetings. And Phoumi Vongvichit warned that the Neo Lao Hak Xat, the Pathet Lao's political party, would not recognize the assembly's authority to grant any powers to the Government of National Union, for this authority would give

34. *Bangkok Post*, September 21, 1962; see also *New York Times*, October 1, 1962.

35. *New York Times*, October 4, 1962.

36. *Department of State Bulletin* (April 15, 1963), p. 568.

37. The text of the Zurich Agreement of July 1961 specifies that the three factions agree that the Government of National Union "will be formed in accordance with a special procedure by direct designation and nomination by His Majesty the King *without reference to the National Assembly*" (italics added), United Kingdom, *International Conference on the Settlement of the Laotian Question, Laos no. 1 (1962), Command Paper* (CMND.) 1828 (London: Her Majesty's Stationery Office [HMSO], October, 1962), p. 14.

the assembly the implied legal powers to topple the coalition government.[38]

Souvanna's cooperation with the Americans and the right wing on the Meo supply question and his decision to recognize the right-wing assembly as Laos' highest political authority (both decisions made without consulting the Pathet Lao) marked a clear break with the previous tripartite agreements. Moreover, Souvanna further compromised his neutralism (even in the eyes of his supporters) by making an official visit to Thailand. Given the close ties between Bangkok and Laotian right-wingers such as General Phoumi Nosavan, this trip had obvious political significance.[39]

On October 22 Takashi Oka reported from Vientiane that Souvanna appeared to have "moved somewhat closer to the rightists" and that the Pathet Lao were "openly unhappy over this relationship."[40] Nor were the Pathet Lao alone in their chagrin over Souvanna's decision to cooperate with the rightists and their American sponsors at the expense of the tripartite arrangement. Many within the neutralist camp, including some cabinet ministers, now believed that Souvanna had compromised the neutralist stance he was supposed to maintain as premier.[41]

There had always been two distinct neutralist tendencies in Vientiane despite their unity after the Kong Le coup of August 1960. (See article 9, by Ackland.) The Santiphab Pen Kang Party, which had collaborated successfully with the Pathet Lao in the election of 1958 (the only free election in Laotian history), probably represented the strongest political organization standing between the army and the Pathet Lao.[42] Some of the most prominent neutralists chosen by Souvanna to fill cabinet posts in the coalition government were identified with this "left-

38. *The Statesman* (Calcutta), October 12, 1962; and *The Nation*, (Rangoon) October 12, 1962; cited in *Asian Recorder* (November 12–18, 1962), p. 1890.

39. *Bangkok Post*, November 10, 1962.

40. *Christian Science Monitor*, October 22, 1962.

41. *Bangkok Post*, November 8, 1962.

42. Shortly before he was assassinated, Quinim Pholsena, head of the *Santiphab*, was said to be the leader of the "biggest single faction of Souvanna's followers," *Washington Post*, February 24, 1963.

neutralist party. These included Foreign Minister Quinim Phol-sena, the leader of the Santiphab, and Colonel Kanthi Sisou-phanthong, Souvanna's choice to head a tripartite police force for Vientiane.

But Souvanna had also established his own personal political party, the Lao Pen Kang, and after the coalition agreement, he tried without success to persuade Quinim and the other Santiphab leaders to merge their party with his.[43] When Souvanna moved to the right in October 1962, the Santiphab neutralists began to dissociate themselves from the premier, declaring themselves "true neutralists." Realizing that Souvanna's only domestic base was the officers and troops of Kong Le's neutralist army, they began to seek support for their position within the military. Kong Le later said that the dissidents had put forward Quinim Pholsena as the leader of the "true neutralists" and had accused those remaining faithful to Souvanna of being "reactionary and pro-imperialist."[44]

The appeals of the "true neutralists" were heard with a good deal of sympathy by many in the neutralist army. And until the beginning of November, the army radio broadcasts, paralleling Pathet Lao broadcasts, cautioned that the rightists wanted to "revive their old regime" with the aid of "bellicose foreigners."[45] In the autumn of 1962, Kong Le himself complained bitterly of the arbitrary arrests of his officers and those of the Pathet Lao by the right-wing police in Vientiane.[46] In this tense atmosphere left-neutralist propaganda gained converts rapidly. The most influential officer to associate himself with the "true neutralists" was Kong Le's right-hand man in the 1960 coup, Colonel Deuane Siphaseuth.

Faced with the sudden threat to his own power by the growth

43. "Appeal by Prime Minister Souvanna Phouma," August 17, 1963, Embassy of Laos, News Release, September 25, 1963; see also "End to Laotian Neutrality?" *Far Eastern Economic Review* (April 25, 1963), p. 210.

44. Interview in *Khao Kongtap* (*Army News*), Vietnam News Agency, Hanoi Radio, March 16, 1963.

45. National Army Station, October 31, 1962; compare with Pathet Lao radio, October 30, 1962.

46. Interview with Kong Le in *Army News*, National Army Station, November 2, 1962.

of left-neutralist influence among his followers, Kong Le turned against his former Pathet Lao allies. As he later put it, he was "forced to carry out adequate counter-measures."[47]

According to Jean Lacouture, the "subversion" of the neutralists from the left was matched by American efforts (using right-wing Laotian agents) to "ensure the complicity of the greatest possible number of supposedly neutralist officers."[48] Another Western observer has written that late in 1962 "non-Communist advisers . . . began to make their appearance again with Kong Le, after an interval of three years during which Soviet influence had been strong."[49]

During this period of polarization within the neutralist ranks, the Soviets, in an apparent effort to exercise some pressure on the Americans regarding the Air America flights, told Souvanna that on November 1 they would end their own unilateral airlift of supplies to both neutralist and Pathet Lao forces stationed on the Plain of Jars. The Soviets offered to give their ten aircraft to the Laotian government, which would then be directly responsible for the flights (although Soviet pilots would continue to fly the planes until Laotian pilots could be trained). General Singkapo, commander in chief of the Pathet Lao forces, announced the move one week later and linked it with Air America flights to the Meo. He charged that the Air America flights were used to support "subversive activities" in Pathet Lao territory and warned that his troops would now feel free to fire on any civilian or military aircraft intruding over airspace which they controlled.[50]

However, Souvanna was apparently persuaded by the Americans to refuse this Soviet initiative and agreed instead to have *American* planes supply the neutralist forces. Nothing could have been better calculated to hasten the polarization already under

47. *Army News,* Hanoi Radio, March 16, 1963.

48. *Le Monde,* April 16, 1963, trans. by *Keesing's Contemporary Archives,* cited in Toye, *op. cit.,* p. 190.

49. E. H. S. Simmonds, "Breakdown in Laos," *The World Today* (July 1964), p. 286. For the communist charges, see Radio Pathet Lao, April 19, 1963; and I. Schderov, "Laos: Anxieties and Hopes," *New Times,* November 18, 1964.

50. *Bangkok Post,* November 7, 1962.

way on the Plain of Jars. This became clear on November 27, when an Air America plane was shot down by the "true neutralist" troops of Colonel Deuane, while preparing to land on the Plain of Jars. The embarrassed Souvanna now publicly confirmed that U.S. aircraft had been taking supplies to the neutralists under an agreement with his government. After the incident, some 400 neutralist soldiers followed Colonel Deuane into the Pathet Lao sector of the joint neutralist–Pathet Lao headquarters on the Plain.[51] After managing a temporary reunification of the neutralist factions, Souvanna apparently reconsidered his earlier decision, called off the American flights to the Plain, and accepted the Soviet planes instead.[52] But it was too late to head off the defection of a large enough contingent of neutralist troops to cause Souvanna and Kong Le difficulties later on. In December followers of Colonel Deuane reportedly took over the radio station and other government offices at the Kang Khay neutralist headquarters and held them for several days before leaving peacefully.[53] Thus relations between the left-neutralists and those remaining loyal to Souvanna grew increasingly tense.

The Pathet Lao reopened the issue of Meo support flights when they shot down another Air America supply plane on January 5, 1963. After receiving a protest note from the U.S. Embassy, Prince Souphanouvong responded by saying that either the American planes had to be given to the coalition government or the flights had to stop. He noted that the Soviets had already turned over their supply planes to the Laotian government and said that if the United States did the same he would say "nothing more."[54]

At this point, Souvanna, beginning for the first time to show signs of uncertainty about forcing a right-wing resolution of the issue, attempted to take a step back from his earlier move to the

51. "The End of Laotian Neutrality?" p. 210.

52. Souvanna revealed his acceptance of the Soviet offer on January 10, 1963. *Washington Post*, January 11, 1963.

53. *Bangkok Post*, December 27, 1962.

54. Agence-France Press dispatch, Vientiane, January 9, 1963, cited in Philippe Devillers, *Chronologie de L'Asie du Sud et du Sud-Est* (Paris: Centre d'Etude des Relations Internationales, July 1964), 1st Trimester, pp. 13–14 (cited hereafter as *Chronologie*).

right. Announcing disingenuously that he had been "totally unaware" that American planes were airdropping food supplies to
the Meo, he disclaimed having any knowledge of an official
Laotian agreement with the United States to carry out such
flights. He further revealed in an interview on January 10, 1963,
that he had asked the U.S. ambassador to give the Air America
planes carrying out "relief operations" to the coalition government, as the Soviet Union had agreed to do earlier.[55]

The following day, the State Department responding with
undisguised irritation, said that the Meo supply flights were
sanctioned by an "undertaking between the two governments
. . . since last October, based on an exchange of letters between
Prime Minister Souvanna Phouma and Ambassador Unger."[56]
But the State Department was conspicuously noncommittal about
Souvanna's request for the aircraft. The whole question of
"methods and channels" for U.S. relief supplies for Laotian
refugees, it declared, "remains under constant review by our
two governments." No decision, in any case, would be reached
until after "considerable study."[57]

This response reflected the reluctance of the United States to
halt the Meo supply operations and foreshadowed the major
policy statement issued by the U.S. Embassy in Vientiane two
weeks later.[58] This statement argued, in effect, that the maintenance of the anti-communist Meo as a political and military
force within the Pathet Lao zone was a condition of American
support for the Geneva Agreement. While the supply of Meo
encampments was justified as "humanitarian" aid, the memorandum alluded obliquely to the political and military significance
of the Meo guerrillas: "The Pathet Lao have long faced a situation which must cause them acute frustration and embarrassment."[59]

The statement further charged that the Pathet Lao were trying to "shift the balance of forces in Laos by seeking to cut off

55. Interview with Associated Press, *Bangkok Post*, January 11, 1963.
56. *Washington Post*, January 12, 1963.
57. *Ibid.*
58. *Department of State Bulletin* (April 15, 1963), pp. 567–572.
59. *Ibid.*, p. 571.

food supplies to isolated refugees, imposing their will on the hill peoples and consolidating what they claim to be the Pathet Lao 'zone.'" The statement concluded that if the Pathet Lao intended to "consolidate their 'zone' rather than to work toward reunification" then both the Government of National Union and the Geneva Agreement "may be in peril."[60]

Thus, the real thrust of American policy in Laos was revealed: the Pathet Lao were not to be allowed to consolidate their control over the territory on their side of the cease-fire line, even though the right wing clearly intended to maintain firm control of all the towns in the Mekong valley for as long as possible.[61] In warning that the Geneva Agreement might collapse if the anti-communist Meo were not maintained within the Pathet Lao zone, the United States was conveying a scarcely veiled threat, not only to the Pathet Lao but to Souvanna as well, that the United States might revert to its earlier commitment to the right wing.

The United States offered to give two C–46 aircraft to the Laotian government (in addition to two others which had been earlier offered on a "charter" basis), so that Air America could make its contract with Souvanna's government rather than with the U.S. Mission.[62] This proposal still left ten planes of Air America's fleet of fourteen carrying out airdrops to those isolated anti-communist outposts under American control.[63] In this way the United States had made clear its determination to maintain the Meo as an effective military force and, in effect, dared Souvanna to do something about it.

Souvanna repeated that he had not been informed of the Air America flights and declared that the agreement referred to by the State Department had been signed by the "previous government."[64] But he did nothing to stop the flights, indicating once again that his freedom of action was limited by his dependence on American political support.

60. Ibid., p. 569.
61. See Stuart Simmonds, "Laos: A Renewal of Crisis," Asian Survey (January 1964), p. 682.
62. Washington Post, January 26, 1963.
63. Department of State Bulletin (April 15, 1963), p. 571.
64. Quoted in Nhan Dan, Vietnam News Agency, February 2, 1963.

During Souvanna's trip to Washington in late February the *New York Times* revealed some American disappointment with his ability to forge a neutralist-rightist alliance against the Pathet Lao. There was discontent with his failure to "check up on the activities of the Pathet Lao Communists in areas which they control." U.S. officials, whose attitudes were reflected in the *Times* article, seemed to regard Souvanna more as a subordinate at some American outpost in Vientiane than as the supposedly neutralist head of an independent government. "American officials," it reported, "expressed concern over Souvanna's comments and indicated they would be closely watching his actions when he returns to Laos."[65]

Meanwhile, the split within the neutralist ranks took violent form in February and March, beginning on February 12 with the left-neutralist's assassination of Colonel Ketsana, the leading officer of the group which reportedly "favored association with the West."[66] The following month, Colonel Deuane's 4th Parachute battalion once again led a defection to the Pathet Lao side and, before the end of March, fighting had broken out between the two factions.[67]

This fighting—on the Plain—coincided with the assassination of Foreign Minister Quinim Pholsena, the leading left-neutralist figure. One week later Prince Souphanouvong fled from the capital to the safety of the Pathet Lao zone in order to avoid a repetition of his 1959 arrest by the right wing.[68]

On April 12 Colonel Kanthi Sisouphantong, formerly associated with Quinim, and the designated head of the still unborn tripartite police force, was assassinated in Vientiane; and Phoumi Vongvichit, the Pathet Lao minister of information, left for Pathet Lao headquarters, leaving two junior officials behind to represent Pathet Lao interests in the coalition.[69] The message from the right was clear: there would be no sharing of power with the Pathet Lao and left-neutralists in Vientiane.

65. *New York Times,* March 1, 1963.
66. Simmonds, "Breakdown in Laos," *op. cit.,* p. 287.
67. *Le Monde,* May 23, 1964.
68. Dommen, *Conflict in Laos,* p. 247.
69. Robert K. McCabe, *Storm over Asia* (New York: New American Library, 1967), p. 36; Dommen, *loc. cit.*

In a series of small skirmishes on the Plain of Jars, involving no more than 100 men on either side, Colonel Deuane's "true neutralists," with Pathet Lao support, pushed back Kong Le's forces.[70] The decision to take the offensive on the Plain reflected the judgment by Pathet Lao leaders that Kong Le and Souvanna Phouma were now clearly aligned with the right wing and the Americans. Therefore, the vital line of communication from the Plain east on Route 7 had to be cleared of Kong Le's forces.[71] The presence of "true neutralists" who were prepared to fight their former comrades facilitated the decision. The military move against Kong Le probably had another purpose as well: to bring pressure on Souvanna and the Americans to restore the coalition government. The Pathet Lao, by keeping two ministers at their posts despite the lack of security in Vientiane, indicated their desire to see the tripartite Government of National Union function as originally planned.

Negotiations were quickly arranged among the three factions and began on April 27, 1963. The Pathet Lao demanded two primary concessions in return for a permanent cease-fire and a retreat by leftist forces from their newly won territory: the restoration of "troika" rule in the cabinet, and the immediate establishment of a tripartite Vientiane police force to guarantee the security of left-wing ministers.[72] But Souvanna was no longer free to negotiate a return to the post-Geneva status quo. Three days before the negotiations opened, the right-wing Directorate of National Coordination, in a move foreshadowing the right-wing coup of April 1964, took over key installations in Vientiane.[73] Souvanna's weakness as the premier of a theoretically neutralist government in a city under right-wing control was dramatically illustrated.[74]

At the same time, the neutralist forces were being reinforced

70. See the interview with Roger Hilsman, *Washington Star,* April 28, 1963.

71. Simmonds, "Laos: A Renewal of Crisis," *op. cit.,* p. 682.

72. *Ibid.*

73. *Washington Post,* April 25, 1963.

74. French journalist George Penchennier wrote later that after Quinim's assassination, Souvanna became "prisoner of his old enemy Phoumi Nosavan." (*Le Monde,* May 23, 1964.)

by right-wing troops (including Meo guerrillas), which now received U.S. arms and logistical support. Air America transport
planes were once again ferrying right-wing troops to the combat
area.[75] Souvanna was unable to prevent the American-supported
neutralist-rightist military cooperation already under way (and
could not break off his collaboration with the right wing and
the Americans. He not only refused to negotiate the Pathet Lao
demands but went before the right-wing assembly to deliver
his first open denunciation of the Pathet Lao as an arm of the
North Vietnamese.[76]

In just nine months, then, the Government of National Union
had been reduced to a coalition between Souvanna and the
right wing. With the capital firmly in the hands of General
Phoumi's Directorate of National Coordination, the United
States was able to maintain paramount influence even though
it had withdrawn its military advisers. In forcing Souvanna to
move to the right in order to accommodate U.S. support of Meo
guerrilla forces and Kong Le's neutralists, American policy laid
the foundation for a Laotian government firmly aligned with
the anti-communist bloc in Southeast Asia. If the cost was splitting the neutralist bloc and forfeiting part of it to the Pathet
Lao, it was worth it. The primary objective was to keep the
symbol of neutralism, Prince Souvanna Phouma, as a figurehead
in a government dominated by military clients of the United
States.

The fighting on the Plain of Jars and the departure of Souphanouvong and Phoumi Vongvichit from Vientiane signaled the
success of the Kennedy administration's strategy of turning
the tripartite arrangement against the Pathet Lao. Roger Hilsman, appearing before a congressional committee in June 1963,
did not conceal his satisfaction with developments in Laos.
Asked about the coalition government, he assured the congress-

75. *Washington Post*, May 12, 1963. Marek Thee, then the Polish
delegate to the International Control Commission, and now living in Oslo,
Norway, recalls that the Commission delegates saw ten Air America planes
unload right-wing troops on the Plain of Jars on April 26, 1963. (Interview,
Ithaca, New York, January 8, 1970.)

76. Simmonds, "Laos: A Renewal of Crisis," p. 682.

men that it no longer existed and explained why, "in terms of U.S. national security," the situation was in some ways "much better" than before: "Six months ago the neutralists and the Communists were working against the conservative forces. Today the neutralists have moved over and are now fighting against the Communists." Moreover, he declared, the anti-communist side had actually gained ground in this political shift. Before conflict broke out, the neutralists had occupied the Plain of Jars together with the communists and opposed the right wing; now, although the neutralists occupied less territory on the Plain, their switch to the anti-communist side represented a net gain.[77]

As for the future, Mr. Hilsman's description of the "short-run policy objectives" of the United States in Laos was apparently considered too sensitive to be made public, since it was deleted from the published transcript.[78] We now know, however, that the United States had already embarked on a new effort to strengthen the anti-communist forces in Laos for another round of civil war, while at the same time fostering close cooperation between the Laotian right-wing military leadership and the military dictatorships in Thailand and South Vietnam.

Very soon after the skirmishes on the Plain of Jars, U.S. military advisers quietly began to filter back into Laos to give military support and advice to the Royal Laotian Army, Kong Le's neutralists (who were completely re-equipped within a few months), and the Meo guerilla army. This time, however, the numbers were considerably smaller than before Geneva, and the advisers were from the CIA rather than from the army.[79]

With new American supplies and full U.S. political support, the Phoumist troops, accompanied by their new neutralist allies, went on the offensive in northern and central Laos in the autumn of 1963. In November right-wing troops in central Laos pushed

77. Testimony in *Foreign Operations Appropriations for 1964, Hearings before a Subcommittee of the Committee on Appropriations,* House of Representatives, 88th Congress, 1st Session (Washington, D.C.: Government Printing Office, 1963), pp. 260–261.

78. *Ibid.,* p. 264.

79. Schanche, *op. cit.,* p. 164.

deep into Pathet Lao territory to capture the towns of Lak Sao and Kham Keut on Route 8, the vital supply route into the Pathet Lao zone from North Vietnam. This Phoumist offensive brought the inevitable Pathet Lao counterattack two months later, inflicting a major defeat (comparable to the debacle at Nam Tha in May 1962) on the rightist-neutralist forces in the region.[80]

The atmosphere of insecurity which continued to envelop Vientiane discouraged any thoughts that Pathet Lao leaders might have had about returning to their posts in the coalition cabinet. On September 9, 1963, Pathet Lao security guards and right-wing forces exchanged fire for three hours as the rightists surrounded the Pathet Lao villa there. The shooting finally stopped, but the right-wing troops and tanks remained around the villa. The embassies of China and North Vietnam were encircled as well.[81]

The Pathet Lao claimed that the incident was caused by right-wing forces which opened fire on their guards before surrounding the villa.[82] The right-wing police, on the other hand, gave two different versions of the incident. The first communiqué accused the Pathet Lao soldiers at the villa of firing on a nearby residence occupied by two right-wing colonels.[83] However, a later communiqué stated that the guards "opened fire with automatic arms and threw grenades in all directions without reason or provocation."[84] In a separate statement Phoumi Nosavan charged that the Pathet Lao had provoked the exchange in order to prevent Premier Souvanna Phouma from leaving the next day for the United Nations.[85]

But the right wing may have had a more compelling reason

80. Denis Warner, *Reporting South-East Asia* (Sydney: Angus and Robertson, 1966), p. 187; *Le Monde,* May 23, 1964.

81. *Bangkok Post,* September 10, 1963; François Cayrac, *Chronologie,* 4th trimester, 1963 (August 1965), p. 33.

82. *Bangkok Post,* September 10, 1963.

83. *Ibid.*

84. Cayrac, *op. cit.,* p. 33. Associated Press correspondent Antoine Yared was reportedly arrested by right-wing police while he was investigating the incident. *Bangkok Post,* September 9, 1963.

85. Agence-France Press, Vientiane, September 11, cited in Cayrac, *Chronologie, op. cit.,* p. 34.

for initiating the incident. Left-wing Minister of Information Phoumi Vongvichit had been in Vientiane for two weeks and, according to his story, had expressed a desire to resume his post at the ministry.[86] Phoumi's faction, which was known to oppose any Pathet Lao participation in the government, may have seen the September 9 incident as a way of reinforcing the message conveyed earlier in the year. Three days after the incident, right-wing troops were still surrounding the Pathet Lao villa.[87]

In December another neutralist official was assassinated in Vientiane: the chief of military intelligence, Colonel Leuang. Although not a well-known left-neutralist like the others, Leuang had been abducted, manhandled, and threatened by right-wing thugs a year earlier. Leuang was killed by a bullet from a .45-caliber gun, and neutralists maintained that the right-wingers were the only ones in Vientiane equipped with these weapons.[88] In March 1964, only one hour after Kong Le himself had threatened to withdraw his forces from Vientiane unless greater security could be guaranteed all officials, an unidentified gunman killed the chief of *right-wing* military intelligence.[89]

Early in 1964, as it became increasingly clear that Souvanna Phouma and the neutralists were *de facto* prisoners of the right in Vientiane, two more neutralist ministers fled to exile in Cambodia.[90] Khamsouk Keola, the minister of health and acting minister of foreign affairs, and Heuame Mongkolovilay, secretary of state for war veterans, did not reappear in Laotian politics until 1965, when they and Pathet Lao ministers signed a joint statement denouncing the elections held by Souvanna's government.[91]

86. *Bangkok Post,* September 14, 1963.

87. *Ibid.,* September 12, 1963. In a letter to Souvanna Phouma on November 13, 1963, Souphanouvong complained of a series of incidents involving a hand grenade, a shot fired into a Pathet Lao residence, and provocative arrests of security guards—all during the month of September. *Asian Almanac* (Singapore), November 24–30, 1963, p. 263.

88. Cayrac, *Chronologie, op. cit.,* 4th trimester, 1963 (August 1965), p. 32.

89. *New York Times,* March 18, 1964.

90. *Asian Almanac* (May 3–9, 1964), p. 534.

91. Pathet Lao Radio, August 15, 1965.

The Pathet Lao continued to press Souvanna and the right wing to provide more security for left-wing officials as the first condition for peaceful restoration of the Government of National Union. By the end of 1963 representatives of neutralists and Pathet Lao had agreed on a plan to transfer the administrative capital to Luang Prabang. The capital would be neutralized by stationing all right-wing troops at least 12.5 miles from the city and establishing a tripartite police force.[92] But the right wing vetoed this plan, insisting that they needed Luang Prabang airport to support their troops in northern Laos.[93]

Meanwhile, the United States was moving rapidly to ensure close cooperation among the military regimes in Laos, Thailand, and Vietnam. In return for American, Thai, and South Vietnamese assistance in the fight against the Pathet Lao and North Vietnamese, the Laotian military and American-backed tribal mercenaries would put pressure on the North Vietnamese supply trails in eastern Laos. The distinctive feature of this military alliance was that it was carried out, as far as possible, in complete secrecy.

The first move was an American request to the Thai government that an Air Force Special Warfare unit be sent to Thailand to train Lao and Thai pilots to fly counterinsurgency missions in T-28 planes over Laos. In March 1964 the unit was dispatched[94] and soon after that, Lao-speaking Thai pilots with Laotian Air Force identification cards began making their appearance in Laos.[95] The United States was in effect importing a foreign air force into Laos until Laotian pilots could be trained.

92. See the communiqué issued after a meeting on the Plain of Jars December 20, 1963. *Asian Almanac* (December 29, 1963–January 4, 1964), p. 322.

93. *New York Times,* April 19, 1964; François Nivolon, "New Crisis," *Far Eastern Economic Review* (May 14, 1964), p. 327.

94. Testimony of former Ambassador William H. Sullivan and Colonel Robert E. F. Tyrrell, U.S. Air Attaché Representative in Laos, *Laos Hearings,* pp. 369 and 457.

95. See the statement by Thai pilot Chein Ban Rung Uom, who was captured by the Pathet Lao on August 18, 1964. *Comment les Impérialistes Américans ont Perpétré L'Agression et Saboté la Paix et La Neutralité du Laos au Lendemain de la Signature des Accords de Genève de 1962 sur le Laos* (Central Committee of the Neo Lao Hak Xat, 1965), pp. 23–24.

At the same time, the Laotian military and the South Vietnamese military regime were entering into a far-reaching arrangement which constituted a *de facto* military alliance. On March 13, 1964, at Dalat, South Vietnam, Phoumi Nosavan conferred with General Nguyen Khanh, head of the South Vietnamese military junta, concerning the use of South Vietnamese troops in Laos and the training of Laotian troops and officers in Vietnam.[96] General Oudone Sananikone, special military adviser to Phoumi, and General Tran Thien Khiem, commander in chief of the South Vietnamese army, agreed secretly that a "disguised" South Vietnamese liaison team would be stationed at the right-wing military headquarters in Savannakhet and that South Vietnamese troops would be used in the southern Laotian provinces of Attopeu and Saravane.[97]

In mid-April a final meeting in Dalat between Phoumi and Khanh concluded the deal. In return for endorsing the covert presence of South Vietnamese forces in Laos, the Laotian military would receive various direct benefits: Regular Laotian army officers and noncommissioned officers as well as Meo tribesmen would receive training in South Vietnam, and financial aid would be provided (from American military aid funds) for training Laotian officers on Taiwan.[98]

Another U.S.-directed covert operation in Laos having approval of the Laotian military was the dispatch of South Vietnamese commandos into Pathet Lao zones to collect intelligence on military positions, fortified villages, and supply trails. Under "Plan Delta," American officers at the Special Forces training center

96. Information obtained from a former U.S. intelligence officer in Vietnam.

97. *Ibid.* In a letter to the co-chairmen of the Geneva Conference, Souphanouvong noted that following the talks between Phoumi and Khanh, "Several units of South Vietnamese . . . troops have appeared in the Savannakhet and Tchepone regions and elsewhere." Pathet Lao Radio, April 4, 1964.

98. *Ibid.* The training of Laotian officers in Taiwan was already under way. General Siho Lanphoutacoul, the right-wing police chief, attended the General Staff school in Taiwan in 1963, and fell under the influence of Chiang Ching-kuo, chief of Taiwan's secret police. *New York Times*, April 27, 1964.

in Nha-trang, South Vietnam, trained and equipped the commando teams. These were then flown into the Pathet Lao areas, with instructions to make their way to a right-wing Laotian post if pursued by the Pathet Lao.[99] Apparently this program was initiated well before the Phoumi-Khanh agreement. According to Prince Souphanouvong, Vietnamese commando teams had been parachuted into southern Laos as early as 1962.[100]

Whether or not Premier Souvanna Phouma gave his explicit consent to these military arrangements is not known. However, it seems clear that Souvanna did not have the power to stop either the integration of Laos into the larger U.S.-dominated alliance of right-wing military regimes or the ultimate merger of neutralist forces into those of the right wing. It is in this context that the right-wing coup of April 19, 1964, must be understood. Its effect was to further tighten the screws on a premier who had *never* had freedom of action or the power to control the military leadership. The coup leaders wanted to do away with Souvanna Phouma's Government of National Union and its two Pathet Lao cabinet posts, not because they felt the need to change either the internal or external policies of the Laotian government, but simply because they saw no reason to tolerate a cabinet which did not reflect the realities of power in the military-dominated government. Moreover, they still did not trust Souvanna Phouma. General Kouprasith Abhay, explaining the reasons for the coup in a speech at the National Defense Department on April 19, complained of appeals by "some people" for negotiations which he said were "only aimed at helping certain Ministers to retain their posts and exert their influence in the country."[101]

A probable third cause of the coup was the excessive power of General Phoumi, who had been given a free hand to organize a variety of lucrative commercial interests, including gambling,

99. See the statements by captured South Vietnamese commandos in *Comment les Impérialistes . . .* , pp. 25–34.

100. Pathet Lao Radio, April 4, 1964.

101. *Asian Almanac*, April 15–19, 1964, p. 510.

opium dens, and a monopoly on the import of gold. General Abhay, a relative of the wealthy Sananikone family of Vientiane, was Phoumi's long-time rival for leadership of the military, while the other coup leader, General Siho Lanphoutacoup, chief of the right-wing police, had been Phoumi's protégé.[102]

Because the whole object of American maneuverings in the previous year and a half had been to confer greater legitimacy on the Laotian government, the U.S. Embassy responded to the coup by pressuring the generals into retaining Souvanna as a figurehead premier. The United States now made explicit its threat to cut off aid, and the coup leaders released Souvanna from house arrest on April 22, asking him to form a new cabinet. A spokesman for the coup leaders explained, "Without aid Laos cannot survive."[103]

The coup leaders were embarrassingly frank about Souvanna's status in the new regime. On April 24 Kouprasith and Siho submitted their demands to a cabinet meeting chaired by Souvanna and said that they would remain in control of the capital until Souvanna complied.[104] When Souvanna finally spoke on May 2 about the future of his government, it became clear that one of the conditions for his remaining in office was the integration of the neutralist forces into the right-wing armies. Souvanna declared that he was assuming control of military affairs and that he would henceforth speak "in the name of the center and right-wing."[105] General Phoumi Nosavan returned the favor by issuing a statement on May 4 that he had "decided to hand over to Prince Souvanna Phouma the post of Minister of National Defense" and that unified rightist-neutralist troops would be under Souvanna's "direct command."[106]

102. McCabe, *op. cit.*, p. 40; Warner, *op. cit.*, p. 190; *Le Monde*, May 24–25, 1964; Parke Fulham, "A Million White Elephants," *Far Eastern Economic Review* (May 28, 1964), pp. 420–421. Phoumi's rivals did in fact prevail, as his financial props were taken away from him. He was defeated in a bid to recover his position in February 1965, and fled to Thailand, along with General Siho.

103. *New York Times,* April 22, 1964.

104. *Ibid.,* April 25, 1964.

105. *Ibid.,* May 3, 1964.

106. *Asian Almanac* (May 3–9, 1964), p. 534.

But this was clearly a charade which masked the capitulation of Souvanna to the right wing. Prince Souphanouvong, after a meeting with Souvanna at Khang Khai on May 5, said, "Prince Souvanna Phouma claimed that he is the leader of both the right-wing and neutralist forces and is in power, but the fact is that he is under the control of the Kouprasith-Siho group."[107] And Souphanouvong was not alone in this view of Souvanna's position. Arthur Dommen, whose book is rather sympathetic to Souvanna, observes that after the coup Souvanna "became daily more of a figurehead in a situation over which he had little control."[108]

On May 13 Souvanna named ten army generals to a committee to reorganize the unified army command.[109] All were rightists except his own military adviser. Prince Souphanouvong had previously warned Souvanna that if he went through with the planned merger of rightists and neutralists, the Pathet Lao would launch a general attack.[110] On May 17 a Pathet Lao offensive began on the Plain of Jars, driving Kong Le's forces from the last neutralist outpost on the Plain within one week.

A major factor in the quick success of this offensive was a new political crisis within the neutralist forces on the Plain, which was triggered by the rightist coup. Many neutralist officers and men would not fight for a government which was now clearly controlled by the right wing, and they rejected the planned merger with the rightist army. (Three battalions of right-wing troops had already been stationed with them at the neutralist headquarters at Muong Phanh.)[111]

In the end, there was another mass defection to the Pathet Lao before the offensive,[112] and it was reported that six of the ten battalions that attacked Kong Le's position were former neutralist troops.[113] Three months later Kong Le admitted his

107. *Ibid.*
108. Dommen, *op. cit.*, p. 258.
109. *New York Times*, May 14, 1964.
110. *Le Monde*, May 20, 1964.
111. Toye, *op. cit.*, p. 192.
112. Warner, *op. cit.*, p. 191.
113. *Le Monde*, May 19, 1964.

concern about the defections when he issued a plea to all officers and troops "who have been deceived by and are cooperating with the Viet–NLHX (Neo Lao Hak Xat), calling upon them to "rejoin the neutralist party."[114]

The collapse of the neutralist position on the Plain brought an immediate escalation of U.S. and Thai military involvement in Laos. With American reconnaissance planes from Thailand and the Gulf of Tonkin providing the intelligence, Thai pilots began flying bombing raids against Pathet Lao positions on the Plain and the supply trails to the east.[115] As many as 25 Thai pilots were flying these combat missions, according to one Western source.[116] When the Pathet Lao shot down an American jet over the Plain of Jars, the Thai strafed Souphanouvong's headquarters at Khang Khai, and U.S. jets escorted them.[117]

The fighter escorts for U.S. reconnaissance missions then began attacking the antiaircraft guns brought onto the Plain by the Pathet Lao. Souvanna Phouma told a reporter that he had not ordered the use of armed escort planes, recalled his earlier disclaimer about supply flights to Meo, and declared he would stop these intelligence flights. A few days later he backed down and supported the flights without reservation.[118]

Even more serious was the deep American and Thai involvement in a major right-wing and neutralist offensive campaign, "Operation Three Arrows," which began in late July 1964.[119] A number of U.S. officers were secretly brought in to advise the Laotian forces, while U.S. Air Force ground controllers guided air strikes by U.S. jets in support of the offensive.[120] Meanwhile, several hundred Thai artillerymen and officers in Lao uniforms were sent into Laos to reinforce Vang Pao's Meo army.[121]

114. Vientiane Domestic Service, August 3, 1964.
115. Charles J. V. Murphy, "Thailand's Fight to the Finish," *Fortune* (October, 1965), p. 126.
116. Warner, *op. cit.*, p. 198.
117. Murphy, *op. cit.*
118. McCabe, *op. cit.*, p. 42.
119. *New York Times*, December 19, 1964; *Comment les Impérialistes . . . , op. cit.*, pp. 14–15.
120. *Laos Hearings*, pp. 457 and 479.
121. Murphy, *op. cit.*

In December 1964 the Pathet Lao charged that two battalions of Thai troops, accompanied by U.S. officers, were stationed at Kong Le's headquarters at Muong Suoi.[122] For many months, newsmen were not allowed into Muong Suoi, and the accusation could not be confirmed. However, early in 1965 neutralist military sources reported that twenty Americans were working at Muong Suoi as military advisers to the "neutralist" and rightist troops stationed there.[123] Richard Dudman of the *St. Louis Post-Dispatch* reported in 1966 that Thai troops were operating in considerable numbers in Laos,[124] and it was generally assumed that Thai battalions shuttled back and forth across the Laotian border regularly.

In addition to the introduction of more foreign military forces, the United States also stepped up its use of tribal mercenaries as guerrilla forces in attacks on Pathet Lao transportation lines in eastern Laos. The CIA's Air America no longer bothered to conceal its paramilitary role, and it increased its supply of weapons to Meo encampments throughout northern and eastern Laos. One indication of the magnitude of CIA operations involving Meo guerrillas is that by the spring of 1965 more than 200 airfields and airstrips had been built for regular Air America supply flights.[125]

Although the Meo were the most important tribal group involved in these American-directed military activities, Black Tai and Kha tribesmen were also employed. A major goal of the guerrilla activity was to inhibit the movement of supplies from North Vietnam to the Plain of Jars and South Vietnam. The Meo tried to prevent the Pathet Lao from capturing territory necessary for the security of the routes, and both Meo and Kha guerrillas, with American advisers, set ambushes on the trails.[126]

122. P. H. M. Jones, "Laos Next," *Atlas* (reprinted from *Far Eastern Economic Review*, March 1966), p. 174.
123. *New York Times*, March 25, 1965.
124. Richard Dudman, *St. Louis Post-Dispatch*, January 11, 1966.
125. Warner, *op. cit.*, p. 199.
126. John Stirling, Observer Foreign News Service, *Saigon Daily News*, June 17, 1965; Reuters dispatch, *Saigon Daily News*, September 21, 1965.

Meo tribesmen fulfilled one other vital military function: despite the fact that Sam Neua province was a primary base area for the Pathet Lao, Meo guerrillas had maintained control of an area in northwestern Sam Neua after the cease-fire of June 1962. Late in 1964, according to an authoritative report, construction began on a radar base for guiding the future bombing of both the Ho Chi Minh Trail and North Vietnam itself. It was located on a mountain called Phou Pha Thi, 17 miles from the North Vietnamese border. At the foot of the mountain a 700-foot landing strip was constructed to serve the teams of Meo mercenaries who operated from the valley. Their mission was not only to protect the radar facility, but to conduct raids into North Vietnam, against Pathet Lao headquarters, and upon the Pathet Lao-controlled town of Sam Neua.[127]

The right wing was not satisfied with combined operations with the neutralist forces, which remained under a separate command. By the beginning of 1965 the right wing began to try to complete the integration of right-wing and neutralist troops. For Kong Le, military cooperation with the right was acceptable, but complete integration, which would eliminate his position as head of the neutralist troops, was not. For a second time, his power was threatened by political polarization, but this time he could not save it by remaining loyal to Souvanna Phouma.

In March 1965 he announced that he had resisted pressures to form a single army with the right.[128] During April, in an effort to bolster his neutralist command, he arranged to have Indonesia provide military supplies to his forces and to take neutralist officers to Djakarta to be trained. Although Souvanna opposed this plan, having already agreed to remove the last vestige of neutralism in Laos, it was implemented in August 1965.[129] In September 1965 Souvanna Phouma declared that the unification of the armed forces would be completed be-

127. T. D. Allman, Times-Post Service, *San Francisco Chronicle,* March 17, 1970.

128. *Le Monde,* March 19, 1965.

129. *Asian Almanac,* September 12–18, 1965, p. 1265.

fore the end of the year.[130] Kong Le delayed his ouster for another year; but he finally lost control over the neutralist forces in October 1966 when his three top officers, whom he later charged were bribed by the United States, spirited him off to Thailand.

The right wing took control of logistics for the neutralists and integrated the neutralist headquarters into their own.[131] This dissolution of the neutralist command in the right-wing army represented the culmination of the American policy of turning the Government of National Union of Souvanna Phouma into an instrument that could be used in the struggle for Indochina. By 1966 Laos had reverted to the situation of 1959–1960 before Kong Le's coup had reintroduced neutralism into the conflict. This state of affairs was only thinly disguised by Souvanna Phouma, who continued to claim the legitimacy of the Geneva Agreement and to keep two cabinet positions (long since taken over in fact by right-wing officials) formally reserved for the Pathet Lao.

The fiction of Souvanna's "neutral" government was preserved long after anyone took it seriously, primarily because of the complicity of the Soviet Union. Although the Soviets frequently attacked the United States for its intervention in Laos and its violation of the Geneva Agreement, Moscow, a co-chairman of the Geneva Conference, continued to recognize Souvanna and by extension the right-wing government as legitimate. As Souvanna himself frankly explained to the national assembly in September 1965, "If we destroyed the structure of the coalition government, . . . we would no longer have the support of the socialist countries, especially, the U.S.S.R."[132]

Thus, one of the ironies of the Geneva Agreement and the abortive experiment in Laotian neutrality is Moscow's tacit acquiescence to the subversion of the tripartite coalition government by the United States.

130. Vientiane Domestic Service, September 7, 1965.
131. *New York Times,* March 24, 1967, and November 22, 1966.
132. Vientiane Domestic Service, September 7, 1965.

PATHET LAO VIEW OF THE MILITARY
SITUATION AT THE TIME OF
THE 1962 GENEVA ACCORD

Under control of Pathet Lao and
Neutralists after 1962
ceasefire

Under control of Right Wing
Party

Provincial boundaries

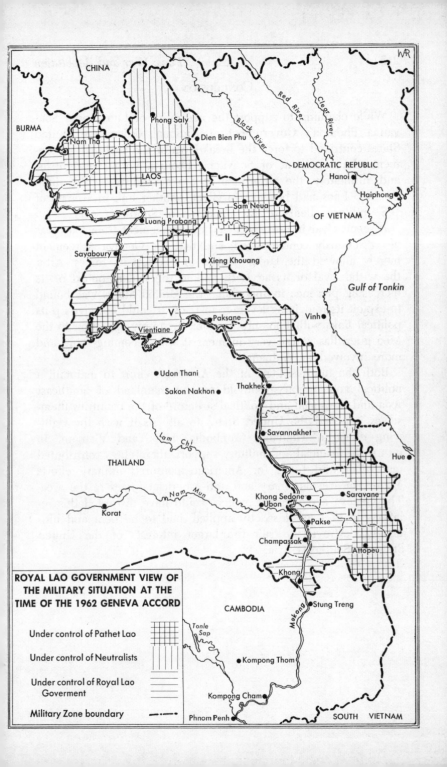

ROYAL LAO GOVERNMENT VIEW OF
THE MILITARY SITUATION AT THE
TIME OF THE 1962 GENEVA ACCORD

Under control of Pathet Lao

Under control of Neutralists

Under control of Royal Lao
Goverment

Military Zone boundary

Conclusion

While claiming to support the neutrality of Laos under Souvanna Phouma's Government of National Union, the United States contrived to force the breakdown of the coalition government, the alignment of Souvanna Phouma with the rightists, and, ultimately, the absorption of the neutralists by the right. By 1965 Laos had become, in effect, another link in a chain of U.S. military clients on the mainland of Southeast Asia.

It seems clear in retrospect that disengagement from Laos was never seriously contemplated, and that the Geneva Agreement merely allowed the United States to regroup its forces. After the withdrawal of its advisers, and in the wider context of its increasing presence in Indochina, the United States was bound to exploit its remaining leverage in Laos. It could not give up its political links with Phoumi's army or its supply operation to the Meo guerrillas at the very moment it was becoming more and more involved in Vietnam.

Both the internal logic of the American effort to maintain a political and military foothold on the mainland of Southeast Asia and the social and political structure of the countries themselves impelled the United States to ally itself with the right-wing elites in Thailand, Cambodia, Laos, and Vietnam. In return for financial and military support, these elites contributed manpower and bases for American-sponsored military efforts against the revolutionary and anti-American forces in the area. The Geneva arrangement, which would have disrupted this relationship in Laos if strictly applied, had to be bent and ultimately destroyed to suit the larger interests of the United States in Southeast Asia.

12

Presidential War in Laos, 1964–1970

Fred Branfman

If the United States intervenes in the third world in the next decade, it is likely to model its actions on its experience in Laos rather than duplicating the frustrations of Vietnam. While the two wars are similar in the destruction and dislocation of civilian populations (although Laos has sustained even greater devastation than Vietnam), the strategies directing them differ significantly. Without introducing its own combat troops into Laos, the United States has waged secretly a more extensive foreign war than any other nation in history. Incorporating the lessons of Vietnam, synthesizing previous Western experience in counterinsurgency, and operating almost exclusively through executive decrees, the American military in Laos has devised a pattern of warfare likely to become the model for all future attempts to fight localized guerrilla conflicts.

As Vietnam has demonstrated, the American military is not geared to combating local insurgencies. Commitment of American troops to Laos has long been opposed by the Pentagon,[1] since this would risk a massive North Vietnamese, or even a Chinese, invasion. Instead, a scheme of warfare has been devised which is characterized by five major operational elements:

1. a massive air war directed, above all, at the destruction of the physical setting and social infrastructure of the enemy;

2. a ground war fought by Asian troops directed and supplied by a relatively small number of American personnel;

---

1. The original discussion in January 1955 dealt with the advisability of enlarging the Lao army. The Pentagon counseled against this, arguing that Laos could not develop a military force capable of resisting its more powerful neighbors. The State Department, however, overrode this on political grounds. It maintained that if the RLG did not develop a greatly enlarged army, it would not be able to resist an internal Pathet Lao victory. See Arthur J. Dommen, *Conflict in Laos* (New York: *Praeger*, 1964), pp. 98–103.

3. the large-scale evacuation of the civilian population to American-controlled zones;

4. the creation of an American-directed civil administration paralleling the existing government structure;

5. a policy of deliberate secrecy designed to give the executive as free a hand as possible.

These techniques take into account problems which have limited the effectiveness of counterinsurgency efforts in other areas. Ground involvement in rural theaters diverts resources from the development of modern conventional and nuclear weaponry, placing emphasis instead on rather low-level technology. At the same time, the impossible task of destroying all enemy sources of supply is attempted and, if necessary, the threat of deploying tactical nuclear weapons is used. But such steps are prevented in the third world arena from Cuba to Vietnam by the threat of intervention by China or the Soviet Union. The United States can only intervene on the ground in such areas if it is willing to risk war with either of the socialist bloc protectors. Lastly, unproductive ground action involves embarrassing battlefield reverses and unnecessary combat deaths. These well-publicized effects have serious domestic repercussions, within the economy as well as in the national psyche. Recognition of these drawbacks by an executive branch nonetheless determined to accept increasing foreign commitments explains not only the evolution of this particular type of warfare but also its secrecy. While neither Congress nor the public opposes foreign intervention per se, expensive operations overseas can lead to what the executive sees as unacceptable limitations on its prerogative. When Laotian-style ventures are openly considered, neither the general public nor the legislative branch are easily persuaded of their value. As Senator J. William Fulbright expressed it:

We got along pretty well in this country for a long time without any interest in Laos at all. . . . What is there about Laos that justifies the spending of a billion dollars . . . ? If we have any sense left we ought to liquidate the mistake (of replacing the French) in the most efficient manner we can and leave it there. . . . I do not think it is of any consequence today whether they (the Vietnamese) control it or not. . . . I do not believe any of my constituents are deeply concerned about whether Laos is independent or not. . . . If I could get up on the floor and say . . . how ridiculous this is, a lot of my colleagues would say, "For goodness' sakes, this is nonsense throwing (deleted) million a year pretty nearly down a rat hole."[2]

The executive branch has at no time informed the general public of the full extent of American activities in Laos. Congress itself received its first formal presentation of information in 1969 when the war was in full swing. And this presentation included numerous distortions; it appeared to have been designed, above all, to defuse possible congressional criticism. Congress was ignorant of the situation because no action regarding Laos had been requested openly by the executive and the war had been conducted almost entirely by executive order to bodies such as the CIA, USAID, USIS, and the armed forces, which are responsible only to the President. The United States has no treaties or written agreements with Laos[3] which would have required congressional scrutiny or approval.

Nixon policy appears to foreshadow application of the Laotian model to other nations of the third world. It calls for precisely the formula developed in Laos: a maximum input of usable American matériel coupled with a minimum investment of American personnel. At this writing (June 1970), moreover, the Laotian model is already being applied to Thailand, though as yet on a far smaller scale. Whether American intervention of the Laotian type will succeed is a moot point. Its strengths and weaknesses, successes or failures, can be debated endlessly. What seems far more to the point is the probability that it will be tried

2. See "United States Security Agreements and Commitments Abroad, Kingdom of Laos," Hearings Before the Subcommittee on United States Security Agreements and Commitments Abroad of the Committee on Foreign Relations, United States Senate, Ninety-First Congress, First Session, Part 2, October 20, 21, 22, and 28, 1969.

3. At the Senate hearings on Laos in October 1969 Deputy Assistant Secretary of State and former ambassador to Laos William Sullivan stated, "The United States has undertaken no defense commitment—written, stated or understood—to the Royal Lao Government (RLG)." *Ibid.*, p. 367.

in other places. The willingness and power of the American executive to intervene, the passive support of the public and Congress, and above all the probable continued threat of local insurgencies to American interests, all suggest that the Laotian experience will serve as the model of third world power struggles in the decade to come. Thus, it is with something more than historical interest that we turn to an examination of the American experience in Laos.

BACKGROUND: A *DE FACTO* ARRANGEMENT

As confirmed in recent testimony before Congress, the primary American aim in Laos since 1964 has been to assist the military effort in Vietnam, regardless of the possible consequences west of the border. United States military activities have been violations of the 1962 Geneva Accords and a direct threat to North Vietnamese security. The United States has used bases in northern Laos to aid in the bombing of North Vietnam and to gather intelligence within that country. The United States has also carried out extensive bombing of southeastern Laos in an attempt to interdict men and supplies moving into South Vietnam from the North. This provocation of Laos' more powerful neighbor for temporary military gains is undoubtedly one of the most monumental of American blunders. Bombing the Ho Chi Minh Trail has also weakened Laos' position. Originally the Trail followed a narrow corridor on the far eastern edge of Laos' frontier with South Vietnam. It had little if any relation to the war within Laos. But, as U.S. bombing of the Trail grew in intensity, it led inevitably to a widening of the war into southern Laos.[4]

The other major American goal in Laos has remained unchanged since 1954: to keep as much Laotian territory as pos-

4. The general in charge of the intelligence branch of the Royal Laotian Army, for example, recently stated in an interview with the author that the supplies first began moving down Route 23, west of Saravane, in March 1968. He, like most other observers, has concluded that this was a direct result of American bombing.

sible within the American sphere of influence. Laos has long been regarded as a key to the security of our SEATO ally, Thailand, and, by extension, to that of the entire Southeast Asian peninsula. Pathet Lao penetration of the Mekong valley, in particular, has been seen as a major threat to American interests for at least two decades. John Kennedy, for example, sent American combat troops to the Thai side of the Mekong border in May 1962, long before North Vietnamese combat involvement in Laos became a real issue.[5]

The pattern of warfare developed by the United States in Laos after 1964 was intended to realize these two goals. Its major operational elements, however, did not derive from prior long-range strategic projections. Rather, they were the outcomes of day-by-day tactical decisions. The escalation of the air war is a good illustration. When it began in 1964, the few sorties flown were directed primarily against supply routes and enemy troop concentrations. But, as more planes became available and Communist forces began to extend their influence, pilots began to bomb the outskirts of inhabited areas, then to stage random air strikes, and finally to engage in saturation bombing of towns and villages. Most other elements in the American war underwent a similar process—with one striking exception. The single most notable development of the Laotian war has been the American refusal to supplement its ground combat advisers with purely American combat units. No nation has ever made such an extensive—and expensive—attempt to control foreign territory without sending in large numbers of its own foot soldiers. This was the subject of much debate within both the Pentagon and State Department and for a number of reasons, it was decided not to intervene on the ground.

The most basic reason was a reluctance to open up a second front directly related to the war in Vietnam. The U.S. Army had warned against getting involved in a ground war in Laos as

5. Hugh Toye, *Laos: Buffer State or Battleground* (London: Oxford University Press, 1968), p. 183. For further discussion of these events, see the article by Jonathan Mirsky and Stephen Stonefield in the present book.

early as 1956 and had reiterated its views in 1961.[6] Their fears were reinforced by the American ground involvement in Vietnam, which demanded their utmost attention. The February 1968 Tet offensive resolved the issue. The United States would not commit extra troops to Vietnam—let alone Laos, where ground intervention might well trigger a North Vietnamese response. And since, as former Ambassador William Sullivan had pointed out, the Democratic Republic of Vietnam (DRV) still had 350,000 troops in reserve in the North,[7] it was clear that in Laos the United States might open a Pandora's box that could be closed no more easily than the one in Vietnam. Similar objections prevailed against the heavy pressure to use ground troops to close the Ho Chi Minh Trail.[8] Even a limited operation would have demanded a commitment of 150,000 American troops (two combat divisions plus support troops). Once again, the United States did not have these troops to spare. Even if they had been available, other obstacles to be considered were communist con-

6. The isues were posed directly for the first time in March 1961, near the end of a successful Pathet Lao dry season offensive. When direct American ground intervention was considered, as Dommen tells it, "The prospects were not good. Admiral Harry D. Felt Commander in Chief of U.S. forces in the Pacific, dispelled any illusions about the complexity of the logistics problems. In the event of large-scale movement of North Vietnamese troops in Laos in response to the commitment of American troops there, the enemy supply line would be short, the American line long . . . a large area would require garrisoning by American troops. The troops would be vulnerable to guerrilla action. In combat against the North Vietnamese, they would be fighting on the defensive against an enemy highly skilled in attritional warfare and intimately familiar with the terrain."—Dommen, *op. cit.,* pp. 188–189. In the end, some 25,000 American ground troops were sent into northeastern Thailand and, although American military advisers continued to fight in Laos, the main force units were not sent.

7. Senate hearings, *op. cit.,* p. 557.

8. The public got some glimpses of this debate during the curious episode of the "McNamara Line" in the fall of 1967. It was announced in October that the United States would install an electronic line across Laos to monitor and prevent North Vietnamese infiltration into South Vietnam. (See "The End of a Myth," *Newsweek,* October 23, 1970.) This led to public criticism that such action would involve sending American ground troops into Laos and thus almost certainly would extend the war. In the end, it appears that the original idea was withdrawn and a compromise solution implemented: Task Force Alpha. (For a partial account of Task Force Alpha, see "Laos: Where the Bombing Goes On," *Newsweek,* March 31, 1969.)

trol of the heights, their superior knowledge of the terrain, and, once again, those 350,000 reserve troops. It was one thing to invade communist sanctuaries in Cambodia, which had become important through convenience rather than necessity, but it was quite another to consider striking the Trail area. There was also the very real possibility that such a move would simply force a North Vietnamese swing to the west, creating the undesirable second front. State Department officials also argued forcefully that American ground intervention would destroy the final shreds of the 1962 Geneva Accords. Although the Accords had been clearly violated by all sides, maintaining some pretense of observing them would make it easier to reach a postwar settlement in Laos.

Finally, a major factor in the U.S. decision not to introduce ground troops into Laos has been the assumption of a basically defensive posture by the Communists. The Pathet Lao have concentrated on building up the zones they control and taking major military bases in or near these zones. The North Vietnamese have focused on controlling the Trail and securing northeastern Laos. They have avoided taking towns held by the Royal Laotian Government forces or making massive forays into the Mekong valley. At present, there are *at the very most* five to ten thousand North Vietnamese combat troops involved in Laos, mostly in the northeast and areas contiguous to the Trail.[9] Their number in Laos has followed the growth of American, Thai, and other foreign military elements on the Royal Laotian Government (RLG) side.

But, although the United States has not introduced ground troops into Laos, it has introduced a different kind of army. After 1962 thousands of Americans came to Laos: CIA operatives, USAID bureaucrats, International Voluntary Services (IVS) volunteers, Air America pilots, Air Force ground technicians and Blue Berets, embassy officials, Army military advisers, USIS functionaries, Bureau of Public Roads road builders, and Bureau of Reclamation dam builders. Their day-to-day jobs were different, but their basic mission was the same: to shore up the

9. See the appendix to this article, pp. 278–280.

inadequate Royal Laotian Government which emerged from the political turmoil of the period July 1962 to February 1965.[10]

The July 1962 Geneva Agreement recognized a coalition government in Laos of the right, center, and left. In the power struggles which followed, the United States consistently threw its military support behind the rightist army and its political support behind neutralist Souvanna Phouma. It was felt that the American-created Royal Laotian Army offered the best hope of securing American military objectives in Laos. And, among the various available Vientiane politicians, Souvanna Phouma was regarded as having the widest domestic and international prestige. This forced marriage of rightist generals and Souvanna Phouma was not without its tensions. The continued friction, however, resulted in some compromise on both sides. The generals retained domestic and military control over Laos. Souvanna, in turn, was allowed some degree of control over the activities of the Ministry of Foreign Affairs.

The chaotic political and military events in Laos occurred as the war next door was intensifying. By February 1965 American ground and air intervention in Vietnam had stimulated a North Vietnamese desire to obtain a Laotian corridor to supply aid to the National Liberation Front in South Vietnam. The battle lines were drawn. The United States found itself allied with a Royal Laotian Government which controlled perhaps 40 per cent of Laotian territory and two thirds of the people. The RLG sphere of influence included the Vientiane plain, Mekong valley, the Sam Thong–Long Cheng area west to Route 13, and various positions in northern Laos.

The basic American strategic objectives were (1) to control northern Laos in order to prevent communist penetration of the Mekong valley; (2) to extend American control of and influence over the Royal Laotian Government throughout the Mekong valley and Vientiane plain; (3) to bomb the Ho Chi Minh Trail; and (4) to use Laos as a base for the air war against North

10. For details and views of this period, see the articles by Jonathan Mirsky, and Stephen Stonefield, D. Gareth Porter, and Wilfred Burchett in the present book.

Vietnam. Communist forces were in control of most of the mountainous regions in Laos. Their basic aims included (1) driving RLG forces out of northern Laos and in particular asserting control over the area down to the Plain of Jars; (2) keeping the Ho Chi Minh Trail open; and (3) working for a Vientiane government in which the Pathet Lao would have a real and, ultimately, a controlling voice.

The battle that ensued had a pendulum-like quality. In the rainy season (April to October), the pendulum would arc north and east as the RLG advanced. In the dry season (November to April), it would swing back south and west as the Pathet Lao launched their annual offensive. Ground fighting on both sides seemed somewhat restrained. During the rainy season, RLG troops would usually advance behind heavy air bombardment. Communist main force units, in traditional guerrilla fashion, generally retreated without engaging in combat. During its offensives, the most typical RLG objective was to evacuate the civilian population from enemy villages and take it back behind friendly lines. During the dry season, the Communist troops' main objective was usually to secure the military bases held by the RLG. Hindered mainly by intensive bombing, they normally succeeded in their dry season goals, because RLG soldiers habitually fled from their outposts or bases prior to the final attack. From 1964 until 1968 this seesaw pattern of conflict, concentrated mainly in northern Laos, was kept roughly in balance, while the outside support given to each side increased year by year. The RLG received increasing American air, Thai Army, and other foreign mercenary combat support. The Pathet Lao received increasing amounts of combat support from the North Vietnamese Army (NVA). In November 1968 each side controlled essentially the same territory that it held in June 1964.

November 1968, however, marked a significant escalation in the war; the United States ceased its bombing of North Vietnam and diverted the newly available aircraft to Laos. Pathet Lao forces were no more active during this period than they had ever been at the beginning of a dry season. There was little if any indication that they now intended to advance much beyond previous limits. Nonetheless, the United States decided to greatly intensify its bombing and to support a ground advance into northern Laos as well.

T. D. Allman, whose *New York Times* reports helped spark the 1969 Senate hearings on Laos, has written of this decision that "observers say the most significant development in the recent history of the Laotian war came in November, 1968, when the full might of the U.S. air arsenal—previously concentrated on North Vietnam—was turned on Laos and the trail . . . the five-fold escalation of the U.S. bombing in Laos, the observers say, convinced the North Vietnamese that they had to meet force with counter-force."[11] Whatever the role of the North Vietnamese,[12] communist forces did indeed reply in force. After a year and a half of escalation and counterescalation by each side,[13] the pendulum has swung farther south and west than ever before. Communist forces are now in a stronger position than at the end of any dry season since 1964. Having driven the RLG out of most of the positions they have held since 1964, the Pathet Lao now control most of the mountainous areas of Laos; the only major enclave remaining under RLG control is a much-reduced Sam Thong–Long Cheng area.

11. T. D. Allman, "Waiting for a Miracle," *Far Eastern Economic Review*, Vol. 67, No. 11 (March 12, 1970), p. 6.

12. The relationship between Pathet Lao and North Vietnamese military high commands is not yet known. Although most observers tend to assume that the North Vietnamese make all basic decisions about military activities in Laos, there is as yet little evidence to support this point of view. Langer and Zasloff claim that this is the case, but their contention appears to be based almost entirely on the revelations of one North Vietnamese officer, a captain named Mai Dai Hap, who defected to the RLG in December 1966. Neither Hap's rank nor role—as adviser to a Pathet Lao battalion—suggest that his testimony affords much solid evidence of the relationship between high commands.

13. November, December 1968—RLG forces launch large offensive into Northern Xieng Khouang and Sam Neua provinces; March 1969—Communist forces take Na Khang, an important RLG base in northeastern Laos; April 1969—RLG takes Xieng Khouang City; September 1969, RLG forces retake Moung Soui and go on to take almost the entire Plain of Jars; September 1969 —RLG forces sweep along Route 9 and take Moung Phine; February 1970—communist forces retake the Plain of Jars and Moung Soui; March 1970—communist forces knock out Sam Thong and launch ground probes against Long Cheng; April 1970—Communist forces take Attopeu; June 1970—Communist forces take Saravane.

The war in Laos today is essentially between Communist ground forces and American air power, for since the 1950s both the civilian and military arms of the Royal Laotian Government have proven to be the most dubious possible instruments for effecting American objectives. Elitist, urban-centered, and riddled with corruption from top to bottom, the RLG today exercises varying control over 13 of Laos' 16 provincial capitals and over a series of district towns and small military outposts. The area between these points is a shadowy no-man's-land. Roving bands of Communist guerrillas regularly cut off the roads; only a few are considered safe for travel. RLG officials generally do not venture more than 10 to 20 kilometers from the provincial and district capitals. Much of their supplies is brought in by air.

Laos has been divided into five military regions, each ruled by a coalition of right-wing generals and traditional ruling families. These five regions operate autonomously and have proven incapable of significant cooperation. Military Region 1, Luang Prabang, is dominated by General Ouane Rattikone, commander in chief of the Laotian Army. His main source of power is his exclusive control over the opium trade from northern Laos. His chief nonmilitary support comes from his alliance with the royal family.

Military Region 2, which includes most of northeastern Laos, is an emerging Meo kingdom led by chief Vang Pao, who is supported directly by the United States. He is closely allied with Touby Ly Fong, an hereditary clan leader whose cousin Faydang is a Pathet Lao commander.[14] Faydang is vying with Vang Pao for the allegiance of the Meo.

Military Region 3, which includes most of central Laos, centers on Savannakhet. It is administered by General Bounphone, the weakest of the five military commanders, but in practice is run

14. Touby, now frequently found in the bar at the Hotel Constellation in Vientiane, recently told a group of journalists about his split with Faydang. He explained that after returning from his studies, Faydang was rightfully entitled to be named chief administrator for his region. But the French did not want him and chose Touby instead. "Faydang never liked the French," said Touby, "I don't know why. As for me, I was proud that they selected me. You know, France is a rich and beautiful country, and I was the first Meo ever to study in a university there."

by Colonel Thao Ly. The real power in the region is the Insisiengmay family, led by Leuam Insisiengmay, vice premier and
minister of education. Phoumi Nosavan retains a strong following and is actively involved in political maneuvering, thanks to
the millions of dollars he salted away during his heyday of
American aid.

Military Region 4, with headquarters at Pakse, includes the
six provinces of southern Laos. This is the traditional fief of the
Na Champassak family whose leader,[15] Prince Boun Oum,
dominates the area. In addition to tradition, his chief sources of
power are extensive commercial interests, ranging from tin mines
to vast landholdings, transport and aviation companies, and arms
trade with the Communists. The commander of Region 4 is
General Prasook Sanly, perhaps the toughest of the Lao commanders.

Military Region 5 is Vientiane province, ruled by perhaps the
brightest of the Laotian military leaders, General Kouprasith
Abhay. He himself belongs to the powerful Abhay family from
Khong Island in southern Laos. He owns a widespread array of
properties and commercial enterprises, mostly acquired during
the last six years. These include forests, sawmills, land and
buildings within Vientiane city, agricultural land seized from
farmers in the Ban Keun area, whorehouses, slot machines, a
bowling alley, and transport contracts. In addition, he is awarded
a percentage of the ownership or profit from most other commercial activities conducted in his area. While he receives American
aid, the foundation of Kouprasith's power is his alliance with the
Sananikone family. Jocularly referred to by American officials

15. Under the French, the ruling families of the traditional kingdoms of
Vientiane, Luang Prabang, and Champassak retained special privileges but
did not have formal powers. Boun Oum, for example, worked his way up in
the French administration, spending most of his early career as a clerk,
secretary, and district chief. His personal fortunes began to rise only at the
end of the Second World War when he opposed the Lao Issara (independence) movement and joined the French forces as they drove up from the
south to retake Laos. In 1947, when the three kingdoms were united under
the king of Luang Prabang, Boun Oum was rewarded with the lifetime title
of vice-regent of the kingdom. It was at this point that he began to acquire
the vast power and wealth he holds today.

here as the "Rockefellers of Laos," the Sananikone clan is predominant in national politics and the economy. Phoui Sananikone, the clan patriarch, is president of the National Assembly. Two other Sananikones are deputies in the Assembly. Two Sananikones are generals, including Chief of Staff Oudone. Ngon Sananikone is minister of public works. A host of other Sananikones are found at lower levels of the political, military, and civil service structure.

The central government has little influence within these military regions, where the word of the military commander, and of the traditional families supporting him, is law. Indeed the open hostility of all the military commanders to "interference" by the central or local civilian government is a major political fact of life in Laos. And the rivalries between military commanders and the families allied with them prevent functional collaboration among regions. (It is common knowledge in Laos, for example, that Prasook and Vang Pao are barely on speaking terms with Kouprasith.) The colonels who control each district capital regard these posts as opportunities for personal enrichment and jealously guard their domains, which they rule with an iron hand.

Neither the king nor the National Assembly wield noticeable influence outside of Luang Prabang. The former has little charisma, for the house of Luang Prabang became the national monarchy only in 1947. The present king is unknown outside the capital, and he is regarded with attitudes ranging from indifference to contempt. U.S. official Loring Waggoner, for example, reported to the Senate that many of the people in his area (only 150 miles south of Luang Prabang) "do not know who the King is, they do not know what he looks like."[16] The author has frequently heard villagers around Vientiane make rather resentful jokes about the king, whom they tend to regard as a symbol of all that they dislike about the RLG. In the south, the king is frequently ridiculed, particularly by Prince Boun Oum. A French friend repeated to this author one of Boun Oum's favorite jests: "[I] would shoot the King in the head, but he's so stupid that it

16. Senate hearings, *op. cit.*, p. 580.

would be a waste of the bullet." Laotians regard the National Assembly as a powerless debating club. Its membership is composed almost entirely of men from the traditional ruling families, who attain their seats in elections controlled by the military and who use them exclusively for personal profit.

Corruption in Laos is omnipresent on every level of the military and civilian hierarchies. One could offer an endless list of types and techniques: land-grabbing, bribes for performing the simplest government functions, appropriating public funds for private use, and selling American-supplied commodities to whomever will buy them, with no questions asked. It costs $70 in bribes to get a driving license in Vientiane, $100 to obtain a commercial license, and thousands—depending on how high one's adversary is willing to go—to win a court case. On a recent trip to southern Laos, the author was told of farmers forced to lay their crops by the side of the road for collection by the local colonel, who sold them in Pakse for his personal profit; of merchants compelled to pay crippling bribes directly to local military and civilian leaders to remain in business; of soldiers deprived of their American-supplied medicine each month because their commanders are selling it; of refugees deprived of American-supplied rice, which was being sold by government officials; and of village girls removed to the provincial capitals by high-ranking government officials to serve as temporary concubines until they ceased to amuse their patrons. Such stories are extremely commonplace in Laos.

Largely as a result of corruption, the Royal Laotian Government raises at most about 40 per cent of its national budget through taxes and duties. The remainder is made up by the United States and several other foreign donors. The proceeds from Laos' two major natural resources, tin and timber, go into private pockets. The tin mines in central Laos belong to Boun Oum and a French company. Timber, Laos' fastest rising export (because of purchases by the American army in Thailand), is controlled primarily by Kouprasith Abhay and the Sananikone family. Tax collections for the public exchequer are a fraction of what they might be. Civilian and military leaders pay virtually no taxes on their considerable incomes. The weak central government refuses to tax the villagers for fear of becoming even more unpopular. Laos' other main source of income is customs duty on imports. Revenues here again are diverted from the central government. Customs officials take a flat 50 per cent of the receipts by falsifying records of imported goods. The customs department is renowned for the unusually sumptuous villas of its department heads and for the practice of giving motorcycles to the noncustoms officials who comprise the bulk of its invincible soccer team.

One of the most critical weaknesses of the Royal Laotian Government has been its structural inability to meet rural needs. Both high-ranking and lower-level officials—even those in such offices as the Department of Rural Affairs or the Ministry of Agriculture—avoid visiting villages. In general, it is more the incompetent or less well-connected officials who are sent to outlying areas. To the extent that there is an interchange between the cities and villages, it is by and large a flow of the resources and the most talented rural youth from the villages into the towns. The RLG devotes little money to rural or productive purposes, using its capital instead for luxury housing, imports, and amusements. This was strikingly illustrated in October 1969, when the director of resettlement pleaded with the international Mekong committee for $300,000 to resettle some 3,000 people who had been forcibly moved from behind the reservoir area of the committee-built Nam Ngeum dam by RLG soldiers and bombing. He requested the funds, which he claimed the RLG totally lacked. On the same day, by chance, Vientiane's first bowling alley had its gala opening. The ceremonies were presided over by its president, General Kouprasith Abhay, and a group of other Laotian officials who composed its board of directors. The price of constructing the bowling alley is reliably reported to be about $300,000.

Laotian villages suffer from classic third world ills: high infant mortality, illiteracy, poor diet, illness—particularly chronic dysentery—and low life expectancy. The elitist educational system offers little to peasants hoping to improve their lot or that of their villages. City life is also hard; young boys and girls, and indeed most of those who are not civil servants work 10 to 14 hours a day, 7 days a week. In return they typically receive room and board and salaries averaging from $6 to $10 a month. Madames purchase village girls from their parents for $200–$400 to work as prostitutes, and those who run away are brought back by the police. Opium dens abound. A young refugee from Pathet Lao zones once explained: "You know, the Pathet Lao always used to tell us that there were more whorehouses and opium dens in Vientiane than schools and hospitals. I never really believed them. But now that I'm here, do you know? They were right!"

But General Kouprasith Abhay once explained to the author:

You know, our Laotian villagers are happy, peaceful people. They know how to cooperate together, in fact they have their own kind of village communism. The best thing for our government to do is to leave them alone. Oh, we can build a few schools, a few roads. But the best thing is to leave them be, allow them to grow their rice and till their fields.

It is no wonder, then, that the RLG has little support from the general population and even less from the people who know it best.

From the American point of view perhaps the most serious problem in Laos has been the consistently poor performance of the Royal Laotian Army (RLA). Their weakness is often attributed to the gentle, pacific Laotian personality, despite the obvious fact that the Laotians on the other side are aggressive, highly motivated, and effective in combat. Former Ambassador William Sullivan was aware of one essential RLA weakness when he told the Senate:

The principal military shortcoming in Laos is leadership. Senior officers are often selected on the basis of family, wealth or political connections. They tend to have limited military training or experience. Aggressiveness and combat proficiency of Lao troops consequently suffer.[17]

He might have added that service in the Lao officer corps is

17. *Ibid.*, p. 371.

regarded first and foremost as an opportunity for personal enrichment. Activities include pocketing American-supplied salaries of nonexistent soldiers, selling arms and ammunition, using military vehicles and personnel for private businesses and farms, collecting bribes and taxes from local businessmen, and forcing levies on farmers. The Laotian officer's interests, psychological and real, lie in avoiding combat rather than seeking it out. Despite 20 years of guerrilla warfare, the Laotian Military Academy in Vientiane still trains its officers in conventional tactics. The director of the Academy feels he should train a Laotian army which falls somewhere "in between the French and American armies."

RLA troops are probably among the least motivated in Asia. The overwhelming majority are village youths who have been forcibly conscripted "for the duration of the war" or, as they often put it, "until we are killed." Their pay is about $5 a month, the food poor and conditions arduous. They constantly complain of the flagrant corruption of their officers, of being employed in a variety of nonmilitary tasks in officers' private enterprises and homes, and of the lack of even the most elementary system of justice. In a classic understatement, Sullivan said: "Since the army's educational level is low, its attitudes are rarely public-minded."[18] RLA troops are greatly feared and resented by villagers, who complain of their bothering village girls, stealing livestock and crops, and pressing them into work gangs without compensation. The educational level has little to do with it. For Pathet Lao soldiers, with as little or less schooling, are invariably more "public-minded."

In contrast to the Pathet Lao, who believe in their cause, RLA troops are convinced that even in the unlikely event of victory the spoils will go to those in power. Appeals to patriotism, calling on them to fight the North Vietnamese (and often the Chinese) tend to frighten more than inspire them. And the introduction of regular Thai Army troops and other foreign mercenaries has undercut these patriotic appeals. The RLA, both officers and troops, remain famous throughout Asia for their propensity to flee the scene of battle.

18. *Ibid.,* p. 371.

The failings of the Royal Laotian Government in every field—economic, political, and military—presented the United States with a basic problem in the early 1960s. To achieve its objectives in Laos, it became necessary to intervene directly and assume control over the functions normally carried out by a sovereign government—warfare, economic management, and domestic development. But the American urge to assume responsibility for Laotian affairs was not uncontrollable: Laos was a desirable base from which to wage war in Vietnam, not an area of primary American interest; at the same time, the RLG had little enthusiasm for this project, so clearly Vietnam-oriented, and their reluctance gave them a way to bargain with the Americans.

The Ho Chi Minh Trail in 1964 was a rather narrow corridor in southeastern Laos running through territory over which the RLG had rarely attempted to exercise its sovereignty. While its use disturbed the United States, it caused few problems for Laos. But if the United States attacked it in force, the RLG feared the communists would respond to the provocation by moving westward and increasing the number of North Vietnamese troops fighting a wider war in Laos. Were their interests not served by the American presence, therefore, the Lao elite could be expected to protest and perhaps effectively prevent American use of Lao territory to fight the Vietnam War.

Therefore a *de facto* agreement was reached. In return for the RLG's acquiescence to its military activities in Laos, the United States would make no attempts to limit the domestic power and prerogatives of the Lao elite. On the contrary, the United States would buttress their position through military assistance and a domestic aid program focused on the villages, an area in which the RLG had little direct interest. This arrangement helped to contribute to the demise of Laotian neutrality. RLG-controlled territory within Laos became a part of an American-oriented, Saigon-Bangkok-Vientiane axis. By allowing the U.S. Air Force to bomb throughout Laos, Thai soldiers to fight there, American CIA advisers to run the "Armée Clandestine" and, above all, by allowing radar sites to be established in northern Laos for use in the bombing of North Vietnam, the RLG became a functional element of the American camp.

THE AIR WAR: "NO PLACE TO HIDE"

Most of the resources devoted to the war in Laos have gone into the air war. Outmanned on the ground, the United States has resorted to continuous escalation in the air in an attempt to preserve its position. The annual cost is in the neighborhood of $2 billion; over 50,000 airmen in bases in Thailand, South Vietnam, and Guam, and on the 7th fleet's carriers are involved. The whole range of the American air arsenal, from the B–52 through the F–4 down to the Cessna, has been employed.

What is most distinctive about this air war is that it has resulted in the most protracted and extensive bombing of civilian targets in history. Beginning in May 1964 the attacks have gradually been extended to cover all Pathet Lao-controlled territory, an area comprising some 50,000 square miles and (according to American embassy estimates) containing over one million people.[19] For the last two years, bombing has been carried out on a continuous basis against the populated portions of this region, resulting in the destruction of most of the villages and towns, disruption of normal life, and a significant number of civilian casualties.

The American air war was begun in 1964, primarily as a tactical bombing effort involving strikes at supply routes and troop concentrations, and offering close tactical air support for Lao troops during battle. All three functions soon became impractical. The important areas of combat are the mountainous regions of Laos, a vast carpet of forest dotted by small villages and towns. Communist forces move in small mobile groups, usually

---

19. This estimate was characterized by the embassy official who gave it to the author in March 1970 as "a very rough one." In the absence of other statistics, however, this is probably the closest approximation presently available. A province-by-province breakdown shows:

Population in Pathet Lao-Controlled Territory

Phong Saly	115,000	Khammouane	78,000
Houa Phans	192,000	Saravane	66,000
Houa Khong	65,000	Savannakhet	14,000
Luang Prabang	263,500	Sedone	15,000
Xieng Khouang	12,000	Attopeu	80,000
Vientiane	18,700	Sayaboury	10,000
Borikane	9,200		

attacking at night. Under these conditions, the pinpointing of "military" targets is most difficult, and random bombing of the forest is clearly a pointless waste of ordnance. And, since the United States had only air power with which to pursue its objectives, it was inevitable that towns and villages would become the prime targets.

The change in emphasis from tactical to saturation bombing was carried out with a number of strategic objectives in mind. These may be summarized as demoralization, deprivation, and destruction—that is: (1) demoralizing the civilian population; (2) depriving the Pathet Lao of rice, vegetables, and livestock; (3) depriving them of porters, recruits, and civil administrative personnel; (4) depriving them of natural locales for regroupment, recreation, and storing arms; and (5) destruction of commerce and trade. The overall aim has been to weaken the Pathet Lao as an effective fighting force by destroying their physical, social, and economic infrastructure. Another major aim of bombing is to slow or stop the movement along the Ho Chi Minh Trail. Thus the saturation bombing campaign has been conducted primarily in two areas of Laos: (1) the northeast, from the southern rim of the Plain of Jars to the frontier with North Vietnam (an area estimated to contain something over 200,000 people); and (2) the mountainous regions of southeastern Laos (with an estimated population of 200,000 to 250,000 people).

In February 1970 some 15,000 ethnic Laotians were moved off the Plain of Jars area into refugee camps in the Vientiane plain; these evacuees had been under Pathet Lao control from May 1964 until September 1969. The author has spoken with more than 300 of these people, from all major towns and more than 50 villages throughout the region. Their reports have, for the first time, given outside observers a clear picture of the nature of the American air war. Every individual interviewed—without exception—has said that his town or village was destroyed by American bombing while he resided there during 1968 or 1969. Each has said that his village was bombed countless times, the bombs continuing to fall even after the village had been totally destroyed. Each refugee added that all of the other towns and villages within the general area with which he is familiar have been repeatedly bombed and are now leveled.

The evacuees describe four main phases of bombing. The first ran from May 1964 until about October 1966. Bombing during this period was rather sporadic, carried out mostly by propeller-driven aircraft, and directed largely against presumed troop concentrations in the forest. Between October 1966 and the beginning of 1968, bombing began to be focused on villages and towns. American jets became more noticeable; in certain areas people began evacuating their homes, and civilian casualties became more numerous. The year 1968 saw a third escalation, with American jets now outnumbering the Laotian Air Force's propeller-driven planes. Bombing was directed primarily against villages and towns and began to be carried out on a regular basis. Most villages and towns were evacuated during this period, and people moved to outlying areas, where they spent much of their time in holes dug in the ground or into the bases of hills and mountains. Most villages suffered direct bombing raids during this period and a number were leveled. Bombing in forested areas was relatively light.

But these people speak most of 1969, after the bombing halt in North Vietnam and the diversion of jets into Laos. During this period jets came over daily, bombing both day and night, dropping 500-pound bombs, delayed-action bombs, napalm, phosphorous bombs and, most of all, CBU antipersonnel bombs. They say that American jets (primarily F–4s and F–150s), which almost entirely replaced the prop-driven aircraft, bombed both the villages and their outskirts, that they themselves spent most of their time in holes or caves, and that they suffered numerous civilian casualties. Everything was attacked—buffaloes, cows, rice fields, schools, temples, and tiny shelters erected outside the villages. The author has also talked with more than 50 evacuees from Pathet Lao zones in southeastern Laos who paint an identical picture of the escalation and ultimate nature of American bombing in their areas. Similar bombing has been carried out elsewhere in Laos, including the Mekong valley. Jacques Decornoy of *Le Monde,* who visited Sam Neua province

in the spring of 1968, is the only non-Communist observer to
have written a firsthand account of life in Pathet Lao territory
(see article 25). His reports of the bombing tally with those of
evacuees from the Plain of Jars and southeastern Laos, although
it appears that Sam Neua has been the hardest hit. It has become
the general rule that any territory taken by Communist forces
will be heavily bombed and that the primary objectives will be
the towns and villages in the area. Evacuees from the Nam
Ngeum dam area in the Vientiane plain, areas east of Thakhek
in central Laos, and Lao Ngam, Thateng, and the Bolovens Plateau in southern Laos, have all reported extensive jet and pro-
peller aircraft bombing in their areas.[20]

The air war is the single most expensive item in the American
war budget for Laos. It was revealed in the Senate hearings that
the cost of one sortie over northern Laos is $3,190.[21] Although the
total number of sorties was deleted, most observers accept the
figures given by Robert Shaplen in the April 1970 issue of *Foreign Affairs*. Shaplen estimated that the United States carried out
an average of 200–300 sorties a day over northern Laos, and
1,200 daily over the southeast.[22] A rather conservative estimate
of the cost would thus be something over $120 million a month,
and a moderate estimate of the cost of all phases of the air war

20. Jacques Doyen gave an eyewitness report of bombing in the Mekong
valley some 25 miles northeast of the Mekong from Saksane: "Our truck then
crossed the twin villages of Nongboua and Nongvieng, bombed on the 17th
of February by T–28's and American F–150's. The Pathet Lao were refuged
there and had organized football games with the population before being surprised by the bombs. The school is in ruins. A blackboard lies on a bench
jutting out from the debris. Here and there are the remains of houses. . . ."
In *Le Figaro*, datelined March 10, 1970, "The Ambiguity of the American
Involvement in Laos," Jacques Doyen and Guy Hannoteau.

21. Senate hearings, *op. cit.*, p. 371.

22. The figure of 200–300 strikes for northern Laos is probably too low.
An American embassy official recently indicated to the author that the same
sorties level over North Vietnam was maintained against northern Laos after
November 1968. It has been reported that Pentagon statistics show that
American sorties against North Vietnam averaged about "12,000 sorties a
month" (*Washington Post*, August 16, 1969, by Stanley Karnow). Thus,
after November 1968, U.S. airplanes were probably averaging at least 400
sorties a day (to this might be added the sorties normally carried out before
the bombing halt over North Vietnam) against northern Laos.

in Laos would be about $2 billion a year. In addition to the daily operational costs of actual air raids, the American air war in Laos has required a sizable investment of overhead capital for bases, planes, and personnel. A conservative guess would be that at any given time there are some 50,000 American personnel involved in the air war in Laos. Udorn Air Force Base alone houses some 10,000 American airmen. In addition to ordnance, servicing, and logistic functions back at the base, their tasks include

a. saturation and tactical bombing.
b. reconnaissance flights.
c. gunship flights.
d. Airborne Control Command squadron flights.
e. rescue missions for downed pilots.
f. spotter flights for American, Thai, and Laotian bombing.
g. military logistic flights.
h. supporting intelligence-gathering missions behind enemy lines by Asian commandos and Air Force Blue Berets.
i. general transport of U.S. military and paramilitary personnel.

For purposes of analysis, the American air war in Laos might be divided into four operations: 7/13th U.S. Air Force bombing against the Ho Chi Minh Trail; 7/13th U.S. Air Force bombing related to the war within Laos; 506th Special Operations Wing activities, which provide propeller-driven aircraft for military support operations within Laos; and the Air America, Continental Air Services, and United States Air Force air support involved in supplying and deploying Asian mercenary ground troops. MACV, Saigon, coordinates 7/13th Air Force bombing of the Trail. It includes B–52 bombing from Guam and Uttaphao in southern Thailand and jet bombing from carriers of the 7th fleet, air bases in South Vietnam, and Korat, Ubon, Takhli, and Nakhorn Phanom air bases in Thailand.

Although in theory jet bombing related to the war in Laos is also coordinated out of Saigon, in practice the effective center is Udorn Air Force Base in Thailand (see Figure 1). Udorn houses the largest air wing in Thailand and is, in addition, head-

Figure 1. Chain of Command for United States' Air War in Laos

Almost all of the activities taking place out of Udorn Air Force Base are carried out in Laos. There is little connection between Udorn and South Vietnam. The following chart gives an idea of the scope of these activities and the planes involved.

Commander
7th Air Force (Saigon)
(COMBAT)

Commander
13th Air Force (Clark AFB)
(COMBAT SUPPORT)

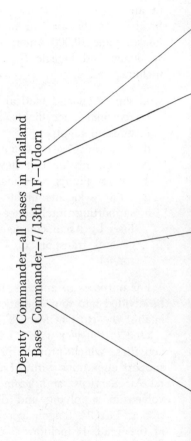

Deputy Commander—all bases in Thailand
Base Commander—7/13th AF—Udorn

432 Tactical Reconnaissance Wing			Air Force Tenants On Base	Air America	Thai AF "T" Squadron
11th Tactical Reconnaissance Squadron (TRS) (RF–4 Jets)	14th TRS (RF–4 Jets)	555 Tactical Fighter Squadron (TFS) (F–4 Jets)	1. 7th Airborne Control Command Squadron (ACCS) (C–130s)	Planes: C–123s C–47s Bell helicopters C–47s Porters Cessnas Dorniers	T–28s
		13th TFS (F–4 Jets)	2. Spooky Squadron (AC–47 and AC–54 gunships)		
Support Squadrons			3. 38th Air Rescue and Recovery Squadron (ARRS) (normal helicopters)		
432 Field Maintenance Squadron			4. 40th ARRS (Jolly Green Giant helicopters, also used as gunships)		
432 Avionics Maintenance Squadron			5. Detachment one 506th Special Operations Wing (T–28s – A–1Es)		
432 Munitions Maintenance Squadron					
621 Tactical Control Squadron					
1974 Communications Group					
1973 Communications Squadron					
432 Transportation Squadron					
432 Security Police					
432 Services Squadron					

quarters for Air America, Continental Air Services, the CIA, and a detachment of the 506th. The base is primarily oriented toward the effort in Laos, while its operations are supplemented by bombing missions emanating from Nakhon Phanom, Korat, Ubon, and Takhli. In addition to F–4 and F–100 series bombers, F–4 and EC–121 reconnaissance aircraft, Huey helicopter gunships, H–134 and "Jolly Green Giant" rescue helicopters are used. There are also C–130s of the Airborne Control Command, at least one of which is over Laos 24 hours a day, coordinating bombing activities. Informed sources within Thailand report that the great majority of the ordnance used are 500 pound-antipersonnel bombs, known as CBUs, "guavas," or "cluster" bombs.

The 506th special operations wing is based at Nakhon Phanom Air Force Base, with detachments at Udorn, Long Cheng in northern Laos, Savannakhet in southern Laos, and Danang, South Vietnam. Its propeller-driven aircraft include T–28 bombers, A–1 "Skyraiders," AC–47 and AC–54 "Spooky" gunships, and a variety of small planes used for spotting bombing strikes. The planes are flown by American, Thai, and Laotian pilots; the American and Thai pilots fly out of Thailand and South Vietnam, while the Laotian pilots begin most of their missions from bases within Laos. Nakhon Phanom also houses the multibillion-dollar Project Alpha, which is designed to coordinate intelligence gathered from electronic sensors dropped on the Ho Chi Minh Trail and to monitor movements between Laos and Thailand. There is speculation that the two computers employed by Project Alpha are the largest in Asia south of the Caspian Sea, reportedly bigger than the ones the Russians lent the Chinese to build their atomic bomb. In any event the most noteworthy thing about them at this point is that they don't work. Their failure helps explain why it costs about $100,000 for each truck destroyed on the Ho Chi Minh Trail.

The Laotian Air Force is a component of the 506th. Consisting of some fifty T–28s and fewer than a dozen gunships, it is divided into five wings within Laos: at Luang Prabang, Long Cheng, Vientiane, Savannakhet, and Pakse. Its Laotian pilots are trained in Thailand by American and Thai instructors. In addition to their salaries, they receive $1 a bombing raid and often fly as many as five a day. The number of sorties flown by the Laotian Air Force varies between 5 and 20 per cent of the daily total. American pilots fly spotter planes for their bombing missions. Major repairs on their planes are done by American, Thai, Nationalist Chinese, and Filipino mechanics at the American air bases in Thailand. Ordnance is supplied from Thailand, and bombs are loaded under guidance from American military advisers.

Air America and Continental Air Services are based at Udorn. They supply equipment to Laotian military and paramilitary forces, rice and arms to Meo refugees grouped into self-defense units, and transport Laotian army troops. Their planes, which include C–123s and C–47 cargo planes, Bell helicopters, and a variety of smaller aircraft are piloted by Americans, usually retired Air Force pilots. Their logistic efforts are often supplemented by U.S. Air Force C–130s.

In theory, the American ambassador is in charge of these operations, approving or rejecting suggested targets. In practice, the U.S. military controls the air war. Lacking independent means of verification, the embassy merely approves targets (of which there is often a backlog), so that the U.S. Air Force can then decide how, when, and how often they will be bombed. The appointment in June 1969 of Ambassador G. McMurtrie Godley, a firm and open advocate of continued bombing, has increased the military domination of the air war and other programs as well. The primary criterion used in setting the number of bombing raids flown over Laos appears to be the number of planes that can be spared from military operations in the rest of Indochina. The level of communist activity at a particular time is weighed, but it is given only secondary consideration. The great jump in sorties in November 1968, for example, occurred during one of the periodic lulls in communist military activity which had followed every rainy season for the past six years; but the cessation of the bombing in North Vietnam had freed jets for use in Laos. Thus, the American rationale behind the escalation, as enunciated by U.S. Deputy Chief of Mission

Stearns, was simply: "Well, we had all those planes sitting around and couldn't just let them stay there with nothing to do."[23]

The reasoning behind the escalating air war has been as vague and contradictory as its results. The aim of disrupting the socio-economic fabric of life in Pathet Lao zones and demoralizing the civilians has been achieved through saturation bombing. Commerce, farming, medical care, schooling, and movement between villages were all seriously hindered by the necessity of hiding from the bombs. Transportation became the Pathet Lao's major problem. Goods which had been previously transported by truck now demanded villagers serving as porters. And there seems little doubt that bombing succeeded in demoralizing a good portion of the civilian population. One evacuee explained to the author, "There never was a night we would go to bed when we thought we would live till the morning, never a morning we would wake up when we thought we would live to the night." An old woman stated: "Oh, yes, we cried all the time. We cried until our tears couldn't come any more." And a 35-year-old villager remembered that "when I was in my cave, I would just sit there in the dark, thinking: 'Oh, please, don't let the planes come any more, don't let the planes come any more, don't let the planes come any more. Oh, please.'"

Despite these American achievements the air war probably has been—on the whole—militarily counterproductive. Communist troops in Indochina have ceded control of the air to the enemy for 25 years and have long since learned to avoid bombing casualties. Evacuees report extensive civilian casualties, but say few Pathet Lao or North Vietnamese soldiers are killed, for, unburdened by families or possessions, they retreat more deeply into the forest. In any given evacuation of civilians from Pathet Lao zones, U.S. officials estimate that approximately 50 per cent of the population remains behind; those who leave the area are those who cannot fight, while almost all men and women of fighting age join the Pathet Lao. The bombing solved a major Pathet Lao problem; mobilization of the rather isolated and near-

23. Senate hearings, *op. cit.*, p. 484.

subsistence-level farmers. In the early 1960s people had had rather limited experience with American intervention and direct exploitation by the Vientiane government. Evacuees estimate, for example, that in early 1965 about 30 per cent of the young men volunteered for the Pathet Lao army in the Plain of Jars area. Five years later, volunteers were on the order of 95 per cent. The attitude was "better to die fighting than die hiding from the bombs." By 1970 the Pathet Lao were the only soldiers in Laos who felt they knew what they were fighting for. Higher morale resulted in increased combat efficiency.

Perhaps the U.S. air war has strengthened the Pathet Lao most by increasing the North Vietnamese stake in the Laotian war game. American actions, including the providing of air support for rainy season offensives (following the line of a possible invasion route to North Vietnam) forced an increase in the number of North Vietnamese soldiers committed to the area. Although in June 1970 only about 5,000 North Vietnamese were actually engaged in combat in Laos,[24] this represented a significant increase over the number present in May 1964, when the United States began its air war. There is little doubt that they have played a significant role in strengthening communist ground power. Direct military damage to the Pathet Lao has been limited mainly to destruction of rice stores, curtailing of rice production, and dislocation of military supply lines, all seriously inconveniencing communist troops. But paradoxically, this has undoubtedly increased their combat efficiency. Normally, "people's armies" are forced to spend a good deal of their time and energy working in farmers' fields in return for rice, building community relations, and protecting the civilian population. Thus, by making Pathet Lao forces increasingly dependent on regular food supplies from North Vietnam, the American air war has freed them for more exclusively military operations.

The ineffectiveness of American air strategy was decisively demonstrated by the February 1970 communist counteroffensive

24. According to American embassy sources, the total number of North Vietnamese in Laos as of May 1964 was 10,000. Given this assumption and following the analysis of troop deployment described in the appendix, this would yield a maximum of 2,000 actually engaged in combat.

to retake the Plain of Jars. In May 1964 the dissident neutralists and Pathet Lao had captured the Plain of Jars in three days. In February 1970, despite six years of saturation bombing and evacuation of the entire civilian population from the Plain area, communist forces captured it in five days.

Despite its many failures, however, reliance on air power still guarantees the achievement of one major aim; bombing will, if nothing else, prevent the Pathet Lao seizure of any major Laotian towns. Past actions lend great credibility to the threat that any and all objectives taken by the Pathet Lao will be destroyed from the air. In the case of Vientiane, the Laotians further assume that there would be heavy artillery bombardment from the Thai side of the Mekong. On one recent occasion the author was present at a discussion between an evacuee from the Plain of Jars and a group of long-time residents of a village just outside Vientiane. The evacuee described in some detail his experiences under the bombing. The villagers' first reaction was typical. "Oh," one said, "but you were lucky, in some ways, you know. You had a lot of hills around, and could hide in the caves. But what about us? It's all flat around here. We have no place to hide." Whether such feelings will serve as a significant deterrent to the Pathet Lao remains to be seen. On the one hand, taking possession of devastated towns and villages is clearly a rather cheerless form of victory. On the other hand, given a choice between living under saturation bombing in two-thirds of Laos, or in all of it, the Pathet Lao just might opt for the latter. The final resolution of this question is some time off. It will depend above all on an end to the Vietnam War and on how the Pathet Lao interprets American postwar intentions.

THE GROUND WAR: "NO BOOM-BOOM, NO RICE"

From 1954 to 1962 a major American objective in Laos was to enlarge and improve ground forces known as the Royal Laotian Army (RLA); primary emphasis was placed on building up an ethnic Lao army. During this period the United States transformed what was essentially a police force into a conventional army whose basic role was and is to provide defense for major towns and military bases. The RLA was expanded from some 15,000 men to approximately 50,000. American advisers supplied full logistics, training, and combat advisory support.[25]

However, once the 1962 Geneva Accords had been signed, the United States made two basic changes in its ground policy. These shifts reflected a change in American strategic thinking and recognition of the legendary weakness of the RLA as a fighting instrument. The United States decided to supplement the RLA in two ways. First, it created a separate army called, appropriately enough, the Armée Clandestine (AC), led by American advisers who were primarily former members of the Special Forces employed in Laos by the CIA. The AC troops consist largely of Meo, ethnic Laotians from northeast Thailand, and a variety of other Asians brought in from outside Laos. Secondly, the United States supported the introduction of regular Thai army units. These two initiatives were designed to make possible a shift to guerrilla tactics, which the RLA was clearly incapable of making.

Colonel Hugh Toye, for example, describes the remarkable process through which the Pathet Lao took almost a third of Laos in late 1959:

Small armed Pathet Lao groups would approach defended villages, sending emissaries ahead to frighten the defenders with stories of approaching hordes. The isolated military posts, not always linked by radio and never particularly confident in this basically hostile non-Lao country, would dispatch runners with reports of massive enemy attacks or movements in order to excuse their own withdrawal. The reports were accepted at the army headquarters in Sam Neua, translated into great red arrows on the situation maps, and forwarded to

25. "Following the signing of the SEATO treaty in September, 1954 . . . the consensus of the Joint Chiefs was that . . . it would be best to reduce the Lao territorial army from its wartime strength of 15,000 men to the level needed for routine internal policing . . . [but in January 1955] the State Department requested the American diplomatic mission in Vientiane to draw up its recommendations for the size of a Lao army. The mission . . . came up with a recommendation for 23,600 men." Dommen, *op. cit.*, pp. 98–99.

Vientiane where they became even bigger arrows on even larger maps
. . . broadcasts of the resulting news items increased further the
nervousness of the men holding out against the tide of panic. As the
little garrisons and petty officials fled, the Pathet Lao substituted their
own, until by mid-September they controlled considerable areas in
half the provinces in Laos.[26]

A decade later, RLA troops had shown few signs of improvement. In January 1968, for example, they lost Nam Bac, the last
large base north of Luang Prabang. Since the United States considered it strategically significant, American aircraft flew in vast
amounts of modern weaponry to the 4,500–5,000 RLA defenders
and daily conducted massive air support missions. The attacking
Pathet Lao and North Vietnamese Army forces were estimated
to number from 2,000 to 2,500 troops. In the end, however, the
RLA defenders broke and ran, and the United States suffered
one of the most expensive losses of manpower and equipment
in the history of the war. In April 1970 Pathet Lao forces took
the strategic provincial capital of Attopeu in southeastern Laos
by the simple expedient of announcing over a loudspeaker that
they were about to do so and offering the RLA battalion defending it the choice of retreat. The RLA quickly accepted.

The Armée Clandestine has been given the major responsibility for offensive ground operations in Laos. Designed to operate in small, mobile units (often only the size of a platoon),
which would attack when they had numerical superiority and,
much like the Pathet Lao, retreat when outnumbered, over the
last six years it has performed two major tasks. First, it has been
the cutting edge of ground offensives launched into Pathet Lao
areas, arranging for the evacuation of civilians to behind friendly
lines. Secondly, it has engaged in commando operations behind
enemy lines designed to gather intelligence and commit sabotage.
There are today some 30,000 AC troops throughout Laos, but the
bulk of these are concentrated in the northeast. The center for
AC operations there is the Long Cheng military base (located
some thirty miles southwest of the Plain of Jars) from which
soldiers are dispatched on operations and to forward mountain-

26. Toye, *op. cit.*, pp. 127–128.

top outposts. The remainder of the AC troops are in camps strung out from the northwestern frontier with Burma down to the Bolovens Plateau in southern Laos. AC troops are relatively well paid; a private earns between $30 and $35 a month, as compared to the $5 to $10 earned by RLA troops. In addition, AC troops receive far better training, arms, and supplies and are also accorded more American air support. The ethnic composition of the AC is a polyglot mixture unrivaled anywhere in Asia. The indigenous troops are mainly Meo from the northeast and other montagnard tribes from the rest of the country. Ethnic Lao from northeast Thailand and some ethnic Thai from central Thailand are believed to make up at least 25 per cent of the total AC. In addition, there are sizable numbers of Cambodian, Burmese, Filipino, Nationalist Chinese, and other mercenaries.

The AC is completely controlled by the American CIA and U.S. Army advisers, who plan strategy and operations, arrange and direct air support and, frequently, lead AC troops into combat. The combat role of the Americans is precisely analogous to that of American army advisers to the Army of the Republic of Vietnam (ARVN) in South Vietnam in the late fifties and early sixties; but the Americans in Laos retain far greater control than did their Vietnam-based counterparts by virtue of the fact that they pay the soldiers' salaries and supply them with arms, ammunition, and rations without working through a Lao "counterpart system." Moreover, they control the air transport facilities of the AC troops.

The Armée Clandestine in Laos is, in turn, a part of a larger American-controlled supranational army extending throughout Southeast Asia. Tammy Arbuckle, perhaps the most knowledgeable of outside observers on this phenomenon, has written of the

American-directed "Secret Army" which operates all through Southeast Asia. Making up its units are Cambodians, Vietnamese, Chinese and Laotians, as well as Thais and various hill tribes, such as the Meo who have been active on the Plain of Jars. Its operations extend into northeast Burma, China's Yunnan Province, North Vietnam, South Vietnam, Cambodia and Thailand. . . . Laos, bordering on all the Southeast Asian nations, is ideal for these U.S. operations. And the Secret Army concept fits neatly into the Guam Doctrine. Americans take care of the leadership, training, planning and logistics. The Asians do the bulk of the fighting.[27]

This army respects no national frontiers, recognizes no government, and is responsible only to its American employers.

Since the mid-sixties, the other major U.S. innovation in Laos has been to support the introduction of regular units of the Thai Army, with both immediate and long-range objectives in mind. In the short run, it was hoped that Thai units could contribute something to the ground fighting. In particular, Thai artillery battalions were brought into major military bases and infantry battalions to the critical points of conflict. However, obvious Thai shortcomings on the battlefield make it seem that the major goals of the Thai intervention were long-term in nature. The Thai are the battlefield joke of South Vietnam. Relegated to guarding a corner of Long Binh air base, and surrounded by American troops in order to avoid politically embarrassing battlefield casualties, their major accomplishment to date has been mastering the complexities of disposing of PX goods on the black market. Looking ahead, the Americans have been interested in offering the Thai troops experience in fighting a guerrilla war, in anticipation of their future combat against insurgency in their own country and elsewhere in Southeast Asia. The Nixon Administration's unprecedented revelation that Thai army troops had been sent to Laos in March 1970, essentially justified in terms of the Guam Doctrine, was implicit confirmation of this contingency planning.

The arrival of Thai troops created a good deal of dissatisfaction within the Royal Laotian Government, with the extreme right alone supporting the move. Laotians tend to resent the Thai, feeling that the latter act with arrogance and condescension toward them. Historically, the Thai have held more territory for longer periods of time than any of Laos' neighbors. It is widely believed in Laos that the more Thai troops are introduced, the more difficult it will be to make them leave after the

27. *Washington Star*, March 25, 1970—"Thais Are Only Part of U.S.'s Secret Army," by Tammy Arbuckle.

war has ended. Furthermore, the Thai are generally regarded by the Lao military as rather fainthearted soldiers, who fight well only when generously supplied in set-piece situations. Laotian generals state quite openly that they consider Thai troops absolutely useless in fighting a guerrilla war. Resentment has also been generated in recent years by the Thai charging excessive freight rates on goods coming through Thailand—the landlocked RLG's only overland supply route.

The Thai themselves were undecided about whether to intervene in Laos. Like the RLG, they originally feared antagonizing the more powerful North Vietnamese and perhaps creating unfavorable international repercussions as well. Above all, they were uncertain what effect intervention would have on the insurgency in northeast Thailand; they feared that the communist bloc might step up support to the insurgents. In the end, it was the Americans who made the decision and imposed their optimistic views. While diminishing their military weakness, the Thai would gain valuable experience in fighting guerrillas as well as generous American cash grants; and the Americans would be a bit stronger on the ground and perhaps a bit closer to the realization of the Nixon Doctrine. Unfavorable internal and international repercussions would be minimized by restricting press coverage as much as possible. There are presently well over 5,000 Thai[28] troops fighting in Laos, divided into 10 to 12 artillery and infantry units numbering about 500 men each. They are stationed primarily in the northeast, in the Long Cheng area, but there are a number of battalions in central and southern Laos as well.

Along with its backing of the AC and Thai, the United States has continued to offer the RLA logistical and arms support. There are now some 60,000 RLA troops, divided more or less equally between the 5 Military Regions and deployed in defensive posi-

28. Writing nine months ago, a journalist stated, "Radio Hanoi's recent charge that Thailand has 5,000 troops on Laotian soil was substantially correct . . ." (Far Eastern Economic Review, "Big Brother Is Watching" by T. D. Allman, October 9, 1969). This figure included both regular Thai army units and Thai "volunteers" in the Armée Clandestine. The number of regular Thai army units has substantially increased since then.

tions near the provincial capitals. The United States has also provided training in Thailand, the Philippines, Guam, or the United States for the vast majority of RLA officers, who later receive extensive assistance in the field. Air America and Continental Air flights deliver supplies to RLA outposts; U.S. ground military advisers plan strategy and coordinate air strikes; American pilots ferry RLA troops about; Americans gather intelligence for the RLA; and the United States directs the operations of the Laotian Air Force. American control of government fighting forces is immediately apparent to even the most casual observer in Laos. The offices of the most senior Lao generals are typically rather bare. They generally contain various ornaments—flags, weapons, medals, and diplomas—a desk clean of any papers, and one or two filing cabinets. Their only military paraphernalia is a huge wall map supplied by the Americans. It is entitled, appropriately enough, "Joint Operations Graphic," and depicts Thailand, South Vietnam, and Cambodia in addition to Laos. Sentries and clerks loll indolently about, and much of the space in Lao military buildings is unused. By contrast, American military offices are a beehive of activity. People rush in and out, radios crackle. Desks, tables, and closets are filled to the overflowing with papers, maps, and "top secret" reports. Not a foot of office space is wasted.

There is considerable ambiguity about both the cost of ground war in Laos and the number of Americans directly involved. Senator Fulbright, however, has indicated that the Armée Clandestine alone devours about $150 million per year.[29] To this must be added the cost of support to the RLA and Thai army units operating in Laos and American ground advisory personnel. A minimum estimate of the total would be in the neighborhood of $300,000,000 annually.

With regard to personnel, President Nixon stated on March 6, 1970, that there were 643 Americans involved militarily in Laos; 323 involved in logistics, and 320 involved in military "advising"

---

29. *Far Eastern Economic Review*, "Allies in the Clouds," Michael Malloy, November 20, 1969.

or "training." It is not known whether this figure includes all CIA personnel involved in direction of the Armée Clandestine and intelligence-gathering activities. The figure certainly did not include, however, the sizable number of U.S. Army and CIA operatives who are formally assigned to Thailand but who commute into Laos on a regular basis. If one adds them to Nixon's figure, a reasonable estimate of the number of Americans involved directly would range between 1,000 and 2,000.

A few hundred million dollars . . . a few thousand men . . . the cost certainly seems small enough, especially when compared to the unpalatable alternative of introducing American ground troops. It has, moreover, scored a few notable achievements. Shifting to more mobile tactics and raising a well-paid army under direct American control have certainly improved military effectiveness. The AC has functioned far better than the RLA could have in the assigned tasks. The general AC/Thai/RLA ground effort has resulted in enemy killed, territory gained, population evacuated, and positions defended.

But, in a war such as the one in Laos, a purely advisory American ground role is at best a stopgap measure, since, motivated by personal or local interest, the AC is not an effective ground army in the full sense of the word. Its polyglot composition leads to serious problems of morale, and it is plagued by disciplinary difficulties. For example, Meo treatment of the civilian population after the capture of the Plain of Jars in September 1969 showed a striking lack of control. Looting, rape and, above all, wanton destruction of property, were rather strange ways of befriending 20,000 people who would later be placed under RLG control on the Vientiane plain.

Armée Clandestine troops do a creditable job in commando-level offensive operations. But, as an American embassy official rather delicately put it, "they are better at attacking than defending." Neither the AC nor the Thai are expected to offer serious resistance to a determined communist ground offensive. The Thai in particular are greatly resented by the Lao military for their performance in their major test to date. Moung Soui, a major RLG base, some 25 miles west of the Plain of Jars, fell to the communists in June 1969. In addition to RLA and AC troops, it was defended by one Thai infantry and one Thai artillery battalion. Laotians complained that the Thai lived apart in more luxurious barracks, coddled with canned food, newspapers, movies, and other comforts flown in from Thailand while the Lao troops subsisted on their usual meager rations. More seriously the Laotians reported that during the final communist attack, Thai infantry units broke in terror from their perimeter defensive positions and retreated inside the base. Abandoned, Laotian troops took to the hills while the Thai were evacuated by helicopters.

The RLA is no more reliable on the ground now than it was a decade ago. A generation of U.S. military advisers have seen their best efforts thwarted time and again by the corruption, indifference, and lack of morale which is the RLA trademark. And RLA resentment of their American mentors is growing. Officers often complain bitterly in private that they are pushed into fighting by their American military advisers; they explain why they comply with the phrase "no boom-boom, no rice." No rice—and no salaries, arms, air support, communications aid, or gasoline either.

And as the war drags on, with neither cause nor end in sight and, above all, as AC/Thai/RLA take more and more casualties, morale sags even lower. The fighting has taken a fearful toll of front-line units in recent years. Journalists visiting the Sam Thong–Long Cheng area in the fall of 1969 were shocked to discover 13- and 14-year-old boys impressed into AC service. Front-line battalions were operating at below 50 per cent strength in many cases. And now, ten months later, this is even more common. Five years ago, America's Asian troops in Laos were greater in number, better paid, and better supplied than their communist adversaries. This is still true today. Yet, despite the massive air war on their behalf, they are in a weaker position vis-à-vis the enemy than at any time since 1964. Clearly, the American ground effort in Laos has done all it could be expected to do. But this has not been enough. Whatever its short-term successes, the American ground war in Laos cannot be expected to serve as a long-term deterrent to communist gains.

Population Relocation: "The Old, the Very Young, and the Afraid"

British experience with the tactic of population relocation in Malaya, where it enjoyed a certain success owing to unique circumstances, led to inclusion of the concept in virtually every Western counterinsurgency program undertaken thereafter. The idea has a simple logic: if one can succeed in separating the civilian population from the armed elements of the insurgency, one ought to be able to isolate—and eventually eliminate—the insurgent. There has been a massive attempt to test this notion in Laos. It is estimated that since 1962 over half a million people have been moved out of Pathet Lao zones into areas controlled by the RLG. This population relocation was intended to deprive the Pathet Lao of rice farmers, porters, and potential recruits; to organize evacuees into paramilitary units; and to secure recruits for the RLA or AC as well as to provide the RLG with a larger manpower base for both political and economic reasons.

The Sam Thong–Long Cheng area, some 30 miles southwest of the Plain of Jars in northeastern Laos, has been the site of major relocation efforts financed by the Department of Defense, USAID, and the CIA. Sam Thong, a collection of quonset huts with an airstrip, was constructed in the early 1960s. It is the center for processing evacuees, has a large school and hospital, contains rice and medical storehouses, and has perhaps a dozen American residents. Long Cheng, 12 miles by road to the southeast, is the major military base in the area. In addition to housing soldiers and ammunition dumps, it is the site of the longest all-weather airstrip in the northeast. In the early sixties some 20,000–30,000 tribal people, principally Meo, resided in this general area. By 1970 an estimated 250,000 Meo and related tribal people had become residents of Sam Thong and Long Cheng, while approximately 50,000–100,000 more had been relocated to the west and northwest.[30] These evacuees were resettled on isolated mountaintops throughout the area. In the interim,

30. These very approximate figures are based on estimates made by Edgar "Pop" Buell during an interview on February 11, 1970.

American personnel had directed the evacuation of Meo and other hill tribes by foot and plane from their homes in northern Xieng Khouang and Sam Neua provinces to a secure oval-shaped area southwest of Sam Thong and Long Cheng. Although the young men were inducted into the AC, families for the most part were kept intact on the theory that the men would fight better if their wives and children were with them. All the mountaintop communities were armed and organized into "self-defense" units called the ADC. Deprived of their traditional livelihood, two thirds of the Meo evacuees were dependent on Air America and Continental airdrops of rice and other basic necessities. The planes also supplied them with arms and ammunition on a regular basis.

The Sam Thong–Long Cheng program is regarded as perhaps the single most important American program in Laos. The Meo outposts are seen as a vital barrier to communist penetration of the Mekong valley; Meo troops are considered the sole ground force of any worth between the Plain of Jars and Vientiane. But the Meo themselves have little allegiance to the RLG. Meo leader Vang Pao's ultimate motive appears to be to fight for a *de facto* autonomous Meo kingdom spreading through most of northern Laos. A man of rather obscure origins, he attained his present position through French support in the fifties, an alliance with the French-backed Meo clan chieftain Touby Ly Fong, and, above all, as a result of direct American support since 1960. A former sergeant in the French army, Vang Pao won both French and American favor by his personal courage, his willingness to fight, his affinity for both the French and the Americans, and his ability to maintain order by dispensing a rather ruthless brand of justice. Hundreds of millions of dollars of American aid over the years have allowed him to build alliances with local clan leaders by providing arms, ammunition, rice, and other forms of aid to the people under their rule.

The Meo have taken very high losses during the sixties, for they have taken the brunt of the casualties in the fighting directed by Westerners. Edgar "Pop" Buell, the former Indiana corn farmer who has been Vang Pao's chief source of support for more than a decade, estimates that 20 per cent of the Meo alone vanished on the early marches from the north down to the Sam Thong–Long Cheng area. Robert Shaplen, for example, quotes Buell's description of the Meo manpower situation in March 1968:

Vang Pao has lost at least a thousand men since January 1, killed alone, and I don't know how many more wounded. He's lost all but one of his commanders. . . . A short time ago we rounded up three hundred fresh recruits. Thirty percent were fourteen years old or less, and ten of them were only ten years old. Another 30 percent were fifteen or sixteen. The remaining 40 percent were thirty-five or over. Where were the ones between? I'll tell you—they're all dead . . . and in a few weeks 90 percent of (the new recruits) will be dead.[31]

The Meo people themselves would undoubtedly prefer retreat or a negotiated settlement to their continuing losses; with their near-total dependence on American support, they do not have the power to reverse the American decision to keep them fighting. The zealousness of Buell and his American assistants is reported to have been a major psychological factor in preventing their resignation from the fray. Don Schanche, who has written the most extensively about the Meo operation, reported that Vang Pao himself was ready to admit defeat by the end of 1968. As Schanche tells it, he was "dejected to the point of total despair" and refused to continue fighting. However, "Buell lectured Vang Pao as if he were a wayward child, urging him to get out with his dispirited troops and rally them for another stand against the Communists. Shocked out of his apathy . . . Vang Pao returned to the field."[32]

The Americans attempted to make similar strategic use of evacuees in southern Laos from 1965 through 1967. The program, called the Sedone Valley Development Scheme, was initiated by American military personnel in the region and carried out by USAID civilian and military advisers. RLG officials had little to do with the project, which reproduced the strategic hamlet program executed in South Vietnam in the early 1960s. The

31. Robert Shaplen, *Time Out of Hand* (New York: Harper & Row, 1969), p. 348.
32. *Washington Star,* April 12, 1970. Don A. Schanche, "Behind Pathet Lao Lines—An Indianan for All Seasons."

area selected was a rough parallelogram, bounded by Khong Sedone and Saravane to the north and Pakse and Paksong to the south. The focus of the program was the village of Lao Ngam, located toward the center of the area, which originally had some 25,000–30,000 people and produced a fair amount of rice. Beginning in 1965, the Lao army moved the people from their villages to Lao Ngam and to an area to the west along Route 13. Evacuees were tightly guarded, and subsisted on rice handouts. Various "inputs" such as schools, wells, and other "community development" projects were engineered in a classic attempt to "win hearts and minds." In December 1967, however, Lao Ngam was taken by the Pathet Lao, who could not be dislodged. Many of the evacuees returned to their original homes while others remained in the refugee camps. The area is now a free-fire zone, and most of the villages have been destroyed from the air.

In addition to the Sam Thong–Long Cheng and Sedone programs, another 200,000–300,000 people have been relocated around the provincial capitals of Luang Prabang, Houei Sai, and Sayaboury in northern Laos, in the Vientiane plain, and along Route 13 in the Mekong valley. These evacuees have either been airlifted out by the Lao army or have come out on their own; but in both cases the principal reason given is American bombing. From 1964 until the beginning of 1969 the number of evacuees on USAID monthly dole averaged a steady 130,000, never dropping below 122,000 or rising to over 145,000. Beginning in February 1969, however, the figure jumped dramatically as a result of the November 1968 bombing escalation. By November 1969 the number of evacuees had reached 230,000, and at this writing it has climbed to *over 250,000*. These are the "old, the very young, and the afraid" who remained in their villages until the RLG forces entered.

Once in RLG-controlled territory, the refugees are generally relocated on poorer, forested land, since the better, cleared land is already occupied. During their first year, while getting in their initial crop, they subsist on American-supplied rice. Invariably they have left behind almost all their livestock, household goods, and farming implements. Once their first crops are harvested, they are taken off the dole and must get by on what they can produce themselves on low-yield land. Evacuees tend psychologically to resist putting down roots in the new locations, for their greatest wish is to return to their native villages when there is peace. It is not only that they were far better off there economically, but it is the place of their ancestors; they know the valleys, rivers, and forests, and they simply are not at home elsewhere.

The $30–$40 made available for each USAID-supported refugee each year is temporary subsistence support, and is used almost entirely to purchase and transport rice. The USAID Refugee Relief branch divides its program into "relocation" and "resettlement." The "resettlement" program, which gives a decent support allowance for each refugee, extends to only about 5 per cent of all refugees. Refugee Relief Chief Guillion explains that "frankly, if the resettlement program extends to 30,000 people by 1974, it will be fantastic."

There is no doubt that the relocation program, like the air war, has created short-term difficulties for the Pathet Lao and short-term gains for the RLG. Evacuation has deprived the Pathet Lao of rice growers, porters, and potential recruits. And it has weakened the population base essential for any "people's revolution," which tries to create a successful alternative to the old society. But again, like the air war, the program does not appear to have weakened the Pathet Lao militarily. The great majority of the men and women of fighting age remain with them, and it seems evident that the great majority of evacuees feel little allegiance to the RLG. It is hard to account for the curious reluctance of the Americans to spend more money on resettling evacuees within the RLG zones. Clearly, a more ambitious attempt to win evacuee loyalties would have contributed to the long-term goals of the relocation effort. Spending $2 billion for the air war and only a few hundred thousand for resettling half a million civilians seems a strange way to wage a battle that is as much political as it is military. In setting its priorities for its war in Laos, the United States has consistently concentrated on the short term. Its population relocation program is no exception.

CIVIL ADMINISTRATION: "THE SECOND PRIME MINISTER"

Counterinsurgency warfare is political as well as military in nature, and the development of an administrative structure is as much a military means as it is a political end. The American effort in Laos thus clearly demanded a reliable civil administration to gather political and military intelligence, process Royal Army conscripts, manage the economy, stabilize the currency, care for evacuees, run the schools and hospitals, and accomplish a hundred other daily tasks which could influence the outcome of the war. Furthermore, to be effective the administration would have to focus on the countryside where 85 per cent of the population lived and the war was being fought. Building, buttressing, or replacing such an administration proved one of the prime problems in Laos.

From 1954 through 1962 the United States had given $290 million in economic aid to the government of Laos. The resulting waste merited a whole chapter in *The Ugly American.* Most of the money had gone directly into the pockets of high-ranking Laotian officials in the cities, and only a tiny fraction trickled out into the countryside.[33] Congressman Otto Passman made the Monument to the Dead—a giant structure erected in the center of Vientiane with American-supplied cement meant for an airport runway[34]—the very symbol of waste and corruption in American foreign aid. The economy was in a shambles; black marketeering and smuggling were rife, imports outnumbered exports 20 to 1, and tax collection was nil. The kip had been devalued from 35 to the dollar, to 80, to 240, and finally, to its present level of 500 to the dollar. In the end, the RLG stood isolated in the Mekong valley towns, artificial islands dependent

33. Toye cites Sisouk Na Champassak's description of the aid program in the latter's *Storm over Laos* (1961): "Corruption and extortion in the customs, banking, foreign trade, police and other administrative departments were commonplace. Black market deals in American aid dollars reached such proportions that the Pathet Lao needed no propaganda to turn the rural population against the townspeople. The Chinese of Hong Kong and Bangkok and a few Lao officials profited from the American aid." p. 117.

34. "USAID Guidelines for First Fiscal Year 71–72 Program Discussion," March 3, 1970, by Charles Mann, USAID/Laos Mission Director.

on outside transfusions for life, surrounded by an indifferent or hostile countryside. In the aftermath of this colossal failure, the United States gave up on the idea of working through the Laotian government.

In 1962 one of the most ambitious attempts at the direct administration of a foreign country in the postcolonial era began. An American administrative structure was established which paralleled that of the RLG in every important respect; it extended throughout RLG-controlled territory and was directly responsible for the vast majority of the goods and services reaching the population. The American effort was headed by the U.S. ambassador, who defined policy and coordinated the activities of the CIA, American military, Air America and Continental, and USAID personnel.

USAID, the key to the operation, established departments of agriculture, irrigation, education, rural development, refugee relief, health, industry, financial affairs, public works, well drilling, and public administration to parallel the respective RLG bureaus. In addition, a requirements office was established to funnel military aid to the Lao army; a public safety office was set up to run the Lao police; Air America and Continental Air Services were given USAID contracts to transport arms and rice to soldiers and refugees; and a USAID "Annex" was created to serve as a cover for CIA direction of the Armée Clandestine and intelligence networks.

A hierarchical structure reaching from Vientiane down to the villages was also set up. At its head was the American ambassador, who delegated the running of USAID to its director (also listed as the economic counselor to the U.S. Embassy). Under him there were five area coordinators (mostly retired military men) stationed in the capitals of each of the five Military Regions. The area coordinators, functional counterparts of the five RLG military commanders, were responsible for all American activities in their respective regions and supervised subordinate American coordinators living in the major district and often in the subdistrict capitals. For the most part these men were assigned to the USAID Rural Development Division or were members of International Voluntary Services, Inc. (IVS). In addition, every

USAID department had a representative in each of the five Military Regions, usually living in the provincial capital and working in liaison with USAID and IVS personnel living in the major villages. These regional representatives were responsible both to the area coordinator and to their department chief. Although Americans controlled the operation from top to bottom, the majority of USAID personnel were Asians. The chain of command within each department generally ran from an American chief, to a "Third Country National"—usually Filipino or Thai—supervisor, to Laotian employees.

The great horizontal and vertical expansion of USAID was accompanied by the 1964 establishment of the Foreign Exchange Operations Fund (FEOF), which stabilized the kip by the simple expedient of making up the annual RLG budget deficit with hard currency. Although FEOF is also backed by France, Japan, Great Britain, and Australia, the United States has made about 70 per cent of the total contribution to date. The United States thus acquired a predominant role in carrying out many of the day-to-day functions of the civil administration. Comparing the sheer numbers of American and RLG personnel demonstrates the relationship. As of October 1969 the United States employed 6,878 people in Laos, of whom 833 were Americans and 6,045 were Asians and other foreigners. The Lao civil administration employed 10,777 persons—of whom about 5,000 were schoolteachers. RLG budgetary funds—60 per cent of which were supplied by FEOF—went almost entirely to recurring expenditures: salaries, housing, and other maintainance needs. Almost all other funds came directly from USAID, which controlled nonrecurring expenditures. From 1962 to 1970 the USAID budget totaled $400 million, or about $50 million annually. It was this money which built the schools and roads, provided the fertilizer, built the administrative buildings, and supplied the vehicles. From the Agency for International Development (AID) official in Vientiane down to the IVSer in the village, Americans retained direct control of most of the AID-supplied commodities.

As pointed out in recent Senate hearings, it is Americans who program Lao radio broadcasts designed to win over the Lao population to the RLG, Americans who make propaganda movies on behalf of the RLG, and Americans who run the leafleting and other "Psy War" operations of the Lao government.[35] Americans have financed Thai-written textbooks for Laotian primary schools, directed the building of schools and dams, the movement and relocation of the civilian population, and the establishment of a dry season rice program. Although usually consulted, RLG officials quite frankly admit that they have little more than an advisory role. As one RLG official once put it, "I drive my jeep, but it is the Americans who gave it to me and to whom I must go to get my gasoline."

The American civil administration has contributed to the war effort in a number of ways. In a memo dated March 3, 1970, USAID Director Charles Mann described USAID's goals and priorities in the following terms:

The objectives of U.S. foreign policy in Laos are to support and maintain the present Lao government and to avoid a takeover by Communist forces. The role of USAID as an instrument of this annual foreign policy may be summarized by the following priority list:

1. *Economic Stability*—Chiefly the U.S. input into FEOF.
2. *War-Related Activities*—
   a. Minimum level of ground transportation . . .
   b. Medical and basic subsistence needs for (war victims) . . .
   c. Air support of RLG civil functions and U.S. Government programs.
   d. Public Safety as it relates to communications and intelligence.
   e. Emergency assistance . . .
3. *Maintenance of Minimum Level of Government Service*—
   This category of programs is intended to preserve the social and economic structure of the RLG as it is. The goal is not development, but preservation . . .
4. *Social Infrastructure* . . .
5. *Economic Development* . . .

For the most part, USAID has succeeded in its three major activities: the kip has been stabilized, the civil administration has aided the war effort, and minimal government services have been maintained where security allows. But perhaps the single

35. Senate hearings, *op. cit.*, p. 578.

most important contribution of USAID has been the creation of a country-wide organization—extending into areas where RLG officials rarely go—capable of effectively gathering intelligence from USAID operatives and IVS volunteers in the field, which is then relayed directly to the area coordinator, who in turn passes it to the CIA or military authorities. USAID field operatives also have authority to call in bombing strikes when the immediate situation seems propitious, and often do.

USAID also often understakes specific intelligence-gathering projects. In June 1970, for example, IVS volunteers were investigating the political attitudes of evacuees from the Plain of Jars, and U.S. Information Service (USIS) was preparing a series of questionnaires to test the political attitudes of villagers near provincial capitals. The area coordinator for Military Region 3 found such activities the single most effective accomplishment of his program. He explained that because of economic aid, villagers in his region had been giving an increasing amount of information; as a result, the effectiveness of air strikes had been greatly increased. Other USAID programs which particularly have aided the war effort are the arms and rice drops to the Meo; road building for strategic purposes; and the population relocation program.

The American civilian administration has probably failed to change village attitudes of indifference or resentment toward the RLG, and may have increased village discontent. The direct channeling of U.S. aid to the villages has highlighted the incompetence of the RLG. Numerous villagers all over Laos have explained to the author, in surprisingly similar terms, that the Americans should not try to pass anything through the RLG officials to the village, for it is sure to be stolen. USAID Rural Development official Loring Waggoner suggested in the Senate hearings that the USAID program raised villagers expectations so that

villagers' reaction to the ineptness of their officials is one of unrest. There is increasing awareness on the part of the villager that he has the right to determine his own future and that certain benefits are entitled him under a central government system. This awareness, the freedom to express his views, and an increasingly better financial position have created social and political problems which the traditional central government authorities find difficult to solve without upsetting the balance of large-family power, army strength, and the favored few.[36]

In October 1969, after 15 years and $647,000,000 of aid to the RLG, a top AID official could say flatly that "the Lao Government operates at relatively low effectiveness at both the national and local level."[37]

USAID effort could not strengthen the RLG, of course, because of the *de facto* arrangement (discussed above) between the U.S. military and the Lao elite, which guaranteed that aid programs would work through and around the elitism and corruption, not change it. Wealth and power remained concentrated in the hands of the tiny elite which had ruled Laos for centuries precisely because "the objectives of U.S. foreign policy in Laos are to support and maintain the present Lao government." Under these conditions the USAID effort was hardly conducive to winning the political support which was the RLG's only guarantee of a political future. And naturally enough, RLG officials were resentful and bitter over the extent to which their prerogatives and functions had been usurped by the Americans. At a public meeting of RLG officials in October 1969 a director in the Ministry of Public Works queried USAID Director Mann:

You know, sir, it is customary among us to refer to the USAID Director as the second prime minister of Laos. He has his own budget, his own cabinet, his own technical departments, his own bureaucracy. Do you think that this is really helping our government to develop? Don't you think it would be better to break down your government, and assign USAID technicians only as advisers to our Lao ministries to help us in our work?

Director Mann's rather diplomatic evasion of the question did not satisfy his listeners, one of whom expressed his discontent with a rather vulgar gesture, presumably picked up in France. For

36. *Ibid.*, p. 569.
37. *Ibid.*, p. 569.

it was more than evident that the American felt the current arrangement was the only possible one which could preserve a functioning civil administration. And what was perhaps most disturbing to his listeners was the fact that he was clearly right.

RLG critics were, of course, quite correct in many of their objections to USAID officials who had, indeed, taken over much of the RLG. On one occasion, for example, former USAID Director Mendenhall wrote to RLG Finance Minister Sisouk Na Champassak:

Dear Mr. Minister:

I am attaching, for your information, copies of a letter to be sent by your Ministry to me and of my proposed reply, both relating to continuation of and support of your country's invisible expenditures.

And the fact is that USAID officials—living apart in what the Laotians regarded as luxurious communities and spending most of their work hours in their air-conditioned offices—have not been particularly well qualified to run a country. Few know the local language, or have much understanding of or sensitivity to local customs and needs. Not surprisingly, there are serious tensions within USAID. Lao employees complain bitterly in private of everything—from being supervised by the well-paid Filipinos and Thai to, in one case, being forced to sign in and out whenever they leave their desks, even to go to the bathroom. Among themselves they accuse their American bosses of being arrogant, patronizing, condescending and, often, racist.

Even the relatively few Americans who operate at the village level and know Laotian fly their food in from the American PX in Vientiane; their homes are generally the only ones in the village powered by an electric generator, and their control over jeeps, gasoline, funds, cement, tin roofing, and a staff of often well over 50 people leads to their being treated with the traditional Lao deference and humility toward more powerful outsiders. They stay in the villages rather briefly, and are evaluated on the quantity—and not quality—of the projects they complete. One of USAID's more highly regarded rural development workers recently summed up the problem this way:

You can't expect a guy in his mid-twenties with a wife, children, college degree and ambition to eat dust and sticky rice out in the villages for more than a few years. He's got his career to think about.

Such attitudes promote neither continuity nor effectiveness in rural programs. By an act of Congress, moreover, almost all USAID commodities must be imported from the United States, although such goods are often inappropriate, hard to get, and overly expensive to maintain.

The contradictions inherent in the USAID Laotian operation were illustrated by an incident which took place in the village of Lahanam, in Savannakhet province, in the summer of 1967. USAID had decided to erect a cement school in the village. The still-serviceable wooden school erected by the villagers was torn down, and USAID materials and technicians were brought in to erect the new school on this site. The villagers needed to construct the school, however, remained indifferent to the project, which required unpaid labor. The Lao district chief, although reluctant to annoy the villagers, was finally persuaded by his American counterpart to exhort them to come out to work. One day, during a religious ceremony, the Lao official called them together and said:

Look, I know you all have a lot of work right now. But you really ought to help the Americans build this school. It is very important to them. If you don't work on the school, they'll take away the cement and the tin roofing and the carpenters. Also, they may refuse to help us much in the future.

Despite the many and accurate criticisms by RLG officials of the Americans' performance, neither group had much of an alternative. By 1970 the American parallel government obviously had worked itself into a job, and would in fact entrench itself further. The prefabricated huts which had served as headquarters for USAID and the U.S. Embassy for more than a decade were being transformed into multistoried cement buildings. A similar expansion of USAID facilities was being carried out in the provinces. Newly arrived American construction companies were busily erecting warehouses, generator rooms, and permanent office buildings. The liberal university graduates and ex-Peace Corps men who had previously staffed the rural program were being replaced by more hard-nosed civilian and military veterans of the Vietnam conflict. And the USAID budget, though cut 10 per cent due to worldwide budget reductions, was still a healthy $45 million. It was the second highest per capita aid program in the world (after Vietnam), and could be cut another 50 per cent without reducing the extent of American control.

Nonetheless, USAID could neither rally the Lao people to the RLG nor mobilize them against the Pathet Lao. In the end, its only substantial contributions to avoiding a "communist take-over" were those which fed directly into the ground and air war. And thus, for all of its air of permanence, it was the military's success in denying the Pathet Lao victory which would determine the length of the American parallel government's stay in Laos.

THE SECRET WAR: "NO WAY TO ASK QUESTIONS

There has rarely been a time in its history when the United States has been so involved in a war with so little public or congressional knowledge. While admitting their attempts at secrecy, American officials justify it on two grounds: (1) that to admit American violations of the 1962 Geneva Accords would give a propaganda advantage to Hanoi, which has never admitted its own violations of the agreement, and (2) that the U.S.S.R. wishes to avoid an extension of the war in Laos. Were the United States to officially admit all that it has been doing, it would make it more difficult for the Russians to continue exercising a restraining influence.[38] Doubt has been expressed about both of these rationalizations. One can only assume that Radio Hanoi's listeners have long ago made up their minds whether or not they believe what they hear and that official American announcements are not likely to change many minds. And skeptics suggest that there is little reason to believe that the Soviet Union exerts much direct influence over the war in Laos or that such

38. *Ibid.*, p. 399.

influence might be affected by disclosure of the American role (something which Moscow—as well as Hanoi and Sam Neua— have been describing in detail for years). It is clear that the secrecy stems less from concern with the communists and more from a desire to avoid domestic pressures and thereby allow American policy makers a freer hand in waging war.

The most concerted attempts to conceal facts have been made regarding the air war (above all the systematic bombing of towns and villages), American ground combat involvement, CIA direction of the Armée Clandestine, American military escalation, and American subsidizing of the Thai and other foreign Asians to fight in Laos. At the same time a major campaign has been mounted to exaggerate both North Vietnamese combat involvement and its hold over the Pathet Lao. U.S. officials continue to believe that a full revelation of protracted American bombing of civilian targets would spark a great deal of domestic criticism besides casting doubt on the official theory that Laotian refugess are fleeing only communist oppression. They fear above all that disclosures—of the 300 civilians who were killed in a cave 6 miles west of Ban Ban in the summer of 1968, of the 63 prisoners killed in a bombing raid on a jail 5 miles west of Xieng Khouang in the winter of 1969, and, most important of all, of the fact that between half a million and a million people have been living underground for years hiding from the bombs —would raise the charge of war crimes both in the United States and abroad. This would limit the intensity and extent of the air war and might help bring about a bombing halt as it did over North Vietnam in 1968.

Officials continue to worry about providing evidence that Laos might become another Vietnam. For, as in Vietnam in the early sixties, armed American CIA and army personnel are leading Asian forces on patrol, advising them during combat, and sleeping with them at forward military bases. As in Vietnam, Americans are raising, training, and leading a montagnard army.[39] Above all, publicizing the facts would not only document Ameri-

39. Schanche, *op. cit.* See also Schanche's recent book *Mister Pop: The Adventures of a Peaceful Man in a Small War* (New York: McKay, 1970).

can overinvolvement but would weaken the case against the North Vietnamese, who are charged with the same offense. The CIA, already widely criticized for everything from its involvement with the National Student Association to its failure at the Bay of Pigs, seems particularly vulnerable. For all of its previous covert paramilitary activities, the CIA has never before raised and directed an army. Its acceptance and tacit encouragement of the opium trade in northern Laos is another highly sensitive issue. Since its only legal function is intelligence gathering, it would be attacked for having exceeded its congressional authorization and, more damaging still, its effectiveness might be disputed. While some would argue it is the organization best suited for such operations, owing to its "mobility" and utilization of "a flexible approach that the bureaucratic hierarchy of the army lacks,"[40] others who have met CIA field operatives, the author included, would argue the opposite. Lacking knowledge of local conditions, unable to speak local languages, and generally insensitive, CIA personnel seem singularly ill-equipped to direct a war like the one in Laos. Such arguments aside, there is little doubt that disclosure of CIA activities in Laos could lead to public and congressional attempts to limit them.

Foreign mercenaries raise another sore point. By 1970 the United States had brought at least 10,000 Asians into Laos, including regular Thai Army troops, and the Thai, Cambodian, Burmese, Nationalist Chinese, and Filipino mercenaries constituting the Armée Clandestine. In addition, thousands of foreign Asians are involved in the air war in various capacities. Widespread publication of these facts could conceivably buttress complaints that the United States had raised an army of mercenaries to fight its war by proxy. More important, it would damage seriously the consistent U.S. accusations that the North Vietnamese have invaded Laos—a claim which is crucial, for it affords the only legal, moral, and political justification for American violations of the Geneva Accords. By tirelessly and falsely proclaiming the invasion of Laos by 50,000–67,000 North Vietnamese, succes-

40. Robert Shaplen, "Our Involvement in Laos," in *Foreign Affairs* (April 1970).

sive administrations have succeeded in planting their version in all the newspapers and imprinting it on the public mind. This public relations coup would be undercut by disclosure of the fact that the number of U.S.-supported foreign Asians was equal to or greater than the number of North Vietnamese engaged in combat in Laos, and that the ratio of foreigners to Lao was approximately equal on both sides.[41]

The executive branch has carried out its elaborate campaign of concealment by simply refusing to allow outside observers to visit sensitive areas on a regular basis after 1962. Frequent visits to the front by journalists such as Dennis Warner had led to refutation of the official claim that the Pathet Lao offensives from 1959 to 1962 were carried out largely by North Vietnamese combat troops.[42] Thus after 1962, and especially after 1964, a policy of deliberate exclusion was instituted at the front and in other potentially embarrassing areas. Reporters, authors, and television teams have repeatedly asked permission to visit Long Cheng, accompany American advisers in operations on the Ho Chi Minh Trail, visit bases under attack by communist forces, participate in RLG offensives, view villages and towns destroyed by American bombing and subsequently taken by the RLG, and visit the CIA training bases strung out throughout the country. All have been refused on the ground of military security, although it is clear that the major reasons are political. Restrictions have been applied to the many activities related to American bombing in Laos, which has been kept as far out of the public eye as possible. Newsmen have been prevented from talking with airmen, viewing installations in Thailand, and participating in air raids

41. At this writing, the 10,000 foreign Asians supported by the United States in Laos are facing a maximum of 5,000 North Vietnamese engaged in combat here. (See also appendix.) Indigenous forces in the RLA and AC total approximately 80,000–90,000 men. Pathet Lao troops number some 50,000 men.

42. Toye cites Warner's visits to the front, for example, in substantiating his account of the 1959 Pathet Lao offensive which, as we have seen, did not involve North Vietnamese units despite American and RLG claims to the contrary. Toye, *op. cit.*, p. 128. It was Warner who made the famous comment that a Laotian army commander "accepted as fact what the most junior Western staff officer would have rejected as fiction." Denis Warner, *The Last Confucian* (London: Penguin, 1964), p. 257.

over Laos. Operating on agreed-upon rules, newsmen and other outsiders have participated in all similar military activities in Vietnam. The domestic dissent which resulted is the main reason they have not been allowed to do so in Laos.

The infrequent visits of newsmen to sensitive areas have been rather carefully managed. American military personnel and foreign mercenaries are withdrawn; a briefing is given by a Laotian general in which the emphasis is on the North Vietnamese invasion of the given areas; American involvement is denied; North Vietnamese prisoners and Pathet Lao defectors are made available for interviews; and stocks of captured communist weapons are exhibited. There have been some exceptions, of course, with a few journalists or authors visiting restricted areas, obtaining franker briefings, or interviewing such key men (normally inaccessible) as Air Attaché Chief Tyrrell, or CIA Station Chief Devlin. But such privileges have been accorded primarily to those known to support the official point of view, or willing to keep the information obtained off the record. Thus in January 1968, for example, a Washington correspondent was allowed to visit Long Cheng with the express understanding that he would not describe what he saw there.

The executive branch has maintained secrecy here by using an even more elementary method: not telling the truth. Seeing the Laotian conflict solely in the context of the Cold War, many American officials view lying not only as a tactical aid but also as a patriotic duty. From 1962 to the present, American officials have consistently denied or distorted the facts in contacts ranging from private interview to public briefing to official statement. From May 1964 until President Nixon's March 1970 statement on Laos, for example, American officials denied, publicly and privately, that the United States was bombing in Laos. Since the president's speech, they have contended that the bombing is confined to the Ho Chi Minh Trail and "North Vietnamese supply routes," and have continued to reiterate all the denials and false allegations dealt with at length earlier in this article. When public pressure finally led to the release of some information, it appeared that official disclosures were intended more to maintain the policy of secrecy than to end it. The author has searched President Nixon's statement in vain for a single paragraph that does not contain either a glaring omission or simple untruth. Among the most relevant misstatements were the contentions that

• "Today there are 67,000 North Vietnamese troops in this small country," [with the added implication that all had come to invade Laos. On the same day, in Vientiane, U.S. military attachés gave the total figure as 48,000; this figure, which I have suggested is far too high, was one they had been using for months, contradicting President Nixon's claim that 13,000 additional troops had been recently poured into the country.]

• "The level of our air operations has been increased only as the number of North Vietnamese in Laos and the level of their aggression has increased." [I have already described the November 1968 bombing escalation, its reasons, and its consequences.]

• "We have continued to conduct air operations. Our first priority . . . is . . . the Ho Chi Minh Trail. . . . In addition . . . we have continued to carry out reconnaissance flights in northern Laos and to fly combat support missions for Laotian forces. . . ." [The 16,000 refugees who had been brought in from the Plain of Jars a month before gave a rather different impression about American bombing in Laos.]

• "No American stationed in Laos has ever been killed in ground combat operations." [This statement was soon discredited when 27 American combat deaths in Laos were documented by reporters. A few days later the number became "something less than 50," while the actual figure remains anyone's guess. No account includes the 200 American pilots missing or presumed dead in Laos.]

• No mention was made of Thai and other foreign Asian involvement on the American-supported side.

• The impression was given that there are only 643 Americans involved in the Laotian war in "advisory" and "logistics" roles.

• And, in a letter prefacing the censored transcript of the Symington hearings, released to the public, congressional aide Pincus objected to deletions from the text of crucial information pertaining to (1) support to Vang Pao; (2) increase in air sorties over northern Laos; (3) the cumulative amount of military assistance since 1962; (4) the millions of dollars spent on U.S. air operations over northern Laos; (5) U.S.-operated Thai airbases; and (6) the financing by the U.S. of third country nationals fighting in Laos.

These are precisely the topics which have been cloaked in secrecy since 1964, not only to deceive the public but also in order to mislead Congress. Senator Fulbright, speaking for his colleagues, acknowledged how little Congress had been told:

I think the surprise that is evidenced by the chairman of the subcommittee and others, that they did not know the extent of this involvement until these hearings, is pretty clear evidence that we were not aware of these activities, although we had had some hearings on it.[43]

The author accompanied two congressmen during their visit to Laos in the summer of 1967. American officials made a consistent attempt to mislead them throughout their stay. Particular emphasis was placed on obscuring American military involvement in the Long Cheng–Sam Thong operation. The attitude of resident officials was illustrated during a visit to Sam Thong. As the congressmen proceeded down a long line of welcoming Meo, who draped them with Hawaiian-style leis, the author joined a group of USAID officials, including the present Deputy Chief of USAID James Chandler and "Pop" Buell. During the course of the conversation, Buell asked Chandler, "Do they know anything?" "Don't worry, Pop," Chandler replied, "Hurwitch [then deputy chief of mission] gave them a beautiful snow job, complete with maps. They were very impressed."

Public and congressional pressure finally resulted in the closed Senate hearings of October 1969, in which, for the first time, congressional leaders were given some of the facts they wanted. However, the senators could not evaluate the truth of what they were being told—as Fulbright put it, "I do not know whether we know all of it now. I have no idea whether we do or not."[44]

43. Senate hearings, *op. cit.*, p. 547.
44. *Ibid.*, p. 547.

In fact, he didn't. The executive branch continued to distort the more sensitive questions of American involvement in Laos throughout the hearings, even in the portion without deletions which has been made public. Former Ambassador Sullivan, for example, stated: "The Lao, of course, placed restrictions on those strikes that would go into populated areas . . . the United States Air Force contribution was limited to striking at the logistic routes, or what were Allied check points on those routes or at points of concentration which fed into the area where that actual ground battling was taking place . . . it was the policy not to attack populated areas."[45] Air Attaché Tyrrell also said that "villages, even in a free drop zone, would be restricted from bombing."[46] The nondeleted testimony is studded with dozens of misrepresentations of the type already analyzed, and includes as well, the remarkable contention that American activities in Laos have been designed to promote the independence of Laos from China and protect the neutrality of Laos within the framework of the 1962 Geneva Accords

The news media were again manipulated during the communist offensive to retake the Plain of Jars in February 1970. Throughout this period the many reporters in Vientiane heard almost nothing except briefings from the office of Colonel Duskin, the military attaché, who unwaveringly contended that almost all the attackers were North Vietnamese and that "no Pathet Lao units had been sighted." To back up this claim, he frequently asserted that no Pathet Lao prisoners had been taken. After the newspapers had printed this account, American embassy officials revealed that the number of Pathet Lao prisoners taken outnumbered North Vietnamese by about "30 to 40" to "8."

Prosecrecy advocates dispute the extent to which information has been controlled here. Robert Shaplen, for example, has gone so far as to state that "nobody was fooled by anything, including that portion of the American public willing to read the newspapers and magazines with a modicum of care."[47] But the secrecy policy cannot be judged this way, for the general sup-

45. *Ibid.*, pp. 481, 500.
46. *Ibid.*, p. 514.
47. Shaplen, *op. cit.*

pression of information has obviously succeeded in achieving the desired aim. There has been minimal domestic opposition to the war in Laos—no demonstrations, no petitions, no marches. The only congressional action has been passage of the rider prohibiting the deployment of American combat troops in Laos, an option long since discarded.

The Vietnam experience indicates, however, that widespread, regular newspaper and television coverage of American activities in Laos would have verified unpleasant facts and led to dissent and attempts to limit the administration's freedom of action. That such might have been the case is indicated by the reaction to revelations of American combat deaths in Laos. As a result, American civilian advisers have been withdrawn from the field, and the combat involvement of CIA and military advisers has been encumbered with added restrictions. Even an informed press might not have led to a curtailment of the American involvement in Laos since the United States was still involved in Vietnam. But the Laotian strategy might have been altered. Some restrictions might have been placed on the bombing of civilian targets or on the population relocation program. The role of the CIA, American army personnel, or a hundred other things might have been changed. However, there can hardly be rising political opposition to policies of which the general public and Congress are unaware.

The policy of executive secrecy has been facilitated by the absence of large numbers of American ground troops. The war in Laos, therefore, is of marginal interest in the United States. Journalists have little leverage over government officials in situations not directly affecting the American public. The president is concerned, after all, with his constituency, not with the networks. And the war in Laos has been played out in the shadow of Vietnam. The extent of American involvement there has ensured that public, journalistic, and congressional interest will be focused on Vietnam. As Senator Fulbright told former Ambassador Sullivan during the Senate hearings:

There is a minimum of enlightenment of this committee by anybody in the executive. . . . We do not know enough to ask you these questions unless you are willing to volunteer the information. There is no way to ask you questions about things we don't know you're doing.[48]

CONCLUSION: THE MOST ENDURING LEGACY

The United States has successfully achieved its primary end in Laos in that for the last six years it has used Laotian territory to aid its effort in Vietnam. This had been accomplished with the agreement of the Royal Laotian Government, thus minimizing legal and political complications. Whether the United States will achieve its other major aim, that of retaining Laos within its sphere of influence, is more doubtful. For after eight years of the bloodiest warfare in its history, the sides in Laos are more polarized than ever. Few knowledgeable observers believe that the RLG and Pathet Lao can ever enter into meaningful, long-term cooperation. If they could not do so in 1956, 1958, or 1962, how on earth could they do so after a decade of conflict? The prospect is for continued fighting until one side achieves decisive battlefield victory, sometime after the Vietnam War has ended.

The American military is unlikely to be the victor in such a conflict, for it must overcome three basic handicaps. First, there is the Royal Laotian Government, which is simply too weak, divided, disorganized, urban-centered, and corrupt to be viable. In order to win the war it has created, the United States must have a far more durable structure on which to base itself. Second, the full-scale intervention described here did not really begin until 1964, when it was already too late to be effective. By that time the Pathet Lao had already built up secure bases in Sam Neua, Phong Saly, and southeastern Laos, set up a clandestine infrastructure in much of the rest of the country, and established itself as a legal, recognized political party. It had thus established its legitimacy and, given the weaknesses of the RLG, there seems no way that it can be destroyed. Third, Laos is an integral part of an Indochinese theater in which the North Vietnamese are

48. Senate hearings, *op. cit.*, p. 547.

the dominant power. Given their demonstrated willingness to support the Pathet Lao, there seems little likelihood that the United States can achieve any sort of lasting victory in Laos.

Rather than trying to overcome such odds, it seems likely that the United States will simply continue its policy of making communist gains as costly as possible. Every territorial objective taken by the Pathet Lao will be destroyed. If things get really serious, there is a strong possibility that the United States will back a full-scale Thai invasion of Laos. While it is recognized that even these extreme measures will probably not result in total victory, it is hoped that they can delay communist gains as long as possible, gain time for the American counterinsurgency program in Thailand, weaken the Pathet Lao and North Vietnamese and, above all, provide a convincing deterrent to revolution throughout the world. In many circles it is also hoped that these tactics will cause a partition of Laos, with the United States retaining the Mekong valley in its sphere of influence. In any event, it is clear that prospects for a peaceful, unified Laos appear confined to the rather distant future. The prognosis for the foreseeable future is—more of the same.

Whatever happens in Laos itself, the most enduring legacy of the war effort seems likely to be the creation of a model for future American counterinsurgency operations in the third world. For American administrations leery of involvement in a post-Vietnam ground war, the Laotian model offers several obvious advantages:

1. It can be carried out without the risk of creating very much domestic dissent, because a large number of American ground combat troops are not involved.

2. The risk of opposition at home can be further reduced by following a policy of secrecy which, as in Laos, will blunt the domestic impact of American deaths, failures, war atrocities, and intimate involvement in the military and internal affairs of a foreign state.

3. It is not overly expensive. Unlike Vietnam, the United States can afford a number of Laoses simultaneously without adverse effects on its economy. In fact, war-related expenditures

for a Laos-type war are not only minimal, but they also will be seen in many quarters as desirable as the economy adjusts to a reduced post-Vietnam military budget.

4. Nor is the investment of American personnel overly burdensome. The total number of Americans needed to run the political and military war in Laos, where a rather strong communist ground force is deployed, is in the neighborhood of 2,000–3,000 men. The need for airmen is, of course, much greater, but they are always available from the air bases planted throughout the third world.

5. It causes maximum destruction of the enemy infrastructure and maximum civilian demoralization at minimum risk to American lives.

6. Such a war combines the advantages of maximum firepower from the air, guerrilla and conventional tactics on the ground, and extensive control of the civilian population. It is clearly the simplest, most rational, and most effective means of intervention possessed by the United States, once introduction of its own ground troops and tactical deployment of nuclear weapons are ruled out.

A Laotian-style war does not, however, come with an unqualified recommendation. It failed, after all, in Vietnam from 1954 to 1964. And it gives every indication of doing so in Laos as well. The essential problem for the United States lies in the very nature of a counterrevolutionary war. Insurgency thrives on the structural and political weaknesses of an existing government which demands a large input of American aid. But the necessity of working through the existing government limits American effectiveness at every turn. All the aid supplied will be counterbalanced or neutralized as long as the insurgents also receive adequate amounts of assistance from outside. Both of these factors contributed to the failures of each of the operational elements of the American war in Laos discussed in detail here.

Stalemate or defeat for the United States in Laos does not reduce the probability that the Americans will apply the pattern in other third world nations in the decade to come, for such a war could conceivably succeed elsewhere. Conditions clearly vary from country to country, and tactics which could not prevail in Laos will not necessarily fail in Malaysia, Mozambique, or Bolivia. An American embassy official here responded to doubts about the effectiveness of Vietnamization by explaining: "Look, by definition Vietnamization must be carried out before you can gauge its effectiveness. There's no way to predict beforehand." A similar "logic" can dictate continued experimentation with this form of warfare, especially if the American executive retains its determination to prevent successful insurgency in other countries, or at least delay victory or cause enough destruction to render the insurgents' triumph as empty as possible.

But we won't have to speculate much longer in the abstract because, as the new decade dawns, the United States has already begun to apply its Laotian brand of counterinsurgency in Thailand. The Meo region in northern Thailand has been turned into a free-fire zone as aircraft carry out blanket bombing in an attempt to move the 500,000 tribesmen off the mountaintops into government-controlled areas in the valley. Most of this bombing, as in Laos in the early stages, is being carried out by propeller-driven aircraft. American advisers are leading Thai units and engaging in combat in the hills of northeastern Thailand. One key area is the hills behind Sakhorakhom, which are thought to be the headquarters of the Thai insurgents. Intensive bombing is being carried out in a concentrated effort to crush the insurgents in that area.

An agency called Accelerated Rural Development (ARD) has been set up to funnel aid directly to villagers and cut through the endemic corruption and sloth of the Royal Thai Government. In addition, the U.S. Army and Air Force have engaged in a good deal of civic action and have also constructed roads throughout the northeast. Direct attempts at population control are also being made in the area. During the last year, an irregular police force has been raised throughout the region. In small villages everywhere, unemployed youths have been given a few months training, armed, and sent back to their native villages as "village policemen." They are well paid and receive a monthly salary approaching that of a village schoolteacher. (Peace Corps volunteers in the area report that the program has been the single greatest failure of the whole pacification effort. The "village policemen" have been invariably among the least motivated and most disliked of the village youths. Capitalizing on their new status, they have threatened villagers, bothered village girls, extorted money, and alienated the villagers. The program nonetheless continues.) Plans for strategic hamlets have been drawn up by American counterinsurgency experts. Vast efforts have been made in Thailand and the United States to equip and train the Thai army. And, as in Laos, a policy of secrecy has been instituted about the more sensitive aspects of the Thai counterinsurgency program. Outsiders have not been allowed into northern Thailand to witness the bombing of civilian targets. American and Thai officials refuse to comment on it when questioned.

The program is just beginning. But, depending on the strength of the insurgency, it gives every indication of developing all the basic elements of the Laotian affair. It is still too soon to make any definite judgments. On the one hand, American intervention in Thailand clearly begins with important advantages lacking in Laos. The Royal Thai Government is stronger, more firmly implanted, and far more capable than the RLG. Moreover, American intervention in Thailand has occurred much earlier than in Laos. The Thai insurgents have not yet had a chance to establish secure rear areas and to set up a functioning administration over a large portion of territory. And, to date, powerful allies have not given much aid beyond some training and logistical support. On the other hand, the Royal Thai Government suffers from the same structural weaknesses as most American-supported regimes throughout the developing world. It is urban-centered, elitist, corrupt, and controlled by an unusually grasping military. Unless the United States can generate fundamental changes in the government, it seems likely that the Thai insurgents will exploit these weaknesses to their advantage.

However, the United States has little leverage for achieving basic alterations in Thai society. American studies have invariably suggested such things as restructuring the army on a regional basis, attempting to reverse the flow of the most talented youth from the rural areas to the cities, and doing more to have power flow from the bottom up instead of the top down. Thai officials have just as invariably rejected these suggestions. The American program in Thailand is greatly complicated not only by the short-sightedness of the Thai regime, but also by the general Thai resentment of foreigners. Increasing American support to the Thai regime will probably be paralleled by increasing communist support to the Thai insurgents. The impulse to do so will be all the stronger because of the Thai regime's close identification with the Western camp and, especially, because of their leasing of air bases to the U.S. Air Force and dispatching troops to Vietnam, Laos, and Cambodia. A scaling down of the Vietnam war will probably mark an increase in aid to Thai insurgents.

American ground intervention in Vietnam posed the dominant question for counterinsurgency in the sixties. For a quick American success there would have augured well for similar attempts to contain revolution throughout the developing world. In the end, however, American ground combat involvement failed. And the excessive cost to the United States—economic, political, psychological—seems to have effectively ruled out similar intervention for years to come. But this will not lead to withdrawal, for neither the interests of the American government nor the reaction of the American public would permit it. Unless the course of the history of the previous 25 years is suddenly and unexpectedly reversed, the new decade will certainly bring many more revolutions, many more American attempts to contain them, and . . . many more Laoses.

APPENDIX

It is most difficult to arrive at any precise figures on communist troop strength in Laos, for soldiers in small groups are constantly on the move. Moreover, as the American government prevents outside observers from visiting the front and observing combat on a regular basis (as they can in Vietnam), eyewitness accounts are hard to come by. After much investigation, the author has concluded that there are at the very most 5,000 North Vietnamese engaged in combat in Laos at this writing (June 1970). I base this on the following:

(*a*) One source is the Black Tai major in charge of RLA intelligence on North Vietnamese involvement in Laos. (The same man—then a captain—was virtually the sole source of intelligence on North Vietnamese activities 1959–1962 for Langer and Zasloff's work *Revolution in Laos: The North Vietnamese and Pathet Lao* [Santa Monica: the RAND Corporation, RM–5935, 1969], pp. 92, 99.) The major estimated in a recent interview that there were some 30 North Vietnamese battalions engaged in Laos, with each battalion comprising between 300–500 men. This would lead to an estimate of 9,000–15,000 involved in support and combat operations. The figure is probably under 9,000 since most observers believe that the average North Vietnamese battalion incorporates fewer than 300 men. General Prasook Sanly, the military commander of Military Region 4, for example, lists the size of one North Vietnamese "combat" battalion in his region as about 280 men. Of the 9,000 or so North Vietnamese involved in Laos at any one time, at least one half are engaged in support functions. The British military attaché estimated that during the communist offensives against Sam Thong and Long Cheng in the spring of 1970, fully three quarters of the North Vietnamese troops were carrying out support functions. Interviews with evacuees indicate that many of these "North Vietnamese troops" are actually girls, older men, and women engaged in porterage. Thus, even if the estimate of 30 battalions given by the major were correct, there would be at most 5,000 North Vietnamese troops actually engaged in combat throughout Laos.

(*b*) The French military attaché maintains that there are a maximum of 30,000 North Vietnamese troops. The RLG military spokesmen give a figure of 70 battalions which, given an average of 400–500 men each, comes to a maximum of 35,000 men. Whatever the total number, all are agreed that at least 60 per cent are involved in maintaining the Ho Chi Minh and Sihanouk Trails, and that perhaps 5 to 10 per cent remain in rear positions in the Laotian war. The majority are not even soldiers but are porters, road repairers, engineers, and the like; at least half are women. The Black Tai major stated that the military units assigned to guard these personnel do not fight unless attacked.

(*c*) According to American embassy estimates, there are some 50,000 Pathet Lao troops fighting in Laos. There appears to be no need for more than a few thousand North Vietnamese troops to stiffen their ranks. The low number of communist troops involved in any given battle also indicates few North Vietnamese troops in Laos. American embassy sources state that the Plain of Jars airfield, the last major outpost, was taken by 400 men; that Saravane was taken by three companies; and that Attopeu was taken by an unknown number of troops. There is no information on the number of troops which took Attopeu, since the RLG forces fled before the attack could take place.

Part III

America in Laos

13

Pawns and Patriots: The U.S. Fight for Laos

Wilfred Burchett

United States intervention in Laos started long before there was any question of "Ho Chi Minh trails" or a war raging in South Vietnam. It started with financial support—up to 80 per cent of all military costs—of France's colonial war against the peoples of Indochina. It continued with heavy U.S. pressure on the Laotian delegation at the 1954 Geneva Conference to refuse to sign the Accords and thus bring down the French government.[1] A huge bribe was paid by the CIA to one of the members of the delegation—today a leading Vientiane politician—to reject the Accords. (Another member of the delegation, Defense Minister Kou Voravong, who insisted on signing the agreements later revealed the details of the bribe and the U.S. sabotage effort to the Laotian National Assembly. He was assassinated shortly afterwards.)

Successive U.S. Presidents and leading officials advanced many pretexts for U.S. intervention in Laotian affairs. The most common one was that the French defeat and withdrawal from Indochina had created a dangerous "power vacuum" which the United States was duty-bound to fill as part of its special mission of defending the Free World. But even before there were any signs of French defeat, strategic policy planners had already marked Laos as an area of special interest. It was in 1949, as Chinese Communist armies were rolling south to sweep the rest of the Kuomintang armies—and their American advisers—off the Chinese mainland, that an Office of Strategic Services (OSS) agent was first sent into Laos. He was Major James Thompson, a key aide of General "Wild Bill" Donovan, who then headed the OSS and who was at that time U.S. ambassador to Thailand. In those days,

1. Premier Pierre Mendes-France pledged to get agreement by July 7, 1954 or resign.

behind-the-scenes U.S. strategic thinking concentrated on the problem of putting Chiang Kai-shek back on to the mainland, or at the very least, of halting an overflow of Mao Tse-tung's armies into Southeast Asia. Both goals were preludes to more direct U.S. military intervention against mainland China itself. A glance at the map shows the interest that Laos had for the military planners. Within its huge Plain of Jars, Laos was capable of accommodating enough U.S. air power to dominate South China up to the Yangtze River as well as all of continental Southeast Asia. Later, when the Korean War broke out, the Pentagon "hawks" of the day toyed with the possibility of a three-pronged attack on the People's Republic of China—from Korea, from Indochina, and from Taiwan (to which Chiang Kai-shek's remnant armies had been transported by U.S. ships and planes). Laos would have played a key role in such plans. But the military setbacks in Korea and the French defeat at Dien Bien Phu put those plans into cold storage.

With the collapse of the French, however, there was renewed interest in Laos for another reason. Vietnam, north of the 17th parallel, had now become "red." If the Chinese wave of revolution had become too big to be stopped, at least the "red tide" could be rolled back in North Vietnam. In such an operation control of Laos, especially the Plain of Jars, could be strategically decisive. Brigadier General James Gavin—who was then U.S. Army deputy chief of staff in charge of plans—has described how plans were drawn up immediately after the 1954 Geneva Conference for an American invasion of North Vietnam, to start with a landing at Haiphong and the occupation of the Red River Delta up to Hanoi.[2] Admiral Radford, chairman of the joint chiefs of staff, the Air Force chief of staff, and the chief of naval operations, approved the plans, which called for the occupation of Hainan Island to protect the flanks of the huge amphibious operation "even if it meant risking war with Red China." The invasion was planned for some time in 1955 or early the following year—well before July 1956, by which time there were supposed to be all-Vietnam elections to unite the temporarily sepa-

2. *Crisis Now* (New York: Random House, 1968).

rated northern and southern zones. Needless to say, Secretary of State Dulles and the CIA were enthusiastic supporters of the invasion plan and firm opponents of elections.

Gavin was sent to Vietnam to assess how large a force would be necessary to carry out the plans. He came up with the figure of "eight combat divisions, supported by 35 engineer battalions and all the artillery and logistical support such mammoth undertakings require." But he himself was against the scheme and so was his immediate chief, General Matthew B. Ridgeway, the Army chief of staff. Ridgeway, with his Korean experience fresh in mind, opposed getting bogged down in a land war with China. He went directly to Eisenhower, bypassing Radford and the joint chiefs, and had the scheme killed.

Because of the enthusiasm shown by Dulles, Vice President Nixon, the CIA, and most of the joint chiefs, a compromise was made when the invasion plan was discarded. As Gavin relates: "We would not attack North Vietnam but would support a South Vietnamese government that we hoped would provide a stable, independent government." The real compromise was that the Saigon regime would be given an army to carry out the invasion of North Vietnam alone, using U.S. air and logistics support. General John "Iron Mike" O'Daniel was sent to Saigon in late 1954 as head of an American mission to work out details with General Paul Ely, who at that time headed the French mission to Saigon. Plans were agreed on for an American takeover without consulting the head of the French government. (Pierre Mendes-France, French prime minister at that time, informed me recently that he tried to repudiate the O'Daniel-Ely agreements, but was warned by Dulles personally that the United States would "ignore" any such repudiation, and the U.S. government applied severe financial pressures to back up the warning.)

If China could not be tackled at the time and "Operation Rollback" in North Vietnam would have to await the creation of Ngo Dinh Diem's new army, at least a start could be made in Laos by wiping out the Pathet Lao resistance forces. During the 1954 Geneva Conference the French had at first tried to deny the existence of any Laotian resistance forces, just as today the U.S. government and the Lon Nol regime in Phnom Penh deny the existence of Cambodian resistance forces. But on the battlefield "recognition" of the Pathet Lao was a daily occurence. Finally it was agreed at Geneva that the Pathet Lao would withdraw from their main bases in southern and central Laos and concentrate their forces in the two northern provinces of Sam Neua and Phong Saly, pending a political settlement between the Pathet Lao and the French-appointed regime in Vientiane. Former Defense Minister Kou Voravong (in his speech to the national assembly referred to earlier) revealed that right-wing elements had drawn up plans to take the Pathet Lao forces by surprise and wipe them out as they regrouped. He also disclosed the fact that he had arranged a meeting between the two half-brother princes—Souvanna Phouma, who then headed the Vientiane government, and Souphanouvong, who headed the Pathet Lao—as the first step toward a negotiated political settlement.

Nine days after Voravong's revelations, he was shot and killed in the home of Phoui Sananikone, whom he had named in the assembly as having accepted the enormous CIA bribe not to sign the Geneva Accords. (Phoui Sananikone has remained one of the most trusted U.S. assistants in Laos until the present time.) The assassination of Kou Voravong created a crisis which resulted in the resignation of Souvanna Phouma and the formation of a new government under Katay Don Sasorith—the first Laotian Ngo Dinh Diem.

Dulles dropped into Vientiane for a personal chat with Katay, at the end of February 1955, following a SEATO meeting in Bangkok. Five weeks later Katay launched a military offensive against the Pathet Lao in their newly established base areas. This marked the beginning of an endless series of attempts to liquidate the Pathet Lao by force of arms. At first, the United States stage-managed from the wings, but they intervened openly from time to time, on an ever-increasing scale, when the right-wing forces of the day were faced with complete collapse.

The South East Asia Treaty Organization (SEATO) was set up at Dulles' insistence to negate the main clauses of the 1954 Geneva Accords. At their inaugural session the SEATO representatives, without consulting the governments of Laos and Cambodia, placed the two countries in a zone of SEATO "protection." Katay and his right-wing successors were always assured of SEATO intervention if things went hopelessly wrong. But in fact France, not relishing the American takeover of its domains, consistently vetoed such intervention and from time to time was backed by Britain and Pakistan. Both Sihanouk and Prince Souvanna Phouma (when he came to power again) rejected any such SEATO "protection" for Cambodia or Laos. But Katay, Sananikone, Phoumi Nosavan, and others accepted continual reassurances from the CIA and the U.S. Embassy in Vientiane that SEATO military support would be supplied if things became really desperate. This happened on a number of occasions. But it was the United States alone that came to the rescue.

With the invariable logic of a well-run people's war, each offensive against the Pathet Lao ended in the latter's forces being stronger militarily—and above all politically—than when the offensive started. They were militarily stronger because of the experience gained, the stocks of modern U.S. weapons that fell into their hands, and the new recruits generated from deserters from the rightist ranks and from revenge-seeking families of victims of rightist atrocities. They were politically stronger because it was clear to the Laotian people that it was the Pathet Lao who were the authentic patriots defending the national interests, while the rightist forces were puppets of foreign interests.

Very important from the start was the fact that, despite vigorous and well-financed U.S. attempts to win over the Buddhists, the Buddhist hierarchy and, above all, the rank-and-file bonzes supported the Pathet Lao. As in Cambodia, the Buddhist bonzes had traditionally played a patriotic role. They had always resisted foreign incursions, and they especially resented American attempts to propagate a Thai version of Buddhism which ran counter to national traditions.

Time and again the Laotian people dramatically demonstrated their support for the Pathet Lao and the latter's consistent policy of national union within the framework of independence and neutrality. One can cite, for example, the May 1958 "complementary elections" held to give the Pathet Lao (now by agreement a participant in the coalition government) a chance for some representation in the national assembly pending nationwide elections. With Katay as minister of the interior and any real electioneering banned as "subversive propaganda," the results seemed a foregone conclusion. Facing its first electoral test, and hoping not to frighten Washington too much, the Neo Lao Hak Xat presented only 10 candidates for the 21 seats at stake. Souphanouvong won his seat in Vientiane with the greatest majority of any of the candidates for any seat. Of 21 seats, the Pathet Lao and its ally, the Peace and Neutrality Party under Quinim Pholsena, won 13, despite electoral procedures heavily weighted against them. Katay and his supporters won only 4 of the 26 seats they contested, and Phoui Sananikone's supporters none. As an expression of public opinion, nothing could have been more dramatic.

It was clear to Washington that under the most scrupulous application of the Western concept of "free elections" and despite Katay's dollar-greased electoral machinery, Souphanouvong and his allies would win a landslide victory in the general elections for the national assembly scheduled to be held the following year. The United States cut off aid, which resulted in Souvanna Phouma being ousted by Sananikone, who then took over as prime minister. The coalition government was wrecked, and the two Pathet Lao ministers forced out. (See article 9, by Ackland.)

In the Sananikone government, Katay was given another chance to "redeem himself" as minister of defense and the interior. With the Pathet Lao forces dissolved except for two veteran battalions which were to be integrated as units into the Royal Laotian Army, with key cadres exposed and defenseless and integrated as members of the administration as provided for in the 1956–57 agreements, Katay was all set to prove his worth. He dispatched troops to seal off the frontiers between Sam Neua and North Vietnam and then the killing started. In some provinces—Phong Saly, for instance—not a single Pathet Lao cadre escaped. In the old resistance bases in Attopeu and Saravane, to which cadres had returned after the 1957 agreements, the heads of murdered cadres were publicly exposed to prove that the Pathet Lao had ceased physically to exist. Katay did not, however, have enough troops and police to concentrate them everywhere at the same time for the arrests and killings, so in some areas small groups started up armed resistance again in self-defense. Throughout the latter half of 1958 and early 1959, the killings went on; Katay was taking revenge for his defeats in 1955 by using his army and police against unarmed patriots who had devoted years to the independence struggle.

Then Katay and Sananikone went ahead with plans for the final coup—the liquidation of the two Pathet Lao battalions. By that time the two battalions had been separated, one stationed near Luang Prabang, the other in the Plain of Jars. On May 9, 1959, they were ordered to line up for the ceremony of "integration" into the royal army, without arms or uniforms—in their underwear!—as they were to be totally reequipped, including uniforms. Simultaneously units of the Royal Laotian Army, accompanied by U.S. tanks and artillery, moved in to surround them. The battalion leaders demanded time to get instructions from their leaders in Vientiane. But by this time, Prince Souphanouvong, Phoumi Vongvichit, and other Neo Lao Hak Xat leaders had been placed under house arrest. On May 18 the two battalions were each ordered to surrender or be wiped out; tank-supported troops moved up for the kill. About one-third of Battalion 1 escaped that night despite the "eyeball to eyeball" encirclement. The following morning, General Rattikone, commander in chief of the Royal Laotian Army, came in person to receive the surrender of Battalion 2—and found an empty barracks. Despite encirclement by units vastly superior in numbers and equipment, Battalion 2 had escaped intact. Rattikone ordered his troops into hot pursuit. Parachute battalions were dropped squarely across the escape route but were soundly thrashed by the Pathet Lao. The whole of Battalion 2 and about one-third of Battalion 1 marched and fought their way back to their old resistance bases. Most of the rest of Battalion 1 hid in the jungle to await instructions. Obviously, the escapes could not have been made without extensive cooperation from the encircling government troops. It was another example of the real feeling in the country, even among officers and rank-and-file troops of the Royal Laotian Army. And the popular support for the Pathet Lao was demonstrated once more by the help the battalions must have received along their retreat route in the way of food, shelter, and intelligence information concerning the activities of the Vientiane garrisons in the areas through which they withdrew.

The escape of the battalion was a horrifying blow to Sananikone-Katay and their CIA–State Department backers. In retaliation, Sananikone put Souphanouvong and other Pathet Lao leaders in jail, where conditions were atrocious. The right wing had no illusions concerning the fighting quality of the Pathet Lao forces nor concerning the popular support they enjoyed throughout the country.

"Phoui [Sananikone]," commented Under Secretary of State for Far Eastern Affairs Roger Hilsman, "asked for more American aid and more American military technicians and advisors, and the United States agreed, announcing that it would send military technicians who would wear civilian clothes in token deference to the Geneva Accords, to help in expanding the Royal Lao Army from 25,000 to 29,000 men."[3] It is impossible to overemphasize that this was in May 1959, eighteen months before the founding of the National Liberation Front of South Vietnam; long before any generalized armed resistance had started in South Vietnam; years before any mention of a Ho Chi Minh Trail and various other pretexts used since to justify U.S. intervention in Laos. And even before this, Hilsman informs us of the duplicity and hypocrisy with which Washington covered up its intervention and violated key paragraphs of the 1962 Geneva Agreements by building up the Lao army to 25,000 men!

To accommodate to the Pentagon's insistence on having a Military Assistance Advisory Group (MAAG) in spite of the provisions of the Geneva Agreements, the State Department agreed to let one be set up in disguise. The PEO, for Programs Evaluation Office, wore civilian clothes—to no avail since the deception eventually became known and hit the newspapers.[4]

In his solitary prison cell on the outskirts of Vientiane, Souphanouvong had been working on the prison guards, awaken-

3. Roger Hilsman, *To Move a Nation* (Garden City, N.Y.: Doubleday, 1967), p. 120.
4. *Ibid.*, p. 112.

ing their patriotism, appealing to their consciences, gradually establishing human contact—very difficult at first because the guards had strict orders not to exchange a word with their captives and to cover their ears if addressed. In March 1960 Souphanouvong's older brother Prince Phetsarath died, but Souphanouvong was not permitted to attend his funeral. Souvanna Phouma returned for the occasion, but was not allowed to see his jailed half-brother. At preliminary hearings, the judges could find no pretext to condemn Souphanouvong and the others. (One judge was so impressed by Souphanouvong's bearing and arguments that he later joined the Pathet Lao.) Early in May 1960 the prisoners were tipped off that there would be no trial. They were to be "shot while attempting to escape" during a pretended transfer to another prison. Shortly after receiving this news, in the dead of night, Souphanouvong led all sixteen detainees out of prison (along with nine prison guards on duty that night, all of them armed and wearing MP uniforms). Eight of the guards had been won over by Souphanouvong's persistent explanations; the ninth—in charge of the arsenal—decided to "go along" with the others. This, on top of the escape of the two battalions was too much! General Phoumi Nosavan, who at this time was the latest American "strong man" in power, raved and ranted and pledged to recover the escapees alive or dead—preferably dead. The police and virtually the entire Laotian army, together with U.S. advisers, were mobilized in pursuit.

Souphanouvong and his comrades were terribly weakened from their year in prison. It was the start of the rainy season. Their route lay over a series of jungle-covered mountains, 300 miles to Sam Neua. To avoid reprisals on villages by the pursuing troops, they slept in the open, soaked to the skin, plagued by leeches and mosquitoes. But they evaded their pursuers, and were passed on from place to place by guerrillas who were by that time already organized, even in the areas adjoining Vientiane province.

The whole story of the escape and of the ideological preparatory work done by Souphanouvong in the seemingly impossible conditions of his imprisonment, is an epic of human determination and courage.[5] It illustrates the extraordinary qualities of this prince turned revolutionary. It also testifies to the real sentiments of the Laotian people, including the military police who were obviously the toughest and most reliable troops that General Nosavan could find for the task of guarding the country's number one prisoner. The escape of Souphanouvong and the other Pathet Lao cadres was a most dramatic illustration that even leading elements within the Royal Laotian Army supported the Pathet Lao, displaying their contempt for the puppets implementing U.S. policies in Laos.

One morning some three months after their escape—still two months from his home base in Sam Neua—Souphanouvong switched on his transistor radio to hear the electrifying news of a military coup in Vientiane, pulled off by an unknown para-trooper captain, Kong Le—unknown, that is, to the outside world and even to most Laotians. Souphanouvong knew who he was and so did his right-hand man Singkapo,[6] who was at his side listening to the radio. Kong Le came from the same village as Singkapo and had studied under the latter at the village school. Later when Singkapo had established his reputation as one of the most brilliant of the Pathet Lao commanders, the CIA chose Kong Le—by then an American-trained paratroop officer—to approach his former teacher and try to win him over, buying his support if necessary. In a series of discussions that lasted over three months, it was Singkapo who persuaded Kong Le of his real duties as a patriot. At their last meeting, Kong Le had said: "When the right time comes you may find support from un-expected quarters. Many of us are sick of this business of kill-ing our brother Laotians on American orders."

When the two Pathet Lao battalions escaped, after the pur-suing 1st Paratroop Battalion had been badly defeated, Kong Le's 2nd Battalion was ordered into action. He managed to smuggle a message to Singkapo in prison, asking for advice.

5. I have described the escape in more detail in Wilfred Burchett, *The Furtive War* (New York: International Publishers, 1963), chap. 10.

6. Colonel Singkapo Chunmali Sikhot, member of the Central Committee of the Neo Lao Hak Xat, head of the Pathet Lao armed forces.

Singkapo said he had no alternative but to go, but advised him "not to expose yourself or your battalion too much." Kong Le, slightly wounded during the first contact, demanded hospitalization. Lacking his leadership, the battalion fled at the first firefight and was withdrawn to garrison duty as punishment.

In their jungle hideout, Souphanouvong and the others discussed the situation. Once the details became clear, it was decided that Singkapo should return with utmost speed and join forces with Kong Le. In seven days, he covered the distance that had taken three months during the escape. He reached a point close enough to Vientiane for Kong Le to be able to send a helicopter to pick him up.

From a moral and political viewpoint, not to mention the subsequent military consequences, the revolt of Kong Le and his paratroop battalion was the bitterest blow of all to Washington. Kong Le was wholly "made in USA"; his battalion was considered to be one of the most "reliable" of all the units in the Royal army. But Kong Le and his men, sick at heart, could no longer tolerate American orders to try and wipe out fellow Laotians, especially those whom they realized were the staunchest of patriots. Two days after the coup which overthrew Nosavan, Kong Le declared at a big public meeting in Vientiane: "Many past governments promised to follow a neutral course, but they never kept their promises. My group and I are ready to sacrifice everything, including our lives, in order to bring peace and neutrality to our nation."

The king invited Souvanna Phouma—who had accepted a comfortable exile as ambassador to Paris after he had been forced out of office—to form a government, which he did. But with his usual genius for vacillation, he brought in Nosavan as deputy premier and—of all posts—minister of the interior. This government was immediately recognized by the United States. But Washington's "other hand" immediately started plotting with Nosavan to overthrow the new neutralist regime by force and arms—which Nosavan eventually succeeded in doing with massive U.S. military and logistics support.

I will pass over here the political events following Kong Le's

1961 coup, as these are dealt with in other articles in this book. My own book on Laos and Cambodia[7] details events up to the U.S. invasion of Cambodia on April 30, 1970 and the subsequent Pathet Lao offensive in the Bolovens Plateau. Those portions of the Senate Subcommittee (Symington) Hearings on Laos so far released supply confirmatory data on the systematic U.S. bombing of Laos, which began in May 1964—three months before the famous Tonkin Gulf nonincident and the first air strikes on North Vietnam—nearly five years before the U.S. public was informed. Note that long after the bombing began and thousands of U.S. "advisers" were taking part in military operations, Souvanna Phouma strenuously denied any U.S. military involvement. Indeed this was one pretext for the heavy censorship of the Symington report.

From May 1964 onwards, of course, Washington could claim— and subsequently did so—that it was "only" bombing the Ho Chi Minh Trail. In fact from that date onward U.S. planes were flying tactical support for rightist military operations. After the start of the systematic bombings of North Vietnam in February 1965 and the landing of the first U.S. combat units at Danang a month later, American intervention in Laos and neighboring Thailand assumed a more dangerous form, the full consequences of which have not yet been felt. The United States in fact forced the governments in Bangkok and Vientiane to commit acts of war against the Democratic Republic of Vietnam. When the bombings were at their height, 80 per cent of the missions were flown out of Thailand, across Laotian airspace, or by aircraft that took off from carriers cruising in the Gulf of Tonkin, bombed, and then flew on across Laotian airspace to the complex of bases in Thailand. Moreover, to support these missions and guide the aircraft to their targets, a network of radar bases was established in Laos, mostly in illegally seized areas deep inside Pathet Lao territory. The Pha Thi and Nakhang radar bases, for instance, were used not only to guide bombers to their targets, but to flash electronic signals to drop the actual bombs.

7. *The Second Indochina War* (New York: International Publishers, 1970).

While the U.S. press was shouting about "North Vietnamese" aggression and intervention in Laos, it was in fact the United States that was carrying out intervention of the most deadly kind in Laos in support of the flagrant aggression against North Vietnam that the bombings represented. Villages were razed to the ground to establish the mountaintop radar bases, while surrounding settlements were bombed out of existence. The Ho Chi Minh Trail on the other hand ran through Pathet Lao-held territory and in itself caused no damage or inconvenience, no loss of lives or property to the local people. Vast areas of Laos were devastated by U.S. planes trying to prevent the movement of what American military experts cited by Hilsman in *To Move a Nation* estimated at 6 to 12 tons of supplies daily. Hilsman, incidentally, recognizes that it was only long after U.S. intervention in South Vietnam that the North really started to help the resistance movement there by sending supplies down the Ho Chi Minh Trail. In referring to the famous State Department White Paper on "Aggression from the North"—used as the pretext to start the bombings—Hilsman comments:

No captured documents, equipment or materials were presented to indicate either the presence of North Vietnamese regular units or of individual North Vietnamese in significant numbers. The White Paper was able to present the case studies of only 4 captured infiltrators who were ethnic North Vietnamese. No evidence was presented of the presence of regular North Vietnamese units except the allegations of two of these and two other captured Vietcong of southern origin.[8]

Hilsman was aware of the methods used to extract such allegations and did not set much store in them.

Washington, in other words, used a double standard in measuring its own activities in Indochina and those of North Vietnam. It reserved the right to conduct an all-Indochina war: waged on the ground in South Vietnam; from the air against North Vietnam; from the air and by "secret war" with U.S. advisers and Green Berets in Laos; and eventually a full-scale invasion of Cambodia. But each of the component peoples of Indochina had

8. Hilsman, *op. cit.*, p. 531.

to stay behind its own frontiers on pain of being branded "aggressors" and automatically marked for destruction.

From the viewpoint of international law, Thailand was guilty of an act of war in lending its territory as bases for a second power to attack a third country. The Vientiane government was guilty of an act of war in lending its airspace for such attacks and for lending ground bases for guiding the attackers to their targets. It is granted that most of the latter were in Pathet Lao-held territory, but the Pathet Lao forces fulfilled their national and international duty by trying to shoot down the planes in transit and wipe out the bases, while the Vientiane government approved the use of its airspace and the setting up of the radar bases.

The question is obvious: If U.S. planes could fly from Thailand over Laotian territory to attack North Vietnam, why could North Vietnamese troops not march across Laotian territory to attack the bases? They would have a hundred times more justification in thus defending their country against aggression. Why should North Vietnamese troops not march into Laos, destroy every radar base and, if necessary, occupy Vientiane and force the authorities to cease granting the use of Laotian airspace to U.S. bombers? Why should they not march on Bangkok and force the authorities there to deny the use of Thai air bases to U.S. bombers? Morally and legally they would be completely within their rights to act in this way.

Another facet of the double standard Washington uses is that it reserves to the United States the monopoly of using foreign troops in their pay against the peoples of Indochina: Thai, South Vietnamese, Kuomintang Chinese, and other mercenaries in Laos; South Vietnamese and Thai troops in Cambodia; the same, plus South Korean, Australian, New Zealand, and Filipino troops in South Vietnam. But for the North Vietnamese to help their closest neighbors and allies in the anti-French colonialist war, or to support their compatriots in the South, was a "crime" to be punished by extermination.

Had the socialist camp acted like the United States, Soviet planes would have been bombing American cities; Soviet and Chinese submarines would be sinking U.S. supply convoys in the Pacific; and Chinese, North Korean, Cuban, Hungarian, etc., troops would be battling the United States and its satellites in Laos and elsewhere in Indochina. This seems far-fetched. In fact the countries of the socialist camp did offer to send pilots and troops to help the North Vietnamese. But from the beginning, the policy of the North Vietnamese was that "the bloodshed should be our blood," the rest of the socialist camp should give material help but continue to "build socialism in peace." At times the temptation must have been strong to use experienced Soviet and Cuban pilots in defense of North Vietnamese territory, or to have Chinese planes bomb the U.S. sanctuaries in Thailand. But the North Vietnamese leaders took a consistently responsible attitude that everything must be done to limit the war, nothing done to extend it: hence they restricted the air war to North Vietnam; the ground war to South Vietnam. It was not their fault that it spilled over into Laos and later into Cambodia. It will not be their fault if it later still spills over into Thailand.

The increasingly large-scale use of Thai troops in Laos and what seems the certainty of Thai intervention in Cambodia presents a grave new situation. (At the time of writing, Thai pilots flying unmarked planes are already bombing Cambodian villages.) The peoples of Indochina have many grievances to settle with Thailand, and the day is fast approaching when some of them seem certain to be settled. On one side of Thailand's western frontier the Pathet Lao holds large areas, and on the other side are Thai of Laotian origin, among whom a guerrilla movement is speedily developing. The use of Thai troops in Laos to defend the Sam Thong and Long Cheng bases south of the Plain of Jars and in attempts to retake the Bolovens Plateau is certain to stimulate Pathet Lao—and probably North Vietnamese —aid to the Thai guerrillas. If Thai troops are sent into Cambodia, there will be similar cooperation and coordination of activities between the Cambodian National United Front and the Patriotic Front of Thailand.

The Summit Conference of the Peoples of Indochina, held in the Vietnamese-Laotian-Chinese border areas on April 24–25, 1970, provided for a united struggle by the Vietnamese, Laotian, and Cambodian resistance movements. It defined the present tasks and established the future relations among the component parts of Indochina. Replying to my question concerning his evaluation of the results of this conference, Prince Souphanouvong, who heads the Neo Lao Hak Xat, replied:

It represents a scathing reply by the peoples of the three countries of Indochina to the adventurous activities of the USA. It is a severe blow at Nixon's thesis of "Asians Fight Asians—Indochinese Fight Indochinese." . . . The Joint Declaration of the conference is a program of unity and struggle against the common enemy and will serve as the basis to reinforce and extend the relations of support, mutual help and long-term cooperation between the peoples of Laos, Cambodia and Vietnam, for intensified coordination and unity of efforts. . . . It is a factor which will raise the struggle of our three peoples to a higher level.

Replying to a similar question, Prince Norodom Sihanouk, who heads the Cambodian National United Front, recalled that solidarity between the three peoples of Indochina had started with the French conquest, had developed during the resistance to Japanese occupation, and went still further in the struggle against French recolonization attempts.

That solidarity [continued Sihanouk] was certainly greatly strengthened by the American invasion of Indochina, in particular South Vietnam. Now U.S. aggression is not only aimed at South Vietnam, but against North Vietnam, Laos and Cambodia. . . . Conscious of our weaknesses, as small countries which have to fight against a very rich and powerful giant, with enormous military strength at his disposal, it is vital for us to unite our efforts, to cooperate closely with each other. This is what we must do to achieve victory. It may take a long time—but we are optimistic as far as the victory of our three peoples is concerned.

Although no formal military alliance was concluded—no general staff established for the various armed forces—the development of military operations in Laos and Cambodia immediately after the conference—which ended only five days before the U.S. invasion of Cambodia—showed that coordination started immediately. The newly formed Cambodian Liberation Army immediately seized a vast area of northern Cambodia which borders on Pathet Lao-held areas in southern Laos and NLF-controlled areas of South Vietnam. The Pathet Lao quickly seized control of the strategic Bolovens Plateau and the whole area leading from there down to the Cambodian frontier. The three forces thus very quickly established a vast base area from which it will be easy to coordinate their efforts and in which it will be easy for the military leaders to consult when necessary. The leaders of the Indochinese resistance movements can thank the Nixon administration for having brought them together and raised their combined struggle to an entirely new level. Their rejection of the idea that it is President Nixon who should decide what should be the relationships between the Indochinese people was perhaps best summed up by Sihanouk in his opening speech to the summit conference:

The cynicism of the United States executive reached its peak when he demanded that the resistance forces of our three peoples of Vietnam, Laos and Cambodia, evacuate their own countries in response to the withdrawal of a part of the United States forces, and especially when our resistance had become "foreign intervention" on our own soil. Where then should our liberation armies go? To the United States? Have the U.S. aggressors, through some operation of the Holy Ghost, become pure-blooded Indochinese?

Since the overthrow of Sihanouk in Cambodia, with its predictable consequences of a widened war, it is difficult to think in terms of separate Vietnamese, Cambodian, and Laotian problems. It is now an Indochinese war. Whether a separate solution can be found for Laos, as distinct from Cambodia and Vietnam, seems more than ever doubtful. Nevertheless, the Neo Lao Hak Xat still insists on a settlement based on the 1962 Geneva Agreements and makes repeated offers to Souvanna Phouma along these lines. The most interesting part of the five-point Neo Lao Hak Xat proposal of March 6, 1970 (see "The Pathet Lao Peace Plan," article 27) was that the "Laotian political parties should set up a consultative conference and a coalition government" pending general elections to a new national assembly. A precondition was the end of U.S. bombings and that any agreement must provide for the cessation of all U.S. military activity in Laos and the withdrawal of all U.S. military personnel.

It seems a fair assumption, however, that just as there is now one war in Indochina, so there can be only one peace in Indochina, based on an American withdrawal from the whole area and the neutralization of South Vietnam, Cambodia, and Laos. Independence based on neutrality is a common plank in the policies of the three resistance movements. At the summit conference this was entirely endorsed by Premier Pham Van Dong, who headed the Democratic Republic of Vietnam (DRV) delegation, and by Premier Chou En-lai for the People's Republic of China in a speech he made at a banquet which followed the closing session.

Someday, some U.S. administration is going to take a close look at the "neutral" solution, perhaps realize that this should have been accepted at the beginning, as provided for in the 1954 Geneva Accords, and take action accordingly. The alternative of "Asianization" or "Indochinization" of the war will spread the struggle over all of South Asia, at least as far as India.

It seems ironic, to say the least, that it is President Nixon who took over Che's slogan of "Two, three and more Vietnams."

14

Air America: Flying the U.S. into Laos

Peter Dale Scott

In the closing days of the 1968 presidential campaign, the Democrats made an eleventh-hour bid for the presidency through a White House announcement that all bombing in North Viet-nam was being stopped and that serious peace negotiations were about to begin. This move was apparently torpedoed within 30 hours by President Thieu of South Viet-Nam who publicly rejected the coming negotiations. Three days later, the Democratic candidate lost to Richard Nixon by a narrow margin.

After the election, it was revealed that a major Nixon fund raiser and supporter had engaged in elaborate machinations in Saigon (including false assurances that Nixon would not enter into such negotiations if elected) to sabotage the Democrats' plan. It was also revealed that, through wire taps, the White House and Humphrey knew of these maneuvers *before* the election and that a heated debate had gone on among Humphrey strategists as to whether the candidate should exploit the discovery in the last moments of the campaign. Humphrey declined to seize the opportunity, he said, because he was sure that Nixon was unaware of and did not approve of the activities of his supporter in Saigon.

The supporter in question was Madame Anna Chennault, and her covert intervention into the highest affairs of state was by no means an unprecedented act for her and her associates. Madame Chennault's husband, General Claire Chennault, had fought in China with Chiang Kai-shek; after the war he formed a private airline company. Both husband and wife have, through

Reprinted from *Ramparts* (Vol. 8), pp. 39–42; 52–54. Published in *The War Conspiracy* (Indianapolis: Bobbs-Merrill, 1970). Copyright © 1970, by Peter Dale Scott. Reprinted by permission of the publishers.

their involvement with the China Lobby and the CIA's complex of private corporations, played a profound role throughout our involvement in Southeast Asia. General Chennault's airline was, for example, employed by the U.S. government in 1954 to fly in support for the French at Dien Bien Phu. It was also a key factor in the new fighting which had begun in Laos in 1959; moreover, it appears that President Eisenhower was not informed and did not know when his office and authority were being committed in the Laotian conflict, just as Nixon did not know of the intrigue of Mme. Chennault. But that is precisely the point of parapolitics and private war enterprise.

In its evasion of Congressional and even Executive controls over military commitments in Laos and elsewhere, the CIA has long relied on the services of General Chennault's "private" paramilitary arm, Civil Air Transport or (as it is now known) Air America, Inc.

How Air America Wages War

Air America's fleets of transport planes are readily seen in the airports of Laos, South Viet-Nam, Thailand and Taiwan. The company is based in Taiwan, where a subsidiary firm, Air Asia, with some 8000 employees, runs one of the world's largest aircraft maintenance and repair facilities. While not all of Air America's operations are paramilitary or even covert, in Viet-Nam and even more in Laos, it is the chief airline serving the CIA in its clandestine war activities.

Until recently the largest of these operations was the supply of the fortified hilltop positions of the 45,000 Meo tribesmen fighting against the Pathet Lao behind their lines in northeast Laos. Most of these Meo outposts have airstrips that will accommodate special Short Take-off and Landing aircraft, but because of the danger of enemy fire the American and Nationalist Chinese crews have usually relied on parachute drops of guns, mortars, ammunition, rice, even live chickens and pigs. Air America's planes also serve to transport the Meos' main cash crop, opium.

The Meo units, originally organized and trained by the French, have provided a good indigenous army for the Americans in Laos. Together with their CIA and U.S. Special Forces "advisors," the Meos have long been used to harass Pathet Lao and North Vietnamese supply lines. More recently they have engaged in conventional battles in which they have been transported by Air America's planes and helicopters (*New York Times,* October 29, 1969). The Meos also defended, until its capture in 1968, the key U.S. radar installation at Pathi near the North Vietnamese border; the station had been used in the bombing of North Viet-Nam.

Further south in Laos, Air America flies out of the CIA operations headquarters at Pakse, from which it reportedly supplies an isolated U.S. Army camp at Attopeu in the southeast, as well as the U.S. and South Vietnamese Special Forces operations in the same region (*San Francisco Chronicle,* October 15, 1969). Originally the chief purpose of these activities was to observe and harass the Ho Chi Minh Trail, but recently the fighting in the Laotian panhandle, as elsewhere in the country, has expanded into a general air and ground war. Air America planes are reported to be flying arms, supplies and reinforcements in this larger campaign as well (*New York Times,* September 18, 1969).

Ostensibly, Air America's planes are only in the business of charter airlift. Before 1968, when the U.S. Air Force transferred its operations from North Viet-Nam to Laos, air combat operations were largely reserved for "Laotian" planes; but it has been suggested that at least some of these operated out of Thailand with American, Thai, or Nationalist Chinese pilots hired through Air America. In addition, many of Air America's pilots and ground crews have been trained for intelligence or "special" missions: a reporter in 1964 was amused to encounter American ground crews whose accents and culture were unmistakably Ivy League. And for years Air America's pilots have flown in a combat support role. As early as April 1961, when U.S. "advisors" are first known to have guided the Laotian army in combat, Air America's pilots flew the troops into battle in transports and in helicopters supplied by the U.S. Marines.

The 1962 Geneva Agreements on Laos prohibit both "foreign

paramilitary formations" and "foreign civilians connected with the supply, maintenance, storing and utilization of war materials"; Air America's presence would appear to constitute a violation under either category. In calling Air America a paramilitary auxiliary arm, however, it should be stressed that its primary function is logistical: not so much to make war, as to make war possible.

THE EARLY HISTORY OF AIR AMERICA

To understand the complex operations of Air America, one must go back to 1941 and the establishment of the "Flying Tigers" or American Volunteer Group (AVG), General Claire Chennault's private air force in support of Chiang Kai-shek against the Japanese. At that time President Roosevelt wished to aid Chiang and he also wanted American reserve pilots from the three services to gain combat experience; but America was not yet at war and the Neutrality Act forbade the service of active or reserve personnel in foreign wars. The solution was a legal fiction, worked out by Chennault's "Washington squadron," which included Roosevelt's "Brain Truster" lawyer, Thomas G. Corcoran, and the young columnist Joseph Alsop. Chennault would visit bases to recruit pilots for the "Central Aircraft Manufacturing Company, Federal, Inc.," (CAMCO), a corporation wholly owned by William Pawley, a former salesman for the old aircraft producer Curtiss-Wright, Inc. and head of Pan American's subsidiary in China. According to their contracts, the pilots were merely to engage in "the manufacture, operation, and repair of airplanes" in China; but Chennault explained to them orally that they were going off to fly and to fight a war.

In theory, the whole contract was to be paid for by the Chinese Government; in practice the funds were supplied by the United States Government through Lend-Lease. The operation was highly profitable to both of Pawley's former employers. Curtiss-Wright was able to unload 100 P-40 pursuit planes, which even the hard-pressed British had just rejected as "obsolescent." Pawley nearly wrecked the whole deal by insisting on a 10 per cent agent's commission, or $450,000, on the Curtiss sale. Treasury Secretary Morgenthau protested, but was persuaded by the Chinese to approve a payment of $250,000. For its part, Pan Am's Chinese subsidiary was later able to use many of Chennault's pilots in the lucrative charter airlift operations over the "hump" to Chungking.

It was agreed that Pawley's new CAMCO Corporation could not take American pilots into the private war business without presidential authorization, and there was some delay in getting this approval. But on April 15, 1941, Roosevelt signed an Executive Order authorizing the enlistment of U.S. reserve officers and men in the AVG-Flying Tigers. Thus CAMCO became a precedent for the establishment of a private war corporation by government decision. It does not appear, however, that the CIA was quite so fastidious about obtaining presidential approval in the postwar period.

After the war Chennault saw that a fortune could be made by obtaining contracts for the airlift of American relief supplies in China. Through Corcoran's connections—and despite much opposition—the relief agency UNRRA supplied Chennault not only with the contracts but also with the planes at bargain prices as well as with a loan to pay for them. One of Corcoran's connections, Whiting Willauer, promptly became Chennault's Number Two man. With the generous financing of the American taxpayers, Chennault and Willauer needed only a million dollars to set up a new airline, Civil Air Transport (CAT), the forerunner of Air America. According to *The Reporter*, CAT was originally bankrolled by T. V. Soong, then Chiang's ambassador to the U.S., whose personal holdings in the United States—after administering Chinese Lend-Lease—were reported to have reached $47,000,000 by 1944. There is no sign that the Soong interest in the CAT-Air America complex has ever been brought out.

The World War was over, but the Chinese Revolution was not. CAT, established for relief flights, was soon flying military airlifts to besieged Nationalist cities, often using the old Flying Tigers as pilots. Chennault himself spent a great deal of time in Washington with Corcoran, Senator William Knowland and other members of the Soong-financed China Lobby: he campaigned in vain for a $700,000,000 aid program to Chiang, half of which would have been earmarked for military airlift.

After the establishment of the Chinese People's Republic in October 1949, Truman and the State Department moved to abandon the Chiang clique and to dissociate themselves from the defense of Taiwan. By contrast, CAT chose to expand its parabusiness operations, appealing for more pilots "of proved loyalty."

To help secure Taiwan from invasion, Chennault and his partners put up personal notes of $4,750,000 to buy out China's civil air fleet, then grounded in Hong Kong. The avowed purpose of this "legal kidnapping" was less to acquire the planes than to deny them to the new government pending litigation. It is unclear exactly who backed Chennault financially in this critical maneuver (Soong denied that it was he). But it is known that shortly before the Korean war CAT was refinanced as a Delaware-based corporation by "a group of American businessmen and bankers." By the winter of 1950–1951 CAT was playing a key role in the airlift of supplies to Korea, and Chennault (according to his wife's memoirs) was into "a heavy intelligence assignment for the U.S. Government" (*A Thousand Springs*, p. 248).

CHENNAULT'S AMBITION OF ROLLING BACK COMMUNISM

Chennault's vision for his airline was summed up in 1959, the year of CAT's entry into Laos, by his close friend and biographer, Robert Lee Scott: "Wherever CAT flies it proclaims to the world that somehow the men of Mao will be defeated and driven off the mainland, and all China will return to being free."

As late as March 1952, according to Stewart Alsop, the Truman Administration had failed to approve the "forward" policy against China then being proposed by John Foster Dulles (*Saturday Evening Post*, Dec. 13, 1958). Yet in a CIA operation in 1951, CAT planes were ferrying arms and possibly troops from Taiwan to some 12,000 of Chiang's soldiers who had fled into Burma. In his book, *To Move a Nation*, Roger Hilsman tells us that the troops, having been equipped by air, undertook a large-scale raid into China's Yunnan Province, but the raid was a "colossal failure." Later, in the "crisis" year 1959, some 3000 of the troops moved from Burma to Laos. On another CIA operation in 1952, a CAT plane dropped CIA agents John Downey and Richard Fecteau with a supply of arms for Nationalist guerrillas on the mainland.

In 1954 Chennault conducted a vigorous political campaign in support of a grandiose but detailed proposal whereby his old friends Chiang and Syngman Rhee would be unleashed together against the Chinese mainland with the support of a 470-man "International Volunteer Group" modeled after his old Flying Tigers. "Once Chiang unfurls his banner on the mainland," promised Chennault, "Mao will be blighted by spontaneous peasant uprisings and sabotage."

Chennault actually had a list of pilots and had located training sites for the Group in Central America, where his former partner Whiting Willauer, now U.S. ambassador to Honduras, was playing a key role in the CIA-organized deposition of Guatemalan President Arbenz. (Willauer was also one of the two chief officials responsible for the planning of the Bay of Pigs operation under the Eisenhower Administration.) Chennault's plan seems to have had CIA support. It was defeated however by opposition in the State Department, Pentagon, and Nationalist Chinese Air Force.

CAT, however, had by no means been idle. It flew 24 of the 29 C–119's dropping supplies for the French at Dien Bien Phu. The planes were on "loan" from the U.S. Air Force, and some of the "civilians" flying them were in fact U.S. military pilots. According to Bernard Fall, who flew in these planes, the pilots were "quietly attached to CAT to familiarize themselves with the area in case [as Dulles and Nixon hoped] of American air intervention on behalf of the French." (*Hell in a Very Small Place,* p. 241).

CAT's C–119's were serviced in Viet-Nam by 200 mechanics of the USAF 81st Air Service Unit. Five of these men were declared missing on June 18, 1954. Thus the CAT operation brought about the first official U.S. casualties in the Viet-Nam war. Senator John Stennis, fearful of a greater U.S. involvement, claimed the Defense Department had violated a "solemn promise" to have the unit removed by June 12.

From the passing of the 1954 Geneva Agreements until Chennault's death four years later, CAT seems to have played more of a waiting than an active paramilitary role. But CAT continued to train large numbers of Chinese mechanics at its huge Taiwan facility. As a right-wing eulogist observed in 1955, they were thus ready for service "if the Communists thrust at Formosa or Thailand or Southern Indochina. . . . CAT has become a symbol of hope to all free Asia. Tomorrow the Far Eastern skies may redden with a new war and its loaded cargo carrier may roll down the runways once more" (*Saturday Evening Post,* Feb. 12, 1955, p. 101).

ALSOP'S "INVASION": AIR AMERICA ENTERS INTO LAOS

The Quemoy crises of 1954 and 1958 were generated in large part by a build-up of Chiang's troops on the offshore islands, from which battalion strength commando raids had been launched. While this build-up was encouraged by local military "advisors" and CIA personnel, it was officially disapproved by Washington. The crises generated new pressures in the Pentagon for bombing the mainland, but with their passage the likelihood of a U.S.-backed offensive seemed to recede decisively. United States intelligence officials later confirmed that the Soviet Union had disappointed China during the 1958 crisis by promising only defensive support. Some CIA officials concluded that the U.S. could therefore risk confrontation with impunity below China's southern border, since any response by China would only intensify the Sino-Soviet split. The fallacy of this reasoning was soon to be made apparent.

After Quemoy, Laos appeared to present the greatest likelihood of war in the Far East, though hardly because of any inherent aggressiveness in the Laotian people themselves. In 1958, the non-aligned government which had been established in Laos under Prince Souvanna Phouma appeared to be close to a neutralist reconciliation with the pro-Communist Pathet Lao. Fearful that this would lead to the absorption of Laos into the Communist bloc, the United States decided to intervene, and Souvanna Phouma was forced out of office on July 23, 1958, by a timely withholding of U.S. aid. Egged on by its American advisors, the succeeding government of Phoui Sananikone declared itself no longer bound by the provisions of the 1954 Geneva Agreements and moved swiftly toward a covert build-up of U.S. military aid, including non-uniformed "advisors." Even so, the CIA and the military were not satisfied with the new government, which the State Department had approved. As Hilsman and Schlesinger have revealed, the CIA organized a right-wing power base under General Phoumi Nosavan and made him a key figure in its subsequent scenarios.

CIA and Pentagon officials were now set upon a course, often opposed to that of the U.S. ambassador in Vientiane, which led to the further destabilization of Laos and hastened the growth of the Pathet Lao. The CIA's plotting on behalf of General Phoumi has therefore frequently been derided as self-defeating. This assumes, however, that the CIA's interest was confined to the rather amorphous internal politics of Laos; in fact the scope of its strategy is far wider.

In December 1958, both North Viet-Nam and Yunnan Province in southern China began to complain of over-flights by American or "Laotian" planes. These charges, which Arthur J. Dommen confirms, may refer in fact to "flights of American reconnaissance aircraft." (Dommen's excellent book, *Conflict in Laos*, was prepared with the aid of the Council on Foreign Relations, published by Praeger, and dedicated to one of the most notorious CIA agents in Taiwan and later in Laos, Robert Campbell James). Soon afterwards, Peking began to complain of U.S.-supplied Nationalist Chinese Special Forces camps in Yunnan Province.

By March 1959, according to Bernard Fall, "Some of the Nationalist Chinese guerrillas operating in the Shan states of neighboring Burma had crossed over into Laotian territory and were being supplied by an airlift of 'unknown planes.'" Laos was already beginning to be what it has since clearly become: a cockpit for international confrontation.

In 1959, following a government crackdown against the leaders

and military forces of the Pathet Lao, the country saw an outbreak of sporadic fighting which General Phoumi quickly labeled
a North Vietnamese "invasion." On August 23, the *New York
Times* reported the arrival of two CAT transports in the Laotian
capital, Vientiane. More transports arrived soon thereafter. On
August 30, a "crisis" occurred which was to be used as a pretext
for a permanent paramilitary airlift operation. (Also, sometime
about this period, before September 30, 1959, CAT, Inc., changed
its name to Air America, Inc.)

All through August, reports from three of Phoumi's generals
created a minor war hysteria in the U.S. press, which depicted
an invasion of Laos by five or more North Vietnamese battalions. At one point, when August rains washed out a bridge,
the *New York Times* reported "Laos Insurgents Take Army
Post Close to Capital," and speculated that they were trying
to cut off Vientiane from the south. As for the August 30 "crisis,"
the Washington *Post* wrote that 3500 communist rebels, "including regular Viet-minh troops, have captured 80 villages in
a new attack in northern Laos." Much later, it was learned that
in fact not 80 but three villages had been evacuated, after two
of them had been briefly blanketed by 81-mm mortar fire at
dawn on August 30. No infantry attack had been observed: the
defending garrisons, as so often happened in Laos, had simply
fled.

After it was all over, the Laotian government claimed only
that it had lost 92 men during the period of the "invasion"
crisis from July 16 to October 7, 1959; more than half of these
deaths ("estimated at 50 killed") took place on August 30. A
U.N. investigating team, after personal interviews, reduced the
latter estimate from 50 to five. Further, as a RAND Corporation
report for the U.S. Air Force concluded, "it is apparent that
the Sananikone government precipitated the final crisis which
led to war in Laos." No North Vietnamese invaders were ever
discovered. Though the Laotians claimed at one point to have
seven North Vietnamese prisoners, it was later admitted that
these were deserters who had crossed over from North Viet-
Nam in order to surrender.

Joseph Alsop, however, who had arrived in Laos just in time

to report the events of August 30, wrote immediately of a "massive new attack on Laos" by "at least three and perhaps five new battalions of enemy troops from North Viet-Nam." In the next few days he would write of "aggression, as naked, as flagrant as a Soviet-East German attack on West Germany," noting that "the age-old process of Chinese expansion has begun again with a new explosive force." Unlike most reporters, Alsop could claim to have first-hand reports: on September 1 at the town of Sam Neua, he had seen the arrival on foot of survivors (one of whom had a "severe leg wound") from the mortared outposts. Bernard Fall, who was also in Laos and knew the area well, later called all of this "just so much nonsense," specifying that "a villager with a severe leg wound does not cover 45 miles in two days of march in the Laotian jungle." (*Street Without Joy,* p. 303). Alsop, by Fall's account, had been a willing witness to a charade staged for his benefit by two of Phoumi's generals.

As on many occasions between 1959 and 1964, Alsop's reports were to play an important role in shaping the Asian developments he described. The London *Times* drew attention to the stir his story created in Washington. Senator Dodd and others clamored vainly that in the light of the "invasion" Khrushchev's impending visit to America should be put off. Though this did not happen, there were three lasting consequences of the "great Laos fraud" of August 1959.

First, on August 26, the State Department announced that additional U.S. aid and personnel would be sent to Laos: thus the military support program was stepped up at a time when a congressional exposure of its scandals and futility had threatened to terminate it altogether. Second, reportedly under a Presidential Order dated September 4, CINCPAC Commander Harry D. Felt moved U.S. ground, sea and air forces into a more forward posture for possible action in Laos. (A signal corps unit is supposed to have been put into Laos at this time, the first U.S. field unit in Southeast Asia.) Third, the planes of Air America were moved into Laos to handle the stepped-up aid, and additional transports (over the approved 1954 levels) were given to the Laotian government. At the same time a

Chennault-type "volunteer air force" of U.S. active and reserve officers ("American Fliers for Laos") was said by the *Times* to be negotiating a contract for operations "like those of the Flying Tigers."

The timing of these germinal decisions is intriguing. On the day of the aid announcement, August 26, Eisenhower had left for Europe at 3:20 in the morning to visit Western leaders before receiving Khrushchev in Washington. At a press conference on the eve of his departure, he professed ignorance about the details of the Laotian aid request, which had just been received that morning. He did, however, specify that the State Department had not yet declared the existence of an "invasion" (something it would do during his absence). The date of the "Presidential Order" on Laos, September 4, was the day allotted in Eisenhower's itinerary for a golf holiday at the secluded Culzean Castle in Scotland. According to his memoirs, which corroborate earlier press reports, "our stolen holiday was interrupted *the following morning* (i.e., September 5) by bad news from Laos." Eisenhower added, "My action *on return to the United States* was to approve increased aid to the pro-United States government" (emphasis added). He is silent about the troop movements he reportedly authorized.

Knowing this, one would like to learn why a U.S. response to an artificially inflated "emergency" on August 30 was delayed until Eisenhower's virtual isolation five days later, even though it could not await his return to Washington three days after that. Once again it is the knowledgeable Joseph Alsop who supplies the corroborating details: "Communications are nonexistent in little Laos. Hence word of the new 'invasion' took more than 48 hours to reach the commander of the Laotian Army, General Ouane Rathikone. There was, of course, a further delay before the grave news reached Washington. Time also was needed to assess its significance."

Bernard Fall rejects this explanation: "The Laotian Army command . . . *did* know what went on in the border posts since it had radio communications with them." The Senate Foreign Relations Committee would do well to investigate the resulting possibility that the first U.S. field unit in Southeast Asia was put in by a combination of deliberate misrepresentation and evasion of proper presidential review. Washington columnist Marquis Childs reported soon after the "invasion" that: "A powerful drive is on within the upper bureaucracy of Defense and Intelligence to persuade President Eisenhower that he must send American troops into Laos. . . . They will consist of two Marine regiments of the Third Marine Division now stationed on Okinawa and components of the 1st Marine Air Wing, also on Okinawa [having been moved up in the course of the crisis]. Notice would be served on the Communists—Red China and North Viet-Nam—that if they did not withdraw in one week, they would be attacked. According to one source, they would use the tactical atomic weapons with which they are in part at least already equipped."

Senator Mansfield asked in the Senate on September 7, whether the President and Secretary of State Herter still made foreign policy, or whether the various executive agencies, like Defense and CIA, had taken over. Today, with Air America deep in Laotian war business, Congress should surely learn more about the arrival of CAT's planes in Vientiane on August 22, more than a week before the U.S. government's two critical policy decisions. The Chennault-inspired "American Fliers for Laos" would violate the provisions of the Neutrality Act quite as clearly as had the Flying Tigers: was there then an authorization from Eisenhower to parallel that granted by Roosevelt? One witness who might be called to testify is Joseph Alsop, who like some of the China hands in the CIA and the Pentagon, had himself worked for Chennault in China during World War II.

AIR AMERICA HELPS TO OVERTHROW A GOVERNMENT

Although the CIA's General Phoumi was largely responsible for the intrigues of the August "invasion," the State Department's Phoui Sananikone was still in office. On December 30, according to Schlesinger, the CIA "moved in" and toppled Phoui.

A few months later, in April 1960, the CIA helped to rig an election for their man Phoumi. Dommen reports that "CIA agents participated in the election rigging, with or without the authority of the American Ambassador. A Foreign Service officer . . . had seen CIA agents distribute bagfuls of money to village headmen." But this maneuver was so flagrant that it discredited the government and led to a coup in August, restoring the old neutralist premier, Souvanna Phouma.

Over the next few weeks, Souvanna Phouma's new government succeeded in winning the approval of the King, American Ambassador Winthrop Brown, and the new right-wing, but pliant, National Assembly. In due course his pro-neutralist government was officially recognized by the United States. Nevertheless General Phoumi, after consulting with his cousin Marshal Sarit in Thailand, decided to move against Souvanna, proclaiming a rival "Revolutionary Committee" in southern Laos. Phoumi's first announcement of his opposition took the form of leaflets dropped from a C–47 over the Laotian capital. Presumably the pilot was an American mercenary, as the Laotians were not known to have been trained to handle these planes.

In the next three months, according to Schlesinger, "A united embassy, including CIA [i.e. CIA station chief Gordon L. Jorgensen] followed Brown in recommending that Washington accept Souvanna's coalition. . . . As for the Defense Department, it was all for Phoumi. *Possibly* with encouragement from Defense and CIA men *in the field,* Phoumi . . . proclaimed a new government and denounced Souvanna. The Phoumi regime became the recipient of American military aid, while the Souvanna government in Vientiane continued to receive economic aid. Ambassador Brown still worked to bring them together, but the military *support* convinced Phoumi that, if he only held out, Washington would put him in power." The words which I have italicized are inexcusably misleading: Phoumi, from the beginning of his formal insurgency in September, had high-level CIA and Pentagon encouragement to oust Souvanna's supporters in Vientiane. The proof of this was that while Sarit's forces in Thailand blockaded Vientiane, Air America was stepping up its military airlift to Phoumi's base at Savannakhet.

"It was plain," writes Dommen, "that General Phoumi was rapidly building up his matériel and manpower for a march on Vientiane. From mid-September, Savannakhet was the scene of an increased number of landings and take-offs by unmarked C–46 and C–47 transports, manned by American crews. These planes belonged to Air America, Inc., a civilian charter company with U.S. Air Force organizational support and under contract to the U.S. Government."[1]

In October, Hilsman reports, Ambassador Brown was telling Souvanna that the United States "had Phoumi's promise not to use the aid against . . . the neutralist forces" in Vientiane. Yet even as he did so, two men "flew to Savannakhet and gave Phoumi the green light to retake Vientiane" (*Saturday Evening Post*, April 22, 1961, p. 89). The two men were not some CIA spooks "in the field," but John N. Irwin II, Assistant Secretary of Defense for International Security Affairs, and Vice-Admiral Herbert D. Riley, chief of staff of the U.S. Pacific Command. Meanwhile the Meo tribesmen, encouraged by the CIA, defected from Souvanna in mid-October, at which point Air America began supplying them with matériel and U.S. Special Forces cadres from Savannakhet. Despite the 1962 Geneva Agreements, this airlift has continued up to the present.

DECEMBER 1960: EISENHOWER O.K.'S AIR AMERICA IN LAOS

Why did top U.S. officials deliberately foment a conflict between non-communist forces in Laos, a conflict which led to rapid increases in the territory held by the Pathet Lao? According to *Time* magazine (March 17, 1961), "the aim, explained the CIA, who called Phoumi 'our boy,' was to 'polarize' the communist and anti-communist factions in Laos." If so, the aim was achieved: the country is today a battlefield where U.S. bombings, with some 400 to 500 sorties a day, have generated

1. Schlesinger, so scathing about "CIA spooks" in Laos, is discreetly silent on the subject of Air America. Even Hilsman, while attacking the "tragedy" of inter-agency rivalry and the CIA's "attempt to 'play God' in Lao political life," says merely that "air transports of a civilian American airline began a steady shuttle to Phoumi's base in Savannakhet" (*To Move a Nation*, p. 124). It is important to remember that Schlesinger and Hilsman (both ex-OSS) were intimately involved with covert CIA operations during the Kennedy Administration.

400,000 refugees. "Polarization," as sanctioned by the Thai block-ade of Vientiane and a U.S. refusal of supplies, forced Souvanna Phouma to request an airlift of rice and oil (and later guns) from the Soviet Union, and in the end to invite in North Viet-namese and Chinese "technicians." The first Soviet transport planes arrived in Vientiane on December 4, 1960; and the Rus-sians were careful to send civilian pilots. As Dommen notes, they were "following the precedent set by the United States."

In late December an American transport was actually fired on by a Soviet Ilyushin 14, and a major international conflict seemed possible. Of course, there were some in CIA and De-fense who thought that a showdown with "Communism" in Asia was inevitable, and better sooner than later. Many more, in-cluding most of the Joint Chiefs, believed that America's first priority in Laos was international, to maintain a militant "for-ward strategy" against an imagined Chinese expansionism. Thus the actual thrust of American policy, if not its avowed intention, was towards the Chennault–Air America vision of "rollback" in Asia.

The last weeks of 1960 were to see ominous indications that anti-communist forces were only too willing to internationalize the conflict, especially with the first reports in the *Times* and *Le Monde* that General Phoumi's forces were being bolstered by Thai combat troops in Laotian uniforms and by Thai heli-copters. The expulsion of Souvanna from Vientiane in mid-December ended nothing; for the next 18 months Laos would have two "governments," each recognized and supplied by a major power.

Did Eisenhower authorize this race to the brink? Years later, in 1966, an article in the *Times* claimed that the President "had specifically approved" the CIA's backing of Phoumi against Am-bassador Brown's advice; the article however said nothing about the Pentagon and Air America's airlift. Eisenhower's own mem-oirs, in an extraordinary passage, state quite clearly that it was after December 13 (*after* the crisis posed by the new Soviet air-lift) that he approved the use of "United States aircraft" to "transport supplies into the area." (Air America's planes are clearly referred to, since the use of Air Force transports was not authorized until April 26, 1961): "As Phoumi proceeded to retake Vientiane, General Goodpaster reported the events to me. . . . He then posed several questions: 'First, should we seek to have Thai aircraft transport supplies into the area? Second, if the Thais can't do the job, should we use United States aircraft?' . . . I approved the use of Thai transport aircraft and United States aircraft as well!"

These last pages of Eisenhower's memoirs reveal how little he was briefed by bureaucrats as they prepared for a change-over to the incoming Kennedy Administration. Just as he knew nothing of the detailed plans for an invasion of Cuba which had been approved by the CIA's "Special Group" on November 4, so he apparently did not know that Thai helicopters were already being used in a combat support role, nor that Air America had been flying missions for Laos for over a year.

This would help explain why a story reporting the crash of an Air America plane in November on the Plain of Jars was not carried in any American newspaper, though it was printed abroad in the *Bangkok Post* of November 28, 1960. (The plane's American pilot was wounded seriously; the Chinese co-pilot, son of Nationalist Chinese Ambassador to Washington Hollington Tong, was killed.)

It also fits in with the fact that U.S. officials announced on December 7 (six days before Eisenhower authorized the flights) that they had "interrupted military air shipments" to Phoumi.[2] After the interruption, Eisenhower was asked to authorize what was in fact a *resumption* of the airlift to Phoumi while apparently under the impression that he was *initiating* it. Thus Air America was "legalized" just in time for the incoming Kennedy Administration. For the purposes of this legalization the Soviet airlift—which Pentagon machinations had done so much to in-

2. *New York Times*, Dec. 8, 1960, p. 7. "At the same time, they added, the United States has accelerated delivery to South Viet-Nam of military equipment needed to fight Communist guerrillas [and] also has recast military training of the Vietnamese Army to emphasize anti-guerrilla operations." The story shows how (as on many later occasions) de-escalation in Laos was balanced by escalation in Viet-Nam; and also how critical military decisions attributed to the Kennedy Administration in 1961 had in fact been made by the Pentagon during the lame-duck Eisenhower Administration.

duce—was not a disaster but a godsend: the airlift could now be justified to the President (as it was to the people) by the formula that, as Sulzberger said, "we are starting to match" the Soviet airlift.

Consciously or not, Air America's operations were leading our country into war in Southeast Asia. And it is hard to believe that Air America's directors were unconscious of this. Retired Admiral Felix B. Stump, until 1958 U.S. Commander-in-Chief, Pacific, and Air America's board chairman since 1959, had told a Los Angeles audience in April 1960: "World War III has already started, and we are deeply involved in it." Later he declared it was "high time" the nation won over communism in the Far East, and he called for the use of tactical nuclear weapons if necessary. Containment was not enough; we must "move beyond this limited objective."

The Admiral was not speaking in a vacuum. Now in one country, now in another, the tempo of U.S. operations in Southeast Asia did indeed increase steadily over the next few years. After a disastrous experiment in the latest counterinsurgency techniques in Laos, for example (with Air America planes and pilots transporting the Laotian army), the Kennedy Administration agreed in May 1961 to a Laotian cease-fire and negotiations. One day later, Rusk announced the first of a series of steps to increase the involvement of U.S. forces, including Air America, in Viet-Nam. A year later the United States signed the July 1962 Geneva Agreements to neutralize Laos. Unfortunately, as in 1954 and 1961, the price for U.S. agreement to this apparent de-escalation was a further buildup of U.S. (and Air America) commitments in Viet-Nam and also Thailand. No diplomatic agreements have ever interrupted this slow but inexorable American buildup in Southeast Asia. Hence it is not surprising that in the Paris talks the other side has been intransigent about the principle of U.S. troop withdrawal, nor that Nixon's public "Vietnamizing" of the war should be balanced by a secret expansion of Air America's role in it.

Despite the 1962 Geneva Agreements, Air America has never dismantled its private war enterprise in Laos. Although the Agreements providently called for the withdrawal of "foreign civilians connected with the supply, maintenance, storing, and utilization of war materials," Air America continued to fly into northeastern Laos, and it appears that some of the uniformed U.S. military "advisors" simply reverted to their pre-Kennedy civilian disguise. The first military incident in the resumption of fighting was the shooting down of an Air America plane in November 1962, three days after the Pathet Lao had warned that they would do so.

What made the Air America coterie with its influential backers in the Pentagon and CIA and its dependent Nationalist Chinese remnants from Burma, hang on in Laos with such tenacity? Hilsman tells us that, at least as late as 1962, there were those in the Pentagon and CIA "who believed that a direct confrontation with Communist China was inevitable," (p. 311). In his judgment, the basic assumption underlying the CIA's programs in Laos, and particularly the airlift to the Meos, "seemed to be that Laos was sooner or later to become a major battleground in a military sense betwen the East and the West" (p. 115).

In 1962, says Hilsman, a CIA proposal for a "'covert' but large-scale landing" on the Chinese mainland itself was turned down; and in June 1962, on the eve of the Laos Geneva Conference, the Chinese Ambassador in Warsaw was informed (for the first time) "that no United States support would be given to any Nationalist attempt to invade the mainland." This apparent rejection of Chennault's old "rollback" proposals did not however put an end to covert operations in Southeast Asia— quite the opposite.

Now that a U.S. attack on China seemed less likely, first Viet-Nam and later Thailand threatened to move toward "neutralism" and a rapprochement with their communist neighbors. Many observers now agree with Tom Wicker of the *New York Times* that one important reason for Diem's removal in November 1963 was "Washington's apprehension that Diem's unstable brother, Nhu, was trying to make a 'neutralist' settlement with the Viet Cong and North Viet-Nam through French intermediaries."[3]

In 1964 the increasing Vietnamese drift toward neutralism

3. Cf. *The Politics of Escalation in Vietnam,* Schurmann et al.

became an ever greater argument for a U.S. escalation, but President Johnson proved unwilling to authorize any dramatic public steps in an election year. Once again, as in the election year 1960, covert war proved to be the easiest answer to the democratic vs. imperialist dilemma: how to appear peaceful at home while intervening abroad.

Once again Laos was the perfect terrain: as in 1960, a CIA-linked right-wing coup, followed by a left-wing reaction, was the moving cause for a major outbreak of fighting. Once again Air America's planes were involved in continuous warfare, as they have been with incremental escalations ever since. They were now joined by jets of the USAF and Navy (on August 5, 1964, the latter were diverted from their Laotian targets for the Tonkin Gulf retaliation). Once again (as in the election year 1960) a covert buildup in Laos supplied the infrastructure and air capability for a subsequent buildup in Viet-Nam.

To an extraordinary extent the history of Air America *is* the history of America's recent involvement in Southeast Asia. The airline has grown with this involvement, so that by 1968 it had amassed a fleet of nearly 200 planes and employed an estimated 11,000 people. (By comparison, its "competitor," the Flying Tiger Line, which was the largest all-cargo carrier in the world when Air America was set up, had only 22 planes and 2089 employees by 1968.)

It is a striking index of the real war strategy of the current administration that Air America's operations, far from being phased out, are on the increase. The main problem Washington sees in Southeast Asian policy is that the war has become too public; the idea now is to hang on by re-emphasizing the covert while publicly "Vietnamizing" the war to dull popular concern. Nixon is again stepping up our undercover involvements in Southeast Asia, with a special focus in Laos, a battlefield rarely penetrated by nosy TV camera teams.

As the *New York Times* reported on September 18, authoritative sources confirmed that "United States B–52 strikes along the Laotian sections of the [Ho Chi Minh] trail have increased greatly in the last two weeks . . . as many as 500 sorties a day were being flown over Laos, and . . . the increase in bombing in Laos was part of the reason for the lull in the air war in South Viet-Nam. . . . United States planes—of Air America, Continental Air Services and the United States Air Force—were flying reinforcements, supplies, and arms to advanced areas, while American Army officers and agents of the Central Intelligence Agency were advising local commanders."

There are clear indications that this upsurge in covert warfare is slated to be an enduring rather than a momentary phenomenon. In October, Air America was making job offers to pilots who had been processed and given security clearances as much as three years earlier, but never employed. One prospective flyer—who was told he would be based in Saigon but could expect to operate throughout Southeast Asia—asked why positions had suddenly become available after such a long interval. The explanation was that Air America's operations had been at a steady level for the last four or five years—including the peak period of the Viet-Nam escalation—but that they were now expected to increase!

And in the wake of the Tonkin escalation, one Washington faction held, as Bernard Fall has written: "That the Viet-Nam affair could be transformed into a 'golden opportunity' to 'solve' the Red Chinese problem as well, possibly by a pan-Asian 'crusade' involving Chinese Nationalist, Korean and Japanese troops, backed by United States power as needed." (*Vietnam Witness*, p. 103).

These strange lusts for conflagration, which do not seem to have been sated yet, have never quite achieved official dominance in Washington. But the old fantasies of rollback have been nourished by Chennault and his successor, Retired Admiral Felix Stump, while each was serving as Board Chairman of CAT and Air America. And the tandem of Air America and CIA did manage to advance the fantasy in Laos—under Kennedy, it seems, as well as Eisenhower—by strengthening the intransigence of General Phoumi while "official" U.S. policy was to induce him into a neutral coalition.

15

Opium and Politics in Laos

David Feingold

On April 25, 1970, an Air Force major—holder of the Air Force Cross—was found guilty by a general court-martial in Saigon. He was convicted on ten counts involving the transportation of 859 pounds of opium alleged to have originated in Thailand. Aside from the value of the haul (worth up to $150,000 in Hong Kong), what makes the case of more than passing interest was the fact that the major had served as pilot for both Ambassador Ellsworth Bunker and General William Westmoreland. A United Press International story of April 26 quotes the testimony he offered in his own defense:

I was under the impression that boxes bound for Hong Kong contained checks and cash and those for Saigon contained dirty movies, books and some medicine.[1]

The strange thing about it is that he may have been telling the truth.

Four years ago Réné Enjabal, a former Air France pilot, fell asleep at the controls of a plane flying from Laos. Much to his surprise and no doubt considerable dismay, he strayed into Thailand, where he was forced down by the Thai Air Force and arrested for violating Thai airspace. In the course of convincing the Thai that he did not represent a major threat to either their sovereignty or security, he explained that he was merely returning from a routine delivery of 1,300 pounds of opium that had been airdropped to a trawler in the Gulf of Siam. Apparently, his explanation was sufficient to justify the short prison term which he eventually received.

In August 1966 some Special Forces troops were surprised to receive a package of opium from their montagnard allies, al-

1. *Chicago Sun Times,* April 26, 1970, p. 30.

though they probably were less surprised than the montagnards were when the package first floated down to them from the sky. It was one small, stray part of the large amount of raw opium that was being smuggled into Vietnam from Laos by plane to be parachuted into drop-zones in the mountains north of Kontum about 260 miles north of Saigon.[2]

In July of 1967 a small opium war erupted in Laos. One of the Shan rebel groups (who have been using opium sales to finance their decade-old fight for independence against the Burmese government) decided to bring its opium into Thailand via Laos rather than by the more usual and direct route—straight across the border from the Shan States in Burma. The aim of this decision was to avoid the territory in the Thai hills controlled by the remnants of the old Kuomintang (Nationalist Chinese) 93rd Division. These Chinese soldiers had been driven out of Yunnan into Burma by the communist forces in 1949, and thereafter caused considerable distress to several Burmese governments. Having refused repatriation to Taiwan, they were forced out of Burma by the government of General Ne Win. They established new headquarters in northern Thailand in 1960–1962, where they have since remained, maintaining themselves by trading in opium and collecting commissions on all opium shipments passing through the areas under their control. The Shan were trying to avoid these payments, which were becoming increasingly irksome and expensive. Not to be outflanked (or outdone), the Chinese struck into Laos and attacked the heavily guarded Shan pack caravan at Ban Nan Nhion, which was north of its destination, the Mekong River town of Ban Houei Sai. The 1,000 Chinese troops and the slightly smaller Shan forces battled for two days. Both were defeated.

The unquestioned victor of the encounter was the Laotian Army commander, General Ouane Rattikone. With a degree of bellicosity and decisiveness rarely met in Royal Laotian Army commanders, he dealt a stunning riposte to this tactless disruption of Laotian serenity: utilizing his force of T–28 planes,

2. *Vietnam Guardian*, August 18, 1966.

he strafed and blasted both sides with an impartiality worthy of the military representative of an avowedly neutral country. The victory yielded some 300 dead Shan and Chinese, as well as spoils to the victor—in this case, about $350,000 worth of opium.

The opium trade in Southeast Asia is very much like a submarine that runs submerged most of the time but can be detected by its echoes, traced by the wake of its periscope, and occasionally caught on the surface. Like a submarine too it can be very deadly. The four incidents outlined above are times that the trade has surfaced; there have been others. In April of 1968 the Senate Subcommittee on Foreign Aid Expenditures issued a report that alleged that four or five years earlier, Colonel (now Vice President) Nguyen Cao Ky, employed at the time by the Central Intelligence Agency, had been active in flying opium from Laos to Saigon.[3] In fact, his pharmaceutical ventures took up so much of the colonel's time and energies that the CIA apparently decided they could get more for their money elsewhere, and sacked him.

In case one should be skeptical of the antiwar fervor of the Senate committee, or should perhaps feel that official participation in the trade and transport of opium is a thing of the past, one need only turn to the *Christian Science Monitor* of May 29, 1970. In the first of a series of ten articles on the international trade in narcotics, the *Monitor* points out, among other things, that both the Laotian Army and Air Force are active participants in the trade and that Lao planes spend a good deal of time hauling the stuff about.[4]

In the politics of Laos, Burma, and Thailand, the influence of opium and the millions of dollars involved in its trade is never very far below the surface. Bizarre military strategies, surprising political alliances, and "irrational" policies often become astonishingly comprehensible when examined in terms of the economics and logistics of opium. Unfortunately, little information reaches the general public. Moreover, because of the

3. *New York Times,* April 19, 1968.
4. *Christian Science Monitor,* May 29, 1970, p. 15.

clandestine nature of the trade, much of what is known is the product of rumor, misunderstanding, and imagination. Even among alleged experts in the field—both official and otherwise—the level of sophistication is sometimes shockingly low; fear of causing embarrassment to well-placed persons has prevented full discussion of what should be publicized. In this brief discussion, we shall attempt to provide an introduction to the various technical aspects of opium production, processing, and use, and examine some of its implications for the political and economic situation in Laos and mainland Southeast Asia.

WHAT EXACTLY IS OPIUM?

Opium is the latex of the poppy *Papaver somniferum*. Of the large variety of poppies (28 genera and about 250 species), only one produces opium. The opium poppy and some of its effects have been known for at least 6,000 years: in Sumerian records it is referred to as the plant of joy.[5] It was not until the beginning of the nineteenth century, however, that a Prussian pharmacist's apprentice, Friedrich Serturner, isolated morphine as the active principle in opium.[6] In fact, morphine is only one—albeit the most important one—of 23 different alkaloids to be found in opium.[7] The biogenesis of morphine is poorly understood,[8] and so is the physiological function of opium in the poppy. The morphine content of opium varies considerably from place to place and from crop to crop. A British survey of the morphine content of opium grown in different years and in different districts of India, for example, found a range from 6.1 per cent to 18 per cent morphine.[9] Most of the opium grown in

5. J. M. Scott, *The White Poppy* (New York: Funk & Wagnalls, 1969), p. 5.
6. F. Meyers et al., *Review of Medical Pharmacology* (Tokyo: Maruzen Asian Edition, Lange Medical Publications, 1968), p. 269.
7. A. Burger, *Medical Chemistry* (New York: Interscience Publishers, 1951), p. 157.
8. D. Ginsburg, *The Opium Alkaloids* (New York: Interscience Publishers, 1962), pp. 88–96.
9. H. E. Annett et al., *A Survey of Indian Poppy Growing Districts for Morphine Content of the Opium Produced* (Calcutta: Agricultural Research Institute, 1921).

Laos would fall closer to the lower end of this range. While very little of the opium produced there goes into the legal world market in analgesic drugs, a good deal finds its way into the contraband trade.

Any contraband trade requires a product with a reliable and accessible market. The product should yield a pleasurable effect for the consumer and create the desire or (better still) the need for repeated use. The product should be scarce and therefore susceptible to a high markup in price; yet the supply must be reasonably reliable. It should not be subject to deterioration, and should have a high value per unit of weight. By nearly every one of these criteria, the opiates are ideal contraband products: the market for the drugs has been expanding at a nearly exponential rate and, despite the supposed tenacity of enforcement agencies, the market has remained frighteningly accessible to those with the desire and technical facility to enter it. The euphoric and habituating properties of opiates have long been recognized, although their mechanisms are little understood. Scarcity is assured by official suppression, as well as by ecological and technological restraints on local production in the regions of highest consumption. (In contrast to growing marijuana, one really can't grow too much opium in one's garden; and heroin is beyond the abilities of the bathroom chemist, particularly since he lacks the morphine base from which to start.) The supply of opium is extremely reliable, since fluctations due to crop failures or confiscation are easily overcome by varying the degree of dilution of the final product. Opium derivatives are stable and may be easily stored for long periods without fear of deterioration and loss of value. In fact, opium appreciates in value with age—the older it gets, the more it's worth. All opiates have a high value per unit of weight, which appreciates astronomically in proportion to the distance from the source. To cite a brief example, in 1969, in one area of Laos, prepared opium was selling for about 4 cents per gram. Prepared opium is obtainable in at least one East Coast city in the United States at 20 dollars per gram. Even allowing for inflation, any product that can be sold at a price 500 times its original value is bound to attract people to handle it.

Given free access to supplies, opium is the preferred choice for most Asian drug users. In contrast to heroin and morphine, which are solitary drugs as a rule, opium is a social drug; that is, while it is sometimes smoked alone, it is usually smoked in groups and tends to promote conviviality. It is for some (although not, unfortunately, for many) a manageable habit, less deleterious to body and mind than either morphine or heroin habituation. Nevertheless, a number of factors have coincided to facilitate the rapid expansion of white drug (morphine and heroin) use, which is now found throughout the urban areas of Asia. Two of the most significant from our viewpoint are related to the regulation of drugs: first, white drugs are more concentrated and compact and are therefore easier and less dangerous to smuggle; second, opium has a very distinctive aroma when smoked, easily detectable by police. The result has been a major upsurge in white drug use, until today heroin habituation is the major narcotic problem in Hong Kong and other Asian cities.

The chain that links a poppy field in the mountains of Laos to a laborer "chasing the dragon" (taking heroin by smoke inhalation off heated tin foil) or "shooting the ack-ack gun" (smoking heroin in a cigarette) in Hong Kong, or to a junkie shooting-up on the West Coast is a long and complex one. It requires the work of numbers of highly skilled, as well as unskilled, workers at each stage to get the drugs to the consumer.

WHO GROWS OPIUM?   AND HOW?

In Laos, as in Thailand and Burma, the opium is grown by so-called minority peoples who live in the hills. As discussed elsewhere in this volume, the ethnic Lao constitute a minority of the population of Laos. Moreover, as is the case throughout Southeast Asia, significant differences in language, sociopolitical organization, and religion exist between the mountain peoples and the valley dwellers, and among the mountain groups themselves. Since not all hill peoples grow opium, we need not concern ourselves in this discussion with more than a few of the vast number of ethnic groups that live in the Laotian hills.

In terms of total output, the various Meo groups are easily

the largest producers of opium in Laos. The Yao (Man), Lahu, Akha (Kha Iho), and, to a lesser extent, members of other groups also grow poppies, but the opium that they produce probably represents less than 10 per cent of the gross production in the country.

It has never been easy to estimate with any precision exactly how much opium is produced in Laos each year. Even for the period of the French opium monopoly in Indochina (see article 6, by McCoy), production figures are highly suspect. To begin with, large amounts of contraband opium were being produced and smuggled from virtually uncontrolled areas of Indochina. Furthermore, the French themselves could often be quite disingenuous regarding production figures. Hardly a leader in the movement for the international control of narcotics, France never ratified the Hague International Opium Convention of 1912. In 1924 a French delegate to an international meeting on the control of opiates maintained—with a straight face—that the whole of Indochina produced only 5 tons of opium a year. He stated that, since the people of Indochina consumed 65 tons per year, and since Indochina was at the mercy of neighboring countries who were major poppy growers, it would be impossible to prohibit the use of opium within the country.[10] The delegate avoided pointing out that the opium monopoly contributed one-quarter of the revenue for all Indochina.[11] More accurate estimates of the pre-World War II opium crops would place them in the range of 40 to 100 tons.[12]

Since World War II, the estimates of the extent of poppy cultivation in Laos have varied considerably. In the late 1950s and early sixties, guesses ran to about 65 tons of crude opium per year.[13] According to some authorities in Bangkok in 1964, this figure is probably low for the period. Subsequently, estimates of yearly production have been revised upward. A United Na-

10. Scott, *op. cit.*, p. 136.

11. L. Roubaud, *Vietnam* (Paris, 1931), p. 205.

12. D. Lancaster, *The Emancipation of French Indochina* (Oxford University Press, 1961), p. 71.

13. F. Lebar and A. Suddard, *Laos: Its People, Its Society, Its Culture* (New Haven: HRAF Press, 1960), p. 205; J. Halpern, *Economy and Society of Laos* (New Haven: Yale University Press, 1964), p. 115.

tions survey team report on the opium-producing areas of Thailand uses the figures of 80 to 150 tons of opium for Laos.[14]

In the past two years the situation has become even more muddled than usual because of the extensive spread of fighting. Production, by all accounts, has been increasing. However, there can be little question that warfare has disrupted production in some regions, particularly those which have changed hands several times. Timing is very important in opium harvesting, and if a field cannot be tapped at the correct time, its entire yield may be lost. Nevertheless, the use of planes to transport opium directly from small landing strips in the hill regions has increased the profit margin. This does not mean that the tribesman gets paid more for his product, but it saves him the difficult task of bringing it to market. Air transport is particularly important during a period when the older-style individual middleman is finding it more difficult to go into the hills to the production sources because of the fighting.

Aside from the war, there are four major techno-environmental factors which govern the extent of opium production:

1. The altitude at which fields are located.
2. The quality of land available for poppy cultivation.
3. The degree of the growers' specialization in opium.
4. The competence of the farming population.

Ecological limitations restrict the growing of poppies to fields above 3,000 feet. Below this level, opium poppies will not grow and produce successfully in Laos. Because of this comparative ecological advantage vis-à-vis the lowlands—an advantage shared by few other crops—and because of its high value per unit weight, opium is an ideal crop for regions whose access to markets is limited by steep mountain trails and transportation by human carriers and packhorses.

The second factor is closely linked to the first; the quality of the land available for poppy cultivation is most often dependent

14. United Nations Survey Team, *Report of the United Nations Survey Team on the Economic and Social Needs of the Opium Producing Areas of Thailand* (Bangkok, 1967), p. 64.

upon the extent to which a particular group or village has chosen to specialize in opium production. Among the various groups of "shifting" farmers who practice poppy cultivation, a decision must often be made between maximizing rice production or opium production. Fields deemed best for rice production are rarely those best suited to poppy growth, and vice versa. In selecting a village site, therefore, it is often necessary to choose between one which has ready access to field sites best adapted to rice and one which is near land best used for poppies. Among groups placing emphasis upon maize production, this is not so much of a problem, because maize is usually cropped in the same fields as poppies. In fact, the growing of maize in a field prior to the planting of poppy will increase the yield of opium. For this reason, even people specializing in opium will plant maize in their opium fields.

Among the Meo, poppy cultivation is the single most significant criterion governing the selection of land.[15] When Meo move their villages looking for good opium land, they pay little attention to the quality of land available for other crops. The Yao also place primary emphasis upon opium production, although a minority seem to show a greater interest in rice production. Among other groups, rice is the crop of primary concern, while opium is a secondary consideration. The Akha, for example, generally give far greater consideration to the selection of rice fields when choosing a village site.

It should be noted that the brief picture given above is, of necessity, highly oversimplified. A considerable amount of intra-group variation exists. For example, there are, as mentioned above, Yao who grow little opium; there are also Lahu villages which grow virtually no rice and whose entire economy is based on producing sufficient cash-crop opium to buy rice from neighboring villages. On the other hand, some Lahu villages grow all their own rice and produce relatively little opium. Moreover, even within a single village, there is likely to be a fairly wide range of choices in labor allocation to various crops among the different village households. The demographic profile of the

15. United Nations Survey Team, *op. cit.,* pp. 36–37.

household will often be a determining factor in the decision to specialize in opium rather than rice; the greater the percentage of women and children in the work force, the greater the tendency to emphasize opium production.[16]

The edaphic (soil type) characteristics of a poppy field are vital factors not only in determining the opium yield of the initial cropping but also in governing the number of croppings possible before severe soil degradation takes place. In relatively high pH (basic), red-brown earth soil, opium may be grown successfully for ten consecutive seasons or more. In other, less favorable, environments, fields will give out in two years or less. It is not surprising, therefore, that the hill farmers consider a careful and thorough investigation of soil type to be of paramount importance in the selection of an opium field. Some groups have native systems of soil classification which place the greatest emphasis upon color, while others consider the taste of the soil to be important. (While it may come as a surprise to many urbanized Westerners, this practice is really quite reasonable and successful; you can taste differences between soils.) Moreover, local topographical features are carefully considered. For the most part, sites which are near outcroppings of limestone are favored, preferably on the western slopes of hills.

The agricultural competence of the local population has been mentioned earlier as the fourth major factor controlling the extent of opium production. It should be pointed out that opium is a sensitive crop, intolerant of error. Poppy cultivation requires several steps, and a mistake at any one can cause the final opium yield to be reduced both in quantity and quality. For the most part, the hill tribes of Laos (as well as the rest of Southeast Asia) practice *swidden* ("slash and burn") agriculture. This means that after selecting a piece of land with the correct edaphic and biotic characteristics, the standing hillside vegetation is cut down and allowed to dry. This is then fired and burned off, the ash residue acting as fertilizer. Planting is

16. D. Feingold, "The Politics of Space: Field Allocation Among the Akha of Northern Thailand." Paper presented to the American Association for the Advancement of Science, (Boston, 1969), p. 6.

usually done with the aid of a dibble stick; plows are never used. As noted above, in the case of opium poppies, maize is planted in the field prior to the planting of the main crop. Most opium is planted in August–September and harvested in January–February–early March, depending on local conditions and the type of opium sown. Some people plant up to three varieties, while others plant only one. These are classified locally in terms of when they are sown and when harvested. The poppy plants are ready to be tapped when the petals have fallen from the pods and the crowns of the pods have just started to turn from green to brown. Tapping is done with a small double- or triple-bladed knife. A shallow vertical incision is made in the poppy pod, and drops of the latex collect along it. On the following day, these are scraped off and collected on a flat, broad-bladed knife. At the time of incision, the opium is milky colored, but gradually turns brown on drying. The opium yield for the day is then carried back to the village, where it may be concentrated through boiling and filtering through cloth, or merely stored for drying. Among many of the groups, most of the tapping is performed by women.

The number of tappings varies from group to group. The Meo generally tap once only, although some will tap a second time as well. The Yao and Akha, on the other hand, will usually use two or three tappings. As would be expected, the amount of opium obtained from secondary tapping is considerably less than that obtained from the primary tap. Among people with large areas under cultivation, it is often considered not worth the extra labor to obtain this marginal portion of the yield. People farming smaller plots, however, tend to farm more intensively and, therefore, show higher yields per area farmed. The Yao are reputed by the other hill tribes to be the most industrious opium cultivators and to produce the best product.

Opium yields vary considerably from group to group and field to field. Dr. Krui Punyasingh, a scholar from the Thai Ministry of Agriculture, conducted yield tests on 190 sampling plots at 23 different locations. He calculated a mean yield of 1,294.76 grams per *rai* (0.16 hectare), with a standard deviation per *rai* of 588.99 grams.[17] While there is no question as to the validity of these figures (approx. 1.3 kg.) for the test plots cited, there is also little doubt that they represent yields which must be considered minimal. Yields of two, three, and among careful cultivators, even four or more times those of the test plots are common. Much depends on the amount of time the grower is willing to invest in weeding and similar care-taking activities.

Significantly, the present productivity of opium agriculture among the hill peoples of Laos, Thailand, and Burma is considerably below what the land will carry. As early as 1901, during a period when the government of French Indochina was seeking to free itself from dependence on opium from British India by encouraging the growth of the crop locally, French agriculturists conducted experiments which demonstrated that improved methods of cultivation could obtain yields equivalent to 8 kilograms per *rai*.[18] Apparently, their lead was not followed; however, the implications for today are not without interest.

At the present time, the United States is the single most important market for narcotics in the world. On the basis of current estimates, about 80 per cent of the illicit opiates entering this country come from the Middle East. (In this regard, our NATO ally, Turkey, makes a major contribution.) This leaves about 20 per cent deriving from opium grown in Southeast Asia. However, in the past few years, some of the attempts to curtail Middle Eastern opium production have met with success (notably in Iran). Given the expanding market for opium-based drugs—not only in the United States, but in Hong Kong, Japan, and Europe as well—it would be reasonable to expect that there would be considerable economic incentive for increased production in Asian areas. More explicitly, since doubling or tripling output merely requires improved organization and incentive, it should not be surprising to see these supplied by those farther down the chain who have most to gain. Furthermore, the expanded production facilities for "999" brick morphine (even illicit

17. United Nations Survey Team, *op. cit.*, Annex 4, Table 2.
18. L. de Reinach, *Le Laos* (A. Charles, 1901). Translation, Human Relations Area Files, Indochina Source No. 148, Appendix.

morphine and heroin are brand-named), as well as newer facilities for the local processing of heroin, have meant that more and more processing is being done in Thailand (though much heroin is still made in Hong Kong). This means that the Laotian opium crop is closer to processing sites, and subsequently greater profits for those who transport it.

It should be noted here that in Thailand these facilities are highly illegal; under Thai law, heroin offenses can evoke the death penalty. Nevertheless, enforcement difficulties, complicated in some cases by local corruption, prevent effective suppression of the drug trade, despite dedicated and energetic efforts on the part of some officials. Moreover, the Thai government has adopted the realistic and humane view that the growing of opium is so vital to the economy of the hill tribes that it would be unwise and unfair to actively repress it until such time as suitable cash crops may be found to replace it. Therefore, the bulk of police activities have been directed against the lowland traders.

The Thai case points up an important feature of the drug trade, characteristic of the situation in Laos: separation of the highland and lowland trades. The opium trade is best understood not as a single trade sphere, but as two distinct trade spheres, meshing with each other at certain key points. In the highlands, opium is used both for currency and consumption. Debts may be paid with it, rice bought with it, and it is acceptable tender in most hill villages from Laos to Burma. Furthermore, opium is widely smoked among the peoples who grow it. Therefore, a certain and sometimes significant percentage of the total crop is consumed at or near its source. The highland trade is usually transacted directly between buyer and consumer. Profits, while significant on a local level, are miniscule compared to the returns of the lowland trade.

In contrast to the opium retained in the highlands, the opium entering the lowland trade enters the world market. It is here that profits are immense and information most difficult to come by. It is clear, however, that the control of this trade has been an important economic asset with major political overtones in the recent history of Laos. In addition to the French activities during the colonial period, the Japanese actively encouraged increased production and in 1945 controlled most of the crop. John McAlister points out that, following the Japanese surrender, the Chinese 93rd Independent Division moved into areas of the Laotian mountains never occupied by the Japanese, specifically to take over the opium crop for that year.[19] McAlister also states that the troops refused to withdraw until September of 1946, because that was when another crop of opium "became available."[20] This latter contention, however, does not ring true. If accepted, it would mean that for the first and only time in history, the hill tribes harvested their opium during the planting season. Unfortunately, the exact process by which this unique ecological transformation was accomplished has never been explained. Donald Lancaster gives a more reasonable timetable of events. He points out that while the majority of Chinese troops had been withdrawn from Tonkin by mid-June 1946, the 93rd Division remained in Laos until the end of the month "to complete the seizure of the opium."[21] If the harvest had been completed by the end of March, it is not unlikely that in the conditions existing at the time, it could have taken three months to collect the opium stored in the various hill tribe villages—especially if the Chinese wanted it boiled.

During the Indochina War, opium from Laos played a key role in financing the operations of the Viet Minh. Opium was used both in direct barter for weapons and to obtain hard currency. Viet Minh agents would barter for opium in Laos and sell the opium inside Vietnam for piasters. Salt, alcohol, and other products were used to obtain opium: 1,000 piasters worth of salt would buy a kilogram of opium, which could be sold to Chinese in Hanoi for 15,000 piasters.[22] The importance of such transactions in Laotian opium to the survival of the Viet Minh

19. J. T. McAlister, *Vietnam: The Origins of a Revolution* (New York: Knopf, 1969), p. 228.

20. *Ibid.*, p. 228.

21. Lancaster, *op. cit.*, p. 150.

22. McAlister, *op. cit.*, p. 249.

during the early period of the revolution should not be under-estimated; it is quite probable that without them the movement would have foundered for lack of resources to buy guns.

Even in the later stages of the war, opium played an important role in Viet Minh strategic thinking. In 1953 the Viet Minh were still dependent upon opium to finance Chinese military aid, as well as a number of internal projects.[23] In fact, the first Viet Minh invasion of Laos in April of 1953 was in part motivated by a desire to capture that year's opium crop; and the troops withdrew to Tonkin on May 7 after harvesting the crop.[24]

Likewise, since the Geneva Accords, the conflicts in Laos have tended to synchronize with the opium agricultural cycle. Throughout the mid-1950s, the Pathet Lao controlled the important opium-growing regions of Sam Neua and Phong Saly. Following the reestablishment of a semblance of Royal Laotian Government (RLG) authority in 1958, conflict broke out again in July 1959—in time to seize the opium that had been collected in the tribal villages.[25]

In the 1960s members of the various Laotian governments have dealt extensively in opium, as have the Pathet Lao. Chinese in Laos and the rest of Southeast Asia have always been extensively involved in the trade. Several British authorities in Hong Kong believe that a number of the more important Chinese secret societies are heavily involved in all aspects of the Asian and trans-Pacific drug trade. This involvement, according to these same sources, does not appear to be limited by ideological barriers.

Economically, there are three things that keep Laos going (if Laos can be said to be "going" at all): U.S. aid, gold, and opium. Laos has received more aid, per capita, from the United States than any other country in the world. The trade in gold and opium provides the only major local assets. Laos allows unlimited imports of gold, against which it levies the incredibly

23. *Le Monde*, November 22, 23, 1953.

24. J. Buttinger, *Vietnam: A Dragon Embattled* (New York: Praeger, 1967), p. 792.

25. H. Toye, *Laos: Buffer State or Battleground* (New York: Oxford University Press, 1968), p. 130.

low duty of 8.5 per cent. Most of the purchases are done through that hardy holdover from the colonial period, the French-owned Banque de l'Indochine. The Banque buys gold on the European gold markets and can guarantee delivery in three days. The duty on gold imports yields about 40 per cent of all local revenues for Laos.[26] More than one ton of gold is flown to Vientiane every week and bought up for resale by people who want to smuggle gold into Thailand and South Vietnam. This makes Laos perhaps the largest transshipment point for smuggled gold in the world. Of the total amount of gold, it is estimated that about 30 per cent goes to Thailand, while 60 per cent ends up in Saigon.[27]

The road of the smuggler is not always smooth, however. Brigadier General Thao Ma was understandably put out at being relieved of his command for refusing to allow his transport planes to be used by high-ranking Laotian Army officers for smuggling. He was further miffed when his complaints of injustice brought no redress. By October 1966 he felt sufficiently resentful of this poor treatment to lead a T–28 air attack on his own army's headquarters.[28] The general then retired to Thailand for reasons of health.

Many of the features of the gold trade in Laos are found in the opium trade. The Banque de l'Indochine, while not openly engaged in opium finance, is rumored to profit extensively from the trade. Laotian military transports are as likely to be carrying opium as troops during certain times of the year. And while opium does not approach gold in providing revenue to the Royal Laotian Government, its total impact on the economy of the country is probably as great, and its political impact is greater.

Official United States policy has approved the gold trade. Not only does the trade help the Laotian economy (which needs all the help it can get), but also, American reasoning runs, the gold absorbs excess dollars in Saigon that might otherwise go

26. *Far Eastern Economic Review 1969 Yearbook* (Hong Kong), p. 216.
27. Louis Kraar, "Report from Laos," in *Fortune* (September 1, 1968), p. 51.
28. *Ibid.*, p. 52.

to Hanoi.[29] The American position on opium is somewhat more equivocal. Publicly, the United States stands four-square for the suppression of opium throughout the world. The U.S. Bureau of Narcotics (which frequently gives the impression of having been dragged, kicking and screaming, from the eleventh century into the twelfth) sees any involvement with drugs as evidence of a pact with the devil—or at the very least, the Communist Chinese. There is much talk among official Americans about eliminating opiates at their source: spraying defoliants on poppy fields; providing support for punitive expeditions— that sort of thing.

Yet on the subject of the opium trade in Laos, there is a curious muting of official pronouncements. In U.S. government-sponsored publications on Laos, one is frequently left with the impression that Laos probably exceeds Iceland in opium production, but not by much. For instance, the *Area Handbook for Laos*, published by the U.S. Government Printing Office "is one of a series of handbooks prepared by Foreign Studies of the American University designed to be useful to military and other personnel who need a compilation of basic facts."[30] In this 349-page collection of political, economic, and social data, three sentences are devoted to opium: one notes that Chinese traders used to exchange swords for Meo opium; a second points out that "this form of trade has virtually ceased"; and the third reveals that Chinese traders and Indian cloth merchants accept Meo opium and duck eggs for their goods in the Xieng Khouang market.[31]

It is widely known that the Central Intelligence Agency supports what must surely be the least clandestine "clandestine army" in the world—the Armée Clandestine of Meo General Vang Pao.[32] It is less widely known, but still an open secret, that, in addition to Laotian Army planes, a number of planes flown by Americans pick up a lot of opium. Most of these are

29. *Ibid.*, p. 52.
30. J. D. Roberts et al., *Area Handbook for Laos*. DA Pam. No. 550–58 (Washington, D.C.: Government Printing Office, 1967), Foreword.
31. *Ibid.*, pp. 249–250.
32. *New York Times*, Oct. 27, 1969.

flown by ostensibly civilian pilots working for what one British observer referred to as "your Terry and the Pirates airlines" (Air America; see article 14 by Scott). Hill people crossing into Thailand from Laos know about it, Nationalist Chinese opium dealers in Thailand know, even British experts in Hong Kong know about it. Therefore, it is highly improbable that the U.S. government is totally unaware of the situation.

This brings us to the extent of official U.S. involvement in the trade. There can be little question that the *de facto* policy in Laos is to wink, at the very least, at transportation of opium locally by American quasi-governmental employees. There is further evidence that designated opium shipments are cleared and monitored by the CIA on their way out of the country by air.[33] (See also article 6, by McCoy.) If this is true, it reveals a major contradiction of America's stated policy on narcotics, as well as a violation of international conventions to which we are party.

Of course, it can always be argued that anyone who gets at all involved with the political economy of Laos ends up involved with opium. The French, Chinese, and the Vietnamese (North and South); the rightist, neutralist, and leftist Lao—all have traded and fought over opium in the past, and most of them continue to do so today. Why should it be any different with us?

33. *Christian Science Monitor,* May 29, 1970.

16

Living It Up in Laos: Congressional Testimony on United States Aid to Laos in the 1950s

Judith W. Cousins and Alfred W. McCoy

The chief instrument of America's attempt to "contain" communism after World War II has been its massive military and economic aid programs designed to strengthen nations on the "Free World's frontier" against external aggression and internal subversion by communist forces. From 1949 to 1959 the program consumed over $65 billion of American tax revenue and created, modernized, and armed military forces all around the "Free World." Of all the nations involved in the foreign aid program, the kingdom of Laos has received the most aid per capita. Under the direction of its American military advisers, the Laotian government has used most of this aid to create one of the most unpopular and corrupt armies in the history of warfare.

Although Laos was established as a neutral nation by the 1954 Geneva Accords, America's Secretary of State John Foster Dulles considered neutralism "immoral" and quickly moved to break the spirit and the letter of those accords by making Laos the "trip wire of Free Asia." Accordingly, in 1955, U.S. military advisers began to develop a 25,000-man Royal Laotian Army which they hoped would be the first line of defense against a southward rush of Communist China's "human waves" long enough to allow a response by America and its SEATO allies. The disproportionately large figure of 25,000 men was determined by State Department estimates of the number of troops needed to hold the Laotian ridges against a Chinese army or suppress internal disruption created by "infiltrating" Chinese and North Vietnamese agents. What these strategists failed to understand was that Laos, being poor and underdeveloped, lacked everything a nation might need to support a modern army. Its self-contained villages were immune to Cold War rhetoric, and its small population would be severely strained if it were forced to support such a costly innovation.

Although the American military made the Laotian army the most expensive (per capita) in the world by giving it $166 million worth of advisers, material, and financial support from 1955 to 1958, American advisers were unable to solve one crucial problem: the average Laotian soldier had nothing to fight for.

The American military sought to substitute money for patriotism—by increasing the salaries of the Lao soldiers at all levels (out of $166 million, $125 million was for troop pay)—but it failed to foresee the consequences of suddenly introducing millions of dollars in cash into what was still little more than a barter economy. The result was massive inflation, to which the Americans responded by trying to create a modern economy overnight. The United States simply gave the Laotian government millions of dollars in cash grants for the import of consumer goods to absorb the surplus currency.

The American response ignored another Laotian reality—a somewhat dishonest government with a potential for unbelievable corruption. The influx of cash grants, soldiers' wages, and consumer goods was just too much to resist, and the result was total corruption within the Laotian government and the spread of bribery, graft, and theft among the American aid officials themselves. (See article 12, by Branfman.)

Although the extent of the American aid program in Laos from 1950 to 1957 was largely kept from public view, in 1958 the corruption became so outrageous that angry congressional hearings were convened, and for the first time American officials were forced to offer a partial explanation of what they were doing in Laos.

The economic means of implementing U.S. strategic goals in Laos was explained in detail by George Staples of the General Accounting Office (GAO) in the House Committee on Government Operations hearings. Staples showed how the economic development program of the International Cooperation Administration (ICA, later U.S. Agency for International Development

[USAID]) was integrated with the CIA–U.S. Army's military assistance programs—an alliance which has been maintained until the present day. His testimony also indicated the enormous cost of trying to create a large army in a relatively poor country.

MR. STAPLES: . . . The aid program as presently administered by ICA dates back to January 1955, when Laos was granted full independence from France. In July 1954, the Geneva Accords had terminated hostilities in the area which was then French Indochina, and brought about the dissolution of the political and economic association between France and the three Indochinese States of Cambodia, Laos, and Vietnam.

The Geneva agreement also had brought northern Vietnam under Communist control. It was at this critical time that the United States decided on separate and enlarged assistance programs to each of the three non-Communist countries, to protect their newly won independence and counter the Communist threat to their security and political and economic stability.

In the 4-year period, 1955–58, assistance to Laos under the administration of ICA totaled $166 million. The level of aid was based principally on the cost of maintaining the military forces of Laos for which the United States had assumed the full burden of support. Close to $125 million was programmed in 1955–58 for the generation of local currency to pay for troop pay and subsistence, ordnance, engineering, and all other military budget costs. This amount is exclusive of military equipment and supplies which were furnished separately under the military assistance program administered by the Department of Defense. The military end-item program is the subject of a separate report by our office and was presented to your sub-committee in a previous session of the current hearings.

MR. HARDY (Congressman): Mr. Staples, I will try not to interrupt you, but I think this will be a good point to try to understand your reference in the previous paragraph to the $125 million programmed for the generation of local currency paid for troop pay, subsistence, and so forth.

The following sentence would imply that it was ICA aid funds as contrasted to military assistance funds. That is not accurate, is it?

MR. STAPLES: That is correct. Military assistance funds were over and beyond the $125 million that I mentioned here.

MR. HARDY: I had understood that direct forces support does not fall in the category of defense support.

MR. STAPLES: That takes a little explaining, Mr. Chairman.

MR. HARDY: The only question I thought we ought to mention and explore at this moment is this one point: Subsistence had normally, as I understood it, come under the military assistance program rather than the economic aid program.

MR. STAPLES: These are local costs connected with the troop pay and subsistence.

MR. HARDY: I understand.

Is it your statement—and this is what I want to be clear on—that defense support funds or ICA's economic aid program went to provide funds for troop pay?

MR. STAPLES: That is correct.

MR. HARDY: I believe that is contrary to other testimony we have had. But go ahead.[1]

Further testimony taken by the House Committee on Government Operations from Assistant Secretary of State for Far Eastern Affairs Walter S. Robertson revealed the morale problems of the Royal Laotian Army. Since the average peasant had little love for his elitist government, American military advisers (in the guise of Program Evalutions Office [PEO] workers) had increased the army's pay scale in an attempt to substitute economic motivation for patriotism. This had increased the flood of currency into Laos, creating spectacular economic problems.

MR. REDDAN (Committee counsel): We also took up with Secretary Dillon the circumstances surrounding the pay raise in January 1959 which apparently was made over the objection of the Department of State. We were interested in knowing what, if any, action was taken because of this apparently precipitate action on the part of the PEO.

MR. ROBERTSON: We didn't know about this until it was a *fait accompli*. In view of the fact that the commitment had been made we stood behind it because we thought the consequences of not doing so would be worse than doing it.

The Lao Government put the greatest importance and emphasis upon raising the pay of the troops because, as indicated before, the Army is one of their principal instruments in civic action operations,

1. United States, 86th Congress, 1st Session, House Committee on Government Operations, *United States Aid Operations in Laos*. Hearings before the Foreign Operations and Monetary Affairs Subcommittee, March 11–June 1, 1959 (Washington, D.C.: Government Printing Office, 1959), p. 252.

as an administrative arm of the Government. They felt that it would make their recruiting problems less difficult if the army had some pay that was better than coolie.

I am saying that we didn't know about it until after the commitment had been made. But when we did find out about it we went along with it because we thought backing out on the commitment might bring about the fall of the Government and in the last analysis this would be worse than the first.

MR. HARDY: That isn't the key to the question Mr. Reddan raised, and the same question was raised with Mr. Dillon.

What happened here is that we were put in an awkward position by the PEO, who without authorization, apparently passed on some information to the Minister of Defense. If that happened here at home, I expect the General Accounting Office would have been right behind the individual who cost Uncle Sam $1 million.

MR. ROBERTSON: But it didn't. That is the point I want to make. The only rationalization I can make is that the Country Team agreed to it on the ground it did not increase the cost to us. It did not increase the military budget. But the Lao Army put such high priority on this, they gave up other things which had been put in the budget.

MR. HARDY: Mr. Secretary, I think you will find that that was an afterthought. At least that is the way I read the record.

MR. ROBERTSON: If it is, I am completely misinformed because as I understand it, when there were objections made to this pay raise, and they had agreed on a budget at a certain level, about $1 million involved, they said, we will take other things out of the budget so you do not increase the level of it. If that isn't true I am completely misinformed.

MR. HARDY: Mr. Secretary, you are either misinformed or I can't read the record, and we spent a lot of time going over this particular point.

If my memory serves me correctly, from the testimony we have already adduced on this particular point, our Government was put in an awful position because the PEO advised the Minister of Defense that CINCPAC [Military Headquarters, Pacific Area] had approved the raise. And it was after that that we were in the position of having either to accommodate ourselves to that situation or, in effect, let the Lao Government down and probably precipitate a very serious condition. Subsequent to that time, according to the way I read the documentation, this device of transferring funds from a transportation account in the amount of $1 million to offset the extra cost of the pay of the army was thought up in order to maintain the budget ceiling.[2]

In further testimony Mr. George Staples (GAO) told the House Committee on Government Operations that the aid program created significant economic dislocations in the Laotian economy, which could not sustain the demands made upon it by a large, modern army or absorb the inflation created by the massive injections of cash from military spending.

MR. STAPLES: . . . The ICA program averaging around $45 million a year during the period 1955–57, was disproportionate in size to the normal volume of economic activity in Laos. The program approximated one-half of the country's estimated gross national product of about $100 million per year—excluding external aid. Laos has an estimated 2 million inhabitants who are predominantly rice farmers producing in general only for their individual needs; about 85 percent of the people are reported to be illiterate. The country is landlocked, largely mountainous, and broken up into small, primitive, and inaccessible villages. Inadequate transportation and communication facilities, within Laos as well as with its neighbors, are an obstacle to the exchange and distribution of goods and seriously hamper economic development.

To provide the assistance considered necessary for the support of the Lao army and police force, essential civilian government services, and development activities, ICA financed a large-scale local currency generating program which involved the granting of dollars regardless of the country's current foreign exchange and import requirements.

During 1955–1957, ICA furnished dollar exchange for an average annual import level of $40 million. Officials in the field considered this level too high and not desirable because it tended to:

(1) Strain transportation and administrative facilities;

(2) Increase pressures for diversion of imports and other malpractices by importers and suppliers; and

(3) Provide more imports than the country can absorb and a living standard higher than Laos can expect to sustain by its own efforts in the foreseeable future.[3]

2. *Ibid,* p. 203.
3. *Ibid,* pp. 258–259.

In these same House hearings, a management consultant, Mr. Howell, who had worked on the foreign aid program in Laos, explained the steps taken to adjust the Laotian economy to the American military programs. If the U.S. military advisers were going to build and motivate an army with money, they had to create a consumer economy capable of absorbing the currency and providing goods which would make a soldier's salary meaningful.

MR. HARDY: What did you do in the period between December 16 and April 10?

MR. HOWELL: Well, Mr. Chairman, we immediately found—we were supposed to make a 90-day survey to find out what the situation really was. And immediately we ran into a chaotic situation that existed with regard to the licenses. We took the time, working with the Minister of Finance, to try to establish a system of licensing and control of foreign exchange which, when the new government was formed, would become operative. And those were all agreed. The record will show that the Government was formed on April 10th, and before the end of April the Government had issued a number of official ordinances putting into effect important changes. Those were all negotiated during this interim period.

MR. HARDY: That was in 1956?

MR. HOWELL: That is correct.

MR. REDDAN: What did you find upon your arrival there with respect to the type of aid program which had been set up, or the part which was contemplated for the future?

MR. HOWELL: The task that was given to us was expressed in this way: that the kip being put into circulation required imports of approximately $3½ million a month to soak up the kip so that there wouldn't be a violent inflation. And we felt that bringing in $3½ million a month was not an impossible task until we had checked to see how it would come in, how it would be distributed after it got in and what was the composition of the program itself.

MR. REDDAN: Do you know how that $3½ million a month had been determined?

MR. HOWELL: Yes.

MR. REDDAN: And who determined it?

MR. HOWELL: It is worked out backward. It is worked out, as I understand it, in this way. Certain commitments were entered into by the Royal Government of Laos as to the force that it would maintain, certain types of force.

MR. REDDAN: Regular forces?

MR. HOWELL: Yes; armed forces, police, and administrative departments and whatnot.

They then computed their budget, and of course they had a deficit. The United States supplied backing for the shortage of kip at the rate of 35 to 1. It is our understanding that that determined the volume of imports that had to be brought in.

MR. REDDAN: In other words, they were forced to bring in that volume of imports to support the overall proposed program, and the imports were necessary not only to generate the kip but also to absorb the kip to stop inflation.

MR. HOWELL: Yes, sir. The theory being that that kip would pass out into the hands of the population, the soldiers and the government people, and that they would want to spend it. Unless enough goods came in, the price of goods would soar out of sight.

MR. REDDAN: When you arrived there, did you find that prior to your arrival any studies had been made to determine the economic validity of a program of that size in Laos?

MR. HOWELL: No, there had been no studies. And I would like to make it clear that it is extremely difficult to make any studies for the simple reason that until 1954 all of the statistics for Laos were considered part of French Indochina. The aid and the French statistics came through Saigon and it was not possible to segregate them. There was no demographic information; there was very little information as to population.

MR. REDDAN: By the "demographic information," does that extend beyond vital statistics?

MR. HOWELL: Yes. That is, we would want to know population in certain areas, age groups, and also with a country that has quite a variety of different types of people, some of whom have rather sophisticated demands but most of whom have no——

MR. REDDAN: This would go to determining the market and nature of it?

MR. HOWELL: Yes. We tried ourselves and we found that practically none of the essentials for a market survey were available.

MR. REDDAN: Did you subsequently make any determination as to the amount the economy could absorb per month?

MR. HOWELL: No. And I would like to point this out: When they say economic need, you must understand I am not a theoretical economist. We ran into difficulties with the economists who said that as long as the money was there, there was an economic need. So we have changed that to consumer and capital goods needs.

We have asserted several times that we felt that the capacity of the people to absorb—that means the goods to come into the country, to be distributed and to be properly absorbed by the people —should not run much over $5 or $6 million a year.

MR. REDDAN: Did you make any estimates as to the number of people that would be necessary to absorb this $3½ million a month?

MR. HOWELL: We did it the other way around. We tried to figure the accessible population by taking the French statistics for certain areas, certain towns, and we came up with, using the utmost liberality in assuming that the goods could be distributed, with about 900,000 people who could be serviced with this money.

MR. REDDAN: Of those people, did you make any determination of which ones would be in the market? In other words, to what extent do they live off the land and to what extent would they be in the market for these imports?

MR. HOWELL: We didn't make any such study. To a considerable extent, a good deal of it was obvious, that the people outside of the small urban areas were practically at a subsistence level and didn't have a latent desire to buy the goods that were coming in from the West.

MR. HARDY: Do you mean they were the kind of goods that the rank and file of people couldn't use?

MR. HOWELL: I think, Mr. Chairman, it is a little bit different. In many countries you will find that the people have a perfectly sound idea of what they would like to have. They just haven't got the wherewithal to get it. We found in many areas of Laos they just didn't know the things existed. There was no demand of any kind. They were completely content. If you supplied them with medicine, blankets in the cold weather, and maybe if they had a rice shortage some rice and fishing equipment, that is about the sum total of their needs. Of course, they learn very quickly to want other things. . . .

MR. REDDAN: I would like to go back just a moment to your estimate of the market which would be necessary to absorb these imports. As I recall, you said that it would take about 900,000 people to absorb them.

MR. HOWELL: No. I am sorry, sir. I said there were 900,000 people capable of absorbing anything that was brought in. In other words, it would have been the other way around. If we could have ascertained that those people needed a hundred dollars apiece for the year, it would be $100 times 900,000.

MR. REDDAN: Of those 900,000 people, do you have any estimate as to the number which had any purchasing power to the extent that they would be considered important in the absorption of these imports?

MR. HOWELL: No, sir.

MR. HARDY: Let me explore this 900,000 figure. That is a rather interesting figure. There were that many people that could conceivably take up a commodity that we were sending in there; is that what you mean?

MR. HOWELL: Yes, sir. That is what led us to question the validity of the $3½ million a month figure, because it is quite obvious that if 900,000 people are going to share in a $30 million program in a country where the annual income, cash income, the best anybody can compute was $70 a year, it is going to involve a vast change in their standard of living.

MR. HARDY: You say that would figure out to about $70 apiece?

MR. HOWELL: No. I say in that country, as in Thailand, the average income is around $70. If we take $30 million and spread it over 900,000 people, that is quite a lot to add to their income, assuming we had it. That adds about 50 percent, which is a lot of money.

MR. HARDY: It adds about 50 percent to their annual income?

MR. HOWELL: Yes.

MR. HARDY: Of course, then, you had the problem of finding any sort of basis which would provide general distribution, and if the types of commodities were not kinds that could be employed generally by the Lao people, it would seem to indicate that if the imports were going to be utilized there would have to be a concentration of them in the hands of a relatively few people; is that correct?

MR. HOWELL: That is correct. That is what happened.[4]

The creation of this modern money economy involved giving the Laotian government millions of dollars in cash grants, the right to sell lucrative import licenses, and control over an inflated currency pegged to the dollar at a profitable exchange rate. The temptation was too much, and Laotian officials began to steal from U.S. aid funds in high enough amounts to create some of the largest private financial empires in Southeast Asia.

4. *Ibid.*, pp. 751–756.

This information was revealed in testimony by Mr. George Staples (GAO) before the House Committee on Government Operations.

MR. MEADER (Committee member): I would like to ask you whether or not, in your judgment from having observed and studied the operation of these aid programs in various countries, if it is not precisely under the situation that existed in Laos that perhaps more than the normal number of controls and supervisory responsibility of ICA should be required to see that the program doesn't get off the tracks?

MR. STAPLES: That has been our contention, yes.

MR. MEADER: In other words, with a fairly well-established government, with statistics and civil servants and procedures, you could expect that controls might be relaxed and still not have disastrous results?

MR. STAPLES: That's right.

MR. MEADER: But where you have no civil service to speak of, and no long-established Government procedures, to relax controls or almost completely remove them could be calculated to result in waste and failure to accomplish the objectives of the program. . . .

MR. HARDY: On page 10, at the bottom of the page, you refer to the issuance in the summer of 1957 of over $12 million of import licenses outside the regular channels.

Do you know what was bought with those licenses?

MR. STAPLES: I don't believe we do. I don't know whether ICA does. I don't recall.

MR. REDDAN: Did ICA ever authorize the issuance of those licenses?

MR. STAPLES: No, sir; they did not.

MR. REDDAN: Do you have any idea at all what was done with that $12 million?

MR. STAPLES: No, we don't.

MR. REDDAN: Has any effort been made to check?

MR. STAPLES: There have been a lot of efforts to check. ICA may have found out later on. I don't know. But the last reading that we had on it they did not know.

MR. HARDY: Do you know who got that $12 million?

MR. STAPLES: No, sir; they were import licenses that were issued, approved and signed by one of the ministers of the Lao Government.

We have the information in case the committee is interested in it. The licenses were approved by one of the ministers of the Lao

Government, rather than passing through the channels of the Import and Export Commission that had been established to screen the applications for import licenses.

MR. REDDAN: Do you know during what period of time that $12 million was withdrawn?

MR. STAPLES: I think it was on two occasions, in the summer of 1957.

MR. REDDAN: Did it cover about a 2-week period?

MR. STAPLES: I believe there were two instances. We have some general information on that. We may have more detailed information in our papers. We can take a check on that, if it is significant to you, Mr. Reddan.

MR. REDDAN: If you would, sir.

(The following information was subsequently submitted to the subcommittee by the General Accounting Office:)

Data on Import Licenses Issued in 1957 Outside the Regular Channels

The subcommittee requested us to submit additional data concerning the issuance, in the summer of 1957, of over $12 million of import licenses outside the regular channels which the Lao Government and the ICA mission had established for a proper allocation of cash grant dollars.

These irregular issuances occurred principally during the latter part of July and the first part of August 1957. One of the pertinent messages from the mission to the Washington office has placed the "deblockage" of corresponding cash grant funds, which were to finance these import licenses, between July 22 to August 20.

The mission was informed by high Lao officials, who accepted responsibility for the action, that the licenses had been issued for domestic, political, and economic reasons calculated to favor the settlement then under way with the Pathet Lao. The mission and the Embassy made representations to the Lao Government and sought to have at least those licenses revoked which involved overpricing or other improprieties.

While some of the licenses issued without mission approval were subsequently canceled, the mission became aware of additional licenses being issued outside the regular channels during September and October 1957. Total import licenses issued between July and October without mission authorization were determined by the mission to approximate $16 million. December 4, 1957, is believed by ICA to be the firm date after which no irregular foreign exchange transactions were allowed by the Lao Government.

The Lao Government reportedly also agreed, in December 1957, to submit the licenses irregularly issued for reexamination by the import commission and to suspend the corresponding dollar allocations. This review action, however, was in fact applied only to licenses totalling about $1.3 million which, the Lao Government stated, were unprocessed at that time at the Lao National Bank. The other licenses, according to Lao officials, were already being processed by commercial banks.[5]

Although many observers speculated that the corruption among American aid missions was rivaled only by that among the Lao elite, American officials on the very highest levels did their best to prevent it from being discovered. As is evidenced by this testimony before the committee, one honest auditor in Laos, Haynes Miller, discovered fraud and corruption amounting to several hundred thousand dollars involving the Universal Construction Co., several high U.S. officials, and high Laotian officials.

MR. CROWL: (U.S. Government official working in Laos): Haynes Miller made allegations which concerned six different contracts with Universal. Miller based his allegations mainly on rumors and related circumstances which in his opinion tended to support the rumors and has offered little firsthand information. We have prepared a summary of allegations made by Miller concerning these six contracts.

Details concerning each of these contracts are set forth in transcripts of interviews of Miller. Basically, these six contracts appear to fall in three categories: one, bribery, USOM personnel. That ties in to four people.

MR. HARDY: That ties in to four people?

MR. CROWL: Yes, sir; in other words, he gave four possibilities. He would not say these accepted the bribes, but he said four people were in a position that they might.

Two, bribery, contract personnel.

MR. MEADER: What do you mean by "contract personnel"?

MR. CROWL: Well, contractors such as Universal Construction Co., Vinnel Co.,—with ICA or with the Lao Government financed by ICA.

MR. MEADER: Of nongovernmental personnel?

MR. CROWL: Four persons.

MR. MEADER: Yes, sir.

Fraudulent certification by the PWI officer that Universal did complete work which in fact they did not do; alleged improper favoritism to Universal by Mission personnel; on the latter, Miller based these observations on allegedly high favorable terms given Universal in their contracts, eliminating other bidders on alleged specious grounds;

5. *Ibid.,* pp. 281–285.

allowing Universal to use Mission equipment, supplies, and materials, without cost or reimbursement.

Then, for Mr. Kelly's information, we sent him pertinent copies of interviews, contracts, and related documents concerning Miller's accusations or allegations. We told him that it was not desired at that time that every circumstance of which Miller is suspicious be made a matter of inquiry but at the present it would appear the following matters require early revolvement which, if inquiry proved Miller correct, then more weight must be given to other allegations.[6]

For his trouble Miller was intimidated, threatened, and finally thrown out of Laos. Not surprisingly, since then no foreign aid official has come forth with similar allegations.

MR. GRIFFIN (Congressman): Who fired you?

MR. MILLER: The Director of the Mission. I put in my resignation orally in August. Then I drew up one several days later when I could get it typed and told them that the resignation would take effect in December because I would have to pay my way home, and I needed to make money to buy the ticket.

The Mission made what I considered to be, I understood to be, two officious offers to promote me and to attach me to another section of the Mission with the implicit understanding that, of course, I had hushed. One of them came through Mr. Guy Forman; another came through Mr. Burke.

Then Mr. Harding said he did not want to accept——

MR. HARDY: Who are the two persons you just mentioned?

MR. MILLER: Mr. Burke was the economic officer of the Mission. Mr. Harding told me that he didn't want me to resign, but if I did want to resign I would have to leave the first of October.

I told him that it was fine with me, that in that case I would be leaving at the Government's convenience and he would have to pay my way home.

He said he would not pay my way home. I told him that that was a violation of ICA regulations, at least as I read the regulations, and that I would sue ICA as soon as I got home, that that was my business and it shouldn't cause me much trouble.

I made my plans to leave on October 1, and got a private passport and bought my ticket and sold my library, or a good part of it, and my guns to get money to buy my ticket. Then 3 days before

6. *Ibid.*, p. 406.

I was to leave I was told that I was fired, that they would pay my way, and that I would not be able to make the hunting trip which I had planned to make before I left; that the Ambassador would see that I got out of the country one way or another, either voluntarily or—

MR. HARDY: Who said that?

MR. MILLER: The Deputy Director of the Mission, Mr. Messagee.

(Continuing) That I would not be able to go hunting as I had planned but that I would have to leave within three days, or else be extradited, I suppose. I think that is the word he used, and that I probably should not appeal, that it would be very dangerous for me to appeal the firing.

They fired me for inability to adjust to overseas life.

MR. REDDAN: Excuse me. Had you had any discussions with the Ambassador concerning your report?

MR. MILLER: Yes, sir. I was called into the Ambassador's office in August, I think August 4. And the Ambassador told me that he had about 20 minutes to give me. He then used about 15 minutes of that time to explain to me how embarrassed he would be if the Universal Construction Co. was not an honest straightforward firm because Washington had asked him earlier in the year if that company was a proper company to receive the contracts they were receiving, from the Lao Government I presume.

And he said—as best I can recall now—

"I should have perhaps gone to my subordinates and made more inquiries than I did make. But I recommended that firm. I knew Mr. Peabody and thought very well of him."[7]

In a later report the House Committee on Government Operations drew this conclusion from its lengthy investigations.

In summary, the decision to support a 25,000-man army—motivated by a Department of State desire to *promote* political stability—seems to have been the foundation for a series of developments which *detract* from that stability.

Given that decision, the minimum size of the necessary aid program was inexorably established at a dollar value far beyond the estimated rate at which the Lao economy could absorb it. From this grew intensive speculation in commodities and foreign exchange,

7. *Ibid.*, p. 322.

productive of inflation, congenial to an atmosphere of corruption, and destructive of *any* stability, political or economic.

With so much of the aid available for Laos earmarked for support of military forces, little attention was paid to programs which might reach the people of the villages. The aid program has not prevented the spread of communism in Laos. In fact, the Communist victory in last year's election, based on the slogans of "Government corruption" and "Government indifference" might lead one to conclude that the U.S. aid program has contributed to an atmosphere in which the ordinary people of Laos question the value of the friendship of the United States.

The army, which was too large for the economy to handle, was inadequate to perform its appointed mission. Against a much smaller force, it was unable to force Communist compliance with the Geneva agreements, which required evacuation of the two northern provinces and their return to the control of the central government. The presence of troops throughout the country may have assisted generally in the maintenance of order, but one may properly question, weighing all factors in the balance, if this was the most effective device.

The inability to remove the Communists from the northern provinces by diplomatic pressure or military force led to a compromise solution which admitted Communists to the Government and which established the Communist Party, Neo Lao Hak Xat, as a legal, aboveground political party.

Recently (January 1959), the Cabinet was given "extraordinary powers" by the National Assembly, which was thereupon dissolved. In effect, this means that for a year the Cabinet exercises dictatorial powers. One of its first acts was to purge itself of Communist members. Other actions since indicate that some housecleaning is underway. In the interim, however, the Communists, being "legal," have acquired a certain amount of prestige in the countryside which will be difficult to destroy.

Another hopeful recent (October 1958) development has been agreement of the United States and the Royal Lao Government upon a realistic exchange rate (80 kip to US$1). This has had the effect of destroying the free market, and it has done so without any of the inflationary effects that "economic experts" had predicted; in fact, its effect has been deflationary, and the cost of living in Laos has dropped about 25 percent since the currency reform.

Foreign exchange is now freely available at the new rate, and the temptations to speculation and corruption are lessened. It is unfortunate that State Department vacillation should have delayed currency reform for 4 years, when it was recognized as one of the key problems in Laos that needed correction.

These recent developments, although they seem to provide an atmosphere in which a better program is possible for the future, do not automatically insure such a program. It is the opinion of the subcommittee that study of the balance of this report will indicate that needed reforms are many in number, and that they are required at all levels of the aid program in Laos.[8]

8. United States, 86th Congress, 1st Session, House Committee on Government Operations, *United States Aid Operations in Laos*. Hearings before the Foreign Operations and Monetary Affairs Subcommittee, June 15, 1959 (Washington, D.C.: Government Printing Office, 1959), pp. 50–51.

17

The Reluctant Counterinsurgents: International Voluntary Services in Laos

John Lewallen

The story of the metamorphosis of IVS/Laos volunteers, from apolitical self-help agents into paramilitary cadre of the American war effort, is a revealing footnote to the story of American involvement in Laos. For in many ways the IVS embodies the best of American character—self-sacrificing service, tolerance of foreign cultures, the desire to elevate the living conditions of the needy. These ideals, when transported to Laos, were transformed into support activities for an ugly, futile little war.

Volunteers of International Voluntary Services, Inc., have been working in Laos since 1957. The evolution of the role of IVS/ Laos volunteers was summarized in the IVS annual report for 1964–1965:

Walt Coward, former team member and Chief-of-Party 1963–1965, fondly reminisced on early days in Laos. "Back in '58," he once commented, "USAID pretty well considered the IVS team 'just a bunch of religious nuts up on the Plain of Jars.'" From this doubtful arrangement, IVS and AID growth has resulted in mutual work together under AID Rural Development and Education divisions throughout the country. As one AID man put it: "IVSers are the scouts in advance of AID's 'front lines' in the provinces."

MISSIONARIES OF DEVELOPMENT

The roots of the International Voluntary Services lie in the pacifist religious sects of heartland America. After World War

---

The research for this article was done with the generous cooperation of the staff of International Voluntary Services, Inc., 1555 Connecticut Ave., N.W., Washington D.C. IVS newsletters, written by volunteers to families and friends, provided indispensable source material. The author is solely responsible for the content of the article.

II, Congress provided that a conscientious objector to war could do two years of peaceful alternate service to fulfill his military obligation. Religious groups such as the Quakers, Mennonites, and Church of the Brethren launched programs of overseas service.

In 1950 the Point Four program was established, and the U.S. International Cooperation Administration (ICA) began technical aid projects in other nations. It was soon noticed that many ICA programs had no relation to the resources, needs, or cultures of the people they were designed to help. Secretary of State Dulles announced, in 1953, that the government would like to contract teams to work in underdeveloped countries with dedication such as members of the church groups exhibited. Men who were leaders in government, business, and religion got together and formed the International Voluntary Services.

IVS was, and is, a private, nonprofit corporation for sending volunteers overseas. It is funded through various contracts, and has supported volunteers through the funds of private parties, the United States government, the United Nations, and foreign host governments. The announced core principles of IVS have always been as follows:

• Volunteers should serve for a minimum of two years, living closely with the people of the host country and earning modest salaries.

• Volunteers should do no political or religious propagandizing.

• The ideal of the volunteer should be to achieve a technical or organizational improvement of the resources at hand. He should strive to achieve small improvements in the world in which he works, and train local people to continue and expand development projects after he is gone.

The first IVS teams were sent to Jordan, Egypt, Iraq, and Nepal. As of March 1970, IVS had 12 English teachers in Algeria, 5 agricultural credit volunteers in the Democratic Republic of the Congo, and 4 range management volunteers in Morocco. But the teams which sustain the IVS are those in Southeast Asia: 48 volunteers in Vietnam, and 56 in Laos. The Vietnam and Laos contracts have always been with the American aid program, first ICA and later the U.S. Agency for International Development (USAID).

In 1957 IVS sent a seven-member team to work in the villages around the capital of Xieng Khouang province in northeastern Laos, a beautiful, mountainous region populated by Meo and other ethnic groups. The climate was comfortable, opium trading flourished, mysterious Frenchmen resided nearby, and a thinly disguised U.S. advisory-intelligence unit was posted in Xieng Khouang. Laotian[1] soldiers of various allegiances coexisted nervously but peacefully. The IVS team headquarters in a village near the capital freely hosted all peoples and armies. In 1959 an IVS volunteer was teaching English to an eager class of commissioned officers of the Pathet Lao!

By all accounts life was pleasant on the Xieng Khouang team. The Tom Dooley mystique was in full flower, and the IVS team included a nurse called Miss Anna who was famed for her untiring efforts to improve health in the area. Other volunteers worked to improve agriculture, livestock, and other aspects of village economy. Dick Bowman, who was on the team in 1959 and 1960, recalls that all his work was with the local people and the Royal Laotian Government, with none of the interference by U.S. aid officials which was to burden IVS in later years.

A second IVS team was sent to Laos in 1959 to help construct and staff the National Education Center, a boarding school being carved from the jungle nine kilometers from Vientiane. This education team trained Laotian English teachers and taught health, agricultural, and technical skills. Their newsletters indicate that they were concerned from the outset with relating Laotian education to village culture.

The peaceful efforts of IVS volunteers to enlist Laotians in the technological twentieth century were interrupted in 1960. On August 9, 1960, Captain Kong Le staged his coup against General Phoumi Nosavan's government. Although by August 19 American dependents had been evacuated to Bangkok, the IVS teams at Xieng Khouang and the National Education Center

1. The term *Laotian* is used to refer collectively to the peoples of Laos, some of whom are of the *Lao* ethnic group.

went on with their work with only minor interruptions. But trouble continued to brew, and by October 19 all IVS volunteers had been evacuated from Xieng Khouang except Dick Bowman and Edgar "Pop" Buell.

On December 13 Phoumi Nosavan began his Vientiane countercoup. IVS volunteers at the National Education Center hosted some of Kong Le's fleeing troops overnight and in the morning saw their campus become an artillery position for Phoumi's forces. Shortly thereafter most U.S. civilians were retrenched in Bangkok. Bowman and Buell intrepidly held out in Xieng Khouang until December 31. As Dick Bowman recalled that day for the author, he and Pop Buell were out in the field in different areas when Meo friends informed them that they should fly away in a hurry. Racing back to their headquarters, they called for an airplane and took off from one end of the runway as mortar rounds were coming in on the other. The Pathet Lao, allied with Kong Le's neutralist troops, had foreclosed their opportunity to carry out people-to-people development in Xieng Khouang.

The end of 1960 was a watershed for IVS/Laos. IVS could have abandoned Laos for more peaceful climes, or continued working as missionaries of development in support of one side in a shooting war. Nothing in the newsletters from that period indicates that an "agonizing reappraisal" was made. The IVS volunteers plunged energetically into the task of stemming what they saw as the "red tide" threatening Laos.

FIGHTING COMMUNISM TO THE LAST MEO

After most of the United States Operations Mission (USOM) fled to Bangkok at the end of 1960, a skeleton task force remained in Laos to carry on USOM programs. Some IVS volunteers were part of this Laos task force, sharing with USOM employees the tasks of developing and propagandizing the Laotians. During 1961 the functional distinction between IVS volunteers and U.S. government employees was not blurred—it was nonexistent. Long after the full USOM mission returned to Laos, IVS volunteers were ordered by USAID to fill gaps in the USOM program. Volunteers became cheap stopgap labor for USAID; they were frequently pulled off their development projects to dispatch airplanes, work in offices, and the like.

One of the tasks assumed by the USOM task force in 1961 was the support of efforts made by a Meo military leader, Vang Pao, to organize his tribe into an anti-communist army. The character of Vang Pao's Meo army, which came to be called the Clandestine Army, was molded by the personality of the most super-extraordinary IVS volunteer of all time: Edgar "Pop" Buell.

"I could write you a book about my adventures," wrote Pop Buell in an IVS newsletter dated November 1960. Don A. Schanche did the job for him in a book titled *Mister Pop*. According to Schanche's account, while Pop Buell was an IVS volunteer in Xieng Khouang he was chosen by the Meo as the American to be informed of a pan-Meo movement in opposition to the Pathet Lao, North Vietnamese, and Kong Le's neutralists. After the takeover of Xieng Khouang by the enemies of this Meo group, Meo loyal to Vang Pao fled to crucial hill sites surrounding the Plain of Jars. The Meo told only one American the location of these sites: Pop. After being evacuated to Bangkok, Mr. Buell mapped the locations of the Meo guerrillas for the American military and CIA. Soon Pop Buell was flying, walking, and parachuting around northeastern Laos, locating Meo and other tribal villages to convert the tribesmen to Vang Pao's cause. Wherever Pop Buell went Air America planes soon followed, dropping supplies to keep dislocated villagers alive. Vang Pao, with the military logistic support of the CIA, organized the young men of Buell's "refugee" villages into a Meo guerrilla army dotted all over Pathet Lao-controlled northeastern Laos. It was the "Pop and Pao Program," with Buell's "refugee" supplies maintaining Vang Pao's army and its dependents. (See articles 11 and 12, by Porter and Branfman.)

Mr. Buell is also described in Schanche's book as training and leading a Meo sapper squad which blew the bridges along Highway 7, near Ban Ban, in December 1962. Schanche repeatedly noted that until 1963 Pop performed all these services for $65 a month—his salary as an IVS agriculture volunteer. At this writing Pop Buell is still in Laos working for USAID and Meo loyal to Vang Pao; he has become a living legend to a dying tribe. For it appears that Mister Pop was prophetic when he wrote in November 1961: "a small minority group known as Meo tribespeople are trying to do the impossible—to keep Laos a non-Communist country."

It is difficult to analyze the Meo position in the multidimensional Laotian war. There are an estimated 300,000 Meo in Laos, living at the highest altitudes in Xieng Khouang and neighboring provinces. The Meo have been called the Gurkhas of Laos, for they are considered to be excellent soldiers. Meo are traditional enemies of all ethnic groups living around them, and of other Meo clans. Opium is the chief cash crop of the Meo, and all wars in their homeland are, to some degree, struggles for control of opium cropland. (See article 15, by Feingold.) Interviews with Americans who have worked with the Meo suggest that the chief objective of Vang Pao's Clandestine Army is the preservation of Meo tribal integrity and control of tribal land.

Since 1961, Meo who support Vang Pao have responded to Pathet Lao–North Vietnamese takeover of their villages by fleeing *en masse* to defensible areas, where they were supported by airdrops directed by Pop Buell. Estimates of death from disease and starvation during these population movements range upward from 10 per cent, depending on the hardships faced in the journey. A decade of fleeing and fleeing again, and of fighting a losing war, has considerably depleted the Meo tribe of Laos. The ranks of the Clandestine Army are heavy with children and old men. Many Meo bands have attained permanent refugee status, and would starve if American supply airdrops ceased.

Meo and others who chose not to run from Pathet Lao takeovers have apparently suffered a fate familiar to Vietnamese villagers. Uncompromising village leaders have been executed. Villagers have been drafted into the Pathet Lao army and impressed as laborers to convey produce to North Vietnam and bring military supplies back. The free-enterprise growing and marketing of opium and other crops have been taken over by the Pathet Lao administration. Associations for communist indoctrination have been organized.

Conversations with Dick Bowman and other Americans who have been close to the Meo "refugee program" indicate that many refugee workers believe they are saving the Meo from genocide at the hands of the North Vietnamese. But, with the exception of isolated incidents of troop riots, which may occur in any army, the Pathet Lao and North Vietnamese have not exterminated Meo under their control. Rather they have assaulted Meo culture, seeking to form a mobilized communist society.

Many IVS volunteers worked with Pop Buell throughout the sixties, locating isolated villages which support Vang Pao, dropping supplies, dispatching airplanes, and so on. Others have initiated development programs, such as creation of fishponds and schools, in an effort to make dislocated Meo self-sufficient. These IVS and U.S. government programs have made a shrinking tribe scattered about northeastern Laos dependent upon American aid for its survival.

In the opinion of this author, who worked with montagnard tribes in Vietnam, the failure of the IVS development approach stands naked in situations such as the Meo "refugee program." Simply stated, the IVS people-to-people development policy should not foster social institutions which prevent the Meo from being integrated with other ethnic groups into a viable nation. IVS (and USAID) projects in Laos tend to shore up doomed social structures. The Pathet Lao can methodically organize all the peoples of Laos. There is some point at which well-meaning economic development efforts, maintained only by an escalating war against the people in Pathet Lao-controlled areas, become acts of criminal madness.

At the end of 1968 the United States began saturation bombing of all man-made structures in northeastern Laos. Many refugees now report that they moved to escape not the Pathet Lao but repeated American bombing raids on their villages. The United States government appears to be willing to pound the land and people of northeastern Laos into dust in order to save the Clandestine Army and Royal Laotian Government from defeat.

THE CLUSTER VILLAGE PROGRAM

The IVS education team was disrupted only briefly by the coups of 1960. Team members returned to the National Education Center near Vientiane in January 1961 and have continued to teach there without being greatly disturbed by political turmoil. After a 1965 coup the National Education Center even provided haven for police officers on the losing side, who surrendered themselves and their weapons to the IVS team.

During 1961 only four development volunteers remained in Laos. These volunteers performed tasks for the USOM task force and worked part-time on development projects in the Vientiane area. The IVS development team remained small until the signing of the Geneva Agreements and the departure of all visible U.S. military advisers on October 6, 1962. At the end of 1961 the IVS contracted with USAID to field 53 volunteers to work with USAID Rural Development Division (RDD) in fighting the peaceful portion of the "secret war."[2]

As described previously, some RDD volunteers worked with Edgar Buell in supplying Vang Pao's Meo. The bulk of the IVS/RDD volunteers were plugged into a USAID counterinsurgency program formalized in September 1963 as the Cluster Village Program.

One IVS volunteer quoted a 1964 article from the *Bangkok World*, written by Martin Stuart-Fox of United Press International, to explain his cluster village work to the folks back home:

To help keep rural peasants on the side of the central government, Laos borrowed an idea from neighboring South Vietnam, establishing cluster villages modeled on Vietnam's 7,000 strategic hamlets. Unlike the strategic hamlets, the five surviving cluster villages (one was

2. The author has found no evidence that IVS has ever been used as a cover for Central Intelligence Agency operations, though USAID/Laos, by admission of its current director, Mr. Hannah, has been used as a CIA cover. IVS does not want to be infiltrated by the CIA, and volunteers who have overtly engaged in military or intelligence-gathering activities have been fired from both the Laos and Vietnam IVS teams.

captured by the Pathet Lao Reds) are not surrounded by trenchworks or bamboo and barbed wire fortifications.

But the Communists show great concern over the cluster villages which were established in September, 1963. The Pathet Lao radio, broadcasting from the eastern reaches of the strategic Plain of Jars, has been denouncing the villages since their start. North Vietnam in recent weeks called the villages a U.S. imperialist plot to establish control over Indochina. The reason the Communists are worried is because the cluster villages, still in their teething stage, mark one of the first steps of the Laotian Government to establish its control in rural areas.

This is the way the program works: An area of relatively dense population is chosen—usually a cluster of villages in a fertile valley. The area's needs are assessed by International Voluntary Services (IVS) workers and U.S. foreign aid officials in cooperation with the Laos Government. A team of three IVS workers, together with their interpreters and Lao officials, then move into one of the villages to take up residence in a Lao-style house. Part of their task is to teach by example: a vegetable patch is marked out, a chicken pen constructed and elementary hygiene in cooking and the disposal of refuse is practiced. Vegetable seeds and improved varieties of rice are distributed. Dispensaries are set up and staffed by Lao nurses until promising young villagers can be trained to take over. In the cluster village programs completed so far, schools have been constructed with the help of the Lao Department of Public Works and the USAID roads department. Wells, irrigation and drainage channels have been built. A new airstrip was built for the Phone Hong cluster, fifty miles north of Vientiane. Finally, village councils have been set up so that the villagers can administer much of the program themselves.

USAID used the Cluster Village Program to gain administrative control of IVS/Laos. As the IVS/Laos annual report for 1963–1964 put it: "The original VARDA [RDD] contract anticipates seven teams of seven IVSers, each with a Team Leader directing activities and maintaining liaison with the IVS Chief-of-Party and USAID personnel. This concept has been changed in the last year with the initiation of the 'cluster village' work and the placing of additional USAID men in the field to provide support and direction."

First, USAID would choose a cluster village site. Then IVS volunteers, often accompanied by a Royal Laotian Army civic action team called Fundamental Educators, would establish themselves at the site. If the place appeared secure and conducive to being developed, a USAID employee would come out and take command. At this point, the IVS volunteer would frequently fade into bureaucratic limbo. As Myron Paine, an IVS team leader, wrote in 1964:

The RDD cluster program also stresses an agricultural demonstration center and agricultural activities. The bind is that this program is a Rural Development program. IVS people are to implement it, yet the technical planning is supposed to be handled by the Agricultural Branch of USAID. So IVS agriculturists who have been living in an area for 5–7 months and struggling to establish housing and the demonstration center are now asked to wait until an Agricultural Technician comes to survey the area, develop plans for it, and turn these plans over to the RLG to implement, if they want to.

USAID completed engulfing IVS/RDD by taking over all supply and support functions, ostensibly to free volunteers for more important work. As one might expect, with USAID in control of IVS program planning, administration, and support, IVS team leaders had little to do but grumble or toady. Team leader Paine wrote: "During the past couple of months, IVS team leaders have tried to be regional representatives of the IVS headquarters. In this role we were to visit several team locations to assist in what ways we could and for 'trouble shooting.' But as another team leader expressed it, 'I get frustrated waiting for trouble to shoot.'" By 1965, after their people-to-people development projects had been totally subordinated to the U.S. pacification effort, IVS/RDD volunteers were primed to be flung into the forward areas of "Free World" Laos.

INSTANT HEARTS AND MINDS

The recent history of Laos reads like a British closet comedy, with Phoumis and Phoumas periodically leaping from the wings and grabbing control. Occasionally a quirky American such as

Pop Buell appears, exuding bureaucratic charisma and gathering enough American resources to do his Laotian "thing" in grand style. Such a character was Colonel Haffner, U.S. Marines (ret.), who hit Laos in mid-1965.

Colonel Haffner was described in a newsletter by IVS volunteer Galen Beery: "At 51, he's a vigorous outdoor type who once did forty push-ups in the Rural Development office to show a paunchy desk-type the value of keeping fit; he finds it hard to sit still for any length of time and enjoys long hikes around Xieng Lom to look at potential projects, keeping up a running commentary on 30 years' military experience and thinking out self-help projects."

"Haff" as he came to be known throughout the mission, decided there had to be a better and faster way than the cluster village program to win hearts and minds in Laos. Why not, he mused, send eager young guys out alone to "semi-secure" areas where they could render the locals agog with short-term, "high-impact" development projects? Intelligence would be a side-product, since each field worker would make regular radio checks, remaining abreast of enemy troop movements in order to stay alive. Thus was born the forward area program. Bob Lovan, a volunteer who worked in Laos from 1964 to 1969, told the author that Haffner first tried to man his scheme with USAID employees. But when a sluggish USAID bureaucracy aborted a forward area training group before it reached Laos, IVS volunteers were placed at Haff's disposal.

The first IVS forward area volunteer, Galen Beery, wrote on June 9, 1965:

For the past month and a half I've been a "forward area" rural development worker in Xieng Lom, an isolated and somewhat forgotten area of northwest Laos, south of the Mekong. This long valley was taken over by the Thai during World War II, returned to Laos, and was held for a short time by the Pathet Lao. Although the military is still operating out of Xieng Lom in the mountains, it's time for the U.S. and the Royal Lao Government to do something that will show the people that they haven't been forgotten. But in light of the security of the area, programs must be simple and completable—to coin a word—and we can't be too extensive in planning. Hence my

presence here—an in-and-out Vientiane-Xieng Lom-Vientiane com-
muter in jaunts of a week or so, as the official IVS-USAID representative and jack-of-all-trades. . . . It's rather pleasant to be greeted as
the minor princes of Laos' medieval eras were greeted—the old men
and women rush to the side of the trails as we bicycle past, doffing
their checkered turbans and bending low to murmur "Lord."

Bob Lovan recalled 1965–1967 as an exciting period in IVS/Laos.
"The forward area program was a quasi-Boy Scout operation,"
he said. "It was great fun being out there all alone. Maybe it
was the best period for IVS/Laos. But I'm sad it ever started. It
looks different in retrospect."

A lot of the charm left the forward area program in 1967, when
IVS/Laos took its first American war casualties (numerous Laotian employees of IVS have been killed by the Pathet Lao). In
1966 one forward area volunteer had drowned, apparently by
accident. In 1967 an IVS volunteer and his Lao assistant were
executed in their forward area home, and another volunteer was
wounded under similar circumstances. Yet another volunteer died
in an Air America crash of undetermined cause. IVS/Washington
dispatched an "agonizing reappraisal" team to Laos.

Richard Peters, a member of the Washington team and now
executive director of IVS, was shocked to find a volunteer who
was flown in and out of the village he worked in during day-
light hours. Mr. Peters described another volunteer as living in
an isolated house next to a lonely airstrip, laughing off danger
but wracked with psychosomatic cramps. The more obviously
idiotic forward area stations were closed, and in September 1967,
IVS participation in the forward area program officially ceased.
However, Bob Lovan, who became IVS/Laos chief-of-party in
1967, said the forward area program went on throughout 1968
under the guise of the cluster village program.

This author, who visited Vientiane in April 1969, noted that
there were still a number of IVS volunteers stationed alone in
insecure areas. These volunteers sported short-wave radios and
"bug-out kits" containing fishhooks, beepers, appeals for help in
several languages, and so on. They had fortified their homes
and were full of "narrow escape" stories. All kept close tabs on

troop movements in their areas; in fact, they were in Vientiane at that time because they sensed the Pathet Lao moving in. They reported that if a Pathet Lao team came for them in their remote homes, the Royal Laotian Government troops would disappear and they would be left to confront the Pathet Lao.

The true end of the IVS forward area program came in mid-1969, after three more IVS/RDD volunteers had been ambushed and killed on the highways of Laos. A volunteer reported Pathet Lao broadcasts calling for the extermination of the "Peace Corps-type spies." The hour had come for forces of reform which had seethed for years within the IVS.

THE RELUCTANT COUNTERINSURGENTS

Reading IVS newsletters written from 1957 to 1970, one begins with happy accounts of unhampered people-to-people development work. Then from 1960 through 1962 an air of Christian anti-communism is present, with volunteers exhorting their friends to support the free world in Laos. From 1963 through 1966, complaints centered around USAID bureaucratic control of IVS mount. In 1967 and later years, large numbers of volunteers criticize U.S. government policy in Laos and the role of IVS in executing that policy.

Volunteer Richard Stern summarized the discontent expressed during a Laos team meeting in early 1968:

The volunteers in Laos think that IVS has essentially prostituted itself to the U.S. Aid program here. At least half of them are quite unhappy about it. They feel that they are subordinate, "junior" employees in AID, forced by that bureaucracy into the materialistic, economic approach to community development instead of the people-to-people, social approach which they originally understood IVS to represent. The Director of AID in Laos admitted under grilling at the meeting that neither he nor the Ambassador, William H. Sullivan, would tolerate the presence in Laos of an organization with as much independence as the Peace Corps! And many IVSers joined because they thought a private organization would be *more* independent than the Peace Corps. Some volunteers feel that they have thus been tricked into a position of supporting a U.S. political program and policy that they were critical of. Some would resign if they were not bound by contracts, draft obligations, the inferred, possible repercussions that quitting could involve. Some are "bribed" by the lucrative fringe benefits that AID offers or by the implicit promise of future employment.

In 1969 an IVS reform movement, which had been brewing for years in the Vietnam team, gained some adherents in IVS/ Laos. Laos volunteer Allan W. Best wrote on October 6, 1969:

IVS is now faced with a major decision: to continue along the lines of the past and be closely associated with USAID and American efforts in foreign countries and be basically an American organization, or to internationalize on all levels. By that I mean to open up membership of IVS volunteers, staff, and Board of Directors to members of any nationality, to field multi-national teams and to find funding for development that will not tie them to any organization or country in a political manner.

The international idea would be hard to implement but would be a most challenging idea. I myself hope the decision is one for internationalization. We already have an American volunteer organization —the Peace Corps—let IVS explore an exciting new concept in volunteer development agencies.

The new executive director of IVS, Richard Peters, told the author that he favors the internationalization of IVS and the seeking of private funding. He feels these goals can be reached while IVS remains in Vietnam and Laos under USAID contract. But like his predecessor, Mr. Peters must balance virtually irreconcilable forces. The IVS board of directors, many of whom are the same Bible Belt pragmatists who founded IVS, tend to consider the volunteers' *objection* to being lackeys of U.S. war policy a major lapse from the apolitical first principles of IVS. The chief-of-party in Vietnam supports ten volunteers who have non-negotiably announced that they will accept no more USAID money after July 1, 1970; while the chief-of-party in Laos appears willing to go along with the USAID "program." USAID contracting officers, Mr. Peters realizes, will support IVS only as long as it appears politically valuable. Finally, private sources of funds and international voluntary organizations look with gimlet eyes at the stain of counterinsurgency on the brow of IVS.

Meanwhile, the IVS/Laos show goes on. The author spoke with one volunteer who was returning to work in Laos. The volunteer was embittered and cynical; and no other cynic is equal to an IVS cynic. He reported that in mid-1969, IVS/RDD pulled its operations back to relatively secure provincial capitals. At a team meeting held then, a number of volunteers voted to withdraw IVS from Laos; but, he noted, all of those volunteers remained in Laos until their contracts expired.

The volunteer's own job was to be an evaluation study of a Royal Laotian Government village leadership training course. "It means a lot of driving along dangerous roads," he said, "and USAID wouldn't be able to get anybody else to do it." His job description included determining the political loyalties of village leaders, but he planned to sanitize his role by refusing to collect political information.

Why was he returning to Laos? "I love the Lao culture," he said. "I hate the war. The Lao have every right to kill Americans, including me. But I feel I can do a little good in Laos. As soon as I feel I can't do any good, I'll leave."

"Don't use my name," he insisted. He was afraid the CIA might kill him for talking about where he worked. Then, driven with self-doubt but ready to compromise with a war machine he hated, the reluctant counterinsurgent was off to Laos.

18

An IVS Volunteer Writes from Laos

T. Hunter Wilson

> The people on the ground kept on shooting at each other,
> and the people in the air kept on dropping bombs all
> over the place, so we decided it was about time to move.
> —Elderly woman in a refugee camp

I visited the refugee camp in Seno yesterday. Driving out with
the four girls from Asian Christian Service [ACS] who run the
clinic and social program there, I realized that this was the
first time I had driven through countryside since the first two
weeks I was in Laos. After we passed the checkpoint at the ENI,
the narrow paved road wound at first through partially cleared
land and brushy young teak plantations. Then a dense forest
rose on either side, nearly overhanging the road and broken
only by an occasional small village and, once, a broad marshy
lake. Several times it reminded me of driving Route 119 to
Vermont, except that there were hundreds of large black butter-
flies flopping out of the jungle and across the road, now and
then coming in through the air vents in the Land Rover. We
went through another small checkpoint and then the one for
Seno itself. That one has been attacked quite often at night—
supposedly the Pathet Lao (PL) have a training school in the
jungle nearby—so there are bunkers of logs and earth; rocket
tubes are lashed to the trees, aimed in a circle outwards; and
the grass in the surrounding fields burned.

Seno itself is a sprawling, dilapidated town (though no place
looks very prosperous at this time of year—so dry). Once it was
the largest French garrison in central Laos, with several thousand
troops, and Savannakhet was only a Mekong port for supplies.
Now the Laotian Army has a sizable military camp there, and
there's an airstrip and a hospital, a post office, a few shops. And
some 3,000 refugees, mostly from around Muong Phin. Nearly

all of them are women and children or old men. Many of them have PL husbands, fathers, boyfriends, and are pro-PL themselves. Like most refugees in Laos, they have left their villages not so much to join the Royal Laotian Government (RLG) side as to get away from the war, particularly the bombing. (The Laotian Air Force consists of some 40-odd T–28s, prop-driven training planes converted to carry bombs and napalm. Ours, of course, is a little bigger.) Huge areas of the Lao countryside are designated free-strike zones, as in Vietnam, and anyone who lives there is a fair target. So there are refugees.

A woman in refugee relief of the World Council of Churches, comparing conditions at Seno with those at other refugee camps, said that they are not bad. By any other standards, however, they're awful. The people are housed in tin barracks abandoned ever since the French left. Inside, there are no partitions save a solid double row of beds, placed head to head down the center, leaving a narrow aisle down each side. Though refugees don't carry much baggage, there isn't room for what they have, so it's strung up in the air over the beds, with the mosquito netting, and jumbled along the wall in the aisle. There's no separate place for cooking, so everything is darkened with charcoal smoke (though a few have built small thatched kitchens outside). There *is* good water, but for 3,000 people there isn't so much as a single outhouse. In small villages with fields and forest all around them, it hardly mattered, but in Seno they're all crammed together so. Of course, they couldn't bring whatever food they had stored, so they have to live on a dole—for about a month, they got rice so bad it stank. The U.S.-run Agriculture Development Organization, generally a pretty good thing, had an attack of poor judgment and bought a lot of rice that had been rained on. They couldn't sell it, so rather than lose the money, they dumped it on the refugees. All things considered, it was no surprise that there was an almost steady stream of patients while the clinic was open—everything from a boy with a gangrenous thumb (sent on to the French hospital for amputation) to women with backaches from clearing the resettlement site (given aspirin and vitamins).

Supposedly, the refugees are not allowed to leave Seno, but

as with most things that are supposed to be in Laos, it isn't, well, "strictly enforced"! Taxi-buses cruise through the camp calling for passengers for Savannakhet. A few families, with relatives in town, have moved here illegally (and were probably represented among the paperless picked up before Tet). And a few have simply packed up and walked back out of camp to rejoin the PL. Not that most of them are particularly unhappy there. Some of the women in the clinic said they prefer it—there are more shops, more things to do, and more people to talk to than in their villages. They work at the resettlement site, three or four kilometers from Seno, clearing land and building houses. Because so many families have no men, work goes very slowly and only 35 houses are finished. In fact, the RLG has been reluctant to improve conditions at the camp for just that reason, lest people get too settled.

And the army's concern is understandable. The PL do come into Seno to visit their wives; so often in fact that the RLG commander has ordered his troops not to fire unless the PL are obviously attacking, instead of just coming in for a night in town. He's worried that if they fire every time the PL are in town, his soldiers will frighten themselves!

At this point, I must introduce Mrs. Nute, who supplies all the gossip about Seno after ACS goes home at three. Mrs. Nute is ACS's Lao interpreter and the closest thing to a genuine eccentric I've met in Laos. As an interpreter, her chief virtue is that she simplifies Lao, for she doesn't speak much English—her most common phrases are "Not very correct, Not very good," and "Not very normale." She is quite tall and stocky (almost burly), which is not simply unusual for a Lao woman—she looks tougher than most Lao men! She knows all the important people in Seno, used to run a bakery, and is reputed to have the best bunker in Seno behind her house. Despite her concern for the "very correct," she used to ride a horse through town wearing shorts (Lao women always wear long skirts) and now goes sky-diving with the paratroopers. She has her opinions, talks a blue streak, and is thoroughly delightful to listen to. She seems to get wind of everything that happens in Seno somehow or other.

One night the PL strolled into Seno smoking cigarettes (which is how the medic who spotted them distinguished them from water buffalo on the lawn). The RLG commander for Seno was in Savannakhet that night, so they took over his house. In a position to do considerable damage, they merely plinked away with rifles at some tanks parked nearby. The five colonels in charge for the night were playing cards down the road a bit. When they heard the firing, they abandoned their jeep (which might show the PL where they were) and ran down the road to Mrs. Nute's house. They woke her up and insisted that she let them sleep on her floor that night. Meanwhile, the RLG soldiers, with no one to tell them what to do, decided not to fire back, since the PL were in the commander's house, and it was a newish house, and since they didn't want to have to pay for it. The PL went away before too long, and Mrs. Nute woke up the colonels with coffee in the morning. It's tales like this that make it easy to believe the stories of the war before all the foreigners joined in. It went for years with practically no casualties. As the PL approached a position, the RLG soldiers would look out and say, "Gee. They've got two companies and we've only got one." So they'd fire a few shots over their heads and retire. It can't have been *just* like that, but then this thing at Seno would be hard to believe too. And if you have to fight a war, that's the way to do it. Nobody gets hurt, you can all get drunk together in town when there's a *boun* [traditional celebration].

The sun no longer sets in Savannakhet; it just fades away. By 4 o'clock it's a yellow blur in the sky that grows redder and redder as it sinks toward the horizon over the river. But it never gets there: it gets dimmer, like a glow from a hot iron, a faint reflection in the water, then fades into the dust altogether. Two weeks ago we had a light sprinkling of rain, just a very few drops, enough to damp the dust—a sharp smell, sweet and acrid at once. It was a shock to realize how much time has gone with not even a smell of moisture.

As you might guess, things have been quiet this month in Savannakhet, since Tet at any rate. So it was startling to sit down this afternoon with the week's papers sent from Vientiane and find Laos on the front page of every issue. The Bangkok papers, at least, are worried. And with some cause, I should think, what with the Vietnamese admitting they're here, the U.S. admitting it used B–52s on the Plain of Jars (apparently without the approval of the Laotian cabinet), and the ICC leasing its helicopters as it packs up to go home.

It's hard to believe here: hot nights talking with friends, standing outside where it's cooler. Even at night, though, the steady rasp of cicadas like a planer in a mill. People pass by singing —where have they been in this dark town? A couple glides by on a bicycle, the woman on the back holding a sputtering torch to one side for light. They pass and a sweet resinous scent reaches us for a moment and is gone.

T. HUNTER WILSON
Savannakhet, Laos
February 28, 1970

19

The CIA's Laotian Colony; or, An Interview with Souvanna Phouma

Douglas F. Dowd

En route to Hanoi in April of 1970, my companions (Noam Chomsky and Reverend Richard Fernandez) and I were delayed for eight days in Vientiane by the bureaucratic inspirations of the Indians then administering the International Control Commission and supervising the weekly plane to North Vietnam. We soon got over being miffed at the delay. Our stay in Laos enabled us to discover at firsthand part of the reality that lies hidden in even the best of the literature available on Laos. Most revealing of all, and also most disturbing, was what came to light in a prolonged interview with Souvanna Phouma, especially when that discussion was contrasted with our earlier interviews with Laotian refugees.

Despite all that has transpired in Laos since 1964—the ever-intensifying bombardment, the massive displacement of the peasantry, the utter corruption of the Royal Laotian Government—it remains tempting to view Souvanna Phouma as the reluctant captive of events but a man still, somehow, neutralist and pacific in his impulses. That temptation was killed for us on April 9, when we spent well over an hour in Souvanna's elegant, air-conditioned, American-style ranch house in Vientiane. Perhaps because he knew we were three antiwar Americans, or perhaps because our questions were not easily turned aside by charming evasions, Souvanna Phouma came out as a savage and voluntary Asian rightwinger. Doubtless there was a time when his neutralism was genuine, and when his basic goal was to prevent the destruction of Laos and its people. That period ended in 1964, when he first gave permission to the Americans to bomb his country; and by now he has found the rationalization to suit the crime.

The question around which our entire discussion revolved

was put to the prince in the first minutes of our interview: "It seems that the two major and realistic alternatives facing Laos are, on the one hand, a political settlement with the Pathet Lao (with the added possibility, as Senator Fulbright has put it, of North Vietnamese hegemony in Indochina) or, on the other hand, the steady destruction of Laos and its people, as the extraordinarily intensive bombing of almost all of Laos proceeds hand in hand with an endless land war. What would your reasons be for acquiescing in the latter rather than the former?"

The steady destruction of Laos and its people has been acquiesced to for many years now, and whatever changes have taken place in the recent past—since the winter of 1968–1969, for example—have been in the nature of sharp intensification of a process that had already been disastrous. Reporters who have been able to fly over or visit the areas in and above the Plain of Jars describe a region reminiscent of the surface of the moon, like the pictures of the no-man's-land created in World War I. Souvanna Phouma eagerly volunteered the information that there are now 700,000 Laotian refugees, and he went on to say that those bombed or killed throughout northern Laos are—not communists, or Pathet Lao—but "North Vietnamese." And he told us that "no cities or villages have been destroyed." "Maybe a few huts." "People flee when they hear that the North Vietnamese are coming." And so on.

A few days before our interview with the prince, we had visited the refugee camps that lie perhaps thirty miles from Vientiane. On each occasion we were accompanied by an interpreter, and the interviews lasted for about six hours on each of two days. The people we interviewed were from the Plain of Jars region. It is important to note that as we left, our interpreter learned, not surprisingly, that the people assumed us to be "American soldiers." After hours of intensive interviewing which involved approaching the same matters from different starting points, we finally emerged with a consistent pattern of facts which squared with the few independent reports of others on the same questions. That the "reports" from Souvanna Phouma, USAID, USIS, and the American embassy—and therefore most news reports—give a qualitatively different picture is to be expected. The following sketch of the recent history of Phonesavan is characteristic of the whole area of northern Laos. Here we will be concerned only with the bombing and the creation of refugees, although the more important as well as the more interesting story is that of life under the Pathet Lao.

Bombing in northern Laos began in May 1964 and hit Phonesavan itself in 1965. Napalm, dropped by F–105s, seems to have been the customary airborne gift. From 1965 to 1967, Phonesavan's residents could still farm; but after January 1968, the bombings were so numerous they could only farm at night. By January 1969 the bombing was so intensive that they could not farm at all, for the bombs fell over the entire twenty-four hour period. The planes used included T–28s, F–105s, and F–86s, but, in that area, there were no B–52s. (However, B–52s became a common carrier in other parts of Laos, farther to the north as well as in southern Laos.) After 1967 the people were afraid to burn firewood for cooking, because of the bombing, and thus ate less frequently. Repeated questioning produced the consistent response that not only were there no North Vietnamese in villages that were bombed, but that neither were there Pathet Lao military units. The refugees from Phonesavan allowed themselves to be removed in February–March 1970. As even American embassy personnel will reveal, in unguarded moments, the characteristic Pathet Lao technique was to place one or two people in a village to organize and educate while participating in the village work. But, in a guarded moment, we were told by American embassy representatives, with something of a flourish, the bombing "denied the fish their water." That, after all, is the American goal in Laos as in South Vietnam: bomb the peasantry out of its homes and lands, and destroy any possibility of a continuing social revolution. Social revolution is, after all, the real enemy in all of Indochina, and not only because it is the sole means of achieving independence from Western rule.

In short, the 700,000 Lao refugees are refugees from American bombing, systematically and persistently laid on them at increasing rates—until, by late 1969, the intensity of American bombing exceeded anything that had taken place in Vietnam or Korea. Now that there are few targets left in Laos, we shall set new

records in Cambodia, where it appears likely that more than
one war will soon be in progress—both that between the Ameri-
can-Saigon forces and the NLF–NVA–Khmer Rouge, and that
between the Saigon forces and those of the Lon Nol Army.
There may even be other combinations in the offing devised by
America in its successful pursuit of the Guam Doctrine—Asians
killing Asians on the ground, while we kill them from the air.

Meanwhile, we are also able to stimulate American academics
to find the silver lining in what might seem to the naïve to be a
dark cloud: As Professor Samuel Huntington has enabled us to
see, the creation of refugees, removing them as it does from
the idiocy of their rural life, is but another way of speeding up
urbanization; a clear advantage. It does not seem so, of course,
to the Lao refugees. When we asked how long they and their
forebears had lived in the regions they left behind, we got an-
swers that always began with laughs, for of course, their lands
were their ancestral lands, going back perhaps thousands of
years. And what has "urbanization" meant to these people? It
means that six or seven hundred of them, mostly old men, women,
and small children, can now live on top of each other in five or
six dreadfully crowded huts, 125–150 to a hut, a hut whose size
would not, I am sure, satisfactorily accommodate Professor
Huntington's family. Nor has urbanization yet meant work to
these people. Perhaps half a mile from their huts are forests,
which they can clear for paddy and which might begin to yield
a harvest in 3 or 4 years if they had the manpower to do the
work—but of course, they do not have the manpower. Meanwhile, the young girls will find a way into Vientiane, where they
will be able to earn a living by catering to the needs of the
Air America crews and those others who have protected them
from the Pathet Lao.

Apart from the reference to Air America, what has all this
to do with the CIA, and the CIA with Prince Souvanna Phouma?
Until the Associated Press dispatch of June 8, 1970, one had to
make speculative remarks, which could be easily brushed aside
by the denials of the State Department, the CIA, and those
Southeast Asian experts who still support the U.S. government.
But the director of the Agency for International Development,

John Hannah—of Michigan State University's Vietnam "assist-ance" program fame—"acknowledged today that the USAID pro-gram is being used as a cover for operations of the CIA in Laos." (See article 24.) This has been alleged and denied for some years now, but everyone in Laos takes it for granted. The same allegation has been made and denied concerning USIS, Air America, the Clandestine Army of Vang Pao, and doubtless many other agencies and nonagencies in and out of Laos, the sum total of whose efforts since the late 1950s has been to make Laos into a genuine colony of the CIA, whose uncrowned ruler is Pop Buell; again, acknowledged by everyone in Laos whom one would dare to ask.

One could not presume to ask Souvanna Phouma, of course; especially if one expected to get on a plane to Hanoi the next day, and could be stopped—that being very possibly one of the few remaining powers left to the once proud prince. He is a man whose pride now comes out as cant, braggadocio, and as a savage aloofness toward his people, his land. Souvanna has been sanitized, pacified—in short, Americanized.

20

A Liberated View of the War:
American Businessmen, Laos . . . and Beyond

Harold Willens

Try to imagine the reaction if several years after public rejection of the Edsel car the Ford Motor Company had attempted to bring it back without as much as modifying a bumper. It would have justified a stockholder's revolt, with fortunate board members hanged in effigy, unfortunate ones in Detroit. The foreign policy engineers who Americanized the Vietnam war saddled the country with a national Edsel. And now, large-scale military involvement in Laos could make the Vietnam tragedy seem small by comparison. The chairman of the Senate Foreign Relations Committee has called Laos "one of the few places worse than Vietnam to fight a war."

Apparently adhering to the theory that even an Edsel can be successfully merchandised if sold with the covering canvas still on, the Nixon administration, like its predecessors, has tried to keep the war in Laos a secret. It is not for me to explore historical, political, or military aspects of American involvement in Laos since articles in this book and elsewhere have already done so. Rather, as a businessman who began to speak out publicly and on a full-time basis against the Vietnam war early in 1967, I hope to describe the changing public attitude toward the Indochina war and the part played in that change by American businessmen.

After what we have already experienced in Southeast Asia, it seems inconceivable that the public will permit Laos to become another Vietnam. The outcry in reaction to our Cambodian invasion supports this assumption, as does the clear probability that three years ago Senator Symington would have found it difficult if not impossible to release the transcript of his committee's closed hearings on Laos. Congress, which passively rubber-stamped escalating American involvement in Vietnam with the Gulf of Tonkin resolution, has at last begun to discover its constitutional responsibilities. The "expertise" of Lyndon Johnson, Dean Rusk, and Walt Rostow—the men most responsible for depicting a national blunder as a national crusade—appears now as nakedly nonexistent as the mythical emperor's clothes. And businessmen who had previously kept their silence have begun to put themselves squarely on the record as opposed to allowing Laos to become another Vietnam.

To me it is especially gratifying to see more and more businessmen come forward and become visibly involved in debating national policy, for I clearly recall how deafening was the silence in the business community only a few short years ago. Businessmen were firmly convinced that foreign policy was the exclusive domain of politicians and soldiers. As I tried to persuade businessmen that a mistaken war which was killing their sons, dividing their country, and damaging their economy was in fact very much their business, I discovered almost immediately that news media people seemed to regard anti-war businessmen as a man-bites-dog story. Whether the press conference occurred in Honolulu, St. Louis, Boston, or Washington, it was always well attended. Soon there were invitations to debate or be interviewed on nationwide television and radio programs. In various parts of the country people read and heard the well-documented and well-reasoned public statements of businessmen, many of them company presidents or board chairmen speaking out against the war. In astonishingly little time the country became aware that there were at least some businessmen of stature who were publicly opposing their country's involvement in the Southeast Asian war. Antiwar businessmen appeared before congressional committees. Mail bearing corporation letterheads landed on White House and Pentagon desks. "Letters to the Editor" cited facts and tore apart Pentagon double-talk.

With growing rapidity in the late sixties, Vietnam became known as the nation's most unpopular war. Administration boasts of victory diminished, followed soon by apologies and promises to do better and ultimately by President Johnson's decision not to seek a second term. This is not to suggest that the appearance of businessmen in the debate made *the* difference. But that we made *a* difference is not in doubt. Protesting adults and youths

helped to tip the balance and turn the question from: How soon
will we win this holy war? to How soon can we extricate ourselves from this unholy mess?

But the job is far from done. Republicans replaced Democrats
on a vow of peace, and the war goes on. Staggering Pentagon
budgets and the persisting death count in Southeast Asia contra-
dict mellifluous vows to end the war. It is plain that additional
and longer-range programs to arrest American militarism are
needed; that we are rapidly approaching the finish line in a race
between education and catastrophe; that to avert ultimate disaster new international realities must replace the fears, fables,
and fallacies upon which our foreign policy is based. And it is
also plain that businessmen/citizens represent a force of vast
potential in the effort to turn the country around before time
runs out. The Vietnam war shows that our country pursues a
foreign policy dominated by military thinking in which weapons
assume greater importance than ideas. It is this type of thinking
that wastes money on weapons which don't work and on nuclear
weapons which work only too well. And it is the military men-
tality which inched us into Vietnam, sent us rushing into Cambodia, and now seeks to sink us further in the quagmire of Laos.

The Businessmen's Educational Fund (BEF) came into being
in 1969 expressly to bring to the attention of the industrial community, the public, and their representatives the excessive mili-
tarization of American foreign policy and the appalling drift to
a militarized state. BEF's essential objective is to widen and
deepen the idea of corporate responsibility by establishing a
channel through which businessmen can strive for more relevant
national priorities and policies. To extricate ourselves from Indochina is imperative. But the Indochina trauma must be recognized for what it is: a symptom reflecting the underlying
misdirection of American policies and priorities. Taking up
Fortune's editorial appeal for a fresh audit of military spending,
BEF has been hammering away at the disproportion between
legitimate defense needs and the apparent uncontrollable pro-
clivity of military leaders to seize everything in sight for themselves. What ultimately happens in Laos will be determined by
the degree to which Americans succeed or fail in curbing the

excessive military influence which brought our country into the Indochina war.

Here and there one notes encouraging confirmation of these essential arguments in publications including *Fortune* and the *Wall Street Journal. Fortune:* "The U.S. is in the grip of a costly, escalating pattern of military expenditures. . . . At staggering costs the military has repeatedly bought weapons and deployed forces that add only marginally to national security." From the beginning we have stressed the relationship of costs and risks to possible gains in our criticism of the Southeast Asian war. But it is no easy task to begin dislodging the firmly implanted myth that war is good for business. The fact is that during the four years prior to escalation of the Vietnam conflict corporate profits after taxes rose 71 per cent, while from 1966 through 1969 corporate profits after taxes rose only 9.2 per cent. The war has weakened the competitive position of the United States in the world market. In 1964 merchandise exports exceeded imports by nearly $7 billion. By 1968 the excess of exports over imports had declined to less than one-half billion dollars.

Since 1964 the Consumer Price Index has increased 16 per cent. Professor James Clayton of the University of Utah has predicted that "the inflationary effect of Vietnam will probably result ultimately in a 10 per cent reduction in the standard of living of the average American." High interest rates and tight money have sharply cut the rate of residential construction, while the credit crunch has cut back spending on automobiles and consumer durable goods.

It has been estimated that by 1990 the interest cost on the Vietnam war debt may reach $35 billion, with the entire principal still outstanding. Perhaps this latter statistic is the most compelling way for a businessman—or any American—to place in proper perspective the economic consequences of a pointless military folly. The only way to hold down the cost of an Edsel is to scrap it quickly.

Even apart from the war, it becomes increasingly clear that military spending benefits relatively few firms while adversely affecting most. A majority of economists today would probably agree with these words of John Kenneth Galbraith: "For the vast majority of businessmen the only visible association with the defense industry is through taxes they pay. Not even a stray sub or sub-subcontract comes their way, and among the important indirect effects are the starved communities in which they must operate and to whose disorders and violence they are exposed, the manpower and the materials they are denied and the regulations on overseas investments which they suffer because of balance of payment difficulties which in turn are the result of military spending." The significance of Galbraith's statement is heightened by a statistic which surprises many: during the fiscal year 1970 *seventy per cent* of the nonfixed portion of our federal budget went to military-related expenditures.

To compound the problem, the Pentagon and its industrial partners, having been left virtually free of meaningful accountability, have become accustomed to spending taxpayers' money with irresponsible abandon. Air Force officials, for example, called the procurement for the C–5A cargo plane "the best contract ever entered into by the Air Force." Perhaps it was. But the cost overruns of this plane are already substantially in excess of $2 billion. The MBT tank was to have cost $250,000 per unit and to have been ready in 1970. The Army has already spent $2 billion on just one prototype, and present estimates are that production will not begin for another four years. Naval experts told Congress that the Mark 48 torpedo would cost $65,000 each. Later it was revealed that the price per torpedo will be at least $1.2 million.

These are just a few examples of the recklessness with which the military spends our money. It is an unfortunate fact that we have now so often heard expenditures described in terms of billions that the vastness of this figure has lost its meaning. It is useful to remind ourselves that a billion (one thousand million) dollars can provide vocational schooling full time for 540,000 youngsters, or send over 100,000 indigent students to a public college or university for four years, including full-time tuition, room, and board. With this in mind we can better appreciate the true cost of the $23 billion we have wasted on missiles and weapons that were built only to be abandoned.

It is now estimated that the B–1 bomber which the Air Force

wants would eventually cost between $15 and $20 billion. In his role as chairman of the joint chiefs of staff, General Earle Wheeler argued for this plane against many experts who regard it as unnecessary in an age of missiles. General Wheeler said: "The main reason for this generation of bomber was to force the Russians to spend more, spending themselves into bankruptcy."

General Wheeler's words illustrate that in foreign policy we have fallen into what businessmen recognize as the deadly trap of competitor-obsession. Fear of underestimating our competition drives us to overestimate the intentions and capabilities of others; what "they" *might* do becomes more important than what we *should* do. The fantasies of our military planners induce escalation of arms which the other side's fantasizers are then compelled to match. Meanwhile, to use a business analogy, our own plant (the environment, the cities, and so on) disintegrates, and our product (free-enterprise democracy) deteriorates. To a businessman, who must live with reality and review both sides of a ledger, however distasteful, it seems clear that this aspect of our foreign policy is self-destructive. In this instance the other side of the national ledger reveals that compulsive competitor-obsession keeps us from the most important business of all: preserving and improving our own national plant and product. It makes little sense to surround our cities with missiles while they are crumbling from within.

We are haunted by Cold War visions of a unified communist monolith, even though clinging to that illusion means shutting our eyes to a world vastly different from that of 25 years ago. Our foreign policy rests more on demonology than on current international realities. We remain blind to the significance of a break between Yugoslavia and Russia, to the Sino-Soviet split, to Rumania's enthusiastic reception of President Nixon, and to the obvious nationalistic aspirations and enmities among communist countries. We have depicted our competitor, whether in Laos, Russia, China, Vietnam, or Cuba, as totally evil. Therefore those who oppose him must be good. We have thus found ourselves embracing, as though they were Jeffersonian models of democracy, the regimes of such hated despots as Batista, Chiang

Kai-shek, Diem, Thieu, and Ky. One wonders how we would respond today to Hitler, that most fervent of all anti-communist crusaders. In our own self-interest it is time to look around; time to admit that there is both good and evil in all political ideologies. Seeing our adversaries as human beings is a necessary first step to avoiding large-scale war in Laos as well as preventing our own nuclear incineration.

Some time ago, addressing himself to the problem of fanaticism, U Thant spoke words which are not a utopian vision but a pragmatic prescription for self-preservation: "We have seen how the great religions of the world, after lamentable periods of bigotry and violence, have become accommodated to each other." While the mutual slaughter went on, theological zealots of old were undoubtedly certain that such accommodation could never occur. They were proved wrong. Practical persons must perceive that peace is not a heaven-sent gift but a structure to be created step by step. In military intervention and arms escalation, each step has been matched by the adversary. Is it not then possible that deescalatory steps will also be matched by adversaries quite well aware that they too are running out of time—and resources?

It is worth a try. For by perpetuating a foreign policy based upon ideological fanaticism we have much to lose at home as well as abroad. Fanaticism inevitably turns its intolerance inward. An overly large, overly rich, and overly powerful military establishment was feared by our Founding Fathers and warned against by Dwight Eisenhower. Such a military bureaucracy could become the most serious threat to the very democracy it is supposed to be protecting. Recently it was revealed that at Fort Holabird in Maryland, the Army was filing and computerizing information on the personalities, beliefs, and lawful political activities of American citizens. Such 1984-type tactics are direct attacks on the constitution of the United States, the same constitution every military officer has taken an oath to defend.

Perhaps we have already gone too far to prevent full-scale war in Laos, repressive erosion of American freedom, or massive nuclear destruction. On all counts a case can be made for giving up the game as lost. But games which were seemingly lost have been won. At all levels of the human enterprise there are moments of balance when a seemingly irreversible tide can still be turned. Left alone, the tide of present events will sweep away everything we value. Effectively challenged, that tide can be restrained and reversed. In looking at Laos and beyond, it strikes me that American businessmen are uniquely equipped to help avert international, national, and personal disaster. I base this statement upon three and one-half years of personal experience in antiwar work as well as two additional considerations. First, since most political leaders follow rather than lead, a relatively small number of enlightened businessmen—to whom people in government are apt to listen—could help bring about constructive change before time runs out. Second, new directions depend upon discarding old orthodoxies, such as fanatical anticommunism. In exposing these to the light of truth, businessmen can best withstand the attacks to which all heretics have at all times been subjected.

Here, then, is the greatest crisis and the greatest challenge ever faced by American businessmen: the rigor of business judgment —pragmatic common sense—must replace unthinking orthodoxy. Our children have the courage to challenge that orthodoxy. But they lack experience and influence. And they are increasingly isolated by the viciousness of certain demagogues in high office. Yet our children are essentially right, as were other powerless heretics, such as Galileo. We cannot blame our best young people for not deferring to the experts who took us into the Southeast Asian war and kept seeing light at the end of the tunnel; experts who invaded Cambodia in search of a nonexistent communist Pentagon; experts clamoring for many more billions to build ABMs considered useless by the nation's best scientists; experts who are quite literally preparing to MIRV us all to death; experts who gobble up the nation's substance by scaring us into believing that Russia is about to roll over Western Europe and that a China barely able to feed itself is about to conquer the world.

As businessmen, as fathers, and as Americans we are confronted by an inescapable choice: our children—or our experts and their myths. How we choose can help determine how the nation makes this fateful choice. That is the great challenge and opportunity confronting American businessmen today. The following words are almost exactly those used over and over again by some of us since early 1967:

"An end to the war would be good, not bad, for American business. . . . We have more than adequate data to demonstrate that the escalation of the [Vietnam] war has seriously distorted the American economy, has inflamed inflationary pressures, has drained resources that are desperately needed . . . and has dampened the rate of growth in profits." The speaker was Louis B. Lundborg, chairman of the board of the Bank of America, the world's largest private bank, and his audience was the Senate Foreign Relations Committee. We have been waiting a long time for Mr. Lundborg and his colleagues in the top tier of the corporate hierarchy to speak out. Mr. Lundborg said that, regardless of who is responsible for the war, "the rest of us have gone along pretty supinely. If anyone is to blame, it is people like me for not speaking up and not speaking out sooner—for not asking, 'what goes on here?' " The president of Formica Corporation, Wallace G. Taylor, told a Honolulu audience that the nation's businessmen are "deaf, dumb, and blind to a hydra-headed new American revolution that is tearing this country asunder, value by value." How, he asked, "can a country whose business is business continue to be deaf to its own youth and blind to a war that is rapidly turning this country into one of the poor nations?"

Messrs. Lundborg and Taylor have said it all. They are now involved. Let us hope the contagion of intelligent involvement spreads on the wings of their words to others in the nobility of American commerce. If enough business leaders lead, we may still find our way safely through the most hazardous period in our nation's history—in Laos and beyond.

Part IV

United States Statements on Laos

21

President John F. Kennedy's
Statement on Laos, March 23, 1961

On March 23, 1961, President Kennedy went before the television cameras to present his program for resolving the Laotian civil war which threatened to create a major Soviet-American confrontation. Using three simplified maps as visual aids, President Kennedy dramatically demonstrated his interpretation of the military situation.

I want to talk about Laos. It is important, I think, for all Americans to understand this difficult and potentially dangerous problem. In my last conversation with General Eisenhower, the day before the inauguration, we spent more time on this hard matter than on any other one thing. And since then it has been steadily before the administration as the most immediate of the problems we found on taking office.

Our special concern with the problem in Laos goes back to 1954. That year, at Geneva, a large group of powers agreed to a settlement of the struggle for Indochina. Laos was one of the new states which had recently emerged from the French Union, and it was a clear premise of the 1954 settlement that this new country would be neutral, free of external domination by anyone. The new country contained contending factions, but in its first years real progress was made toward a unified and neutral status. But the effort of a Communist-dominated group to destroy this neutrality never ceased, and in the last half of 1960 a series of sudden maneuvers occurred and the Communists and their supporters turned to a new and greatly intensified military effort to take over. These three maps show the area of effective Communist domination as it was last August—in December—and as it stands today.

In this military advance the local Communist forces, known as the Pathet Lao, have had increasing support and direction

393

from outside. Soviet planes, I regret to say, have been conspicuous in a large-scale airlift into the battle area—over 1,000 sorties since December 13, 1960, and a whole supporting set of combat specialists, mainly from Communist North Vietnam—and heavier weapons have been provided from outside, all with the clear object of destroying by military action the agreed neutrality of Laos. It is this new dimension of externally supported warfare that creates the present grave problem.

The position of this Administration has been carefully considered, and we have sought to make it just as clear as we know how to the governments concerned. First: We strongly and unreservedly support the goal of a neutral and independent Laos, tied to no outside power or group of powers, threatening no one, and free from any domination. Our support for the present duly constituted government is aimed entirely and exclusively at that result, and if in the past there has been any possible ground for misunderstanding of our support for a truly neutral Laos, there should be none now.

Secondly, if there is to be a peaceful solution, there must be a cessation of the present armed attacks by externally supported Communists. If these attacks do not stop, those who support a genuinely neutral Laos will have to consider their response. The shape of this necessary response will of course be carefully considered not only here in Washington but in the SEATO conference with our allies which begins next Monday [March 27]. SEATO—the South East Asia Treaty Organization—was organized in 1954 with strong leadership from our last Administration, and all members of SEATO have undertaken special treaty responsibilities toward any aggression against Laos.

No one should doubt our own resolution on this point. We are faced with a clear threat of a change in the internationally agreed position of Laos. This threat runs counter to the will of the Laotian people, who wish only to be independent and neutral. It is posed rather by the military operations of internal dissident elements directed from outside the country. This is what must end if peace is to be kept in Southeast Asia.

Third, we are earnestly in favor of constructive negotiation—among the nations concerned and among the leaders of Laos—which can help Laos back to the pathway of independence and genuine neutrality. We strongly support the present British proposal of a prompt end of hostilities and prompt negotiation. We are always conscious of the obligation which rests upon all members of the United Nations to seek peaceful solutions to problems of this sort. We hope that others may be equally aware of this responsibility.

My fellow Americans, Laos is far away from America, but the world is small. Its 2 million peaceful people live in a country three times the size of Austria. The security of all of Southeast Asia will be endangered if Laos loses its neutral independence. Its own safety runs with the safety of us all—in real neutrality observed by all.

I want to make it clear to the American people, and to all the world, that all we want in Laos is peace, not war—a truly neutral government, not a Cold War pawn—a settlement concluded at the conference table, not on the battlefield. Our response will be in close cooperation with our allies and the wishes of the Laotian Government. We will not be provoked, trapped, or drawn into this or any other situation. But I know that every American will want his country to honor its obligations to the point that freedom and security of the free world and ourselves may be achieved.

Careful negotiations are being conducted with many countries in order to see that we take every possible course to ensure a peaceful solution. Yesterday the Secretary of State informed the members of Congress and brought them up to date. We will continue to keep the country fully informed. . . .

QUESTION: Do you know how much time the supporters of the Laos Government might have for diplomacy, in other words is there a danger of a quick takeover by the Communists?

ANSWER: We are hopeful that we can get a quick judgment as to what the prospects are going to be there. I think that every day is important.

QUESTION: Mr. President, there appears to be some national unawareness of the importance of a free Laos to the security of the United States and to the individual American. Could you spell out your views on that a little further?

ANSWER: Well, quite obviously, geographically, Laos borders

on Thailand, which is, to which the United States has treaty obligations under the SEATO agreement of 1954; it borders on South Vietnam—it borders on Vietnam—to which the United States has very close ties, and also which is a signatory of the SEATO pact.

The aggression against Laos itself was referred to in the SEATO agreement, so that given this, the nature of the geography, its location, the commitments which the United States has assumed toward Laos as well as the surrounding countries—as well as other signatories of the SEATO pact—it's quite obvious that if the Communists were able to move in and dominate this country, it would endanger the security of all of Southeast Asia.

And as a member of the United Nations and as a signatory to the SEATO pact, and as a country which is concerned with the strength of the cause of freedom around the world, that quite obviously affects the security of the United States.

QUESTION: Mr. President, the United States has made the position all the way through on this that we want a neutral Laos. But isn't it true that Laos has a nonviable economy and it can't exist as an independent country?

ANSWER: Well, I think it can exist. That was the premise under which the 1954 agreements were signed. It may require economic assistance, but there are many countries which are neutral which have received economic assistance from one side or the other, and many of those countries are in Southeast Asia and some of them are geographically quite close to Laos, so that I don't think that the final test of a neutral country is completely the state of its economy.

The test of a neutral country is whether one side or another dominates it and uses it—a phrase I referred to—as a pawn in the Cold War. We would like it to occupy a neutral category as does Cambodia.

QUESTION: Mr. President, what is your evaluation of the theory that perhaps the Russians are so active in Laos to keep the Chinese Communists out?

ANSWER: Well, I wouldn't attempt to make a judgment about a matter in which we have incomplete information. I think that the facts of the matter on which we have external activity and that it has helped produce the result you see on the map and this is of concern to us. [*sic*]

I'm hopeful that those countries which have been supporting this effort will recognize that this is a matter of great concern to us and that they will be agreeable to the kind of proposals which we have made in the interest of peace. . . .

QUESTION: Mr. President, in the event that your strong efforts to reach a neutral Laos go unheeded, would you possibly consider it necessary then for SEATO to intervene, or would you spell out a little more clearly what would have to take place?

ANSWER: I think a careful reading of my statement, I think, makes clear what the various prospects are and the critical nature of them.

QUESTION: Mr. President, if these responses aren't forthcoming and aren't favorable to your proposals here, would you, and we have to shoot, would you use your executive orders and authority, or is the presence of Mr. Rusk going to the senators a preparation of asking for a declaration of war in case it really becomes a shooting war out there?

ANSWER: I think that it would be best, that, er, to, er, consider it as I stated it in my statement the prospects alternative responsibilities. I've stated them, I think, as clearly as today they can be stated. We will know a good deal more in the coming days.

QUESTION: Mr. President, could you please tell us, sir, what in your opinion this country has obtained out of its roughly $310,-000,000 worth of aid sent in the past six or seven years to Laos?

ANSWER: Well, Laos is not yet a Communist country, and it's my hope that it will not be.

QUESTION: Mr. President, because it was such an obvious move, could you tell us what Mr. Salinger handed you just then? (laughter)

ANSWER: Well, he handed me—I will not draw the cloak of executive privilege around it. The point was made that Vietnam —these are the sort of things he knows—that Vietnam is not a signatory of the SEATO pact, but is a protocol country under the SEATO pact. (laughter)

22

"Laos and the Southeast Asian Crisis": A Congressional Speech by Senator Thomas J. Dodd, May 21, 1962

The crisis of Laos represents a crisis of the first magnitude for the whole of southeast Asia. Indeed, it is no exaggeration to say that it represents a crisis of the first magnitude for the whole free world.

The countries of southeast Asia are rich in natural resources. But it is their strategic importance, rather than their economic importance, that makes them primary targets of Communist aggression.

If the Communists ever succeed in establishing their dominion over the whole of southeast Asia, they will, in effect, have cut the world in half. The western Pacific land mass will be theirs from the Bering Straits to Singapore, while the control of the southern island chain, from Sumatra to New Guinea, would give them command of the entrances from the Pacific Ocean to the Indian Ocean.

The Communists' conquest of southeast Asia would produce so serious a shift in the world balance of power that our very ability to survive would be called into question. . . .

As matters stand today, I believe that our policy in South Vietnam is in conflict with our policy in Laos, that our policy in Laos, as a matter of fact, is undermining the affirmative and courageous policy we are endeavoring to follow in Vietnam.

I think we would all have less difficulty in understanding the world situation if we studied our maps more frequently. In the case of Laos, its strategic importance should be instantly apparent from a look at the map.

From the *Congressional Record*, 87th Congress, Second Session.

If there is any one country that may be described as the geographic heart of southeast Asia, it is Laos. For Laos has common frontiers with virtually every country in the area—with Communist China and North Vietnam, with the neutralist nations of Cambodia and Burma, and with the two committed nations of the southeast Asia mainland, South Vietnam and Thailand. . . .

One of the excuses that has been offered for our own inaction in Laos is that the Lao people and the Lao Army have shown no will or ability to resist the Communists. This [is] coupled with the assertion that the Communists apparently have far more popular backing than does the Royal Lao Government.

Even if these assertions were completely true—which they are not—it would, in my opinion, still be necessary to defend Laos; even if we were not interested in the fate of the Lao people, the defense of Laos would still be a strategic necessity because, ultimately, the fate of all southeast Asia, and our own security may hinge on it.

But I do not accept the theses that the Lao people are indifferent to communism and the Royalist forces are incapable of fighting. . . .

As of 2 years ago, it was probably true that few Laotians knew the meaning of communism or felt very strongly about it. But, as of today, the evidence is that the Laotian people have learned the meaning of communism the hard way, from their actual experiences under Communist rule in those portions of the country that have been overrun by the Laotian and Vietnamese Red forces. . . .

On the Western side, the events in Laos provide us with still another dramatic illustration of our amateurishness in the field of total warfare; of our perennial desire, despite all disappointments, to believe that some kind of accommodation with the Communists is possible; of our willingness, despite their repeated betrayals, to trust their diplomatic promises; of our readiness, despite numerous historic lessons, to foster coalition governments; of the bewitchment which has led us to accept the one-sided rule that the cold war must be waged always on the territory of the free world, and never on the territory of the Communist world, no matter how recently this territory may have been annexed.

If we persist in this sentimentality and these ambiguities that have up until now characterized our policy in Laos, then the positions remaining to the free world will be overrun or eroded, one by one, under the unrelenting attacks of world communism.

But if we now learn the lessons of Laos and apply them to the world situation it will, I am confident—at least, it can, I am confident—mark a turning point in the cold war. Once we have digested these lessons, Laos can be saved and southeast Asia can be saved. But far more important, we will never again make the mistake of retreating before a Communist challenge, in the hope that this will somehow ease tensions and reduce the danger of war. Because it does just the opposite.

We will, on the contrary, move to the total mobilization of resources and energies and spirit that alone can assure the triumph of our free society in the life and death struggle with the godless forces of communism. . . .

23

President Richard Nixon's March 6, 1970, Statement on U.S. Policy and Activity in Laos

In light of the increasingly massive presence of North Vietnamese troops and their recent offensive in Laos, I have written letters today to British Prime Minister Wilson and Soviet Premier Kosygin asking their help in restoring the 1962 Geneva Agreements for that country.

As co-chairmen of that conference, the United Kingdom and the Soviet Union have particular responsibilities for seeing that its provisions are honored. My letters note the persistent North Vietnamese violations of the accords and their current offensives; support the Laotian prime minister's own current appeal to the co-chairmen for consultations; urge the co-chairmen to work with other signatories of the Geneva Accords; and pledge full United States cooperation.

Hanoi's most recent military build-up in Laos has been particularly escalatory. They have poured over 13,000 additional troops into Laos during the past few months, raising their total in Laos to over 67,000. Thirty North Vietnamese battalions from regular division units participated in the current campaign in the Plain of Jars with tanks, armored cars, and long-range artillery. The indigenous Laotian Communists, the Pathet Lao, are playing an insignificant role.

North Vietnam's military escalation in Laos has intensified public discussion in this country. The purpose of this statement is to set forth the record of what we found in January 1969, and the policy of this Administration since that time.

When we came into office, this Administration found a highly precarious situation in Laos. . . . There had been six years of seasonal Communist attacks and growing U.S. involvement at the request of the Royal Laotian Government. The North Vietnamese had steadily increased both their infiltration through Laos into South Vietnam and their troop presence in Laos itself.

Any façade of native Pathet Lao independence had been stripped away. In January 1969, we thus had a military assistance program reaching back over six years and air operations dating over four years.

Since this Administration has been in office, North Vietnamese pressure has continued. Last spring, the North Vietnamese mounted a campaign which threatened the royal capital and moved beyond the areas previously occupied by Communists. A counterattack by the Lao government forces, intended to relieve this military pressure and cut off supply lines, caught the enemy by surprise and succeeded beyond expectations in pushing them off the strategic central plain in north Laos known as the Plain of Jars.

The North Vietnamese left behind huge stores of arms, ammunition, and other supplies cached on the plain. . . . The size and nature of these supply caches the Communists had emplaced on the plain by the summer of 1969 show clearly that many months ago the North Vietnamese were preparing for major offensive actions on Laotian territory against the Royal Laotian Government.

During the final months of 1969 and January 1970, Hanoi sent over 13,000 additional troops into Laos and rebuilt their stocks and supply lines. They also introduced tanks and long-range artillery.

During January and February, Prime Minister Souvanna Phouma proposed to the other side that the Plain of Jars be neutralized. The Communists' response was to launch their current offensive, which has recaptured the Plain of Jars and is threatening to go beyond the furthest line of past Communist advances.

The prime minister is now once again trying to obtain consultations among all the parties to the Geneva Accords, envisaged under Article IV when there is a violation of Lao sovereignty, independence, neutrality or territorial integrity.

In this situation, our purposes remain straightforward.

We are trying above all to save American and allied lives in South Vietnam which are threatened by the continual infiltration of North Vietnamese troops and supplies along the Ho Chi Minh Trail. Hanoi has infiltrated over 100,000 men through Laos since this Administration took office and over 500,000 altogether. Our air strikes have destroyed weapons and supplies over the past four years which would have taken thousands of American lives.

We are also supporting the independence and neutrality of Laos as set forth in the 1962 Geneva Agreements. Our assistance has always been at the request of the legitimate government of Prime Minister Souvanna Phouma, which the North Vietnamese helped establish; it is directly related to North Vietnamese violations of the Agreements.

We continue to be hopeful of eventual progress in the negotiations in Paris, but serious doubts are raised as to Hanoi's intentions if it is simultaneously violating the Geneva Agreements on Laos, which we reached with them largely on the basis of their own proposals. What we do in Laos has thus as its aim to bring about conditions for progress toward peace in the entire Indochinese peninsula.

I turn now to the precise nature of our aid to Laos.

In response to press-conference questions on September 26, December 8, and January 30, I have indicated:

- That the United States has no ground combat forces in Laos.
- That there were 50,000 North Vietnamese troops in Laos and that more perhaps are coming.
- That, at the request of the Royal Laotian Government, which was set up by the Geneva Accords of 1962, we have provided logistical and other assistance to that government for the purpose of helping it to prevent the Communist conquest of Laos.
- That we have used air power for the purpose of interdicting the flow of North Vietnamese troops and supplies on that part of the Ho Chi Minh Trail which runs through Laos.
- That, at the request of the Royal Laotian Government, we have flown reconnaissance missions in northern Laos in support of the Laotian Government's efforts to defend itself against North Vietnamese aggression and that we were engaged in "some other activities."

It would, of course, have posed no political problem for me to have disclosed in greater detail those military-support activi-

ties which had been initiated by two previous Administrations
and which have been continued by this Administration.

I have not considered it in the national interest to do so because of our concern that putting emphasis on American activities in Laos might hinder the efforts of Prime Minister Souvanna
Phouma to bring about adherence to the Geneva Agreements by
the Communist signatories. In recent days, however, there has
been intense public speculation to the effect that the United
States involvement in Laos has substantially increased in violation of the Geneva Accords, that American ground forces are
engaged in combat in Laos and that our air activity has had the
effect of escalating the conflict.

Because these reports are grossly inaccurate, I have concluded
that our national interest will be served by putting the subject
into perspective through a precise description of our current
activities in Laos.

THESE ARE THE FACTS:

• There are no American ground combat troops in Laos.

• We have no plans for introducing ground combat forces
into Laos.

• The total number of Americans directly employed by the
U.S. government in Laos is 616. In addition, there are 424
Americans employed on contract to the government or to government contractors. Of these 1,040 Americans, the total number,
military and civilian, engaged in a military advisory or military
training capacity numbers 320. Logistics personnel number 323.

• No American stationed in Laos has ever been killed in
ground combat operations.

• U.S. personnel in Laos during the past year has not increased, while during the past few months, North Vietnam has
sent over 13,000 additional combat ground troops into Laos.

• When requested by the Royal Laotian Government, we have
continued to provide military assistance to regular and irregular
Laotian forces in the form of equipment, training, and logistics.
The levels of our assistance have risen in response to the growth
of North Vietnamese combat activities.

• We have continued to conduct air operations. Our first priority for such operations is to interdict the continued flow of troops and supplies across Laotian territory on the Ho Chi Minh Trail. As commander in chief of our armed forces, I consider it my responsibility to use our air power to interdict this flow of supplies and men into South Vietnam and thereby avoid a heavy toll of American and allied lives.

• In addition to air operations on the Ho Chi Minh Trail, we have continued to carry out reconnaissance flights in north Laos and fly combat-support missions for Laotian forces when requested to do so by the Royal Laotian Government.

• In every instance our combat air operation has been increased only as the number of North Vietnamese in Laos and the level of their aggression has increased.

Our goal in Laos has been and continues to be to reduce American involvement and not to increase it, to bring peace in accordance with the 1962 Accords and not to prolong the war.

That is the picture of our current aid to Laos. It is limited. It is requested. It is supportive and defensive. It continues the purposes and operations of two previous Administrations. It has been necessary to protect American lives in Vietnam and to preserve a precarious but important balance in Laos.

Peace remains the highest priority of this administration. We will continue our search for it in Vietnam. I hope my appeal today to the Geneva Conference co-chairmen will help in Laos. Our policy for this torn country will continue to rest on some basic principles:

• We will cooperate fully with all diplomatic efforts to restore the 1962 Geneva Agreements.

• We will continue to support the legitimate government of Prime Minister Souvanna Phouma and his efforts to deescalate the conflict and reach political understandings.

• Our air-interdiction efforts are designed to protect American and Allied lives in Vietnam. Our support efforts have the one purpose of helping prevent the recognized Laotian Government from being overwhelmed by larger Communist forces dominated by the North Vietnamese.

• We will continue to give the American people the fullest possible information on our involvement, consistent with national security.

I hope that a genuine quest for peace in Indochina can now begin. For Laos, this will require the efforts of the Geneva Conference co-chairmen and the signatory countries.

But most of all it will require realism and reasonableness from Hanoi. For it is the North Vietnamese, not we, who have escalated the fighting. Today there are 67,000 North Vietnamese troops in this small country. There are no American troops there. Hanoi is not threatened by Laos; it runs risks only when it moves its forces across borders.

We desire nothing more in Laos than to see a return to the Geneva Agreements and the withdrawal of North Vietnamese troops, leaving the Lao people to settle their own differences in a peaceful manner.

In the search for peace we stand ready to cooperate in every way with the other countries involved. That search prompted my letters today to the British prime minister and the Soviet premier. That search will continue to guide our policy.

24

An Interview with Dr. John A. Hannah, Administrator of USAID

On June 7, 1970, Dr. John Hannah, director of the United States Agency for International Development, was interviewed by Dan Blackburn of Metromedia News and A. D. Horne of the Washington Post. Dr. Hannah discussed the future of the U.S. aid program and made some surprising revelations about the relationship between the war effort and USAID in Southeast Asia.

AL HORNE: Well, Dr. Hannah, one of the Peterson Task Force recommendations was for the separation of the security assistance from the development assistance. Do you believe that this concept will help in revitalizing congressional support or is it likely to cause more trouble perhaps in the House?

DR. HANNAH: Well, I think it will have an uneven result. . . . I believe that it should be separated, for the reason that it distorts the role of aid. You see, a substantial fraction of all the money appropriated to us is being spent in Vietnam, Laos, and Thailand for supporting assistance. There are lesser amounts for Korea and malaria programs and so on. Now these military and political objectives are important. I think that they should be carried on, and of course many of the things that we do in Vietnam and Laos are normal aid programs designed to help these people increase their food production, improve their school systems, and be concerned with the health of their people, and all these things. But I am certain . . . that these political-military operations ought to be handled by the State Department and the Defense Department rather than through aid under whatever name.

DAN BLACKBURN: I'd like to raise a question along this line. Do you feel that the involvement in Vietnam, where any look at the foreign service register will show that AID has a really staggering number of people compared to the number of people in other countries, and more recently, the action in Cambodia, has under-

---

This interview was aired on the Metromedia Radio News show "Profile."

mined the credibility of the aid program in the other countries overseas?

DR. HANNAH: Well, I don't know if it has undermined it or not, it certainly has not helped. Our critics, the other nations, are critical of this country and, of course, like to use it. A decision was made back in 1962, that the Defense Department was going to fight the war and that AID was going to be responsible for trying to control inflation and be concerned with the operation of refugee camps and civilian hospitals and increasing agricultural production and providing schools and all this sort of thing. Although I don't think it is appropriate for those of us in AID to be critical of the original decision, it was probably the right decision to be made at the time. It is our role to do what we are supposed to do and do it as well as we can. Now the only way that we have been able to carry on this responsibility is, as you know, to actually draft people that have been in our mission staffs all over the world and actually require them to spend a year in Vietnam, and this has nothing to do with a foreign attitude, but it has complicated our programs all over the world and I would welcome a separation. . . .

DAN BLACKBURN: Doctor, how do you respond to complaints that the AID program is being used as a cover for CIA operations in Laos?

DR. HANNAH: Well, I just have to admit that that is true. This was a decision that was made back in 1962 and by administrations from now until then, and it is the only place in the world that we are. I don't like the way that CIA cover, but we have had people that have been associated with the CIA and doing things in Laos that were believed to be in the national interest, but not routine AID operations.

DAN BLACKBURN: Doesn't this bring back the question I raised earlier about the effect on the credibility of the AID program in other nations?

DR. HANNAH: Yes, it does, and you know that I did not deny it. I said that it might. Certainly, our preference is to get rid of this kind of operation, that is in the Peterson Task Force recommendation, and I am sure that it is going to be in the president's recommendation for discussion. I hope it is going to be in the legislation one that is submitted. . . .

Part V

The Pathet Lao

25

Life in the Pathet Lao Liberated Zone

Jacques Decornoy

We have just come from Hanoi—but have we changed countries? The Soviet-built command car advanced hiccuping over a terribly difficult track, crevassed by bombs, made slippery by rain. It took almost two whole nights to get here, after hours of skidding in the mud and delicate encounters with lorries obstructing the little mountain road with their bulk.

Two feeble lights appeared in the darkness, indicating the high site perched in a cave. We left the main track to penetrate a terrain turned over hundreds of times by explosions and no longer resembling anything at all—a chaos of red earth, broken rocks, devastated trees. As in Vietnam, indeed, and yet we had really crossed the border. We were in Laos, in a sector of the Sam Neua region, in the "liberated zone" which is controlled by the extreme left, the Neo Lao Hak Xat, otherwise known as the Pathet Lao. . . .

Owls in the Grotto

Right up to the last few feet of the journey, it was necessary to steer the car between bomb and rocket craters. A wooden ladder propped against the chalky rock gave access to the grotto hotel, a natural hole in the mountain "improved" by dynamite. The traveler passed from one "suite" to another, walking along a "floor" of sharp pebbles, to arrive finally at his "room." From his bed he can see the sky through a break in the mountain. He

These articles originally appeared in *Le Monde,* July 3–8, 1968. All material reproduced is copyright © by *Le Monde* and Opera Mundi.

This translation first appeared in the *Peace Press* (June–July, 1969), which is published by the Conflict Education Library Trust, 6 Endsleigh St., London, England.

can feel a fresh wind, but it would be extraordinary bad luck if a rocket landed in this cave. In any case, the foundations of this shelter are perfectly protected from bomb explosions. A tiny motor distributes a commodity almost unknown in "liberated Laos"—electricity.

This retreat for hunted guerrillas is managed by Mme. Kempeth Pholsena, a graduate of Moscow University, French-speaking, and a daughter of Quinim Pholsena, Laotian minister of foreign affairs and neutralist leader, who was assassinated in April 1963. Life, here, is of the simplest kind. A wash basin is set on the rocky platform which forms the entrance to the grotto. A dangerous place if one puts one's nose out of the mountain: sometimes one cannot finish shaving because of the jets raiding from Thailand. Then one lies flat on the floor of the grotto with a bit of the sky and a few flower pots attached to the rock by a thread of wire for a view. A difficult life but still possible in this season. When the rainy season begins, water penetrates the chalky mass and drips into the "hotel." It is a world without noise, for the surrounding villages have disappeared and the inhabitants live hidden in the mountains. A few buffalo and a few pigs walk below our feet between the craters made by American bombs. At the end of 1957, several large bombs fell two meters from the grotto: it is dangerous to lean outside at any time of the night or day.

THOUSANDS OF BOMBS

A "routine" day . . . at 7 o'clock, an AD–6 plane prowls above us. It hangs around for about ten minutes, then leaves. At 7:30 the plane returns, flies over once, and, three times, drops its cargo a few kilometers from the "hotel." There is a flight of jets at 8 o'clock and at 8:30 jets and bombs. The same operation at 9 o'clock. In the afternoon we hear planes again on several occasions. It is not surprising, in these circumstances, to watch the breathless arrival at the "hotel" of a secretary of state in the defunct Government of National Union. Papers in his hand, he has run from one cave to another. In this region which they control and administer, the Laotians of the left seem to be an underground in their own land, the guerrillas camouflaging themselves in the shelter of the rocks, as if the enemy rules the valley, though he is only master of the skies.

It seems that the intensity and density of the bombing is even greater in the province of Xieng Khouang in the Plain of Jars. Its persistence in this zone of grottoes raises the problem of the real motives of the Americans. Prince Souvanna Phouma told us in Vientiane (*Le Monde,* February 23) that the raids were aimed less at the Laotians than at the North Vietnamese at their point of entry into the country. It is certain that the U.S. Air Force attacks the trails. But such a relentless attack on the region where we were can only be explained if the target is the Neo Lao Hak Xat central administration itself. For three years, thousands of bombs have fallen on a small area two to three kilometers long. In front of the cave where Prince Souphanou-vong received us, the craters were so close together that they cut into each other. In this forgotten war, these raids, unlike the attacks on North Vietnam, have never been officially reported, but only, with much delay and discretion, "admitted." The Americans are trying to "break" the Laotian left, both psychologically and, if possible, physically.

In Vientiane (and the prime minister cannot be unaware of it), the Pathet Lao, which know that he encourages these offensives, is not ready to forgive him. They also blame Thailand, from which all the bombers fly, as well as the governments supporting American intervention or maintaining a complete silence on the subject. To declare, as Prince Souvanna Phouma has done, that the Neo Lao Hak Xat "will rejoin the national community" when it is "liberated" from "North Vietnamese ascendancy" is to misunderstand completely the views of the leaders of the left, who ask, on the contrary, that Vientiane should disengage itself from the enormous American influence and that the Americans no longer intervene in their country.

One of the officials of the Sam Neua district told us that between February 1965 and March 1968, 65 villages had been destroyed. A number impossible to verify for a short report, but it is a fact that between Sam Neua and a place about 30 kilometers away where we stayed, no house in the villages and hamlets had been spared. Bridges had been destroyed, fields up to the rivers were holed with bomb craters.

SHELTERS IN THE HILL

Life in the caves has its inconveniences for the peasants. It is even more serious for the political and administrative personnel who have to rule an immense, mountainous country, stretching from China to Cambodia, where distances are counted less in kilometers than in days and nights of marching. Nevertheless, the people work on without any sign of giving in. "Owls by day, foxes by night" goes the Laotian proverb. During the day the owl goes to earth in the shadow, but at night the fox comes out.

Taking risks at night, even when one is a fox, presents problems. At three in the morning, we had to leave for Sam Neua, but the command car skidded at the foot of a bomb crater. The journey had to take place at dawn—a delicate moment.

We could not stay on in this village. Camouflaging the command car, we left on foot, by a mule path, and crossed a river on a bamboo bridge to arrive finally in the forest at a hut of poor planks covered by a roof of corrugated iron, with a "floor" of beaten earth: the office of the chairman of the district administration. Attached to a wall by a nail is a map of this region of the province, broken by bomb splinters, drawn by hand, without scale—one sign among others of the great poverty of the Neo Lao Hak Xat. In another hut close by we ate glutinous rice, which forms the basis of the Laotian diet, surrounded by men and women of the militia who were busy reinforcing a shelter hollowed out of a hill under the trees. Several times in the afternoon American planes flew over us. Profiting from a break in the clouds, reconnaissance planes passed over again and again. From above Sam Neua, they could see only the motionless ruins and deserted houses.

The first real raid against the population center itself was launched on February 19, 1965. Very serious attacks were made on it recently on March 17 and 19, 1968. The town looked like one long street, bordered with European-type houses which were built at the time of French colonial rule and with traditional Laotian dwellings of wood and bamboo. The two ends of the town were razed to the ground. The old ruins of 1965 have disappeared; those of March 1968 were still "smoking" when we visited them. Branches of trees lay all along the length of the river, and houses were totally burned out (phosphorus had been used).

At the other end of Sam Neua, the sight was even more painful. Everywhere there were enormous craters, and the church and many houses were demolished. In order to reach the people who might be living there, the Americans dropped their all-too-famous "bombes à billes" (fragmentation bombs). Here lay a "mother bomb," disembowelled, by the side of the road. All around, extending over a dozen meters, the earth was covered with "daughter bombs," little machines that the Vietnamese know well, unexploded and hiding hundreds of steel splinters. One of them had rolled into a shelter, under a mat, mortally wounding the three people who had taken refuge there.

The inhabitants dispersed into the forest, but only to find very thin protection there. As night fell, one saw them emerge, walk around, and feed their cattle. Some ventured as far as the town to collect the remains of beams or doors—the wreckage of their destroyed homes, not completely burned—which they carried off into the forest. There were no traces of DCA (antiaircraft units) —these are as mobile, apparently, as in Vietnam—but units are to be found in the region since the March raids. About two kilometers from Sam Neua, one can see the debris of a downed plane; the pilot was torn to pieces by the bombs which he did not have time to release.[1]

All the inhabited zones situated around the population center have suffered greatly. One district official tells the litany of their misfortunes:

---

1. The Pathet Lao claims to have shot down more than 800 planes, which seems very exaggerated. Their DCA do not have shells larger than 37 millimeters. In this field at least, the aid they receive from the socialist countries seems modest (these countries, among them, North Vietnam, China, and the U.S.S.R., have diplomatic representatives in Vientiane).

March '66:	15 killed in such and such a village
November '66:	15 killed in another
The same month:	a pagoda destroyed; 6 monks killed
September '67:	8 killed
November 1 :	7 killed
November 19:	16 killed
February '68:	4 killed

To which we must add the many wounded. The inhabitants ask the reason for this deluge of fire and steel. "I don't even know where America is," said a peasant mother whose daughter had just been killed and who had lost all her belongings. A peasant said: "I understood nothing before when we were told that we should not accept American aid and when people spoke against the United States. After the raids on my village, I know what they mean." Everything American, far and wide, is hated by the people.

THE FACTORIES OF THE NIGHT: BANE KANG

"During the course of the last two months, American planes have dropped almost as many bombs on Laos as on North Vietnam," *Time* reported on March 22. In these conditions, rare are the oases where it is not necessary to live permanently underground, hidden in the forest or sheltered in a cave.

The village of Bane Kang is one of these, and one knows the reason for this very well. Some unexploded bombs lie about around it, overflights are frequent, but we have been able to sleep without fear in one of those houses on piles, beneath which flocks of ducks and black pigs wander by day and night. In the afternoon, when it it hottest, the men and women go to the river to take a bath, each in a different place. On the opposite bank, officials proudly showed us the rice paddies: the second harvest this year is growing there. This is revolutionary in Laos, though normal in the Vietnamese countryside.

The village is prosperous, a little more prosperous, it seemed, than the hamlets we saw in Sam Neua. Here there is no lack of glutinous rice, nor of fruit, nor of poultry. There was no school here before 1954. Today all the children are in school. They are seen at work in their small classes near the houses where the women sew their dresses. The men who are not working in the fields smoke a water pipe or drink from jars of rice alcohol. The fight against illiteracy among adults continues. Nurses care for their patients. The village is kept impeccably clean. There are no signs of undernourishment or of endemic disease.

Here and there on the houses are a series of pictures vaunting the successes of the Pathet Lao, friendship among ethnic groups, or showing the burial of an American plane by a militia team. In this "liberated Laos," spread out over fantastic distances difficult to cross, central directives can only travel slowly. But the village has two transistor posts which receive Radio Sam Neua. No loudspeakers, as in Vietnam or China. "We have tried, but the people did not like it," an official told us. It is a matter of temperament; the philosophy of life remains gentler here, in spite of everything, than in the neighboring countries. People like noise in these hamlets, but they make the noise themselves by singing, drumming, or playing the *khene,* a little bamboo instrument the sound of which is like that of a harmonica or an accordion. They dance the *lamvong* with slow steps and a graceful twisting of the arms and fingers. They sing "greetings to the DCA" or "The victory of Nam-bac," which was won in January 1968 from the forces of the right, to music suitable for celebrating love in the shade of the coconut palms, or under the juicy mango trees. Someone gets up and improvises a poem to a traditional theme and rhythm. Each time, the author or singer announces the origin of the song: for example, "Province of Phong Saly" or perhaps, "the Meo minority of such and such a district."

A VIRULENT NATIONALISM

The deeprootedness of this peasant community is clearly stressed. The poem does not stop at the frontiers of the hamlet of its origin. It tells of the Laotian nation, of Prince Souphanouvong, of the "puppets" of the capital city, of the "American aggressors." In the sad night of Vientiane, American pilots recreate the atmosphere of Saigon with their blackmarket sales and prostitutes. Do they know that a rural people are forging a Laotian nationality in the villages and caves they have just overflown or bombed, that they dance only Laotian dances and make their own culture, as well as their political ideology, a weapon against foreign intervention?

"Yes, indeed, but they are Communists," reply the good apostles, forgetting that if the kids "cheer the DCA," it is because the American planes ceaselessly threaten their lives. However, are they Communists? Certainly the Pathet Lao does not work hand in hand with Hanoi and the Socialist countries "for nothing." But they are Laotian, as the Vietnamese are Vietnamese, which says a lot. We know nothing precise about the influence of Hanoi on the Pathet Lao, but we have been able to verify, on every occasion, the virulent nationalism of education in geography and history; a nationalism of culture, a nationalism of methods and social organization. The need to work together and to master the water supply for the second rice harvest necessarily reinforces the cohesion of the villages and collectivizes work at the centers of the cooperatives, though today they practice only a simple system of mutual aid. The political philosophy impressed on the cadres has the flexibility of a young bamboo. Conversations are never marked with the rigidity of analysis which one finds in North Vietnam or among the leaders of the NLF in the South.

The Pathet Lao insist on the necessity of reinstating the Government of National Union born of the Geneva Accords of 1962, which has never really functioned. Until this wish is realized they have to administer and develop the areas they control: two-thirds of the territory and 50 per cent of the people (about 1.5 million inhabitants) according to them; according to Vientiane, one-third. This is why, in January 1968, they held their first "financial and economic congress" agreeing on a three-year plan, 1968 to 1970, the main lines of which were explained by Mr. Nouhak Phonsavane, a member of the central committee. One of the key ideas of this program is to give the country, and all intermediate levels, from the hamlet to the province, as much economic autonomy as is possible, in all areas. In this way, it can partly compensate for the absence of rapid communications and increase production.

One cannot, however, scatter or create little industrial centers or important schools everywhere. Hence the existence, in the province of Sam Neua, of nuclei of production and education, established by the central committee. A visit to them, at the end of a night's journey, sometimes slowed down by overflights of planes, brings surprises for the visitor.

WEAVING AND GEOGRAPHY

Somewhere in the region of Sam Neua we left our command car to clamber up piles of rocks, to jump over the bamboo hedges protecting the fields from the greedy buffalo, arriving at last at little very feebly-lit straw huts. It is here that both modern and traditional pharmaceutical products are made. Work is carried out only at night, because the smoke has to be camouflaged. Behind the workshops is an enormous cave, in which work goes on continuously. About a hundred women are working there, many of whom come from the minority ethnic groups. If a foreigner is not surprised by such a mixture of vitamins, he cannot hide his apprehension at swallowing a concoction of monkey bones or deer horns. It seems that these frightful juices soothe and cure. In Hanoi, moreover, very serious research is also carried out on the lines of traditional pharmacopoeia.

In another area of the province we made our way along a path carved out by the flow of a torrent. Near individual caves, youths practiced high jumping. Then we passed near houses destroyed in bombing raids before climbing to a series of caves which hid iron works. The raw material comes from Vietnam, from unexploded American weapons recovered on the spot and from worn-out trucks. Out of these workshops come domestic appliances, farming implements, machetes. In these humid, rocky, secret places, buzzing with mosquitoes, men and women workers sleep during the day and work during the night. The Americans are not popular here either.

It is at the spinning mill and the weaving factory that a visitor finds the greatest cause for astonishment. Here the enterprise is not hidden in a cave at the foot of a mountain, but is much higher up, in a very inaccessible place which can be reached only by scaling sheer rock cut into deep steps and marked out with bamboo. Another mountain directly faces this cave. No bomb or rocket can possibly reach these workshops from which come materials both for dresses and for military uniforms. In about eighty meters one passes from Chinese machines, silent because they are electric, to the most ancient spinning wheels. On the left, in a small rocky enclave, girl bookkeepers balance their books.

Everything has been brought here, installed, built by the textile workers, men and women. Previously there was nothing here in this wild ravine, in this countryside of thickets—huge trees interlaced with bamboo. At the foot of the mountain a village has been created out of all kinds of bits and pieces, including dormitories for girls, dormitories for boys, straw huts for the families of officials, a carpenter's workshop to make wooden looms, a dyeing shop, a parade ground for meetings, dances and Ping-pong, a cave for the electricians, etc. Textiles are made for eight hours a day, but the work does not stop then. Houses must still be built, wood must be found in the forest (11 tons a month), a guard must be mounted, rice and cassava cultivated, pigs and poultry tended, and professional, cultural, and political courses studied. At midday on Saturday, the machines stop. After a short meal, we see the workers disperse, pencils and notebooks in hand. The carpenter's shop, the canteen, and other straw huts as well, are transformed into classrooms, where they study geometry, algebra, and geography. Later on, when night falls, there is dancing. In North Vietnam there is, particularly in the administration, a permanent system of education which gives a solid grounding of general culture. On a much more modest level, they are trying to do the same in "liberated Laos." The laboratory for this—one has to go and look for it—in the caves, of course—is the school for training teachers and schoolmasters. One can see the pupils scattered over the area, studying. They made the tables, the benches, the houses, the pictures, the roads to the rocky classrooms. Rooms where it is difficult to study. Young people seated near the cave opening can write by natural light, but most must make do with a tiny gas lamp. The instruction aims to be as complete as possible: everyone cultivates his own vegetables and rice, everyone raises his own cattle. The goal is to be self-sufficient. Until this is achieved, they still receive rice from the central administration.

The director of education in the "liberated zone" and the headmaster of the school showed us their work and talked of their ideas. It is from them that we heard the most "committed" exposition of "national progressive education," even more than in discussion with other Pathet Lao leaders. The school serves, of course, to raise the level of culture, but also to defend the country, to "serve the people," to "hate the Americans."

The teacher must be a propagandist of the people. He must know how to run a meeting, how to explain the central political line, he must be a shooting instructor and link manual work with theoretical teaching. Weaving, ironmongery, education, culture of burned fields must have no secrets from him.

On the other hand, he must know how to adapt himself to local conditions; it is for this reason that, since 1965, a Meo script has been used. There are not enough books. Research is being carried out now on the possibility of publishing new textbooks on the history and geography of Laos in the national language. No one wants to depend on French or other languages any more. The country remains open to the foreigner, but they believe that everyone must go through the same mill of national culture . . .

ENORMOUS POVERTY

Can the Pathet Lao, quiet but coherent in its political program, militarily powerful, take the destiny of the country rapidly in hand if it wishes? It seemed to us, visiting a part of the territory they control, that they lack technical and even political staff. Their dispersion, the geographical and often mountainous terrain they rule, the meager heritage left them by colonial rule, these elements partly explain a certain misery in their kingdom. Compared with "liberated Laos," North Vietnam appears fabulously rich, intellectually and spiritually. At Sam Neua there is rice and pork, but no one sees any foreign newspapers or books. A well-known doctor told us he would like to be able to use French technical journals. Many of the staff and many of the leaders, in spite of their harassing work, the air raids, the lack of electricity, could read and learn in their caves, but they have absolutely nothing. Their very difficult living conditions, their self-denial, their ideas, remain unknown, "forgotten," like the war they are waging. One of them said to us: "Sometimes I ask myself what I am doing here. . . . I could be in Vientiane with money, girls, and cars. But, no, it is here that I must be."

This human handicap can slow down the political and military actions of the Pathet Lao, for their ideals and their certainty that they are right are not a substitute for everything. It is true that a great many of these people—avoiding guesswork percentages— have lived in this territory too long for going back to be possible. And since the system prevailing in the rest of the country opens up no future prospects, a political evolution in Laos must logically follow a settlement of the Vietnam conflict. When their skies are free of the terrifying presence of American planes, and when the military advisers have left, it will, perhaps, be possible for Laotians to map out their own future. A stay among the Pathet Lao leads one to suppose that, rejecting an American orientation, they will take no more inspiration from the example of Vietnam than the Vietnamese mimic the Chinese or Soviet pattern . . .

An Authentic People's Force

A diplomat with a post in Southeast Asia estimated recently that "the Laotian problem will be more difficult to settle than the Vietnamese problem." The outcome in Laos, which has already been mentioned during the Vietnam talks, risks offering arguments to partisans of the "domino theory." In fact, a solution cannot be found, short of perpetuating the civil war and foreign intervention through the same sort of agreement as that of 1962— which was based on a vain hope for mutual respect between the participants and presupposed an accord between forces which had nothing in common.

On the contrary, everything on the home front moves toward

a victory for the Pathet Lao: the seriousness of its social and political organization and of its nationalism; the courage and self-denial of its militants, as well as the built-in incompetence of the opposing regime, not to speak of its leaders. It would be wrong, therefore, to say that if Vietnam "falls," Laos must also "fall."

Will this evolution, if it takes place, be accepted by the Americans? Will it be accepted by Thailand, a powerful country, itself in the throes of a struggle, the importance of which is too often forgotten in political analyses of the region, just as its very firm links with elements of the Laotian right are also forgotten? Foreign intervention must end, in any case, for Laos to become self-sufficient, and it will be essential that the incessant bombing of the Pathet Lao by American planes and Washington's grip on Vientiane end some day. Then, as everyone in Vientiane knows, with or without the aid of Hanoi, the Pathet Lao will carry the day. Their strength comes less from outside than from the growth of authentically popular social forces. If the "domino theory" is played out in Laos, it will not only damage the Free World—today, above all, represented by the thousands of bombs it scatters there—but it will also damage the feudal clans desperately relying on a foreign air force to perpetuate the circumstances of another age.

26

The Birth of the Pathet Lao Army

Tran Van Dinh

In 1478, one hundred and twenty-five years after the founding of the kingdom of Lan Xang, Vietnamese soldiers swept into the country and captured the capital, Luang Prabang. Since that time, Laos has suffered from constant diplomatic and military pressure from its neighbors, Thailand and Vietnam. In 1700 Sai Ong Hue, a Lao prince who had lived in exile in Vietnam, marched on Vientiane at the head of a Vietnamese army; he took the city and proclaimed himself king. Two hundred and forty-five years later, another Lao prince, named Souphanouvong, was escorted back to his country by a contingent of Vietnamese military officers and soldiers in order to begin building an independence movement now known as the Pathet Lao (Lao State). I was a member of that contingent.

Prince Souphanouvong had arrived in Hue on the afternoon of September 30, 1945, bringing with him a letter of recommendation (which served also as an order) to the Resistance and Administrative Committee for Central Vietnam (*Uy Ban Khang Chien Hanh Chinh Trung Bo*—the Viet Minh administration in Central Vietnam).[1] That night a full alert was declared in the ancient imperial city and capital of Central Vietnam. The local Viet Minh committee had received information that the Japanese troops, who were still in *de facto* control of the city while they waited for the Allied powers to arrive and disarm them, were planning to round up the Vietnamese revolutionaries and promote a pro-Bao Dai coup. I was then 22 years old and was deputy director for special operations of the *Giai Phong Quan*

1. Hue was at that time the seat of the government of Tran Trong Kim, which had been formed after the Japanese *coup d'état* of March 9, 1945. The Tran Trong Kim government resigned after the Japanese defeat, and the Viet Minh took power in Hue on August 22. Emperor Bao Dai abdicated August 24, 1945.

(Liberation Army) General Staff. In the dim light of my command post located in the garden of the General Staff headquarters—formerly the home of the French Résident—I was introduced for the first time to Prince Souphanouvong.[2] He spoke in perfect French. I directed him and his aide-de-camp to a safe place where they spent the night. The next day, October 1, 1945, six other officers and I were called to report to the director of special operations.[3] We were told that we had been selected "to escort His Royal Highness Prince Souphanouvong of Laos back to Vientiane," in accordance with the instructions of President Ho Chi Minh. We were permitted to take with us five other soldiers, 15 old rifles, and one equally old Bren machine gun—a degree of foreign assistance which was indeed generous considering the resources of the Liberation Army at that time.

We left immediately; I did not even have time to say good-bye to my parents, who were then living about 12 miles south of Hue. We were all packed into a ten-year-old bus which stopped nearly every other mile. We were often forced to push it, and we all had to walk, Lao Prince and Vietnamese commoners alike. I was not at all familiar with Laos, except that it was said to be "a land far away from home where the climate is inclement and malaria raging." (This proved to be incorrect: the weather in Laos was better than that of my hot and humid hometown of Hue, and there were fewer mosquitoes.) We made our first stop the following day at Khe-sanh.[4] There, in a solemn voice Prince Souphanouvong ordered all of us to take off our Liberation Army insignias (a gold star against a red back-

2. I had immediately recognized his aide-de-camp *cum* personal secretary as Le Phung Thoi, a classmate of mine from high school in Hue. Le, born in Laos, had been a medical student at the University of Hanoi.
3. The Directorate of Special Operations was in charge of analyzing all military intelligence and organizing commando attacks.
4. In Quang-tri province at the borders of Vietnam and Laos, and the same place where the U.S. Marines were besieged in 1968 by the North Vietnamese Army and NLF forces. According to Richard J. Barnet, director of the Institute for Policy Studies, President Johnson gave "serious consideration to the use of nuclear tactical weapons to relieve the garrison." Barnet, Address at Business Executives Move for Peace Meeting in Washington, D.C., May 20, 1970.

ground) and to replace them with the Laotian badges (a three-headed white elephant on a red background) which he had had made in Hanoi. From that moment on we became his personal guard.

Our relationship, which had been very formal the first day, grew more intimate. On stops along the road after an uneventful patrol, we would sit down beside a stream and he would tell us about his country and his people, and about the Lao kings of the past whom he admired: Fa Gnoum (r. 1353–1373), Souligna Vongsa (r. 1637–1694), Sai Ong Hue (r. 1707–1735) and Anou, for whom Souphanouvong's second son was named. He would tell us of his admiration for President Ho Chi Minh and for the young Army of Liberation of Vietnam. Although he was not yet the master of his country and his future seemed uncertain at best, Prince Souphanouvong was already preparing plans for the development of the Mekong valley and the Bolovens Plateau.[5] (His plans were not very different from those of the present UN project for the area.) His patriotism was intense and his dreams for the future of Laos were boundless. He talked very little, however, about himself or his family. The vital details of his background are matters of public record. Born on July 12, 1912, Prince Souphanouvong was the youngest of twenty sons. (His father, Prince Boun Khong, had several wives.) One of his half-brothers is the 68-year-old prime minister of Laos, Prince Souvanna Phouma. Souphanouvong first attended the prestigious Lycée Albert Sarraut in Hanoi and later went to France to study engineering at the famous Ecole des Ponts et Chaussées. He was politically active in France during the period of the Front Populaire and made friends with many Vietnamese students.

In 1939 after his graduation, he returned to Indochina, and entered the French Public Works Service, where he was "as-

5. In 1910, the fertile Bolovens Plateau became a center of resistance, led by the Komadom clan, against the French. Sithon Komadom is now deputy commander of the Pathet Lao Army and is considered one of its best fighters. In May 1970, after the U.S. invasion of Cambodia, the Pathet Lao occupied the two key towns of the area, Attopeu and Saravane, thus opening a river supply route from North Vietnam through southern Laos to northern Cambodia.

tonished to see the piteous position which the Indochinese administration was offering its most gifted children" (as he wrote in an autobiographical article in 1943). He was posted in Nhatrang, a lovely beach town in South Vietnam, and there he met Le Thi Ky Nam, the beautiful daughter of a hotel owner. Contrary to many stories circulated in the West—for example, that Souphanouvong "married a Vietnamese girl from Hanoi who is said to have been a committed Communist"[6]—she came from a bourgeois family in the South and had attended an exclusive girls school in Hue. They were married in 1939.

Three years later he was posted to Vinh, Vietnam. Already an ardent nationalist, he contacted his old friends who were now members of the Ho Chi Minh cabinet, particularly Dao Trong Kim, minister of public works. Through them he was introduced to President Ho Chi Minh, who subsequently decided to assist him.

Souphanouvong was strongly built, handsome, and had an enormous appetite. He worked very hard, and even in the jungle he would spend the whole night reading and writing. Although he was democratic and easy in his manners, he was very conscious of his title and of his position as a leader of Laos. We would always address him very politely as "Your Royal Highness." Although his life and his survival depended on us, he made it clear that he was the only boss and that we should report all our activities to him.

On the evening of October 7, 1945, after brief stops in Phalane and Dong Hene, we arrived in Savannakhet. We had covered 200 miles in seven days. There we were given perhaps the biggest reception of our whole journey. My first impression of Savannakhet was that it was a Vietnamese town: we heard Vietnamese voices, and the crowd of thousands who greeted us was largely Vietnamese. We were housed at the chao khoueng (governor's) residence, and we prepared immediately to work on putting together the skeleton of the Lao Liberation Army.

6. Bernard B. Fall, "The Pathet Lao," in Robert Scalapino, ed., *The Communist Revolution in Asia* (Englewood Cliffs, N.J.: Prentice-Hall, 1965), p. 175.

Prince Souphanouvong's position was not an easy one. Savannakhet had already been "liberated" by Oune Sananikone, of that powerful Sananikone family which played such an important role in postwar Lao politics. Oune was a former veterinarian who had fled to Thailand during the Thai-French conflict in 1940–1941 and been commissioned as a lieutenant in the Royal Thai Army. During World War II, he worked with the Free Thai (Serei Thai) under Pridi Phanomyong.[7] After the defeat of Japan, he returned to Laos and with Thai help had begun to organize the Laotian resistance movement in his hometown. He had a number of followers among young Laotians and challenged Souphanouvong's role as leader of the Laotian independence movement.

The Viet Kieu Cuu Quoc Hoi Thai Lao (Vietnamese Overseas Association in Thailand and Laos for the Salvation of the Fatherland)[8] was also well organized in Savannakhet, and had

7. After the Japanese defeat, Pridi became prime minister. He was overthrown by the military, and has lived in Canton (China) since 1949. He is reported (*Le Monde,* May 28, 1970) now to be in Paris.

8. In May 1941 the Indochinese Communist Party (ICP) convened the 8th session of its central committee in Tsin Tsi at the borders of Vietnam and China. Presided over by Ho Chi Minh, the meeting resulted in the formation of the Vietnam Doc Lap Dong Minh Hoi (Allied Association for the Independence of Vietnam) popularly known as the Viet Minh. The policy of the Viet Minh was to create numerous Hoi Cuu Quoc (Associations for the Salvation of the Fatherland) which served as a broad national united front against the Japanese and the French.

In the same year, in Udorn (a town in Thailand, opposite Vientiane in Laos) the Viet Kieu Cuu Quoc Hoi Thai Lao (VKCQHTL) was formed in exactly the same pattern as the Viet Minh at home. Many of the VKCQHTL were veteran revolutionaries. The various VKCQHTL worked openly in Thailand and secretly in Laos until 1945. The VKCQHTL headquarters previously located in Sakon Nakhon (northeast Thailand) moved to Laos, to Thakhet, a town opposite the Thai city of Nakhon Phanom. In November 1945 it moved to Vientiane, the administrative capital of Laos.

Once established in Laos, where there lived over 100,000 Vietnamese (mostly businessmen and officials in the former French administration), the VKCQHTL grew very fast. The Vietnamese emigrés and the young Vietnamese born in Laos had always retained their emotional attachment to Vietnam. For them, dreams of independence, liberty, and happiness became realities with the Viet Minh achievement of power in Hanoi. They supported Ho Chi Minh wholeheartedly and organized themselves politically and militarily. Arms were purchased from Thailand. At that time, the Pridi

its own armed self-defense units. There had been incidents between the Vietnamese and the Lao. The Vietnamese community was naturally very proud of us, the revolutionaries from home, and most of them thought of us as the vanguard of the coming conquering army. The Laotian leaders (except Prince Souphanouvong, who always trusted us completely) looked upon us with great suspicion. We had not anticipated these new factors, and they made our job very delicate and difficult. At first, our anomalous position (as Vietnamese in Laotian uniforms) was understood by neither the Laotians nor the Vietnamese.

Eventually we sat down and negotiated. After two days of debates and compromise, it was decided that an Army for the Liberation and Defense of Laos should be formed. Decree number 46/Issara signed on the second day of the rising moon of the eleventh month of the Buddhist year 2488 (corresponding to October 8, 1945) by Prince Souphanouvong was the birth certificate of what is now the Pathet Lao Army. Thao Oune and Souphanouvong merged their men to form the command and the staff of that army. The commander in chief was Souphanouvong. Thao Oune, a very proud, even vain, but goodhearted man, had sensed that Souphanouvong had our support and the support of the leaders of the well-organized and prosperous Vietnamese community, and had accepted a position of "commandant en second." The chief of staff at that time was

---

government and the Thai people, emotionally anti-French, were sympathetic to the Vietnamese struggle for freedom. The leaders of the VKCQHTL kept in close touch with members of the Thai government such as Nai Tieng Serikan, Thong In Buripat, Thawi Udorn, Chamlong Daoruang, and Thong Kantatham. After the overthrow of Pridi, these leaders, all of them from the northeast region of Thailand at the Lao border, were accused of having separatist tendencies. They were mysteriously liquidated by the Thai police in 1951.

The most important leaders of the VKCQHTL were members of the Indochinese Communist Party. Some had fled Vietnam after the failure of the 1930 uprisings against the French and the onset of the "White Terror" repression in the rebellious provinces. Ho Chi Minh himself was in Bangkok in August 1928 and had spent some time in Thailand organizing among his countrymen. He lived in Udorn, Sakon Nakhon, and Nakhon Rashima. He left Thailand in June 1929 and returned the next year for a quick visit to Udorn.

Phoumi Nosavan, a trusted follower of Thao Oune.[9] His adviser was Nguyen Chuong, an officer in my contingent from Hue and commander of Souphanouvong's personal guard. There were the usual army services: personnel, armament, equipment, liaison, cadre training, supply, transport, and the *Service de Renseignements* (Intelligence Service), officially headed by a Lao named Thao Toulane.

As in other services, the Vietnamese officers who were in Prince Souphanouvong's personal guard became advisers. With two other Vietnamese officers, I was named adviser for the intelligence service. This was later to grow into an almost independent agency similar to the CIA and under the direct control of Souphanouvong. We were kept very busy, working and training the Laotians and the Vietnamese in the daytime[10] and going on military operations most of the nights. We had information at the time that the French were returning and dropping men and equipment into the jungle; however, we did not have any serious engagements with them. Looking back, I am amazed that we could do so much in such a brief time with limited means, but revolutionary fervor was high.

We stayed a week in Savannakhet and then proceeded north by motor launch on the Mekong River to Thakhek. The Vietnamese community there was even more prosperous than in Savannakhet, and Souphanouvong did not meet with any serious challenge. He was very happy because his wife and two sons had just arrived from Vietnam. This was accomplished through the courtesy of the Chinese Kuomintang army. Although there were very few Japanese in Laos, the Chinese army sent in two divisions to disarm them. Madame Souphanouvong came to Laos with an advance group of Chinese officers.

We immediately investigated the military situation, recruited

9. He was a physical education instructor at the time. Later, as general, he became the right-wing leader in Laos. He is now living in exile in Bangkok.

10. The training of the Lao was done mostly in French, and all papers and orders were also in French. However, we all learned Lao, and most of us could speak it after a month or so.

more Laotians,[11] and planned to extend the radius of security beyond at least twenty miles. The French who had been parachuted back into Laos after the Japanese defeat were building their resistance zones, the strongest of which was at Lamplaimat, about 10 miles north of Thakhek. The second day we were there, we planned the assault on Lamplaimat. Two days later, Prince Souphanouvong held a Lao ceremony of well-wishing, called *baci,* for the important people of Thakhek, and at midnight, when the *baci* was over, we left for the fight. We attacked the French post at 4 A.M. on October 26, 1945. Prince Souphanouvong led us in his first battle, accompanied by his eldest son Ariya.[12] We decided to withdraw no later than 6 A.M. in order to avoid being pursued by French planes. The attack was a success, for the French were caught by surprise, but we lost several very bright young Vietnamese. We did not know the extent of the French casualties. They did not know that they were being attacked by the general staff and entire army of the newly independent Laos, not more than 100 officers and men in all, including Prince Souphanouvong and his son. Our attack in true guerrilla fashion was somewhat ridiculous, but we had little choice. We needed to enhance our prestige and to build the morale of the population. The situation in Laos at that time was such that the French occupied the countryside and waged guerrilla warfare with modern weapons, while we occupied the cities and waged conventional warfare with primitive arms.

From Thakhek, we moved to Vientiane, again by motor launch, and arrived on October 29. There, in the administrative

11. One of these recruits was Singkapo Chounlamany, who was to replace Phoumi Nosavan as chief of staff in November 1945. Singkapo is now commander of the Lao Army of which Souphanouvong is commander in chief. Another recruit from Savannakhet was Kaysone Phomvihan, Souphanouvong's present minister of defense. Born of a Vietnamese mother and a Lao father he studied in Hanoi (medical school) and was close to Vietnamese revolutionaries.

12. He was then 6 years old, and very intelligent. (His brother Anou was 4.) He was trained in Moscow and China. Recent rumors say he was killed in a battle in the Plain of Jars.

capital of Laos, a Lao Issara (Free Lao) government had been
in existence for two months (since August 18, 1945). The
prime minister was Phaya Khammao, a former governor who
greatly distrusted the Vietnamese. The real leader, however,
was Prince Phetsarath, the viceroy, who was Prince Souphanouvong's eldest half-brother. Souphanouvong's position was difficult, and his main problems were to make himself accepted by
the government, to legalize his military organization, and to retain military control of the army. Here, as in Savannakhet, the
support he enjoyed from the local Vietnamese community (and
its guerrilla soldiers and self-defense units) was instrumental
in the success of his negotiations.

Eventually, he was officially recognized as the legal commander of the Army of the Liberation and Defense of Laos
which was officially recreated by Decree Number 63 of October 30, 1945, signed by Prime Minister Khammao. Prince Souphanouvong also became minister of foreign affairs. Another half-
brother, Prince Souvanna Phouma, became minister of public
works. I remained the adviser to the Service des Renseignements, which was reorganized and provided me with a powerful
base of action.[13] On October 30 a Convention militaire was
signed between the Laotian government and the Democratic
Republic of Vietnam.[14] This was in fact a formalization of the
existing realities and a private arrangement between the Vietnamese and Prince Souphanouvong, the only Laotian leader
completely backed by the Vietnamese.

In November we received alarming news of an imminent attack on Thakhek by the French. Souphanouvong left Vientiane
for Thakhek on November 5, along with his entire Vietnamese
staff. He had long thought that Thakhek was the key city in Laos

13. The Service was given power over all police and intelligence networks,
and the power of the adviser was also greatly strengthened. The Lao director
could not take any actions without his presence and approval. (See decree
Number 1/ALD, dated November 1, 1946.)
14. The Democratic Republic of Vietnam was represented in Vientiane by
Tran Duc Vinh, a young leader of the VKCQHTL. He had participated in
the Viet Minh National Congress on August 6, 1945, at Tran Trao, north
Vietnam. (He was killed in 1948, on one of his trips between Laos and north
Vietnam, by a French air raid.)

for the development of his revolution, since it was the center of communications with the Vietnamese Fourth Military Interzone (i.e., the northern part of Central Vietnam). On the eve of his departure, he called me in for a private conversation. He gave me 5,000 Vietnamese piasters (we had never received any salary) and asked me to stay on in Vientiane. He said, "You must remain in Vientiane because the situation here is very complex. I know that besides your military abilities, you are also a good diplomat. Your duties will be to represent me in the government, to report to me on all governmental activities, and above all to organize the *Service des Renseignements*." He handed me a copy of Decree Number 1/ALD, which provided for the reorganization of the *Service*.

I felt very sad, almost rejected. I was the only Vietnamese officer from Vietnam who was left behind. However, I found consolation in the warm support and affection I received daily from my own countrymen. Their patriotism was very touching and very deep. Practically all Vietnamese, men and women, old and young, were enrolled in the Quan Du Kich (guerrilla army) of the Dan Quan Tu Ve (People's Self-Defense Army). The Viet Minh forces in Vientiane were strong and well organized; their commander, Vu Huu Binh, was very capable and spoke fluent Lao, Thai, French, and some English.[15]

In order to coordinate all Laotian and Vietnamese military activities I organized the Lao-Viet Allied Armies General Staff (Tong Bo Tham Muu Lien Quan Lao Viet), headquartered in the former home of the French general who had commanded French forces in Laos. Officially, I was the adviser to the general staff; in reality, I was the actual head. My Lao colleague was not really competent and only signed papers; however, there were many young capable Lao officers.[16] Our immediate problem was armament. I often went to Thailand to buy weap-

15. Born in North Vietnam, he was a warrant officer in the French Indochinese Guard in Vientiane. He deserted to Thailand during the French-Thai conflict of 1940–1941 and was commissioned as a lieutenant in the Thai army. He joined the Viet Minh organization in Thailand in 1941. In 1963 he was Consul General of North Vietnam in Rangoon.

16. One of them, Khamking Souvanlasy, was to become Laos' ambassador to Tokyo and to Washington in the 1960s.

ons, traveling as a civilian Lao, under the name of Thao Somsanith. The money came from the Vietnamese community; the Laotian treasury was empty, or nearly so. We tried to extend our control of the area around Vientiane, which was itself relatively secure. The biggest battle we fought was in early 1946 in order to occupy Tha Deua, a landing post opposite the Thai town of Nong Khai.

As much as I wished to spend my time with the troops, especially with the young Laotian officers, most of my days, even nights, were taken up by diplomatic negotiations. There was a plot among some Laotian cabinet officials aimed at excluding Souphanouvong from the government, and I had to deal with this. Friction between Vietnamese and Laotians increased, apparently for no serious reason. I was trying to promote the closest possible relations between our two peoples and convinced Prince Souvanna Phouma (then acting prime minister) to create (by Decree Number 82 of January 20, 1946) a Lao-Vietnamese Bureau headed by myself and staffed with both Vietnamese and Lao. On November 30, 1945, a governmental decree had already established the Vientiane Defense Staff; this staff was strengthened by another decree of January 26, 1946. Its Laotian members included Thao Sing, minister of defense; his deputy, Thao Tham; and two senior Laotian officers. On the Vietnamese side were Vu Huu Binh; his deputy Tran Van Hoan; and myself, again as an adviser.

Another problem was relations with the Nationalist Chinese Army of Occupation. We were aware that they were not friendly to the Viet Minh; however, we wanted their departure postponed, and used them to delay the return of the French and allow us more time to consolidate. One day in November a Chinese three-star general asked me to come and see him. He demanded that I pay him (not his government) two million Vietnamese piasters in gold; otherwise, he said, his troops would disarm "the Viet Minh guerrillas." I told him politely that I had no money and no power, but that I would report the matter to the "highest authority" in Hanoi. After a moment he said, "You'd better forget it." However, we had our plans ready for any emergency which might be provoked by the Nationalist Chinese;

we did not take them seriously and thought that we could disarm their 300-man garrison any time we wished. I proposed the declaration of martial law, which the Laotian government accepted and signed on November 13, 1945.

Submerged by work, I had had no time to make contact with anyone back home. This had not been necessary; however, on December 29, 1945, I sent the following telegram (we could still send cables through the normal post office) to Phan Tu Lang, the chief of staff in Hue:[17]

1. The Front against French imperialism enters a decisive period. Enemy wanted to extend his control but had to restrict his activities because of heroic resistance of Lao-Viet Liberation Armies. French troops are using most barbarous methods, burning houses, destroying property to terrorize population in the countryside. Our troops' morale very high. Have applied methods of guerrilla warfare with success. Population strongly supports the army.

2. Lao people begin to be conscious of their role and to fight for independence. Our compatriots sacrifice lives and fortunes in struggle for the liberty of Indochina. Economic situation very grave. Please make our problems known at home and help us find a solution to economic problems. Please also publicize the fighting spirit of the Lao troops.

3. Vietnamese community very eager to receive news from home and absolutely obey orders from government.

4. Lao-Viet cooperation progressing well in all fields. Anti-French Front could be enlarged. Please make our people at home aware of importance of Lao-Viet unity and of heroism of Lao-Viet troops.

Tran Van Dinh
General Staff
Joint Lao-Viet Army,
Vientiane

The Tet (traditional Vietnamese New Year) of 1946 was the first I had spent outside my own country and away from home,

---

17. The commander of Central Vietnam Liberation Army was Tran Van Tra, now identified as Tran Nam Trung, commander of the National Liberation Forces in South Vietnam. He was born in Quang-ngai (South Vietnam) and organized the guerrilla base in Ba-to (Quang-ngai) in the 1930s.

but I found country and family in the warmth of my countrymen and their affection toward me. On New Year's Day (January 29, 1946), I sent the following cable to the Government of
the Democratic Republic of Vietnam in Hanoi: "On the occasion of the New Year of Independence of Vietnam, on behalf of
the Lao-Viet armed forces, I would like to send my respectful
wishes to President Ho Chi Minh and the members of the Government. May the New Year bring to our country total independence and progress." These were the first and last communications which I sent to Vietnam from Laos by regular
post. War broke out in Hanoi in December 1946.

On March 21, 1946, the French troops, now strongly reinforced, attacked the town of Thakhek with tanks and planes.
The attack began at 10 A.M. After a fierce battle, the Lao-Viet
regular troops crossed the Mekong into Thailand. Their retreat
was covered by the heroic fighting of the local self-defense
units, which were composed totally of young Vietnamese. The
French bombing and artillery left thousands of casualties among
the civilian population of the town. Prince Souphanouvong was
himself wounded by a bullet from a French plane (a British
Spitfire) when he crossed the river.[18] Thakhek was perhaps the
bloodiest battle fought on Laotian territory.

By March, Vientiane had also been encircled by the French.
We had decided not to fight, and careful preparations were
made to move the entire government and all of the civilian
population to Thailand. This evacuation began in the middle of
April, and on April 24, 1946, the French troops entered Vientiane. All the cities in Laos were then in French hands. The
Thai government and people, who were still very hostile toward
the French, provided us with all kinds of assistance; within a
month, we were able to function again. Although the circumstances were different, we were happy to have the time to organize ourselves politically and militarily for the long protracted war which was the only war we knew how to fight,

18. A Vietnamese officer who was with him was killed. He was Le Thieu
Huy, a former student in Hanoi and the son of a famous scholar, Le Thuoc.

rather than having to conduct part-guerrilla, part-conventional warfare from old French houses.

After a few weeks in a hospital in Nakhon Phanom (the Thai town opposite Thakhek), Prince Souphanouvong was in good physical condition again. In the middle of April, he went up to Nong Khai (the Thai town opposite Vientiane) to talk with the members of his government, now in exile. I saw him there often. His spirits were high, and his optimism was evident, in contrast with his colleagues in the government, who were dispirited. He prepared his plans for the long war. He wanted to organize an intelligence service all along the Mekong River which would gather data on the French in Laos before guerrilla warfare was begun against them. On April 29 he signed a certificate (written in Lao, not in French as before) which entrusted me with that heavy duty.

Prince Souphanouvong was well aware of the fact that sooner or later his exiled government would compromise with the French and return to Vientiane. More than ever before, he was confident of his success and of the help he would receive from the Vietnamese revolutionaries. At the end of 1946 he and his family moved to Bangkok, where the Laotian government-in-exile had established its headquarters. Prince Souphanouvong and his family lived in a house on Sathorn Road, a few blocks from the American and Russian embassies; the government headquarters was on Ron Ruang Road near the Central Railway Station.

On October 24, 1949, three years later, as Souphanouvong predicted, the Lao Issara government-in-exile announced its dissolution. The following month a French air transport plane brought Prince Souvanna Phouma and 25 members of the Laotian resistance back to Vientiane. Leaving his wife and children behind in Bangkok (they later joined him, coming via Hong Kong), Prince Souphanouvong set out on foot for the headquarters of Ho Chi Minh in the jungles of North Vietnam. With Vietnamese assistance, he set up the Lao Liberation Committee. On August 13, 1950, he convened the First Resistance Congress somewhere in the jungles of Laos. This congress elected a National Resistance government, which he headed. It adopted a twelve-point manifesto, at the bottom of which appeared the words "Pathet Lao" (Lao State). Pathet Lao henceforth became the name of the Laotian resistance movement, first against the French and then against the United States.

The last time I saw Souphanouvong was late in December 1949; however, my admiration and respect for him have continued throughout the subsequent years. Having followed his activities since that time at a distance, I have no doubt that he still is what he started out to be—a staunch Laotian patriot. He is not a puppet of anyone, neither his own party nor Hanoi. Having an acute sense of history and of reality, he is cooperating with the Democratic Republic of Vietnam in order to build a peaceful, prosperous, and neutral Laos. Under his direction, the Pathet Lao and its army is a force to be reckoned with, a fact that sooner or later the United States will have to recognize.

27

The Pathet Lao Peace Plan

Translated by Brian Fegan

Liberated Zone of Laos
March 6, 1970

For a number of years, the American imperialists have pursued a ceaseless policy of intervention and aggression in Laos, with the intent of converting this country into a neocolony and a military base of the United States in Southeast Asia.

In contravention of its obligations under the Geneva Accords of 1954 and those of 1962 on Laos, the United States has trampled on the independence and sovereignty, and undermined the peace and neutrality of Laos. In the course of the last eight years American intervention and aggression in Laos have become increasingly brazen. The United States has, by a military *coup d'état,* overthrown the Government of National Union, which had received the royal investiture and had been recognized by the 1962 Geneva Conference on Laos; it set up a puppet administration, headed by Prince Souvanna Phouma and practicing a so-called peace and neutrality policy. It is through the agency of this administration that the United States has conducted a "special war" in Laos, carried out bombing of Laos' territory, and used puppet troops to multiply attacks on the regions controlled by patriotic Laotian forces.

Faithful to the aspirations of the Laotian people for a peaceful, independent, neutral, democratic, unified, and prosperous Laos, the Laotian Patriotic Front has always strictly observed the 1962 Geneva Accords on Laos. In close alliance with Laotian patriotic neutralist forces, and together with the whole people, it has, using its right to legitimate self-defense, struggled reso-

---

From the Central Committee of the Laotian Patriotic Front concerning a political solution to the Laos problem. (Made public by Phao Phimphachan, director of the L.P.F. Information Bureau in Hanoi, and circulated by the *Bulletin of the A.V.I.* of March 6, 1970.)

lutely against the U.S. "special war," fought against the encroachments of the Americans and their lackeys, inflicted on them well-justified blows, and scored victories of ever-increasing magnitude.

While struggling against American intervention and aggression, the Laotian Patriotic Front has repeatedly shown its willingness for a peaceful solution to the Laotian problem. Its 12-point political program and the maintenance of its delegation in Vientiane are clear proof of that willingness.

But the United States and the Vientiane administration have turned a deaf ear to all the reasonable and logical proposals of the Laotian Patriotic Front. Especially since Nixon became president, the United States has escalated the war in Laos with increased obstinacy.

The United States has brought to Laos reinforcements of American and Thai troops, armaments, and military supplies. They have expanded the puppet army, and the "special forces" under the command of Vang Pao have hurled ceaseless attacks against regions controlled by patriotic forces from the north to the south of the country. They have, moreover, mobilized a modern air power to carry out saturation bombing against Laotian territory, thus committing crimes of unprecedented savagery against its people.

Since August 1969, the United States has put into action around fifty battalions of puppet troops and Thai mercenaries, and launched operation *Cukiet,* with the aim of grabbing the Plain of Jars in the Xieng Khouang region. Meanwhile they unleashed numerous encroaching operations into the liberated regions in central and lower Laos. More seriously, since February 17, 1970, they have carried out massive bombing by B–52s and other aircraft against the Plain of Jars–Xieng Khouang liberated zone, thus destroying, in the same way as in middle and lower Laos, hundreds of villages and hamlets and savagely massacring the civilian populations.

But the Laotian armed forces and population, firmly resolved to defend the liberated zone, have smashed all the attacks launched by the Americans and their lackeys in the Plain of Jars and other regions. They have also annihilated a significant proportion of the "special forces" commanded and organized by the United States and dealt a severe blow to the prestige of the U.S. Air Force.

With the aim of disguising the Nixon administration's escalation of the war in Laos, the United States and the Vientiane administration have carried on a campaign of slander against the Laotian Patriotic Front and the Democratic Republic of Vietnam, while trumpeting their assertions of "peace" in order to deceive American and world public opinion, which nevertheless actively condemns the Nixon administration for its policy of intensifying the war of aggression in Laos.

This escalation of the war of aggression by the Nixon Administration has provoked the present worsening of tension in Laos and presented a grave threat to peace and security in Indochina and Southeast Asia.

In the face of the present tension in Laos, the Laotian Patriotic Front declares the need to put an end to the American war and to find a political solution to the Laotian problem.

The Laotian Patriotic Front's position is that the peaceful settlement of the Laotian problem must be based on the 1962 Geneva Accords on Laos and the realities of the present situation in Laos. In more specific form:

1. All countries must respect the sovereignty, independence, neutrality, unity, and territorial integrity of the kingdom of Laos, in accordance with the provisions of the 1962 Geneva Accords on Laos. The United States must end its intervention and aggression in Laos and its escalation of the war; it must cease all bombing of the territory of Laos, withdraw from Laos all American advisers and military personnel with their arms and military supplies, and renounce the use of military bases in Thailand and Thai mercenaries for the purpose of aggression in Laos. The United States must cease to use Laotian territory for purposes of intervention and aggression against other countries.

2. In conformity with the 1962 Geneva Accords, the kingdom of Laos is to abstain from being a member of military alliances with other countries and to permit no foreign country to set up military bases on its territory or to introduce troops and military personnel.

The kingdom of Laos is to apply an external policy of peace

and neutrality, establish relations with other countries on the basis of the five principles of peaceful coexistence, and accept aid which is not tied to political conditions from all countries. It is to establish relations of friendship and neighborliness with the other countries of Indochina on the basis of the five principles of peaceful coexistence, the 1954 Geneva Accords on Indochina, and the 1962 Geneva Accords on Laos. In regard to the DRV and the Republic of South Vietnam, it is to respect the independence, sovereignty, unity, and territorial integrity of Vietnam. In regard to the kingdom of Cambodia, it is to respect its independence, sovereignty, neutrality, and its territorial integrity within its present frontiers.

3. It will respect the throne, organize free and democratic general elections, elect a national assembly, and form a democratic government of national union truly representative of the Laotian people of different ethnic groups, build a peaceful, independent, neutral, democratic, unified, and prosperous Laos.

4. In the period between the reestablishment of peace and the general elections to form a national assembly, interested parties will hold, in a spirit of national harmony, equality, and mutual respect, a political consultative conference constituting representatives of interested Laotian parties to settle Laotian affairs and form a provisional coalition government. The parties will agree to the establishment of a security zone to permit the normal functioning of the political consultative conference and the provisional coalition government, and to smash all attempts at sabotage or pressure from forces within or outside Laos.

5. The unification of Laos will be achieved by consultations between the Laotian parties, based on the principles of equality and national harmony. Until the unification of Laos, each interested party must refrain from the use of force to violate or encroach upon the zone placed under the control of any other party. The pro-American forces must withdraw immediately from the regions that they have illegally occupied. As for the populations which they have forced to leave their villages, the pro-American forces must return them to their places of origin and compensate them for all the misery which has been inflicted on them. Each party agrees to refrain from all discrimination

and reprisals against persons having collaborated with any other party.

The position set forth above by the Laotian Patriotic Front concerning the solution to the Laotian problem is a response to the ardent aspirations of the Laotian people and accords with the interests of peace and security in Indochina, in Southeast Asia, and in the world. It is the proper basis for settlement of the Laotian problem.

The Laotian problem must be worked out between the interested Laotian parties. In order to create conditions which will permit the interested Laotian parties to meet, the United States must immediately end its escalation of the war and completely and unconditionally cease bombing Laotian territory.

The Laotian people profoundly desire independence, liberty, and peace. If the United States persists in its aggressive aims, the Laotian Patriotic Front, the Laotian patriotic neutralist forces, and the Laotian people are resolved to carry on the fight until victory is complete.

The Laotian Patriotic Front earnestly calls on all ethnic groups among the Laotian people to close ranks around the fighting alliance formed by the Laotian Patriotic Front and the Laotian patriotic neutralist forces, to redouble their vigilance, and be ready and determined to smash all military stratagems and deceptive maneuvers by the United States and its lackeys, so that they may defend the liberated zone, safeguard their fundamental national rights, and contribute to maintenance of peace in Indochina and in Southeast Asia.

The Laotian Patriotic Front earnestly calls on all governments dedicated to peace and justice, the American people, and the peoples of the world to give their powerful support to the just struggle of the Laotian people and to demand firmly from the United States the cessation of the war of aggression in Laos, and cease immediately all bombing against Laotian territory.

Strengthened by the immense sympathy and powerful support of the peoples of the world, the entire Laotian people, closely united, will undoubtedly crush the American aggressors and their lackeys, and will successfully build a peaceful, independent, neutral, democratic, unified, and prosperous Laos.

28

The Pathet Lao's Revolutionary Program: Noam Chomsky Interviews Phao Phimphachanh

In April 1970, Professor Noam Chomsky interviewed Phao Phimphachanh, member of the Pathet Lao Central Committee and director of their information office in Hanoi. Although the following is a direct transcript, there is a certain amount of distortion since the exchanges were first translated from Lao into Vietnamese and then into English.

QUESTION: Could you explain to us the background of the present situation in Laos as you see it?

ANSWER: We have passed through our fifth long year of struggle against the U.S. aggressors, and we have scored a certain number of successes. We rely on ourselves and have the support of all the progressive peoples of the world, including those of the United States. Please convey our greetings and best wishes to the progressive American people. We have had lots of trouble and difficulty, but despite our long struggle little is known about our situation outside of Laos.

Laos is situated in the Indochina peninsula. It is a large country with a small population. Most of Laos is mountainous, but there are small plains along the rivers. There are three majority peoples and about 60 minority peoples. The majority peoples are Lao, and they belong to three groups: Lao Lung (lowland), Lao Tung (middle altitudes in the highlands), and Lao Xung (high altitudes). It is a potentially rich country, but we had to live under French rule for over 60 years.

Since the end of French rule, there has been a period of continuous struggle. The three majority peoples struggled during the colonial period, but they had different leaders which led separate struggles against the French. There was no unity, and therefore the struggles failed. In 1945 the first success was achieved. However, the French returned and a second struggle ensued for nine years until the 1954 Geneva Conference ended the fighting.

After 1954, the French withdrew and the Americans came. The Americans wanted to make Laos one of its new Southeast Asian military bases, and they used many maneuvers to disguise their goals and to sabotage the revolutionary forces. That is why we can say that the U.S. imperialists did not abide by the 1954 and 1962 agreements and why the United States threatened the independence and territorial integrity of Laos. The U.S. imperialists use Laotian to fight Laotian, and they have continually intensified the war.

When Nixon came to power he continued the policy of the former administration. Since Nixon came into office, American intervention has become deeper and deeper. The puppet army now has 60,000 men, with 12,000 "advisers," of which 1,200 are Green Berets. Formerly, in Laos there were only the rightist forces, but now there is also Vang Pao's army which carries out the direct orders of the Americans. The U.S. imperialists are building the Vang Pao forces into a strong army, totally supported and trained by Americans. It now numbers 30,000 and its headquarters are at Udorn Air Base in Thailand, code number HQ333.

QUESTION: How have matters changed under the Nixon administration?

ANSWER: Since the Nixon administration came to power it has tried to strengthen the areas of Sam Thong and Long Cheng and make them the second capital of Laos. These mountain bases did not even exist before 1964. Before the Nixon administration took office, the Vang Pao forces were bandits whose work was sabotage in the liberated areas, but now they have been consolidated and are building up their forces under CIA direction.

Since May 1963 there has been bombing in Laos. The number of sorties at that time were about 20–30 a day, but by now there are 630 sorties a day of which 24 are flown by B–52s. They are using all kinds of weapons—bombs, phosphorous, and chemical defoliants. That about sums up the military situation today.

QUESTION: Could you outline for us the present political situation in Laos?

ANSWER: The Vientiane government is reactionary, but not enough for Nixon. Therefore, he is trying to overthrow it. Since

Nixon came to power, he has tried to consolidate the military forces and the reactionary forces and begin an attack on the liberated zones from both the ground and the air. He uses propaganda to hide these actions. Although he speaks about peace, he has introduced more Thai troops recently. He makes allegations against the DRV [Democratic Republic of Vietnam]. Previously, during the "nibbling campaign" [reference is to 1964–1968] there were only 1,000 Thai troops, but during the *Cukiet* campaign the number was raised to 10,000.

QUESTION: Would you describe for us what took place during the *Cukiet* campaign?

ANSWER: The *Cukiet* campaign began in 1969 and ended in February 1970. The name *Cukiet* was used by the United States and RLG [Royal Laotian Government], and it means "save their honor." The meaning is, of course, to save their honor after numerous defeats. The *Cukiet* campaign was full of atrocities. This campaign was the largest they have ever launched, and it followed the plan of "kill all, burn all, destroy all"—the three alls.

The *Cukiet* campaign is the realization of the new Nixon Doctrine. There were new tactics; for example, the helicopter transport of soldiers. Participating in the campaign were 100 planes and 30–50 battalions of Thai troops, all under CIA direction. In this campaign severe crimes were committed. They burned down villages and forced the population into concentration camps. However, we have already defeated the special forces and our people can defeat this as well.

In the light of the military situation described above, we realize that even after heavy setbacks they still want to continue the war; even after we have defeated the *Cukiet* campaign. We would like to stress that although the United States and right-wing forces are big, with the spirit of our people we can win.

We have combined our forces and now fight in close combat. We will take on the best of the enemy and defeat them. Throughout the country, our military strategy is always to harass them day and night.

QUESTION: What is your program at present?

ANSWER: Inside the country we are leading a struggle for independence and territorial integrity, and to the outside world we are demonstrating our peaceful intentions. Accordingly, we have put forth our Five Point Program [see article 27 of the present book] for a political solution based on an independent, neutral, and prosperous Laos.

The U.S. intervention is demonstrated by Nixon's statement as follows. Seven hours after our Patriotic Front issued the Five Point Program, Nixon admitted that the United States had more than 1,000 troops in Laos and that American planes had bombed Laos. The Nixon statement contained three additional points. First, it made allegations against the DRV. Second, it recognized the Phouma government as the legal government of Laos. And third, it stated that the United States had sent troops at the request of the Phouma government. Therefore, we can say that Phouma is a reactionary and a tool of the U.S. imperialists.

QUESTION: Why do you say that Souvanna Phouma is no longer a progressive and now a reactionary?

ANSWER: In 1956 and 1958 we tried to form a coalition government, but Phouma refused to cooperate and became a reactionary and a U.S. puppet. During the first coalition government we tried to show them our sincerity and we integrated our armed forces into the government army.

When Phoui Sananikone's government was in office in 1958–1959 they tried to surround our forces and jail our leaders. But with the help of the Lao people we were able to free all of them.

When our leaders escaped from the surrounding rightist forces, we had nothing to fight with but our empty hands. We started our own military, and by 1962 we held two-thirds of the total area of Laos.

Then came the Geneva Accords, which led to a coalition with the three forces. We thought that Phouma was a progressive and, therefore, chose him as premier. The first coalition had been sabotaged by the United States, and the same thing happened with the second coalition government of 1962.

However, the situation is now different and we can reunify the country and the people. In our struggle we have scored many successes since we rely on ourselves and on the socialist, pro-

gressive countries. The reasons for our success are that we know
how to rely on ourselves, how to bear hardships, and how to
struggle, through our own efforts, with good policies, and with
the clear-sighted leadership of the party.

QUESTION: What kinds of programs do you plan in the social
and economic domain?

ANSWER: Though our country is small and has many different
peoples, we have learned how to unite. We have a strong determination to fight to win. Let me add one point: we know how
to differentiate between our friends and enemies. We fight and
build at the same time; we are building up the countryside in
the liberated areas. Our country is very backward and, because
of the French policy of obscurantism, about 95 per cent of the
people are illiterate. During the French period, the Lao language hardly existed in schools or in books. Since then the level
of education has increased six times. There were about 11,000
children going to school under the French. In the liberated areas
we have worked to raise the educational level, and there alone
60,000 children are now going to school in the first to third
grades. In the field of hygiene there was one doctor and 200
beds in the whole country. Now there are 20 doctors and 1,700
beds in the liberated zones. In the field of agriculture, there was
then only one crop a year; now there are two crops.

Regarding the mountain peoples, the Lao Tung and the Lao
Xung, we can help them move to the plains to make their living
easier. We are trying to establish communal ties, to make improvements in the field of animal husbandry, to increase their
standard of living, and to reduce infant mortality.

Despite the difficulties because of the war, we are laying the
first foundations for industry. There are now a few small factories, weaving, printing, and mechanical shops. Our people fight
and work at the same time. They have faith in the party and,
therefore, we shall ultimately achieve victory.

QUESTION: We understand that the mountain tribesmen, such
as the Meo, have been enlisted by the CIA to fight against the
Pathet Lao. Is there a deep antagonism between the Meo and
the Lao that will stand in the way of reunification and reconciliation?

ANSWER: As for the Lao-Meo antagonism, it is true that contradictions existed during the French period. While the United States is trying to deepen this antagonism, the politics of the party are to unite all of the people in the country. Every minority has its own leaders, for example, Faydang of the Lao Xung. They have political and military forces under their own leaders, and as a result the majority of the Meo are with the Pathet Lao. The Meo forces of Vang Pao include minorities from Burma and Thailand, brought in and paid for by the U.S. imperialists.

QUESTION: What is the situation in the areas controlled by the Lao government?

ANSWER: In the occupied zones, in the towns and concentration camps, people have met many difficulties and the conditions are very severe. The only way for the people to overcome these difficulties is to rise up and take arms against the imperialists.

Inspired by the example of the liberated zones, people in the towns and camps are taking up the struggle. Therefore, military forces are needed to repress them and guard the RLG zones. In the zones temporarily occupied by the right wing, people still believe in our policies and follow the leadership of our party. Our friends in Vientiane live under the very guns of the rightist U.S. forces, but they have the protection of the people.

The town of Vientiane is now being subjected to neo-colonialism and is being used as a strategic base from which to attack our forces. Formerly in Vientiane there were only five or six two-story buildings, but now there are many high buildings. Before the United States arrived the population of Vientiane was 10,000, but now it is 60,000. There are 20,000 Thai and several thousand Vietnamese and Chinese as well. If you understand the Thai language you get the impression in Vientiane that you are in a Thai town. The languages are similar, but the differences are easily noticed. Another big change near the cities is the growth of large concentration camps which are used to draw the water so as to kill the fish, that is, the revolutionary forces.

The U.S. intervention caused all of these difficulties, and if it were not for the United States we could re-create the national concord of 1958–1959, or realize the national union of 1962. The Central Committee of the Patriotic Front would like to see a coalition government which would lead to a neutral, independent, and peaceful Laos. We oppose all U.S. intervention or escalation of the war and would much rather have a peaceful solution to the conflict.

Therefore, we have put forth the Five Point Program. It conforms to the aspirations of the people of our country and receives support even from the police and members of the government. The officers of the puppet army are the only ones who oppose it. The fundamental point of the Five Point Program is U.S. withdrawal and an end to all intervention. If the United States will stop the bombing, the three parties can meet as they did in 1958 and in 1962 to solve their differences peacefully. We know that the Five Point Program will eventually be successful.

Fierce fighting lies ahead, but our people have learned how to fight and will be willing to sacrifice. We may be a small people, but we have a great fighting spirit.

QUESTION: How do you foresee relations developing between Laos and Thailand?

ANSWER: Thailand is a country with a population of 30 million, but there are 10 million Laotians in Thailand who were forcibly abducted in feudal times. The north and northeast formerly belonged to Laos, but they too were seized in feudal times. Although the Lao people of Thailand have joined the struggle against the U.S. imperialists and have the support of the Lao people of Laos, there is absolutely no truth to the allegation that the Neo Lao Hak Xat [Pathet Lao] want to invade Thailand.

29

The Pathet Lao and the People of Laos: Noam Chomsky Interviews a Lao Refugee

In April 1970, Professor Noam Chomsky of M.I.T. interviewed a Lao refugee from the Phonesavan area about living conditions in a Pathet Lao zone. The interview was conducted in one of Laos' many refugee camps, near the Mekong River not far from Vientiane.

QUESTION: Could you tell us a little of your personal history?

ANSWER: I was born in northern Laos and came to Phonesavan, in the Plain of Jars, in 1958. I am now 25 years old. Phonesavan was a town of about 1,000 people, about 200 families. It was one of the three major towns in the Plain of Jars.

QUESTION: What was the outcome of the 1958 election in Phonesavan?

ANSWER: There were two candidates, a right-wing candidate and a man who ran as an independent. The independent candidate won, with about 60 per cent of the vote. Shortly afterward, he was assassinated by the right wing, and the right-wing candidate went to the National Assembly. At that time the Pathet Lao[1] was clandestine in this area. When they revealed themselves later on, we found out the independent candidate who won and was then assassinated was actually a member of the Pathet Lao.

QUESTION: What happened after the election?

ANSWER: At that time the Pathet Lao worked together with the Kong Le forces. They took over all of Xieng Khouang province and the Plain of Jars in 1960. Basically, Kong Le kept the structure that existed under Phoumi Nosavan in 1959. In 1961, the Pathet Lao began talking to the people cautiously and without revealing themselves unless they found people sympathetic to them or hostile to the government. The Pathet Lao explained

1. This informant always used the term "Issara" to refer to the Pathet Lao. So did the refugees in the refugee village.

451

to the people that they began in 1949 with 25 men. They refused to work with the French and they captured weapons from the French. Now, they said, they are working with Kong Le and against Phoumi. They explained what they thought should be done. There should be a new administration. The people should not pay such high taxes to the government. Everyone should farm the way he likes. The big farms should be broken up. There were big farms with absentee landlords living in Vientiane until 1960. Tenants had to pay 50 per cent of their rice crop to the landlord. In the land reform of 1960, there was redistribution, and everyone got an equal share, each person got as much as he could farm. The land reform took 2 or 3 months, and the farmers got individual plots. No farmers had to lose any land, because there is plenty of land in the area, plenty of rich land.

QUESTION: Was there any resistance to the land reform?

ANSWER: No, there was no resistance. There were always explanations before anything was done. The Pathet Lao would say, "The land belongs to everyone—you can farm as much as you want. But you should only take as much land as you can farm yourself." There were no real disputes about who got what land, because long explanations always preceded action. The Pathet Lao always spoke nicely. They were very patient. They always explained everything until people agreed.

QUESTION: Were the Pathet Lao natives of the area?

ANSWER: In the beginning they came from Vientiane or Sam Neua. They were intellectuals. Many had studied in France. At first people didn't like the intellectuals, but then the intellectuals used self-criticism and said: "We want to work with the people." The people accepted this and didn't resent the intellectuals. Later, when the Pathet Lao and Kong Le separated, the intellectuals went with Kong Le, and the Pathet Lao were mostly peasants from the area. Up until 1967–1968, there was a mixed administration, partly local people, partly outsiders. In 1966–1967, there was a sudden change. The outsiders all left and the administration became only local people.

QUESTION: How did the split take place between the Pathet Lao and Kong Le?

ANSWER: In 1961, in principle this was Kong Le territory.

The Pathet Lao cooperated with Kong Le, but they also spoke to the people and began to organize among the people. They would say: "You should like us more than Kong Le." But there was real cooperation until after the Geneva Accords in 1962. It was then that the split occurred.

QUESTION: Why did the split occur?

ANSWER: From 1960 to 1962 the Kong Le troops would ride in cars and trucks. The Pathet Lao would always walk. They didn't criticize the Kong Le troops. They would say: "It's all right. They're corrupted by the imperialists. We're peasants and we've had a harder life." But then the Kong Le officers prevented arms from going to the Pathet Lao. Then there was a split among the Kong Le (neutralist) forces. Colonel Deuane split with the other colonels. They were vying for power. After Geneva, the Americans sent arms. The right-wing neutralists confiscated the arms and wouldn't let any of them go to the Deuane soldiers. They weren't getting arms or pay. Then they shot down an American plane, and the real fighting started.

The American arms all went to Ketsana, a right-wing neutralist. He was Kong Le's right-hand man. When the fighting started between the troops of Ketsana and Deuane, the Americans started aiding Ketsana. Really, a lot of the problem was the bad and undisciplined behavior of Ketsana's troops. Deuane's troops had good relations with the people and with the Pathet Lao. The Pathet Lao stayed out of the conflict between the two groups of neutralists. The Pathet Lao wanted to give political instruction to the soldiers. Deuane agreed, but Ketsana refused.

So the Deuane troops were fighting against Ketsana, who had American aid. Then there was a truce, but it was uneasy. The Pathet Lao still stayed out of it. Then Ketsana assassinated Quinim [Pholsena] in April 1963 in Vientiane. That was known right away. The Deuane forces assassinated Ketsana in retaliation.[2]

The Pathet Lao didn't get involved until several months after the assassinations. But they pulled out of the government at this

2. In fact, it was the other way around. Ketsana was assassinated, then Quinim.

time. There was plenty of fighting going on then. The people didn't know what was going on. They just stayed out of it. During this period (1960–1963) the Russians supported the Pathet Lao and Kong Le. There were no taxes taken from the peasants at all in those years.

QUESTION: What was happening in the political realm during this period?

ANSWER: In town, there were no changes. There was a lot of political speech-making. The Pathet Lao and Kong Le speakers were always together. They would say: "We're cooperating—we're here to help you. We get aid from outside but they are not pulling the strings. It is different now from the way it was under the French."

Basically, they just tried to set up an adminstration that would work properly, a legitimate administration.

QUESTION: What kinds of changes were introduced in the peasants' lives during this period?

ANSWER: In the old days, before 1960, the landowners got a very high part of the crop, sometimes even two-thirds of the crop. After 1960, the peasants got everything. There was also some mutual aid, but real cooperation didn't begin until after 1964. After 1964, people would say: "I'll help you work on your field and you help me work on my field, but then you'll get your whole crop and I'll get my whole crop."

QUESTION: Was there a money economy at that time, with cash transactions and credit?

ANSWER: There was before 1960, but only in the towns. A very poor man might have to borrow rice, say, before the harvest. If he borrowed 50 *meun* before harvest he would have to pay back 60 *meun* after the harvest. But there was no money economy in the countryside.

Most of the townspeople were very poor. There were two or three who were very rich, mostly high ranking officials like the provincial governor. Before 1960 there were only 30 or 40 schools in the whole district. They had grades one to three. About 60 to 70 per cent of the children went to school.

QUESTION: Tell us more about the changes that took place in the lives of the people.

ANSWER: Before 1960, there was no cooperation. Everything was competitive. People were always arguing, fighting, stealing, insulting one another, disputing over everything. It was just like Vientiane is today (gesture of distaste). From 1960 to 1964 when Kong Le was still there, it remained pretty much the same. Kong Le directed the administration. The Pathet Lao tried to ameliorate the conflicts. The Pathet Lao never said anything against Kong Le. They did keep talking to the people, however. They told the people not to say "Doyk'noy"[3] or "Tan K'noy." They told them not to be afraid of big people. This was very important. It has real symbolic significance to the people.

The Pathet Lao cadres came before 1960, and they lived with the people. At first they claimed to be Phoumi [Nosavan's] soldiers. They would reveal themselves only when they had won the people's trust, or when someone would complain about the Phoumi soldiers. They geared their actions to the situation. If the Phoumi soldiers would bother girls, telling them dirty jokes, and then go away, the Pathet Lao cadres would approach the girl and talk against the Phoumi soldiers. Of if the cadre heard people talk against the Phoumi soldiers very strongly, he would identify himself as a member of the Pathet Lao. They were very cautious and prudent.

QUESTION: Please tell us more about the history of the period just after 1963.

ANSWER: The Pathet Lao pushed Kong Le off the Plain with the help of the Deuane soldiers. Most of the recruiting in the Plain before May 1964 was done by the neutralists. Many soldiers went to study in China, Russia, or Hanoi. Often, men whose parents had been killed by Phoumi's soldiers were chosen to go to study. But this was in about 1962. By late 1963 the fighting was really between the Pathet Lao and Kong Le. The Pathet Lao soldiers came mostly from southern Laos (Kha) and from the two provinces of the Pathet Lao, Sam Neua and Phong Saly. By May 1964 the Pathet Lao and the Deuane neutralists had taken over the Plain.

---

3. "Yes, sir," a term used by inferiors to superiors, ubiquitous in Vientiane today.

QUESTION: Did they introduce any changes then?

ANSWER: Yes, they changed many things. The Pathet Lao soldiers helped the villagers farm rice and build houses. They gave rice to people who didn't have enough. Then they changed the status of women. Women became equal to men. Women became nurses and soldiers. They told the wives not to be afraid of the husbands any more.

QUESTION: Didn't the husbands become angry?

ANSWER: Sometimes they did. But they were taught that there is not to be any more oppression. People agreed. The Pathet Lao would say: "Look, she's human, you don't have special rights." Most husbands agreed that it was a good idea. They would think, it's good for me too.

They changed everything, so many things. I can't finish telling you how many things. For example, take money. Before, in the town, everything was for hire. If you were sick and wanted to go to a hospital, you had to have money and spend your money. Now it was free. No money was necessary.

Now people began to cooperate. The Pathet Lao trained doctors and sent them to the villages. Up until 1967–1968 the doctors were soldiers. There were civilian medics after 1967–1968.

Old men and old women and all children went to school. The Pathet Lao gave them books. The teachers were villagers, not Pathet Lao cadres. Mainly, the instruction was literacy and some political instruction at first.

QUESTION: How did the cooperation come about?

ANSWER: Well, cooperation began among the peasants. This was the job of the Pathet Lao cadre in the village. He was supposed to work with the peasants. No force was used.

Say, for example, that there were three families and two of them agreed to cooperate. Then the cadre would go to talk to the third family. He would get the other two families to come and help the third one who was uncooperative. Then they would talk about it. The two families would say: "We helped you so why don't you help us too?" They tried to shame him into helping.

The Pathet Lao cadres formed Phouak Khana Louk (awakening groups). There was generally one cadre in each village. During harvest, two or three others would come to help. They were sent from outside to the village. The cadres are rotated. The government supports them. They bring their own rice, just like the soldiers.

Every village had communal land. It was for the soldiers or the poor people, or people whose field had been bombed and destroyed. Five or ten families would work one piece of land, and then they would divide the harvest. The cadres and the soldiers worked land too. The cadres sent their harvest to the government. The soldiers would keep the harvest. Each family had private holdings too.

If someone would refuse to help or cooperate, they would try to use the shame technique. If they still refused, the cadres would come and say: "You have time. Can't you help poor people? All Laotians are brothers. What will happen to you if you are poor some day?"

The Pathet Lao would never insult anyone. They were very intelligent. They always speak softly and make you like them. They never take out guns or money to impress people.

QUESTION: How did the collective farming develop?

ANSWER: In 1964 very few people agreed to take part in collective farming. In 1965, about 30 per cent of the people took part. In 1966, it was about 50 per cent. By 1967, everyone took part.

In 1967, they suddenly replaced outsiders with local cadres completely. During 1965 and 1966 they had picked out the best workers and made them a new awakening group. They took them away for a month now and then. They were between 18 and 40 years old. The average ones were in their early thirties.

QUESTION: How were the villages organized and governed?

ANSWER: There were lots of organizations: military, political, administrative, defense (police), young boys, young girls, women's cleanliness, education, cooperation. They were social organizations, and everyone belonged. Each one would elect a leader. Every village had all of these organizations. Even a village of 25 families. In 1967 a new set of organizations was added. They dealt with technical matters, such as irrigation, livestock, agriculture. They managed to produce a second crop of dry-season rice for the first time. They would build dams. The North Vietnamese must have provided the initiative for this. There were also committees to deal with adult literacy programs and with forestry. In the technical committees they would pick a representative to make contact with experts from the outside. For example, they would pick a representative from the irrigation committee to meet with the irrigation expert for the district. He would organize the larger projects, and the irrigation representative from the village would be responsible for arranging for people to work on these large projects. The district irrigation expert taught the village representative, who would then take the local responsibility. Other villagers would work in his fields, so that he could be free to do this.

It was the job of the cooperation organization to work all of this out.

QUESTION: What was the job of the political organization?

ANSWER: The political organization would be in charge of political education. They would teach people to hate the Americans who come from so far away to bomb you. They would make the people angry so that they would take up arms. They explained by comparing the Americans with the French. When an American pilot was captured, they would parade him through the village. They would say: "He has come to kill you. But he is not bad. His chiefs are the ones who are bad. He doesn't know what he is doing." The people understood this.

QUESTION: When did the bombing begin?

ANSWER: The bombing started in 1964, in May. That was the first bombing. There had been no bombing under the French. Then there were F–105s. They bombed with explosives and napalm. First they bombed the road between the two towns. Phonesavan was bombed for the first time in 1965. From November 1968 to January 1969 the bombing was very heavy. The town was evacuated completely. It was all bombed out. Everyone had to hide in the forests. They stayed as near to the village as possible. By September, everything was destroyed. Every refugee I have met says that everything was destroyed.

The Vang Pao Army came to Phonesavan in September 1967.

QUESTION: What did you do then?

ANSWER: I didn't go with the Pathet Lao in August 1969.

QUESTION: What about the North Vietnamese? When did they come?

ANSWER: In 1964 and 1965 there were very few North Vietnamese. There were many by 1969. Soldiers had very strict discipline. They kept away from the villagers. The civilian advisers were paid and supported by the North Vietnamese because they were not permitted to have any contact with the Lao people.

QUESTION: What about the anti-Vietnamese feelings of the Lao? Didn't they object when the North Vietnamese came?

ANSWER: The Pathet Lao taught them that the North Vietnamese were their friends. The North Vietnamese helped them to survive. They showed them how to build dams and gave them arms. They helped them to plant fruit trees and they helped with agricultural programs. They also gave them educational materials.

The people were very impressed with the North Vietnamese whom they knew. For example, once a North Vietnamese irrigation adviser killed a buffalo who charged at him. The Pathet Lao condemned him to death. The people objected and complained to the Pathet Lao officer. They said it was not fair and he should be released. But the general decreed that the man would have to die. There might have been trouble. But the North Vietnamese adviser went out and killed himself.

The people regarded the North Vietnamese with awe.

30

Laos' Role in the Indochina War: Douglas Miles Interviews a Member of North Vietnam's Central Committee

Douglas Miles has spent most of the last ten years on field research in Southeast Asia. He is presently a lecturer in Asian anthropology at Sydney University and writes after a recent visit to North Vietnam, Laos, and Cambodia. The article opens with a question he directed at one of Hanoi's leading strategists on March 13, 1970.

"A few years ago the Western press published a report that Ho Chi Minh had switched from Camel to Salem cigarettes. Would you care to make some comment on that?" Hoang Tung, Central Committee member of the Lao Dong, North Vietnam's Communist party, looked through the window at Hanoi's bicycle traffic below and then indicated that he understood exactly what I was getting at. He replied:

"American intelligence organizations must give the public the impression that they really know what is going on inside my country. But can they read the simple meaning of what the Vietnamese and their brothers are doing now and what the present implies for the future? There are 87 U.S. journalists in the Laotian capital at this moment. I've heard most of their reports about events on the Plain of Jars. But even America's best analysts seem to have failed to comprehend what some of those children playing down there on the street could tell you."

In our discussion Hoang Tung had admitted the presence of North Vietnamese regulars on Laotian soil. He had then told me of Senator Mansfield's statement, two days before, expressing great pessimism about Nixon's policy of Vietnamization as a cure for the United States' major headache. The North Vietnamese

Reprinted with the author's permission from *Tharunka*, journal of the Students Representative Council, University of New South Wales, Australia.

was even more definite than Senator Fulbright in last Thursday's forecast.

"Vietnamization will fail. The events on the Plain of Jars have proved this. You know of course, that the recent routing of Laotian troops is detrimental to the Pathet Lao's current interests."

I did not know and asked him to explain.

"Let's look at history. The military defeat of the French at Dien Bien Phu would have been of little political significance had it not occurred in accordance with [General Vo Nguyen] Giap's dictum 'at the right time and the right place.' We perhaps could have inflicted greater losses on the French in earlier battles but the means should justify the end. So we waited. At Dien Bien Phu we not only killed a lot of legionnaires; we ended French colonialism on Vietnamese soil.

"The Pathet Lao have sacrificed their immediate and short-term interests by moving at this time. But they have done so in full consciousness of the fact. The important thing to recognize is the relationship between the Plain of Jars and the wider and long-term implications of recent events for the defiance of all Indochinese peoples against foreign aggression."

I still did not understand so he peeled a mandarin and continued.

"The Pathet Lao's sacrifice is for the sake of their oppressed comrades elsewhere. They are selflessly acting prematurely and postponing the reaping of their own benefits till after the defeat of the Americans in South Vietnam.

"Consider Nixon's policy of Vietnamization as a solution to his problems. It aims at nothing other than the old Kennedy formula ("special war") under a new name. Up until 1965 the Americans had few experts here and the bulk of the fighting on their behalf was by local troops. This did not get them very far so Johnson introduced a new strategy and poured half a million G.I.'s through Saigon under the delusion that they would soon flush the Liberation Forces out of the whole country. The Pentagon does not like to throw away used equipment so it shifted the apparatus for "special war" to Laos and hired it out to Souvanna Phouma as if it was a piece of useful artillery.

"According to Nixon the logical outcome of his Vietnamization policy will be the substitution of indigenous soldiers for the 400,000 Americans who will be repatriated; also the maintenance of Washington's supervision and control through the agents who will remain.

"But this indigenized model, call it what you like, is the very piece of apparatus which the Americans have persuaded Souvanna Phouma to use today in Laos. Nixon himself underscores the fact everytime he talks about the paucity of U.S. advisers in that country and of Souvanna Phouma's dependence on the mercenaries and conscripts he employs.

"Last week we demonstrated that this piece of American equipment is useless. It is not the first time we have done so. But we need to remind Kennedy's successors that its employment will be as futile in South Vietnam in the future as it is in Laos today and as it was in South Vietnam in 1965. And of course, Nixon does not have the same options open to him as his predecessors. He can't bring in more G.I.'s."

Selected Bibliography

by Leonard P. Adams II

GENERAL READING

Burchett, Wilfred, *The Furtive War: The US in Laos and Vietnam.* New York: International Publishers Co., Inc., 1963. An excellent account based on firsthand observations from the Pathet Lao and NLF areas. Burchett has information not obtainable elsewhere. Sympathetic to the communist point of view, as are all his works.

Burchett, Wilfred, *Mekong Upstream: A Visit to Laos and Cambodia.* Hanoi: Red River Publishing House, 1957. An excellent firsthand account.

Burchett, Wilfred, *The Second Indochina War: Cambodia and Laos.* New York: International Publishers Co., Inc., 1970.

Devillers, Philippe, and Jean Lacouture, *End of a War: Geneva 1954.* New York: Frederick A. Praeger, Inc., 1969. A fascinating, detailed and accurate account by a major historian of Indochina and a well-regarded journalist.

Dommen, Arthur J., *Conflict in Laos: The Politics of Neutralization.* New York: Frederick A. Praeger, Inc., 1964. A carefully researched and readable exploration of the issues and the problems of American response from a conservative point of view.

Fall, Bernard B., *Anatomy of a Crisis: The Laotian Crisis of 1960–1961.* Garden City, N.Y.: Doubleday & Company, Inc., 1969. An excellent, readable account, published posthumously with an epilogue by Roger M. Smith.

Fall, Bernard B., *Street Without Joy: Insurgency in Indochina 1946–1965.* Harrisburg: The Stackpole Company, rev. ed., 1966. The best book to appear on French military and political strategies and their failure. The implicit and explicit comparisons with America's Indochina War are impressive and extremely valuable.

Lederer, William J., *A Nation of Sheep.* Greenwich: Fawcett World Library: Crest Books, 1961. Pages 11–26 entitled "The Laos Fraud" recount the 1959 U.S. scare over fictitious threats to Laos.

Scott, Peter Dale, "Laos: The Story Nixon Won't Tell," in *The New York Review of Books,* Vol. 14, No. 7, April 9, 1970. Contains a carefully documented analysis of President Nixon's March 6, 1970, statement and summarizes the evolution of the American policy of intervention in Laos.

Toye, Hugh, *Laos: Buffer State or Battleground.* London: Oxford University Press, 1968. A well-written and complete introduction written by a former British military attaché in Laos. Includes a comprehensive bibliography.

OTHER MATERIALS

The Committee of Concerned Asian Scholars, *The Indochina Handbook.* New York: Bantam Books, Inc. Scheduled to appear in Fall 1970.

Fall, Bernard B., "The Laos Tangle," in *International Journal* (Toronto) Vol. 16, No. 2 (Spring, 1961), pp. 138–157. A good summary of events from the first Geneva Accords to the second.

Fall, Bernard B., "The Pathet Lao, A 'Liberation' Party," in *The Communist Revolution in Asia; Tactics, Goals, and Achievements,* edited by Robert Scalapino. Englewood Cliffs, N.J.: Prentice-Hall, Inc., 1965. A good short account based on field research as well as careful documentation. Contains a selected bibliography.

Friedman, Edward, and Mark Selden, eds., *America's Asia.* New York: Pantheon Books. Scheduled to appear Spring 1971. Contains a longer version of Mirsky and Stonefield's article.

Gettleman, Marvin and Susan, and Larry and Carol Kaplan, eds., *Conflict in Indochina: A Reader on the Widening War in Laos and Cambodia.* New York: Random House, Inc. Scheduled to appear in Fall 1970. Brings together widely scattered sources, analyses, and documents and contains a useful chronology.

Grant, Jonathan S., Laurence A. G. Moss, and Jonathan Unger, eds., *Cambodia: The Widening War in Indochina.* New York: Simon & Schuster. Scheduled to appear Winter 1970. Contains original articles as well as reprints of significant articles and documents.

Halpern, Joel, *Government, Politics, and Social Structure of Laos.* New Haven: Yale University Southeast Asia Studies Monograph Series No. 4, 1964. A basic reference written by an anthropologist. Deals only with a limited range of issues.

Halpern, Joel M., "Observations on the Social Structure of the Lao Elite," *Asian Survey,* Vol. 1 (July 5, 1961), pp. 25–32. A discussion of why and how the traditional Lao elite has failed to adapt to present challenges.

Kundstadter, Peter, ed., *Southeast Asian Tribes, Minorities and Na-*

tions. Princeton: Princeton University Press, 1967. Contains articles on the mountain tribes in Indochina. Written for scholars.

LeBar, Frank M., and Adrienne Suddard, eds., *Laos: Its People, Its Society, Its Culture.* New Haven: Human Relations Area Files, 1960. Contains 21 chapters on all aspects of Laotian affairs. A good deal of the information on economy and politics is now outdated.

Robequain, Charles, *The Economic Development of French Indochina.* New York: Oxford University Press, 1944. The best basic reference dealing with all economic issues and groups, including the overseas Chinese in Vietnam, Cambodia and Laos.

Sisouk Na Champassak, *Storm Over Laos.* New York: Frederick A. Praeger, Inc., 1961. An account by a rightist Royal Laotian Government official of Laotian political development and international relations.

Smith, Roger, "Laos," in George McT. Kahin, ed., *Governments and Politics of Southeast Asia.* Ithaca, N.Y.: Cornell University Press, 2nd ed., 1964, pp. 527–592. An excellent introduction to the history, politics, and major problems of Laos.

Thompson, Virginia, *French Indochina.* New York: Octagon Books, Inc., 1968. A large comprehensive survey using only Western sources and surveying the area from an American perspective before World War II. A useful reference.

Pathet Lao Publications

Neo Lao Hak Xat Publications, *Rains in the Jungle: Lao Short Stories* (1967). Stories about revolutionary cadres in the Pathet Lao liberated zones, more interesting for their point of view than their literary merit.

Neo Lao Hak Xat Publications, *Twelve Years of American Intervention and Aggression in Laos* (1966). The "other side" presents its point of view.

Phoumi Vongvichit, *Laos and the Victorious Struggle of the Lao People Against U.S. Neo Colonialism.* Neo Lao Hak Xat Publications, 1969. Basic for an understanding of Pathet Lao politics.

Periodicals and Organizations Publishing Occasional Articles Relevant to an Understanding of the Indochina Wars

Asian Survey
Bay Area Research Institute Occasional Papers

Bulletin of the Committee of Concerned Asian Scholars
Far Eastern Economic Review
Foreign Affairs
Le Monde (weekly summary in English)
Leviathan
The Nation
National Guardian (contains a weekly column by Wilfred Burchett)
The New Republic
The New York Review of Books (articles by Noam Chomsky, Peter
     Dale Scott, Jonathan Mirsky, and others)
Pacific Affairs

Contributors

LEN E. ACKLAND is a graduate student at Johns Hopkins University who has done research for the RAND Corporation in Vietnam. He is the editor of a forthcoming book on Vietnam. LEONARD P. ADAMS II is a graduate student in Chinese history at Yale University, has traveled widely in Asia, and was a Fulbright Fellow on Formosa in 1966. NINA S. ADAMS is a graduate student in Vietnamese history at Yale University, has published several articles and a bibliography dealing with the area, and was a Fulbright Fellow on Formosa in 1966. FRED BRANFMAN, formerly with IVS, has lived in Laos since 1963 and is presently a journalist in Laos. WILFRED BURCHETT, the author of numerous books on Indochina including *Mekong Upstream* and *The Second Indochina War: Laos and Cambodia,* is a free-lance journalist well known for his continuing coverage of the Indochina war from "the other side." NOAM CHOMSKY is a professor at the Massachusetts Institute of Technology. A noted linguist, Professor Chomsky is the author of *American Power and the New Mandarins* as well as many articles on the U.S. involvement in Southeast Asia. His latest articles have appeared in *Bulletin of CCAS* and *New York Review of Books.* GEORGES CONDOMINAS, professor of anthropology at l'Institut des Hautes Etudes, is the author of numerous books on Indochina including *Nous avons mangés le forêt.* His articles have appeared in many journals, including the *Journal of Asian Studies.* JUDITH W. COUSINS is a graduate student in Asian studies at Central Connecticut State College. JACQUES DECORNOY is the head of the Southeast Asia section for *Le Monde* and has visited and reported on Indochina for several years. PHILIPPE DEVILLERS is director of Southeast Asian studies at the Center for the Study of International Relations in Paris, and professor at the Institute for Political Studies there. He was a correspondent for *Le Monde* in Indochina in 1945–1946. He is the author of four books on Asia including *Histoire du Vietnam 1940–1952,* and, with Jean Lacouture, *End of a War: Geneva, 1954.* DOUGLAS F. DOWD is professor of economics and former chairman of the Economics Department at Cornell University. He is the author of several articles on American involvement in Southeast Asia. DAVID FEINGOLD has done fieldwork among the Akha of Thailand, an opium-growing tribe, and is a doctoral candidate in anthropology at Columbia University. RICHARD S. D. HAWKINS is a former co-chairman of Yale CCAS and holds an M.A. in Southeast Asian studies from Yale University. JOHN LEWALLEN is a former IVS volunteer in Vietnam and presently works as a writer in California. ALFRED W. McCOY is a graduate student in Asian history at Yale University and is a national coordinator of CCAS. JONATHAN MIRSKY is professor of Chinese language and literature at Dartmouth College, Hanover, New Hampshire. He is a frequent contributor to the *New York Review of Books* and *The Nation* and is a member of the editorial board of the *Bulletin of Concerned Asian Scholars*. GUY MORECHAUD teaches at L'Ecole Française d'Extrême-Orient, Paris, and has done fieldwork among the Meo of Laos. D. GARETH PORTER has published articles in *The New Republic, The Nation, Commonweal,* and *Christian Century.* He was also a contributor to *The Viet-Nam Reader,* edited by Bernard B. Fall and Marcus Raskin. He is now a Ph.D. candidate in the Southeast Asia Program at Cornell University, and chairman of Cornell CCAS. PETER DALE SCOTT is professor of English at the University of California, Berkeley. He is the coauthor with Franz Schurmann of *The Politics of Escalation in Vietnam* (Beacon) and a contributor to *Ramparts* and *The New York Review of Books.* STEPHEN E. STONEFIELD is a graduate of Dartmouth College where he majored in Asian studies. MAREK THEE was formerly the Polish representative to the International Control Commission in Laos and Vietnam, and is now doing research at the International Peace Research Institute in Oslo, Norway. TRAN VAN DINH fought with the Viet Minh Liberation Army against the French and served in Laos as an adviser to Prince Souphanouvong. He held several prominent diplomatic posts in the government of Ngo Dinh Diem and is presently a free-lance writer and lecturer. JOHN K. WHITMORE is assistant professor of Southeast Asian history at Yale University and the author of a forthcoming book on classical Vietnamese history. HAROLD WILLENS is the national chairman of the Businessmen's Educational Fund and a co-founder and past national chairman of Business Executives Move for Vietnam Peace.

Index

Abhay, General Kouprasith, 203–204, 224, 226–227
quoted, 228
Accelerated Rural Development (ARD), 276
Ackland, Len E., 43, 139
Adams, Leonard P., ii, xi
Adams, Nina S., 38, 100
Agricultural Development Organization, 373
Agriculture, 331
of the Lao, 10–12, 84
of the Meo, 86, 327, 330, 332
Air America, 87, 153, 183–184, 191–194, 207, 219, 238–239, 248, 252, 257, 301–321, 339, 361, 380–381
early history of, 304–306
Eisenhower's endorsement of, 315–318
and Laos, 308–315
war waged by, 302–304
Air war, the, 231–242
Air America and, 302–304
in North Vietnam, 297
U.S. chain of command in, 236–237
Akha, the, 328, 330, 332
Allman, T. D., quoted, xvii, 222
Alsop, Joseph, 304, 310, 313
quoted, 311–312
Alsop, Stewart, 306
American advisers, 161, 164, 243, 245, 248–250, 253, 272, 276, 294–295, 309, 319, 321, 341, 343, 346, 364, 445, 462
American aircraft, 158, 201, 206, 231, 239, 295–296, 309, 315–317, 321, 376, 386–387, 423, 440, 447
American airdrops, 188, 252, 260
American airlifts, 315
American air power, 223
American bases, 44–48, 231, 235, 445

American businessmen, Laos and, 382–390
American combat deaths, 269
American embassy, 43–44, 49, 157, 193, 257, 287
American imperialists, 439
American military mission, xvi
American public, 271–272, 406
American PX, 262
American Volunteer Group (AVG), 304–305
Americans, 119, 139, 159, 197
in Laos, 219, 257–259, 275, 404, 445, 462
as aggressors, 417
hatred of, 458
unpopularity of, 419, 421
in Thailand, 235
Angkor, 53, 55
Anglo-American understanding, 125
Anglo-French-American understanding, 125
Annam, 56
Annamite Chain, 5–6
Antiaircraft units, 415, 418
Anti-Communism, 369
Anti-Communists, 140, 149, 181–182, 194, 198, 315, 361, 388
Arbuckle, Tammy, quoted, 245–246
Armée Clandestine (AC), 230, 243–245, 247–249, 251, 257, 265, 338, 361–363, 381
morale of, 249
Army for the Liberation and Defense of Laos, 429, 432
Army of Liberation of Vietnam, 426
Army of the Republic of Vietnam (ARVN), xxii, 245
Asia (see Southeast Asia)
Asian Christian Service, 372
Assam, 30–31
Attopeu, 244, 280
Austronesian peoples, 31, 37